The Analytics Edge

The Analytics Edge

Dimitris Bertsimas
Allison K. O'Hair
William R. Pulleyblank

Dynamic Ideas LLC
Belmont, Massachusetts

Dynamic Ideas LLC
43 Lantern Road
Belmont, Mass. 02478
U.S.A.

Online information and orders: https://www.dynamic-ideas.com

Cover Design: *Patrick Ciano*

Publisher's Cataloging-in-Publication Data

Bertsimas, Dimitris, Allison K. O'Hair, William R. Pulleyblank
The Analytics Edge
Includes bibliographical references and index
1. Analytics. 2. Data Science.
3. Applications. I. Title.
T56.B44 2016 519.8

ISBN 978-0-9899108-9-7

To my past, present and future doctoral students

D.B.

To my parents, for their encouragement and advice

A.K.O.

To the three people who have taught me the most: Diane, Morgan and Oliver

W.R.P.

Contents

Preface

The world is rapidly moving into an era of unprecedented data and computational power. Technology adoption rates are accelerating at an astonishing pace. There are tremendous opportunities to be realized by combining the realms of data, modeling, and decisions.

Analytics is the science of using data to build models that add value to decisions made by companies, institutions and individuals. It is emerging as one of the fastest growing fields of our time. A major force in the growth of analytics is the availability of data in electronic form in a large variety of industries.

Evidence of the growth and importance of analytics includes the fact that the number of Chief Data Officers in companies doubled from 2012 to 2014. Additionally, a study of 330 public North American companies found that companies in the top third of their industry in the use of data-driven decision making were, on average, 5% more productive and 6% more profitable than competitors [91].

Our purpose in writing this book is to provide a unified, insightful, modern and entertaining treatment of analytics and its impact. Another objective of the book is to inspire readers to use analytics to materially change their institutions, their companies, their lives and the world. The philosophical underpinnings of the book are that real world problems are usually complex and often ill defined; they do not come with labels, meaning that they are not necessarily regression problems or optimization problems. The only objective reality is data, which itself may be incomplete and of questionable quality, and the role of models is to facilitate the solution of real world problems.

Problems and data play a leading role in this book, while models play an essential but supporting role. This is in contrast with the vast majority of books and classes available today, in which methods play the leading role. Correspondingly, most chapters in this book start with a real world problem (typically from our experience) and a data set, and then use a variety of methods to address the problem.

This book is organized by application areas in which analytics has had a significant impact. It is structured in seven parts:

- In Part I (Chapters 1-3), "Humans and Machines," we discuss the competitive edge of models and machines versus humans in a variety of sometimes unexpected areas: predicting the quality of wine, assessing quality in healthcare, forecasting supreme court decisions, beating the world champion in chess, and beating the best human players in the game show *Jeopardy!*.
- In Part II (Chapters 4-6), "Sports and Games," we present how analytics can be used in a variety of sport and game decisions. Specifically, we present how to evaluate championship players in both professional baseball and basketball, how to optimize the structure of the National Hockey League and how to provide an edge in blackjack.
- In Part III (Chapters 7-10), "Healthcare," we show the impact that analytics has had in healthcare. We start with the Framingham Heart Study, which is to a large extent responsible for what we know today about heart disease. Then we demonstrate how analytics can be used to predict future healthcare costs, predict heart attacks, reduce mortality in infants and design an efficient and fair national policy for kidney allocations.
- In Part IV (Chapters 11-13), "The Internet," we show how analytics is influencing the internet. We describe the heart of Google's search engine, how to optimize revenue from online advertising and how a variety of internet companies provide online recommendations.
- In Part V (Chapters 14-16), "Combating Crime," we show how analytics can be used to combat crime. We describe how analytics can detect medicaid fraud, how to predict where crime will occur and how social networks can help reduce gang crime.
- In Part VI (Chapters 17-18), "Management of Operations," we show how analytics provide an edge in operations management. We discuss revenue management in airlines and casinos, and how to improve emergency room operations of a major hospital.
- In Part VII (Chapters 19-20), "Finance," we show how analytics has had a substantial impact in finance and especially in the areas of asset management and the pricing of options.
- In Part VIII (Chapters 21-22), "Methods and Exercises," we briefly discuss some of the analytics methods that are used in the book, and provide exercises to help the readers put analytics into action.

Using this Book in Course Design

This book can be used to teach several different types of courses to a variety of students. We have used this book to teach a one semester class at the

Massachusetts Institute of Technology (MIT) Sloan School of Management for an audience that included MBA, undergraduate and graduate students. We also taught a shorter class for Executive MBA students focusing on Chapters 1, 3, 4, 7, 8, 9, 11, 13, 14 and 19. A pre-requisite of these courses was a basic class on regression, probability and optimization. However, we have also created a Massive Open Online Course (MOOC) through edX (15.071x), based on this book that teaches the material with no assumed background knowledge.

There are some sections in the book marked with a star (*). These sections are more mathematically challenging than most of the sections in the book, and are intended for a more advanced reader.

In addition to going through the chapters in order (by application area), we also envision using this book for a course on analytics methods structured by method that covers:

(a) Predictive analytics methods: Linear regression (Chapters 1.1, 4, 21.1, 22.1), Logistic regression (Chapters 1.2, 7, 21.2, 22.2), Classification and Regression Trees (CART) (Chapters 1.3, 8, 21.3, 22.3), Random forests (Chapter 9, 21.3, 22.3), Clustering (Chapters 8, 9, 14, 16, 21.4, 22.4), and Simulation (Chapters 6, 18).

(b) Prescriptive analytics methods: Linear Optimization (Chapters 10, 17, 21.6, 22.6), Integer Optimization (Chapters 5, 12, 20, 22.7), and Stochastic Optimization (Chapter 19).

Table 1 shows the analytics methods used in each chapter.

Material for Qualified Instructors

Many materials, including data sets and software tutorials, are available in the Online Companion for the book (www.dynamic-ideas.com/analytics-edge). Please note that all of the data provided with this book has been modified for use from its original source. The organization or individuals who provided the original data make no claims as to the content, accuracy, timeliness, or completeness of any of the data or applications provided in this book.

Qualified instructors can request the Instructor's Resource material from the publisher (analytics-edge@dynamic-ideas.com) that contains the Solutions Manual and slides. The Solutions Manual provides answers to all the exercises in Chapter 22. Slides detail the concepts presented in each chapter and are designed to enhance lecture presentations.

Software

This book does not rely on a specific software for either predictive or prescriptive analytics. We have used the language R for predictive analytics

Table 1: Analytics methods used in each chapter.

Ch.	Subject	Method
1	Models vs. Experts	Linear and logistic regression, CART
2	Deep Blue	Decision trees
3	IBM Watson	Natural language processing
4	Championship Players	Linear regression
5	League Structures	Integer optimization
6	Blackjack	Simulation
7	Framingham Heart Study	Logistic regression
8	Healthcare Costs	CART and clustering
9	Medical Monitoring	Clustering and random forests
10	Kidney Allocation	Linear optimization and regression
11	Google Search	PageRank (Markov chains)
12	Online Advertising	Integer optimization
13	Recommendation Systems	Collaborative and content filtering
14	Fraud Detection	Clustering
15	Predictive Policing	Miscellaneous methods
16	Network Science	Clustering
17	Revenue Management	Linear optimization
18	Emergency Department Operations	Simulation
19	Options Pricing	Stochastic optimization
20	Asset Management	Integer optimization

in classes we have taught and we have designed a reference manual for using R that can be downloaded from the Online Companion (www.dynamic-ideas.com/analytics-edge).

Acknowledgements

We thank the following colleagues and former students who have participated in the development of cases, exercises, and other material in this book: Margret Bjarnadottir, David Czerwinski, Chris Darnell, Iain Dunning, Vivek Farias, Michael Frankovich, Michael Kane, Angie King,

Natasha Markuzon, Velibor V. Mišić, Clay Noyes, Kimberly Shenk, John Silberholz, Nikos Trichakis, and Nataly Youssef.

We would also like to thank the following friends, family, students, and colleagues for reading earlier versions of the chapters and giving us comments that helped us improve the book: Ross Anderson, Chaithanya Bandi, Lauren Berk, André Calmon, Murray Campbell, Martin Copenhaver, Jack Dunn, Iain Dunning, Robert Freund, Vishal Gupta, Steven Horton, Nathan Kallus, Ed Kaplan, Nikita Korolko, Jerry Kung, Jourdain Lamperski, Sébastien Martin, Velibor V. Mišić, Nishanth Mundru, Yeesian Ng, Michele O'Hair, Kelly O'Hair, Colin Pawlowski, Georgia Perakis, Oliver Pulleyblank, Prabhakar Raghavan, Brenna Richards, John Silberholz, Brad Sturt, Joel Tay, Larry Wein, Alexander Weinstein, Julia Yan, and Ying Zhuo.

We also thank all of our former students at the MIT Sloan School of Management, and especially our former teaching assistants, whose feedback in the class *15.071: The Analytics Edge* has shaped our educational philosophy towards the teaching of analytics and has significantly influenced our approach to writing this book. But mostly, we are grateful to our families for their patience, love, and support in the course of this multi-year project.

Dimitris Bertsimas
Allison K. O'Hair
William R. Pulleyblank
Cambridge, November 2015

Part I

Humans and Machines

Chapter 1

Models Versus Experts

Always listen to experts. They'll tell you what can't be done and why. Then do it.

– Robert Heinlein

Contents

On March 4, 1990, the *New York Times* announced that a Princeton University economics professor can predict the quality of wine without tasting a single drop. This professor believes that his predictions are more accurate than those of the world's most influential wine critic, Robert Parker, who called the predictions "ludicrous and absurd." These predictions have nothing to do with assessing the aroma, looking at the color, or determining the flavor profile of the wine; they are the results of a mathematical model.

Meanwhile, in a completely unrelated field, a study was being performed that ultimately reported shocking statistics about the quality of healthcare in the United States. One of the results of this study was the discovery that over half of 2,000 diabetic adults did not have a dilated eye exam in the past year, although diabetes is the leading cause of new cases of blindness among adults. They stated that "the dominant finding of our review is that there are large gaps between the care people should receive and the care they do receive." In research at the Massachusetts Institute of Technology, two analytics professors and a physician developed a mathematical model to assess the quality of care of patients in a fraction of the time that it takes a physician.

Mathematical models have even disrupted the fields of political science and law. In 2004, two law professors and two political science professors published an article claiming that a statistical model is better at predicting the results of Supreme Court cases than the collective opinions of experts. They predicted the affirm/reverse decisions of every Supreme Court case in the October 2002 term, cases including deep issues such as the constitutionality of affirmative action and various free speech rights. Lawyers, legal academics, and specialized journals that follow the Court closely have had little success in consistently predicting Supreme Court decisions in advance. However, these professors claim that the unbiased and unemotional nature of a model can better capture the decisions of the court.

In this chapter, we explore the possibility that predictive mathematical models can outperform expert human judgment by analyzing three different examples. While people are not always consistent in their opinions, are often emotional, and get tired, models are consistent, unemotional, and fast. We will show in this chapter that these characteristics lead to a competitive edge when models are used, especially if they are constructed using human expertise and judgment.

1.1 Predicting the Quality and Prices of Wine

Orley Ashenfelter made his prediction for red wine that is produced in the Bordeaux region of France, commonly referred to as "Bordeaux wine." He sought to address the mystery that while this wine has been produced in much the same way for hundreds of years, there are differences in price and quality from year to year that are sometimes very significant. Bordeaux wines are widely believed to taste better when they are older, so there is an incentive to store young wines until they are mature. The main problem is that it is hard to determine the quality of the wine when it is so young just by tasting it since the taste will change so significantly by the time it will actually be consumed. This is why wine tasters and experts are helpful; they taste the wines and then predict which ones will be the best several years into the future. However, Ashenfelter observed that "bad" vintages are usually overpriced when they are young, and "good" vintages may sometimes be underpriced when they are young. Realizing that the advice of experts was making the market for young wines inefficient, he developed a different system for judging the wines.

Ashenfelter discovered two explanations for the variation in prices: the age of the vintage, and the weather. He hypothesized that since older wines have been held longer, they must be more expensive than younger wines. The fact that the quality of the grapes depends on the weather was widely understood. However, Ashenfelter pointed out that weather in the Bordeaux region can vary dramatically from one year to the next. Figure 1.1 is a scatterplot of the average growing season temperature (in degrees Celsius) versus the amount of harvest rain (in milliliters) in Bordeaux from 1952-1980. Each point is a year, and the years with higher than average prices are shown as triangles. (A year is marked as higher than average if the price is higher than the average price across all years in this dataset.) In this figure, and throughout the rest of this section, the price for a year is computed according to a price index developed by Ashenfelter. His price index took into account the results of several thousand auction sales for wines from many different wineries in the corresponding year. For more information, see the references in Section 1.5.

Figure 1.1 establishes that it is hot, dry summers that produce vintages in which the mature wines obtain the higher prices. Additionally, the data is fairly consistent; there are very few cases that do not adhere to this rule. This observation led Ashenfelter to build a linear regression model for the price of mature wine as a function of the age of the vintage and the weather. For more about linear regression, see Chapter 21.

A sample of the data he used is in Table 1.1. The regression equation is for the logarithm of the average price of the year, normalized relative to the highest selling year in the data, 1961. For more about why Ashenfelter used the logarithm of price, see Section 1.5. The "Price" variable referenced here is the price index developed by Ashenfelter.

Using this data, Ashenfelter published what is now known as the "Bordeaux equation":

$$\begin{aligned}\text{Log(Price)} = &- 12.145 + 0.001173 \times (\text{Winter Rainfall})\\ &+ 0.616 \times (\text{Average Growing Season Temperature})\\ &- 0.00386 \times (\text{Harvest Rainfall}) + 0.0238 \times (\text{Age of Vintage}).\end{aligned}$$

The units for each of the independent variables are given in Table 1.1. This regression equation has an R^2 value of 0.83 and all variables are statistically significant. Ashenfelter experimented with additional variables, but the predictions were remarkably robust to the addition of any other variables.

While this regression equation predicts the logarithm of the average price index of the wine when it is mature, it can be thought of as an equation to predict the quality of the wine. By the time the wine is mature, the quality has been realized, and it is generally believed that the price of the wine reflects the true quality.

In response to Ashenfelter's equation, Britain's *Wine* magazine said "the formula's self-evident silliness invites disrespect." The Bordeaux wine industry was outraged; how can this man claim to know anything about wine that he has never tasted? You would never listen to the opinion of a food critic who had never tasted the food, or to a movie critic who had never seen the movie. To almost everyone, Ashenfelter's approach was just as absurd.

The Weather Makes the Wine

To the surprise of many, Ashenfelter went on to prove that his predictions for the quality of wine are surprisingly accurate. Using his Bordeaux equation, he was able to predict the quality of vintages that had just been bottled and had never even been tasted by comsumers. In 1991, he predicted that the vintages

Figure 1.1: Average growing season temperature and harvest rain in Bordeaux 1952-1980. The years with an above average price index are shown as triangles. The price index was constructed by Ashenfelter to represent the results of several thousand auctions sales for many different wineries in the Bordeaux region.

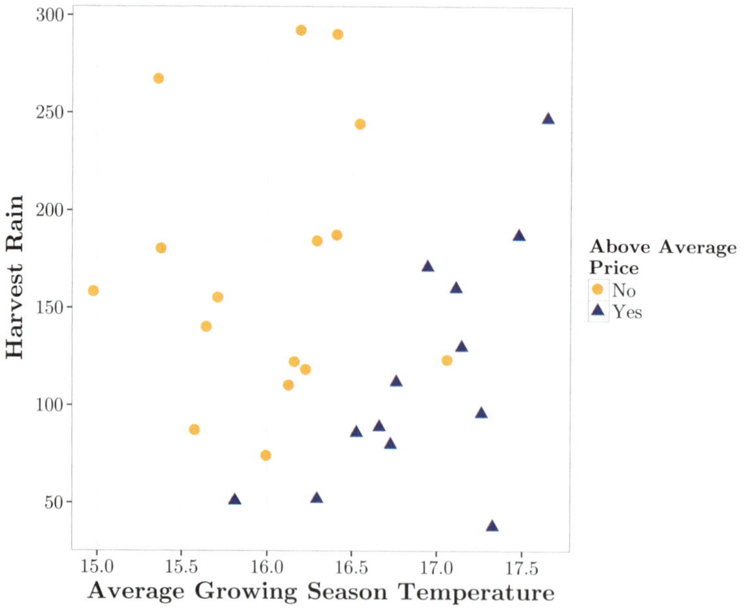

Table 1.1: Vintage and weather data used for the regression equation. The years 1954 and 1956 do not appear here because they were generally considered the worst in their decade and were no longer sold at the time Ashenfelter built his model.

Vintage	Log of Price	Winter Rain (ml)	Average Growing Season Temp (°C)	Harvest Rain (ml)	Age of Vintage (yrs)
1952	-0.99868	600	17.1167	160	31
1953	-0.45440	690	16.7333	80	30
1954		430	15.3833	180	29
1955	-0.80796	502	17.1500	130	28
1956		440	15.6500	140	27
1957	-1.50926	420	16.1333	110	26
1958	-1.71655	582	16.4167	187	25
1959	-0.41800	485	17.4833	187	24
1960	-1.97491	763	16.4167	290	23
1961	0.00000	830	17.3333	38	22
1962	-1.10572	697	16.3000	52	21
1963	-1.78098	608	15.7167	155	20
1964	-1.18435	402	17.2667	96	19
1965	-2.24194	602	15.3667	267	18
1966	-0.74943	819	16.5333	86	17
1967	-1.65388	714	16.2333	118	16
1968	-2.25018	610	16.2000	292	15
1969	-2.14784	575	16.5500	244	14
1970	-0.90544	622	16.6667	89	13
1971	-1.30031	551	16.7667	112	12
1972	-2.28879	536	14.9833	158	11
1973	-1.85700	376	17.0667	123	10
1974	-2.19958	574	16.3000	184	9
1975	-1.20168	572	16.9500	171	8
1976	-1.37264	418	17.6500	247	7
1977	-2.23503	821	15.5833	87	6
1978	-1.30769	763	15.8167	51	5
1979	-1.53960	717	16.1667	122	4
1980	-1.99582	578	16.0000	74	3

of 1989 and 1990 would be exceptional. Many professional wine critics did not agree with him at the time, but there is now a virtually unanimous agreement that 1989 and 1990 are two of the best vintages of the last 50 years. Ashenfelter further predicted that the 2000 and 2003 vintages are in the same league as the 1989 and 1990 vintages. These years have also been praised by the influential Robert Parker who has said "2000 is the greatest vintage Bordeaux has ever produced." He has equally praised the 2003 vintage. Without tasting a single drop of wine, Ashenfelter was able to come to the same conclusion about the quality of the vintages as the man considered to be the most influential wine critic of our time. Additionally, his method does not require any tasting of the wine; just the use of a simple equation.

1.2 Assessing Quality in Healthcare

Perhaps no other domestic policy topic in the United States has spawned more debate in recent years than healthcare. However, even though there is a significant amount of disagreement about healthcare policies, the ultimate goal of politicians, physicians, hospitals, and patients is the same: *quality* healthcare. But what exactly is quality in healthcare? How is it defined, measured, and improved? One possibility is for an expert physician with many years of experience to look at cases and assess the quality of healthcare that patients have received. Clearly, this is impractical if one wants to make this assessment available for every patient in the healthcare system, as it takes an expert physician approximately an hour to read and understand each case before making an appropriate assessment. Also, how does the physician get the information to make this assessment?

Dimitris Bertsimas and David Czerwinski (two analytics professors), together with Michael Kane (a physician), built a model that assesses the quality of healthcare received by a group of patients. In this work, they define good quality care as healthcare that improves outcomes, educates patients, coordinates care among all doctors that see a patient, and controls costs. The goal is to capture the concerns of the patient, physician, and hospital.

This model is built using the opinion of a physician, and it is intended to accurately predict good or bad quality of care on cases not seen by the physician. With this method, an expert's opinion is used to assess the quality of care, but a model is developed to extend this opinion to all patients, without requiring the expert to evaluate each individual case. For this model, the researchers set the goal of predicting the opinion of Dr. Michael Kane, an internal medicine physician with over 40 years of experience. Keep in mind that the model could easily be extended to predict the average opinion of a committee of physicians, or to predict the opinion of a set of guidelines (this is discussed more later in this section). The key observation here is that the model predicts the opinion of a *domain expert*; this concept could be extended to many other applications and problems.

Claims data, the data that healthcare providers submit to insurance companies to be paid for various services, provides the data for this model. This was the most easily accessible and sufficiently large set of data available electronically and up to date. This data is not 100% accurate, and under-reporting is common, but other data sources are not very accessible. With the increasing use of electronic medical records, there is potential for more accurate and complete data in future calibrations of the model. We will also see claims data used for different applications later in this book.

The first step in building the model was asking a physician, in this case Dr. Kane, to rate the quality of care of a set of 101 patients. The patients selected were diabetic and between the ages of 35 and 55 with annual healthcare costs between $10,000 and $20,000. The creators of the model decided to test it with diabetic patients since there is a wide range of tests, medications, and complications associated with diabetes. The age range was to ensure that the patients should receive similar care (an 18 year old and an 81 year old will probably need very different care, partially due to their age difference), and the cost range was to insure that the patient had enough data to make an accurate assessment, but not so much data that it was impractical for Dr. Kane to review.

Dr. Kane rated the quality of care for each patient on a two point scale: poor care, or good care. He also gave his level of confidence that the patient was indeed receiving that quality of care. These ratings are summarized in Table 1.2. He also wrote a paragraph for each patient, explaining his reasoning. The following paragraph gives an example:

> Male on glucophage, had sporadic medical visits and labs. Did have eye exam 4/05. His primary problems were back pain and narcotic use. He had monthly percocet prescriptions in addition to an NSAID and a muscle relaxer. No diagnostic studies. Had a few physical therapy visits in October and November 2003. No other significant diagnostic or therapeutic initiatives. Poor care with high confidence.

From Dr. Kane's assessments, 80 different variables were defined that fell into six different categories: (1) diabetes treatment (e.g. number of glycated hemoglobin tests); (2) utilization (e.g. number of office visits); (3) markers of good care (e.g. mammogram); (4) markers of poor care (e.g. narcotics); (5) providers (e.g. number of doctors); and (6) prescriptions (e.g. number of different drugs). Since blindly classifying every patient as receiving good care gives an accuracy percentage of 78%, the goal was to be more accurate than this. In addition to accuracy, the types of errors that occur are also significant: the percentage of cases classified as poor care that are actually good care and the percentage of cases classified as good care that are actually poor care. Errors of the first type (good care mistakenly classified as poor care) may cause unnecessary expenses to investigate and treat perfectly fine patients. But errors of the second type (poor care mistakenly classified as good care) can be very dangerous. These errors mean that we are overlooking patients that need help, and might cause serious health issues in the future. Understanding the trade-off between the different types of errors for any model is critical in deciding how useful the model will be in practice.

The model uses logistic regression to predict the binary variable "Quality," which takes value 1 if the patient received good quality care according to the

Table 1.2: The quality of care ratings given by Dr. Kane, along with his level of confidence.

	Low Confidence	**High Confidence**
Poor Quality	5	17
Good Quality	19	60

assessment of Dr. Kane, and takes value 0 otherwise. Logistic regression is a predictive method used when the outcome variable is binary, and produces a vector of coefficients similarly to linear regression. For more about logistic regression, see Chapter 21.

In this case, the best logistic regression model uses only three different independent variables: a binary variable for whether or not the patient was started on a combination of drugs to treat their diabetes (Started on Combination), a variable for the number of glycated hemoglobin tests the patient was given (Hemoglobin Tests), and a variable for the fraction of time the patient refilled a prescription to treat an acute condition within 30 days of the prescription running out (Acute Refills). The predictive equation is given by:

$$\begin{aligned}\text{Logit(Quality)} =& 1.66 - 4.23 \times (\text{Started on Combination}) \\ &+ 0.34 \times (\text{Hemoglobin Tests}) - 0.26 \times (\text{Acute Refills}).\end{aligned}$$

This is the *log-odds*, or *logit*, of the model, and is described in more detail in Chapter 21. If we look at this equation, we can see that Started on Combination has a negative coefficient. This means that if everything else is equal, a patient who is started on a combination of drugs (versus a single drug) to treat their diabetes is more likely to have poor quality care. Similarly, Acute Refills has a negative coefficient, so a patient who is repeatedly refilling a drug to treat an acute condition is more likely to have poor quality care. On the other hand, Hemoglobin Tests has a positive coefficient, meaning that more hemoglobin tests is predictive of good quality care. This makes sense, since it is recommended that even healthy diabetics receive this test at least twice a year.

Outcomes

The accuracy of the model for the quality of healthcare is given by the classification matrix in Table 1.3. The rows are labeled by the actual classifications and the columns are labeled by the predicted classifications. Of the cases that were actually classified as poor care, 12 of them were predicted to be poor care and 10 of them were predicted to be good care. Of the cases that were actually classified as good care, 4 of them were predicted to be poor care while 75 of them were predicted to be good care. Approximately half of the poor care patients were classified correctly, and almost all of the good care patients were classified correctly. This gives an 86% success rate, compared to the baseline of 78%.

To test the model out-of-sample, Dr. Kane rated the care of 30 additional patients that were not used to build the model. The baseline success rate (by blindly rating all patients as good care) in this case was 63%. The accuracy of the model was 80%. This shows that only a simple model is needed to capture half of the cases of poor care.

This model can be used on all patients in the system without having the expert rate all of the patients and classify them accurately. As mentioned earlier, this model could also be extended to predict the quality ratings of a committee of physicians, by having them each rate the quality of care of every patient. The ultimate ratings could then be the most common rating across all physicians. This work shows that a simple model has the potential to be used to replicate the opinion of experts when assessing quality of care.

Table 1.3: The classification matrix for the logistic regression model, comparing the actual outcomes to the predicted outcomes.

	Predicted Poor	**Predicted Good**
Actual Poor	12	10
Actual Good	4	75

1.3 Forecasting Supreme Court Decisions

In many political decisions, predictions are abundant. In the months leading up to a presidential election, predictions are made over and over about who will win. But when it comes to the Supreme Court, predictions are not typically made. However, in 2002, Theodore Ruger, Pauline Kim, Andrew Martin, and Kevin Quinn (two political science professors and two law professors), set out to predict Supreme Court rulings. Most people thought that models did not stand a chance against expert predictions, including the authors themselves. They thought that knowledge of the details of each case and the qualitative aspects of the Court would enable experts to predict much better than any statistical model.

These professors decided to use classification trees as their statistical model, due to the need for a flexible method for pattern detection in a situation with many variables that might not have a linear relationship. For more about classification trees, see Chapter 21.

The ultimate goal was to predict, for each case argued by the Supreme Court in the October 2002 term, whether the Supreme Court Justices would affirm the case (uphold the lower court's decision) or reverse the case (overturn the lower court's decision). The predictions made by the model were only allowed to depend on six different independent variables: (1) the circuit of origin of the case; (2) the issue area of the case; (3) the type of petitioner; (4) the type of respondent; (5) the ideological direction of the lower court ruling; and (6) whether or not the petitioner argued that a law or practice is unconstitutional. See Table 1.4 for an explanation of the possible responses for each of these variables. These variables were chosen because they are easily observable prior to the oral argument of the case, and they reflect insights into the key factors in previous decisions.

Hoping that the observable patterns in the Justices' past behavior would hold true for their future behavior, the authors used data from 628 cases that had been argued and decided prior to the October 2002 term by this same Supreme Court (the same set of Justices) to train the classification trees. This was a very rare dataset; the Supreme Court Justices are appointed when needed, and so the set of Justices changes at various times. This particular set of Justices had served together for seven years, which was the longest period of time with the same set of Justices in over 180 years.

The final model consists of eleven distinct classification trees. Two of them predict whether the case is likely to be a unanimous "liberal" decision or a unanimous "conservative" decision. These two trees are the first step in the model. If either tree concludes that a unanimous decision is likely, then the process ends. If neither conclude that a unanimous decision is likely (or both, with conflicting results), then nine different trees, one for each Justice, are used to determine the majority ruling. These trees vary significantly from Justice

Table 1.4: Possible values for the variables used in the model. All of the variables used here are categorical variables.

Variable	Possible Responses
Circuit of origin	1st – 11th, Federal, D.C.
Issue area of the case	Criminal procedure, civil rights, privacy, etc.
Type of petitioner	An employer, an employee, the United States, etc.
Type of respondent	An employer, an employee, the United States, etc.
Ideological direction of the lower court ruling	Liberal or Conservative
Whether the petitioner argued that a law or practice is unconstitutional	Yes or No

to Justice. For example, Figure 1.2 shows the classification tree for Justice O'Connor.

Figure 1.3 shows the classification tree for Chief Justice Rehnquist (recall that this study was for Justices in the October 2002 term). Note that the classification trees can depend on the decisions of other justices; for example, the tree for Chief Justice Rehnquist depends on the predicted decision for Justice Thomas, requiring that the prediction for Justice Thomas to be made first.

For most people, the simplicity of these classification trees further supported the hypothesis that the experts would do much better than the models. How can it possibly be true that a model using only four yes or no questions can predict the decisions of Justice O'Connor better than experts in the field?

To compare their statistical model to expert opinion, the researchers recruited 83 participants who were considered experts in the field of law. To

Figure 1.2: The classification tree for Justice O'Connor.

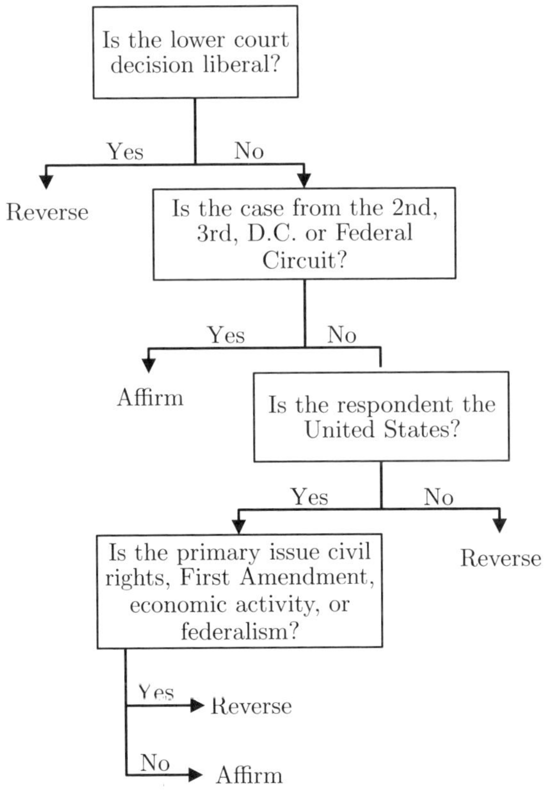

Figure 1.3: The classification tree for Chief Justice Rehnquist.

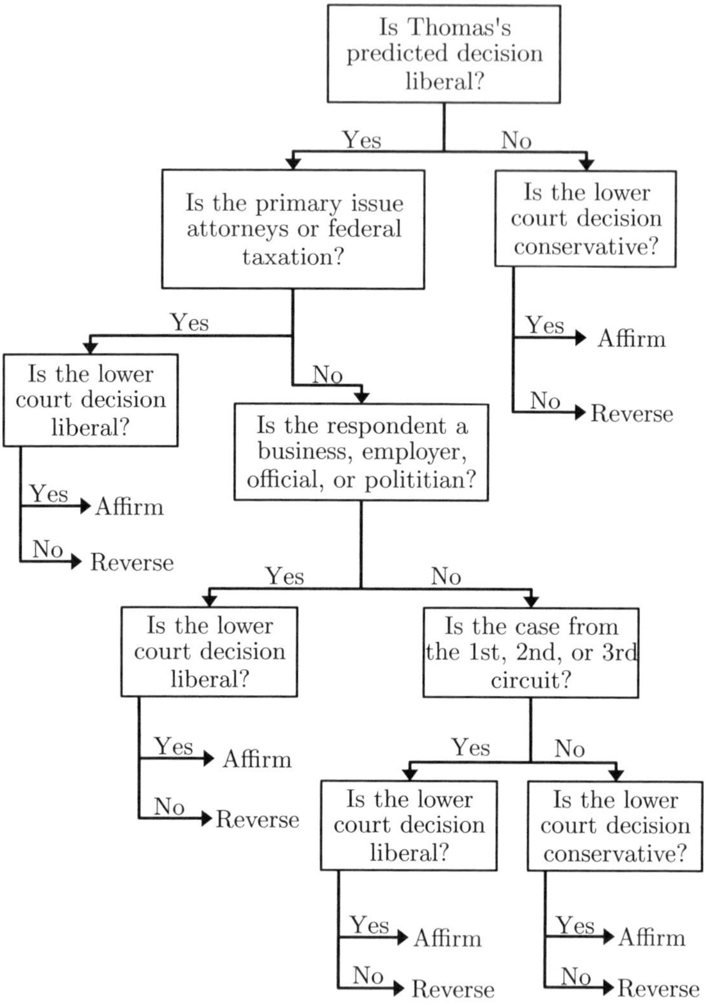

determine whether someone qualified as an expert, they assessed the person's writings, training and expertise, referrals, and experience with the Supreme Court. The group consisted of 71 academics and twelve appellate attorneys, including 38 former Supreme Court law clerks, 33 chaired professors, and five current or former law school deans. The experts were asked to predict the outcomes of the cases that fell into their area of expertise. More than one expert predicted most cases, and the experts did not communicate about their predictions. They were asked to make predictions for the Court as a whole and for each individual Justice. They were allowed to use any materials to make their decisions, as well as the specific knowledge that they have gained from years of experience.

Predicting the Unpredictable

When the Supreme Court term started in October 2002, the model had been run and the experts had reached a decision. These predictions were posted publicly on a website, so many people were able to watch with interest as case after case was decided. To the surprise of almost everyone, the model was more accurate at predicting the decisions.

The models and experts were compared using 68 cases for the overall case outcome forecasts (affirm or reject) and 67 of these cases for the individual vote predictions (one case had to be eliminated due to ambiguous individual voting). Since multiple experts assessed the same cases, there were more expert predictions overall (one prediction for each expert and each case). Table 1.5 gives the accuracy of the model and experts in predicting the case outcomes.

The statistical model greatly outperformed the experts in predicting the overall case outcomes (affirm/reverse). An alternative measure of the experts' success takes the majority prediction on each case as the experts' prediction. Even using this more generous measure of the experts' success, their accuracy rate was only 65.6%, still significantly lower than the model's accuracy rate of 75%. These results were shocking; how could such simple models out-predict experts in the field?

The study also compared the success of the model and of the experts in predicting the decisions of each individual justice (Table 1.6). The model and experts were very close in how accurately they predicted the decisions of the individual justices. However, the model and experts were each best at predicting the votes of different Justices. This is shown in Figure 1.4, which compares the proportion of correctly predicted cases by both methods for each individual justice.

The experts were much worse at predicting Justice O'Connor's votes, which is believed to be due to the fact that she is widely viewed as moderate

Table 1.5: The overall accuracy of the model and the experts at predicting the overall case outcomes. Note that since multiple experts assessed each case, there are more expert predictions overall.

	Correct	**Incorrect**
Model	51 (75.0%)	17 (25.0%)
Experts	101 (59.1%)	70 (40.9%)

by observers of the Court. However, the statistical model was able to correctly predict her votes much more frequently. This shows that the model was able to capture patterns in her decision making that were not obvious to the experts. On the other hand, the experts were able to more accurately predict the votes of other justices, in particular those that are thought of as more conservative.

The success of the model to predict the more "unpredictable" justice votes confirms the belief that models are able to see patterns in data that humans have a harder time discovering. However, the success of the experts in predicting the more "predictable" justice votes shows that intuition and human reasoning of experts can be a better tool in certain cases. This example shows that a mixture of models and experts might be the best approach; the unemotional

Table 1.6: The overall accuracy of the model and the experts at predicting the decisions of the individual justices. Note that some justices did not vote on some cases, and are therefore excluded from this analysis.

	Correct	**Incorrect**
Model	400 (66.7%)	200 (33.3%)
Experts	1015 (67.9%)	479 (32.1%)

Figure 1.4: Model and expert accuracy percentages for individual Justices.

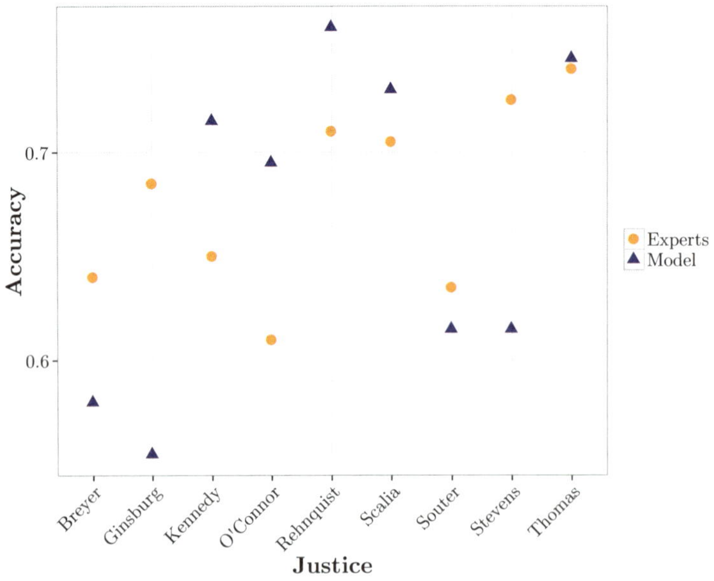

and consistent nature of a model mixed with the intuition and knowledge of an expert gives a much stronger prediction than either of the two alone.

1.4 The Competitive Edge of Models

These three examples provide insight on using models to make predictive decisions. Most importantly, we have learned that:

1. A model does not replace an expert. Expert human judgment is needed to develop a model, interpret the results, and adjust the model when necessary.

2. To make predictions on a large scale, the only option is a model. This was very clear in the healthcare example, since it is impossible for a physician to read and understand millions of patient records before making an accurate assessment.

3. In many cases, models can provide an edge over expert human judgment. People are very good at understanding and analyzing small amounts of information, but good models are able to look at all of the known information quickly and accurately. Models can also aggregate the opinions and assessments of many people into one final unbiased and unemotional prediction. A good model allows the expert to make a more informed decision, as well as gives the expert more time to work on other tasks that a model or computer can not perform as well.

The use of models to make predictions that have typically been made by experts has been a source of controversy; the experts do not like the idea of feeling unnecessary, and in general, people are uneasy with listening to the opinion of a computer program rather than the opinion of an expert in the field. But these examples have shown that the model is not replacing the expert; the model is just performing tasks that can be more efficiently and accurately performed by a computer.

1.5 Notes and Sources

1.1. The information on the Bordeaux equation comes from the academic article [7] and from the *New York Times* article "Wine equation puts some noses out of joint" [113]. The data presented here can be found on the *Liquid Assets* webpage, the wine journal published by Ashenfelter [8].

In this model, Ashenfelter chose to predict the logarithm of price, instead of directly predicting the price of the wine. This is a common practice in the field of economics, and captures what is called the *real product rate of return.* A useful property of the natural logarithm is that it converts an exponential growth pattern to a linear growth pattern. Due to inflation and potentially other factors, the price of wine is expected to increase exponentially over time. By taking the logarithm, the dependent variable (price) shows a more linear pattern from year to year, which makes it more suitable for predicting with a linear regression model.

1.2. The study assessing the quality of care in the United States is published in *The Milbank Quarterly* [125]. The recommended actions for diabetic care are from the American Diabetes Association [3]. The model for assessing the quality of care is described in more detail in the doctorate thesis of David Czerwinski [39] and in the paper by Bertsimas, Czerwinski, and Kane [18].

1.3. The Supreme Court study is described in the academic papers [117, 118]. The figures and diagrams here are reproduced from the results in these papers.

Chapter 2

How Do You Make a Grandmaster Blink?

The way a computer can outperform a human is to find a thing that computers do better than people and then do it.
– Jean-Pierre Uhry

Contents

In May of 1996, a historic event was taking place in Philadelphia. The world chess champion, Garry Kasparov, was playing a series of games against Deep Blue, a chess computer built at IBM Research. The winner of the series would receive a cash prize of $400,000 and, more importantly, bragging rights in the latest round of the attempts by computer scientists to build a computer capable of competing successfully against a chess grandmaster. The loser would receive $100,000.

Initial responses to the announcement of this match were mixed. This was the first time that the current world champion had played against a computer under tournament conditions. Moreover, Garry Kasparov was widely recognized as the strongest world champion of all time. When he retired from competitive chess in 2005, he had been ranked #1 by The World Chess Federation (FIDE) for a total of 268 different months, almost three times longer than any other ranked player [35].

On the other hand, IBM had hired the team behind Deep Thought, Carnegie Mellon University's computer chess project, to form the core of the IBM Research project. There was some interest in seeing what would happen when the Deep Thought team would have access to the resources of IBM, but it was generally believed that they would have little chance to win against Kasparov.

2.1 1996 - Deep Blue vs. Garry Kasparov in Philadelphia

The match was to consist of six games. The winner of each game would receive one point and the loser would receive zero points. In the case of a draw, each would receive $\frac{1}{2}$ point. After six games, the player with more points would be declared the winner.

The games were played under tournament conditions, meaning that the players were timed by a chess clock. A chess clock consists of two timers, one for each player, connected in such a way that once the game starts, the timer for one of the two players is always running. As soon as a player makes a move, the player presses a button on his clock, stopping the player's clock and starting the opponent's clock. Each player was allocated two hours of clock time for the first forty moves, one hour for the next set of twenty moves and then thirty minutes for all remaining moves. If a player's clock ran out of time while time remained on the opponent's clock, the player would lose. Each game would, therefore, end after at most seven hours, but could end much earlier if either player won outright or if both players agreed to a draw.

The young, but rapidly expanding, internet provided an interesting sidebar. Kasparov had insisted that the game be broadcast live on the internet, which was in the early stages of its exponential growth in 1996. Members of the organizing committee were doubtful that there would be much interest, but IBM agreed to host a website.

In a chess game, the player with the white pieces plays first and is believed to have a small advantage. In tournaments the player with white typically wins between 52% and 56% of the points awarded.

The first game, with Deep Blue playing white, was played on February 10. The result shocked the chess world. Deep Blue won. Suddenly, global interest in the match soared. IBM was faced with a problem: the website that the corporation had built for the match had inadequate capacity even for the first game. Moreover, after the first game result, clearly the load on the site was going to increase by several orders of magnitude. Fortunately for IBM, in 1996 the corporation was the IT provider for the Atlanta Summer Olympics, which would take place in August. This included building the servers that would host the website for the world coverage of the Olympics. Within twenty-four hours, IBM was able to move the Deep Blue-Kasparov website to their Olympic servers which had the capacity to handle the load.

The second game, the next day, was a reversal. Kasparov played white and won what turned out to be a seventy-three move, six hour battle. The next two games were draws and then, in Game 5, the Deep Blue team decided not to accept a draw offered by Kasparov and lost the game. (As had been agreed with Kasparov prior to the match, the decision whether Deep Blue would accept an offered draw was made by the team.) By the final game, Kasparov seemed to have figured out Deep Blue. In a game that turned out to be anticlimactic, Deep Blue resigned on its forty-third move.

Garry Kasparov had won the match 4 to 2, with three wins compared to Deep Blue's single win and two matches drawn.

2.2 Lunch at IBM Research

Shortly after the Philadelphia match, Garry Kasparov and team members Frederic Friedel and Owen Williams visited the IBM Research TJ Watson Research Center in Yorktown Heights, New York. Their agenda included a talk in the research center auditorium, a meeting with the Deep Blue team, and a luncheon with a group of IBM Research personnel. At the lunch, following introductions and congratulations, a question was put to Kasparov.

"Garry, how did you feel when Deep Blue won the first game?"

"I was devastated," replied Kasparov, "for two reasons. First, I could not believe that we had already reached the time when a computer could defeat the world chess champion. But second, I was stunned when Deep Blue had offered a sacrifice of a piece at move 23, in exchange for a positional advantage. Computer programs never did that. They keep material at all costs. It seemed that I was having to play against a new generation of chess programs and I was very worried."

Friedel added, " Garry was very upset after. But while he was resting after the game, we analyzed the game and after some time, realized that the move was not a sacrifice of material for position, but Deep Blue had been able to look ahead seventeen moves and see that it could win back the material. When we told Garry, he was greatly relieved."

Somehow, the challenge of playing a machine that could look ahead seventeen moves was much less intimidating than playing a machine that would sacrifice material for position.

Kasparov was then asked what it was like to play against Deep Blue. "Does Deep Blue have a personality?"

Kasparov replied that one confusing aspect of Deep Blue was that it seemed to have no consistent persona. "Sometimes Deep Blue played like a grandmaster. Sometimes it played like a lost child. But sometimes it felt like I was playing against God. Deep Blue did things that I had never seen or imagined."

In fact, as we discuss in following sections, this was a result of the way that Deep Blue was designed. It was never intended to simulate a human grandmaster or any human player. It was not a so-called "expert system." Rather it was designed to exploit the things that computers do well, particularly, when a computer was equipped with a large number of parallel processors. The non-humanness of Deep Blue had another consequence which differed from all its human opponents: even after a devastating loss, it was instantly ready to play again. It never brooded over a loss or a bad move.

The last question for Kasparov was simply "What's next?"

Kasparov became very animated and described his idea that he called "Advanced Chess." Chess could be played between teams – each team consisting of a human player and a computer assistant. "I believe that this could raise chess to a level never before seen!" he explained.

The idea of forging such a human-computer partnership is interesting. Presumably, the human would make the final decision regarding the move. What information would a computer have to provide to convince the human to follow an innovative line never seen before? How could the human provide strategic insight and human intuition to the computer?

Kasparov's final meeting during his visit to IBM Research was with the Deep Blue team to discuss the feasibility and possible arrangements for a return match to be played one year later.

2.3 Strategy and Decision Trees

Chess is a game with perfect information. Each player (and spectator) can look at the position on a chessboard, be told whether black or white is next to play, and know everything that could affect the ultimate outcome. This is different from card games where players know the cards in their hands but not their opponent's cards or games such as backgammon where random events, like rolls of dice, are part of the play.

For a game of perfect information, it is possible, in principle, to completely analyze all possible move sequences by a player and opponent and then choose a winning move if one exists. If such a winning move does not exist, then the game will be a draw or the opponent will win if no mistakes are made. In this case, a player will often try to create a confusing situation for the opponent that, hopefully, will result in the opponent making a mistake that will enable the player to get into a winning situation.

A *strategy* is a set of rules that take as input the current game situation and prescribe the next move to be made by the player. In some games the moves available to a player may differ depending on whether they are the first or second to play. A *winning strategy* for a player is one that guarantees the player using it can win, whatever moves are made by the opponent. In this case, for every game situation that can occur, the player will have a *winning move* specified by the strategy.

Tic-Tac-Toe (also known as *Noughts and Crosses* or *X's and O's*) gives a simple example. Most players of the game have discovered that if both players play carefully, every game will end in a draw. Figure 2.1, due to Robert Xiao [154], describes an optimal strategy for player X. At the highest level, the figure is a 3×3 grid corresponding to the nine squares of a Tic-Tac-Toe game. The large red X in the upper left corner specifies that the first player should play an X in the upper left cell.

The possible replies by O are shown in the remaining eight unoccupied cells. Each of the corresponding squares of the strategy grid deals with one of these cases and has a large O in the corresponding position. An optimal move for X for each of these is also specified in the corresponding square of the grid. For example, suppose O's response was in the center row, right hand column. Look at that cell in the strategy grid. It is subdivided into a smaller 3×3 grid and the first plays by X and O are shown by the largest black letters and the recommended next play by X is shown as the largest red X (X should play in the center square). Note that if the next move by O is anywhere but the lower right cell, X has an immediate win by playing in the lower right cell.

The strategy continues in this subcell as each possible response by O is shown in the corresponding subsubsquare, and so on.

Note that only two sequences of moves by O (both starting with center, top-right, left-mid) lead to a draw, with the remaining sequences all leading to wins from X.

A strategy can be represented by a *decision tree*. This is a tree whose nodes represent the different states of the game and whose edges correspond to possible moves. The node at the top (depth 0) corresponds to the current state of the game. At the beginning, this will be the initial set up of the pieces plus the specification of who is to play. The children of the depth 0 node (depth 1) correspond to the states which could result after each possible next move by the first player. The descendant nodes of these (depth 2) represent the states which could result from the next possible moves by the second player, starting from each depth 1 node. Notice that each node with even depth will be a board position where the first player is to move. Each node with odd depth will be a board position where the second player is to move.

Figure 2.1: A complete strategy for first player in Tic-tac-toe.

If we were constructing a decision tree for X for Tic-Tac-Toe, the depth 0 node would correspond to the nine square Tic-Tac-Toe game with an X in the upper left corner. There would be eight depth 1 nodes corresponding to the eight possible plays by O. Each of these would have a depth 2 "child" node corresponding to the prescribed reply for X as in Figure 2.1. Then, for each of these, there are six squares not yet played in the game. So each of these nodes would have six depth 3 "child" nodes corresponding to the possible next moves by O, and so on.

We illustrate this concept with a simple game called *Fox and Geese* played on the light colored squares of a standard chess board. There are four *geese* who begin on the light squares of one side of the chess board (Rank 1) and a single *fox* starts on square e8. See Figure 2.2. The geese and the fox always move diagonally, to an adjacent white square. However, each goose can only move upwards, that is, to a higher rank. The fox is permitted to move up or down.

Two players alternate moves in the game. The geese player must select and move one goose at each turn. The fox player must make one move with the fox at each turn. The game finishes either when the fox reaches Rank 1, having escaped, or has no possible legal move, being trapped by the geese. In the first case, the fox player wins. In the second case, the geese player wins.

It could happen that the geese have no legal moves, being clumped at the top of the board while the fox is free to move towards Rank 1. This is also counted as a win for the fox. So if the fox ever reaches the lowest rank occupied by any goose, then it will win, and can be declared the winner at that point.

Figure 2.3 shows examples of winning positions for the fox (the black piece) and for the geese (the white pieces).

Now let us see how we can analyze a board position. Suppose it is the fox's turn to move and we have reached the position in Figure 2.4. The fox has two legal moves, to either c8 or e8. In each of these cases, the geese will have six possible moves. Can you see what they are? Which move should the fox make?

In Figure 2.5 we show part of the decision tree, beginning with the position of Figure 2.4. We follow the usual convention of computer scientists and grow the tree downwards from the root corresponding to the situation at depth 0. This node has two children corresponding to the two possible moves for the fox (black). Each of these two children has six children corresponding to the six possible replies by the geese, of which two are shown.

If there is a winning strategy for the fox starting from the position of Figure 2.4, it would specify which of the two options should be taken. It would then specify for each of the six possible moves by the geese what move should be taken and so on.

Some of the moves make sense and others are of no value, but how do we decide which is the case? The answer is that we could continue the analysis. For each of the legal goose moves shown in Figure 2.5, the fox will have one or two legal moves. If we consider each of the resulting positions to be a starting

Figure 2.2: Starting position for *Fox and Geese.*

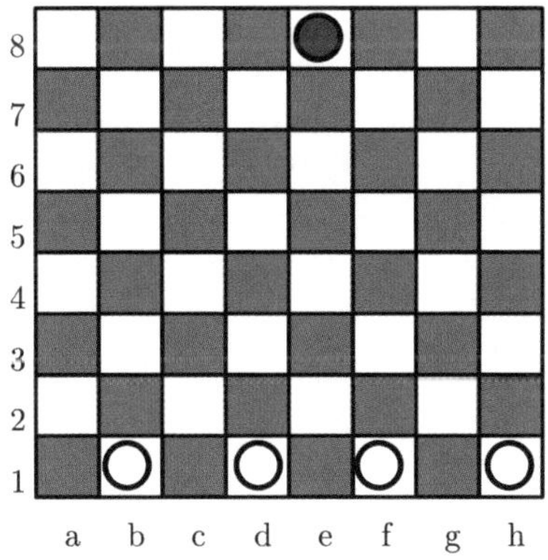

Figure 2.3: Sample winning positions.

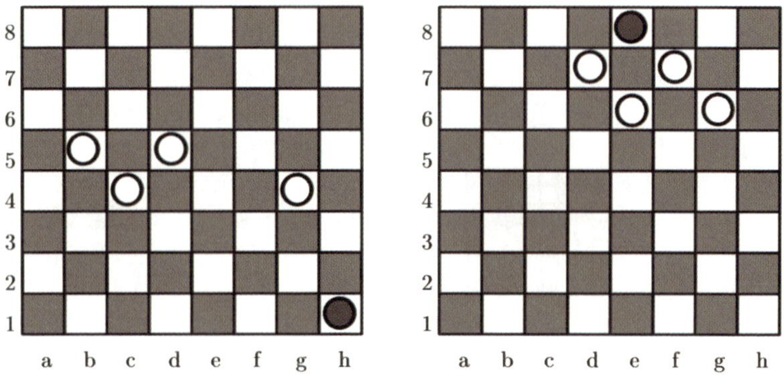

Win by the fox

Win by the geese

Figure 2.4: A game situation.

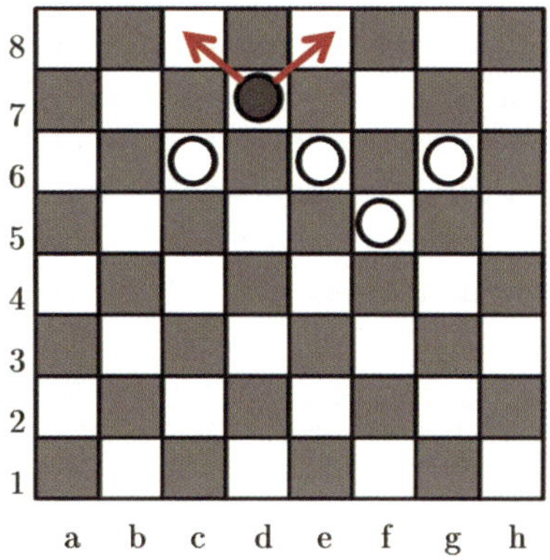

position, we can analyze them in the same way that we did for the position of Figure 2.4.

Because the geese can only move upwards, each goose can only make at most seven moves during a game. Therefore, any play of the game will finish after at most twenty-eight goose moves and so at most fifty-six moves in total. If we continued to grow the tree until every branch ended, we would have a complete analysis of all possible plays of the game. This would be a very large, but finite, tree.

A *leaf* of the tree is a node with no descendant. It corresponds to a position where whichever of the fox or the geese is to play has no legal move, and so loses the game. After all leaves have been categorized as fox wins or geese wins, we could now move up the tree to a nonleaf node v for which all

Figure 2.5: Part of a decision tree.

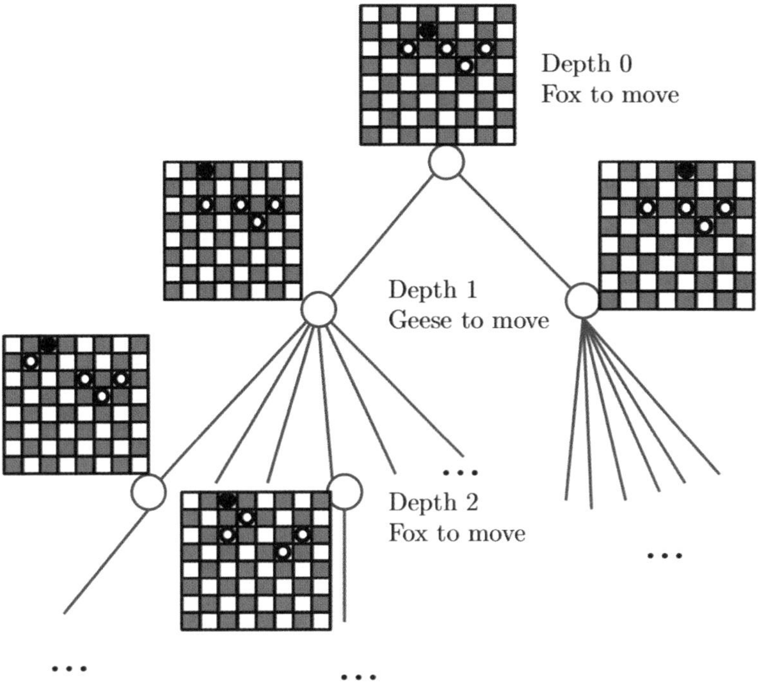

descendants are leaves. Suppose that v corresponds to a goose-to-move position. If a descendant node w corresponds to a position where the fox will lose (and so the geese will win), the geese player could make a move to that position. In that case, v would be labeled as a geese-win node. If no such winning move exists, then v would be labeled as a geese-lose node. If the corresponding position is reached in a game, every legal move for the geese results in a position where the fox can win by playing correctly. A similar set of rules provides a classification of the fox-to-move positions. For example, the position in Figure 2.4 would eventually be classified as a node representing a loss by the fox and a win by the geese.

We can continue this process, locating a tree node which has not been labeled but for which all descendants have been labeled until finally we reach the node of depth 0. At this point, we will know whether the first player to move, in this case the fox, can force a win by perfect play.

Although this decision tree approach works in theory, it is generally not directly applicable in practice because the decision trees quickly become too large to analyze exhaustively, even using a computer. Figure 2.1 described a winning strategy for X in Tic-Tac-Toe. A complete decision tree for *Fox and Geese* could be created using a computer, or with a large amount of patience. However for a game as complex as chess, the size of the tree is prohibitive. Claude Shannon, often referred to as the "father of information theory" estimated the number of different games of chess to be approximately 10^{120}. By contrast, the number of atoms in the observable universe is estimated to be approximately 10^{80}.

What is needed is a shortcut for deciding which player has the advantage and how much of an advantage for a node in a decision tree. Most computer chess programs work by generating a small part of a complete decision tree, typically limiting their analysis to positions within a fixed number of moves from the current position. They complement this with a position evaluator. This is a heuristic program that analyzes a situation and estimates how good it is for Black or White. This evaluation typically uses factors such as the material possessed by each player and positional advantages. When the decision tree reaches its depth limit, it uses the evaluator to estimate the relative advantage for White and Black of nodes of the decision tree below that depth. It then uses these estimates to compute estimated advantages of nodes higher in the tree.

2.4 The Anatomy of Deep Blue

Deep Blue had five critical components:

1. **The Deep Blue Chess Computer.** The Deep Blue SP2 parallel computer consisted of two cabinets containing 36 RS/6000 computers. Each was designed to support sixteen chess chips, but due to the limited number of workable chess chips fabricated, each node had only six chips for a total of 216 chess chips. These chess chips were designed to rapidly evaluate board positions. Deep Blue was able to evaluate approximately 100 million positions per second.

2. **The opening book.** Tournament level chess games normally begin with standard openings, and variations of the openings, played by both players. These openings have been extensively studied over many years. This enables both players to make a number of very good moves at the beginning of the game while using a minimal amount of time on the clock. At some point, Deep Blue would decide that it could no longer play the standard opening and would begin selecting moves based on its decision tree.

3. **The endgame database.** Deep Blue had analyzed many possible endgames. For each it knew an optimal sequence of moves. If it was in a winning position, it would play perfectly. If it was not in a winning position, it would play in such a way as to make its opponent use as much time as possible and, hopefully, make a mistake.

4. **The evaluation function.** Deep Blue had a sophisticated, parameterized, evaluation function used by the chess chips. It based its evaluation of a position on a large number of factors, such as material, mobility, king safety and center control. Optimal values for some of these parameters were determined by the system itself, by analyzing thousands of master games.

5. **Clock Management.** Because the games were timed, played with chess clocks, it was essential that Deep Blue used time well. It was crucial not to waste time, but in a difficult or promising situation, it could use extra time for a deeper examination of the decision tree. In addition, Deep Blue had to keep a time reserve in case it had a hardware or software problem from which it had to recover during the match.

There was one more challenge that had to be faced by the Deep Blue team. Could they engineer the hardware and software so that all the parts worked together, presenting its opponent with a unified adversary with no discoverable gaps?

2.5 Constructing Deep(er) Blue

At the end of the visit to IBM Research in 1996, Garry Kasparov and his team began negotiations with IBM for a rematch to be held in 1997. Shortly after this, the Deep Blue team members decided on the improvements that they would make to Deep Blue. The internal working name was "Deeper Blue." All technical components would be strengthened.

The chess chips were redesigned, made faster and had features added which sped up the evaluation function and increased its strength. The RS/6000 processors were replaced with next generation processors that were twice as fast. The end result was a massively parallel RS/6000 SP system with 30 nodes. Each node had a general microprocessor, plus 16 redesigned VLSI chess chips. These chips typically enabled Deeper Blue to evaluate positions to a depth of six to eight moves, but could support it investigating certain lines of play to a depth of twenty or more moves. This gave it the ability to analyze deeper in the decision tree than its predecessor. The new Deeper Blue could analyze 200 million board positions per second, double what could be done by the original Deep Blue.

The endgame database had been improved, some errors had been removed and all possible endgames with five or fewer pieces on the board, and many with six pieces, had been analyzed.

The evaluation function itself underwent further development. This was a key component. It enabled Deeper Blue to select promising lines of attack and defense without having to explicitly generate the impossibly large complete decision tree. When interviewed after the 1997 match, the Deep Blue team summarized the evaluation function by first identifying the four basic chess values that Deeper Blue considered before deciding on a move: material, position, king safety and tempo [69].

Material is evaluated in a way similar to what beginning chess players learn: a knight or a bishop is worth three pawns, a rook is worth five pawns and a queen is worth nine pawns. However, this is refined by adding a variety of adjustments such as retaining both bishops in the endgame generally increases their value beyond six pawns.

Position is more difficult to evaluate. One way to estimate offensive strength is by counting the number of safe squares that a player's pieces can attack. The more squares they control, the stronger the position. King safety is a defensive counterpart. How many of your opponent's pieces can attack the king's position now, or after a defined number of future moves?

Tempo can be measured by the number of moves it takes players to get their pieces into the current position. It penalizes wasted moves.

The challenge was to find the right combination and weighting of these factors so that they were consistent with the outcome of the game. This included analysis of thousands of master level games with the goal of refining the weighting of the various parameters and detecting and removing anomalies that could cost a game.

During the fourteen months between the first and second match, Joel Benjamin, a grandmaster who worked extensively with the Deep Blue team, played many games and analyzed Deeper Blue's play in a wide range of situations. This included every aspect from the validity of the evaluation function to the opening book database itself. These were significantly improved through his insights. (In Philadelphia in 1996, Game 6, Kasparov played a standard opening, but purposely made the moves out of the normal sequence. This had no effect on the subsequent positions, but it confused Deep Blue which did not recognize this. As a result, the original Deep Blue wasted valuable clock time looking for good moves, which were no better than the moves in the standard opening).

As part of the preparation, the new Deeper Blue also played many games against the original Deep Blue. As spring of 1997 approached, the new Deeper Blue was dominating these games.

2.6 1997 - Deep Blue vs. Garry Kasparov in New York

The return match was scheduled for May of 1997. The Deep Blue team believed that Deeper Blue was ready for the first game of the rematch. Garry Kasparov had also prepared for the rematch by playing games against a variety of computer chess programs. The stakes had been raised. The total prize money was now $1,100,000 with the winner receiving $700,000, and the loser receiving $400,000.

The rematch was to be held at the Equitable Center in New York City. The Center featured a 480 seat auditorium outfitted with three giant projection screens. The games themselves were played in a room on the 35th floor of the Center, and transmitted via a closed circuit video feed to the auditorium. Three expert commentators were on stage in the auditorium and provided ongoing analysis of the progress of the games. The auditorium was filled to capacity throughout the match.

The first game began at 3:00 PM on May 3, 1997, Kasparov playing White. He had won the last two games of the 1996 Philadelphia match. How would the new improved Deeper Blue do one year later against the world champion? The Deep Blue team was guardedly confident. There was no shortage of external predictions of the outcome of the match, most calling for another Kasparov victory.

Typically, computer chess programs were at their best when playing a precise tactical game. Their ability to look ahead, and not miss anything, made them strong opponents. Where they often had troubles was when there was no immediate threat and they had to select a move with a nonspecific long term objective. Kasparov had mentioned this in discussions following the 1996 match. In the first game of the rematch, it appeared that Kasparov was playing a conservative "anti-chess" style to feel out Deeper Blue and see if it exhibited this characteristic.

The game progressed in this fashion until the 33rd move when a situation arose which was not handled well by the Deeper Blue logic, involving two linked passed pawns and an offered trade of queens. Kasparov emerged with an advantage and Deeper Blue's position went downhill. An elusive bug in the software re-emerged in Deeper Blue's 44th move and then, after Kasparov's next move, Deeper Blue resigned.

The score in the rematch was Kasparov 1, Deeper Blue 0. Moreover, the Deep Blue team had lost its last three games – two in 1996, one in 1997 – to Kasparov.

In Game 2, played the next day, the situation reversed with a surprising twist. Deeper Blue, playing White, tried a different opening, hoping to avoid the problematic situation that had arisen the day before. After Deeper Blue's 45th move, Kasparov resigned and the match was tied at one game each. That night, some chess analysts believed that Kasparov had missed a line of play that could have resulted in a draw. Subsequent analysis made this less clear, but in any case, the match was now tied at one game each.

In Game 3, Kasparov, playing white, played an unusual opening, possibly seeing whether Deep Blue could handle it. The game resulted in a draw.

In Game 4, late in the game, Kasparov was running into time problems. Because of this, he probably made sub-optimal moves which may have cost him a win. The game ended in another draw.

Game 5 was another draw, this time due to an unusual move made by Deeper Blue, followed by a brilliant endgame.

The score was now tied at $2\frac{1}{2}$ each, with one game to play.

In Game 6, Deeper Blue offered a knight sacrifice, which Kasparov accepted. After this, Deeper Blue was able to destroy Kasparov's defenses. He resigned after nineteen moves. This was the only game of the match which did not go past the 40th move.

The Deep Blue team had won the rematch, $3\frac{1}{2}$ to $2\frac{1}{2}$.

2.7 Aftermath

Following the match, there was great interest in having a third match between Garry Kasparov and Deep Blue. There is a story, possibly apocryphal, that a delegation from IBM Research called on the Chairman, Lou Gerstner, and presented a vision: IBM could cement its position of being the world's greatest chess playing corporation now and in the future through further investment! However, in 1997, senior executives in the company decided that the time had come to refocus activities on other projects that could exploit what had been learned in the Deep Blue project and which had broader relevance to the company's customers. So Deep Blue retired.

The main Deep Blue system was run on a two tower IBM RS/6000 SP computer. One tower functioned as the primary and the other as the backup. They both still exist, although they are no longer in game condition. One is housed in The Smithsonian Museum in Washington DC and the other is in the Computer History Museum in Mountain View, CA.

The backup tower was considered essential. Match rules specified that if Deep Blue encountered a hardware or software problem, the chess clocks would not stop but continue to run. This meant that a problem that took time to resolve could result in Deep Blue losing a game because clock time ran out. During the match both towers of Deep Blue ran identically so that if a hardware problem occurred in the primary, there could be a fast crossover to the backup. No problems actually occurred during the match to require a crossover.

There were several factors that contributed to Deep Blue's success.

1. The core of the Deep Blue Team, Feng-hsiung Hsu, Murray Campbell and Thomas Anantharaman, was the Carnegie Mellon University team that had built Deep Thought, the world's number one chess computer in 1989. They were brought into IBM Research to create the chess computer project and they gave it an extraordinary launch. (Shortly after joining IBM, Anantharaman left Research for a position on Wall Street. He was replaced by Joe Hoane, who rapidly became a core member of the Deep Blue team.)

2. By incorporating the latest semiconductor technology, and by great creativity and innovation in the software, Deep Blue was very fast. This provided some advantage in the depth of the search tree that could be explored. It also had the significant advantage that Deep Blue's moves could be made faster. Games were played with a chess

clock, and a player lost if their time expired. Players obviously continue their analysis while either their own or their opponent's clock is running. That meant that by doubling the speed of Deep Blue, not only could it choose a move using less of its own time, but also it was providing a smaller amount of time to be used as "free" thinking time by the opponent. Kasparov often felt under time pressure later in the games of the 1997 rematch.

3. The Deep Blue computer and software was designed with one function in mind – to play chess at the level of the world champion. The machine that defeated Gary Kasparov in 1997 was a fourth generation evolution of the architecture that had its origin at Carnegie Mellon University ten years before. The chess chips used to rapidly explore parts of the search tree contained enough logic to manage the subtree and evaluate positions in hardware. Deep Blue combined the raw speed possible on a specialized hardware device with the flexibility and power provided by the sophisticated search-and-evaluate software that ran on the host system, which was itself a state of the art parallel system. Over the period of time between the 1996 and 1997 matches, the team was able to refine the many components and subsystems that made up Deep Blue to create an integrated whole.

4. Joel Benjamin, a grandmaster who had played very well against computer chess programs, worked extensively with the team, especially during the period between the two matches. He probed for weaknesses and made many suggestions that strengthened its play, particularly against an exceptionally strong player such as Garry Kasparov. This enabled significant improvements to be made to the board position evaluator so that Deep Blue's assessment of the strength of a position was closer to that of a grandmaster.

5. Deep Blue was free of emotion and never got tired. At the highest levels, there is a psychological component to chess. Deep Blue, being a computer, was oblivious to this.

Since Shannon in 1950, the creation of a computer capable of playing chess at the level of a human expert had been an elusive goal. Great progress was made over the next 40 years. In 1989, Deep Thought, a predecessor of Deep Blue, was the first computer to have played a tournament at a grandmaster level. There still remained the challenge of creating a machine capable of playing at the level of the world's top player. The Deep Blue team met that challenge.

The two matches in 1996 and 1997 between Deep Blue and Gary Kasparov generated an enormous amount of media coverage. Many people view Deep Blue's success in 1997 as a major milestone in the development of Artificial Intelligence and, more broadly, in the growth of computer science. The Deep Blue team emphatically differentiated what Deep Blue did from Artificial

Chapter 3

What is Watson?

Mr. Watson, Come here. I want you.
– Alexander Graham Bell

Contents

On February 14, 2011, another eagerly anticipated human vs. machine event was about to take place. There would be an exhibition match between the top two (human) winners in the history of the game show *Jeopardy!* and a computer, named "Watson," created over a five year period by a team at IBM Research. The human contestants were Ken Jennings and Brad Rutter. Jennings holds the record for the longest winning streak on *Jeopardy!* (75 days) during which time he won over two million dollars. Rutter is the biggest money winner of all time, having won over $3,500,000. Watson was a powerful supercomputer with a massive amount (terabytes) of memory and 3,000 processors.

This chapter is about the success of Watson, and how the supercomputer was designed and built. While Watson heavily depended on natural language processing and text mining, it also provides an example of the power of combining multiple analytics methods to achieve a desired result.

3.1 February 14, 2011 - The Game is Afoot

Jeopardy! is a popular television quiz show first launched in 1964. Basically, it is a trivia competition between three contestants who are presented with a set of questions covering a broad range of subjects – music, art, history, literature, science, pop culture, movies, ... – and they race to be the first to answer each question.

Part of the popularity of the show, which has contributed to its longevity, is due to the complexity and cleverness of the clues. They feature puns, combinations of ideas, uncommon words and obscure facts.

Ever since Deep Blue's success at playing chess in 1996 and 1997, Paul Horn, Director of Research at IBM, and his executive team had been looking for another suitable "Grand Challenge" for Research. It had to be something that might be possible, but something sufficiently difficult that most people would think that it could not be done. Also, ideally, it should be a problem that would have broad general interest. Some natural candidates, such as checkers, the Japanese game of go, backgammon or poker were ruled out, either because the game seemed too difficult or too specialized or because there were already many teams working on these problems. In 2004, a candidate was discovered.

IBM Vice President Charles Lickel and a small group of co-workers were having dinner in a restaurant. Early in the meal, the restaurant fell silent. All around the IBM group, people left their tables and went into the adjacent bar to watch what was on television. Lickel was intrigued. He and his colleagues followed the exodus into the bar to see what was going on. The show that was attracting everyone's attention was not a sporting event, but *Jeopardy!* The intense interest was due to the ongoing winning streak of Ken Jennings.

Lickel took the idea of developing a computer system to play *Jeopardy!* back to Horn. This game seemed to have all the desired properties. It certainly had universal interest, and no computer based question answering system existed that could even come close to being able to compete with humans under the rules of Jeopardy. The big question was whether it would be possible to build a system that could accomplish this.

In general, supercomputing challenges are of two types. In some cases, such as simulating the folding of a protein, the issue is whether a system can be built with enough power to run a known algorithm sufficiently quickly and whether the algorithm would work on problems of the desired scale. In other cases, even with virtually unlimited computing power, no method is known which can be shown to solve the problem. Playing Jeopardy clearly fell into this second category.

In 2005, Horn decided to launch the project. Nobody had any idea how to beat humans at this game, or even if it was possible, but there was a significant upside to trying: even if the goal of beating humans at Jeopardy was out of reach, almost certainly enough would be learned from trying to make the project worthwhile.

Now, six years later, a two game exhibition match was about to start. It would be broadcast over three shows and would consist of two separate games of Jeopardy. Each game of Jeopardy consists of three rounds: Jeopardy, Double Jeopardy, and Final Jeopardy. At the end of the three rounds, the contestant with the largest amount of winnings is declared champion for the night and is invited to return the next day and play against two new contestants. The first show would consist of the Jeopardy round of the first game. The second show would be the Double Jeopardy and Final Jeopardy rounds of the first game. The third show would be the entire second game. The winner would be the player, Jennings, Rutter or Watson, with the largest total winnings.

The match was termed an "exhibition," but the prize money was substantial. The winner would receive $1 million, the second and third place finishers would receive $300,000 and $200,000 respectively. (IBM had announced that they would donate 100% of Watson's winnings to charity; Jennings and Rutter announced that they would each donate 50% of their winnings.)

Jeopardy has the unusual feature that each question is presented in the form of an answer and the contestant has to answer in the form of a question. For example, the correct response to the clue:

> MUSIC FANS WAX RHAPSODIC ABOUT THIS HUNGARIAN'S TRANSCENDENTAL ETUDES.

is "Who is Franz Liszt?"

The clues for each of the first two rounds are presented in six categories, each with an often cryptic hint to the subject matter of the category. Each category contains five clues. For (simple) Jeopardy, each category contains a clue with dollar value $200, $400, $600, $800, and $1,000. For Double Jeopardy, the values are doubled. The dollar values of the clues in each category are intended to roughly correspond to their difficulty. For each game, the categories and dollar values of the clues are displayed on a large board.

The above clue was under the category "Etude Brute."

Each of the contestants has a buzzer. One contestant selects a category and a clue dollar value. The host of the show reads the clue then turns on a signal light. At this point, the contestants can buzz in if they think that they know the answer. The first contestant to buzz in gets to answer. If the answer is correct, then the dollar value of the clue is added to his or her total winnings. If incorrect, the contestant loses that amount from their winnings.

Presenting clues to Watson was a challenge. Human players are shown each clue on monitors in front of them as it is read out loud. Because the match was intended to test knowledge and natural language understanding, not speech recognition, it was agreed that each clue would be given to Watson in text form at the same time that it was shown to the human players. When the host turned on the signal lights in front of each human contestant, a signal was sent to Watson. At this point Watson and the human players could race to buzz in. To be fair to the humans, Watson had been furnished with a robotic hand that pressed a buzzer identical to the ones used by human contestants. Players who buzzed in too early, before the signal lights came on, were locked out from buzzing in for 1/4 of a second. (Watson never made this mistake.)

Host Alex Trebek and the three contestants, Ken Jennings, Watson and Brad Rutter were introduced and the match began.

Figure 3.1: The match begins.

The clue categories for the first game were "Literary Character APB," "Beatles People," "Olympic Oddities," "Name the Decade," "Final Frontiers" and "Alternate Meanings." Rutter had won the draw to select the first category, and he chose "Alternate Meanings" for $200. The clue was

> 4-LETTER WORD FOR A VANTAGE POINT OR A BELIEF.

Rutter buzzed first and gave the correct answer of "What is a view?" winning $200.

Rutter, being correct, was given the next choice of category. He chose "Alternate Meanings" for $400. The clue was

> 4-LETTER WORD FOR THE IRON FITTING ON THE HOOF OF A HORSE OR A CARD-DEALING BOX IN A CASINO.

This time, Watson buzzed first and gave the correct answer "What is a shoe?" winning $400.

Now Watson was given the choice of category and chose "Literary Character APB" for $800.

A siren sounded signaling that this clue was a Daily Double. In the Jeopardy round, one of the clues on each board is secretly designated as a Daily Double. In the Double Jeopardy round, two clues are designated as Daily Doubles. A player who selects one of these is given the exclusive right to answer the clue. However, before seeing the clue, the player must wager an amount on being able to provide a correct response. The bet must be at least $5.00 but can be as much as the larger of the player's current winnings and the largest clue dollar value on the board.

"$1,000, please," replied Watson. The clue was read:

> WANTED FOR KILLING SIR DANVERS CAREW; APPEARANCE - PALE & DWARFISH; SEEMS TO HAVE A SPLIT PERSONALITY.

Watson answered "Who is Hyde?"

"Hyde, yes, Dr. Jekyll and Mr. Hyde, either one," replied Trebek.

Watson's winnings total was now $1,400.

The round continued on until all clues on the board had been selected. At the end of the round, the score was close: Rutter and Watson were tied with winnings of $5,000 and Jennings followed with winnings of $2,000. There still remained two rounds to play in the first game of the match: Double Jeopardy and Final Jeopardy. These would be played in the next show, broadcast the following day.

In the next round, Double Jeopardy, Watson started by buzzing in and correctly answering the first six clues. The seventh was a Daily Double. At this point, the winnings were Jennings: $2,000, Watson: $14,600, Rutter: $5,000.

An important strategic decision is how much to wager when a contestant selects a Double Jeopardy square. The category was "Cambridge." Watson's wager was not a multiple of $100 or $1,000 as was normally bet, but $6,435. Trebek paused, raised his eyebrows and responded "I won't ask." The clue was

> THE CHAPELS AT PEMBROOKE AND ST. CHRISTOPHER'S COLLEGE WERE DESIGNED BY THIS ARCHITECT.

When Watson correctly answered "Who is Sir Christopher Wren?", its total had grown to $21,035.

The next clue, worth $1,600 under the category "The Art of the Steal," was

> IN MAY 2010, FIVE PAINTINGS WORTH $125 MILLION BY BRAQUE, MATISSE & 3 OTHERS LEFT PARIS' MUSEUM OF THIS ART PERIOD.

Watson buzzed in and answered "What is Picasso?" This was incorrect. Jennings answered "What is Cubism?" which was also incorrect. Rutter tried "What is Impressionism?" also incorrect. The correct reply was "What is Modern Art?" All three contestants lost the same amount, $1,600.

Throughout the rest of the Double Jeopardy Round, Watson continued its domination of the game, including correctly answering the second Daily Double. When the round ended, the standings were Jennings: $2,400, Watson: $36,681, Rutter: $5,400. Watson had taken a commanding lead.

The last round of the first game was Final Jeopardy. In this round the category is revealed to the three contestants. Before the clue is revealed, each must write down how much of their winnings they are willing to wager on being able to answer correctly. Then the clue is revealed and the players are given 30 seconds to write down their proposed answers. (Not coincidentally, this is the same amount of time that it takes to play the musical theme from Jeopardy.)

The category was "US Cities." The clue was

> ITS LARGEST AIRPORT IS NAMED FOR A WORLD WAR II HERO AND ITS SECOND LARGEST FOR A WORLD WAR II BATTLE.

The proposed answers are revealed by the players in increasing order of winnings. Jennings wagered $2,400 and Rutter wagered $5,000 on the same answer "What is Chicago?"

When Watson answered "What is Toronto?????" there was an audible gasp from the audience. That was incorrect. The string of question marks indicated that Watson was very unsure about the answer. The amount wagered, before the clue was revealed, was $947.

At the end of the first game, the scores were Jennings: $4,800, Watson: $35,734, Rutter: $10,400. Watson's lead heading into the second game, to be played in the next broadcast, was large, but perhaps not insurmountable.

3.2 Natural Language Understanding and Text Mining

Most of us have used an internet search engine such a Google or Yahoo to try to find the answer to a question. We quickly learn that it can take considerable skill and creativity to find a sequence of words that will result in a web page containing the desired information appearing near the top of the list of URLs returned. A person looking for a Hilton hotel in Paris might be quite surprised by the result obtained by typing in the name of the city followed by the name of the hotel chain. Try using your favorite internet search engine to determine which car manufacturer has seen the largest percentage increase in sales over the first decade of the 21st century. People may not know the answer, but at least they (generally) understand what is being asked for.

Natural Language Understanding is a branch of Artificial Intelligence that deals with understanding the meaning of human language. The problem was recognized as early as 1950 when Alan Turing proposed the challenge of building a computer that could carry on a "human-like" dialogue with a person. The goal was to carry on a dialogue such that the human could not decide whether it was speaking with a machine or a person. This is the so-called *Turing Test*.

This distinguishes between transcribing recorded speech such as a stenographer might do (speech recognition) and understanding the thoughts expressed by the speech (natural language understanding). The test proposed by Turing focused on the latter, and proposed that communication between the person and the computer or another human should take place by means of typed text. The requirement for the Jeopardy clues to be given to Watson in machine readable form were consistent with this.

Turing also discussed the things that a machine or human could be expected to know and what sorts of calculations each could typically make. For example, a machine would have no difficulty multiplying ten six digit numbers together. It would have no difficulty in providing an alphabetical list of the capitals of all countries belonging to the United Nations. That would be much harder for (most) humans. However, it is difficult to imagine a machine responding to the question "Why are you feeling sad today?" with the answer "I was thinking of my father, who was poor but honest."

The difficulty of understanding text varies tremendously with the complexity, context and grammatical correctness of the text. Simple commands are often easy to understand, for example "Turn off the light," or "Mr. Watson, Come here." But more elaborate texts, such as volumes of poetry, may require expert literary critics to interpret, and often the critics cannot agree.

Jeopardy adds a new dimension to this problem. The clues and category names are often constructed in ways designed to obfuscate the meaning and even disguise the subject matter under consideration.

Text Mining is a general term for methods designed to extract meaning from a body of text. In the simplest case, it may involve looking for keywords appearing in the document. A more sophisticated method may look for combinations and sequences of words with which it may associate synonyms that do not appear in the text. This becomes important when responding to a question which may require combing facts from a number of documents which have different vocabularies. An even more sophisticated method may attempt to extract underlying ideas from the phrases and sentences in the text.

Grammar based Natural Language Understanding (NLU) systems usually include the following components:

1. A *lexicon* of the language. This is a dictionary of the words contained in the language. It may also contain an *ontology* which describes the relationship between different words, for example "Water" is a "clear liquid," but there are "liquids" that are neither "water" nor "clear." "Water" is also a "fluid."

2. A *parser* and language rules that can identify the functions of words within the text. For example, what are the functions of the words "flies" and "like" in the sentence, attributed to Groucho Marx, "Time flies like an arrow; fruit flies like a banana."?

3. A *semantic model* that enables the extraction of meaning from the lexicon, the ontology and the parser. This contrasts with a syntax that specifies the admissible form for a text sample. The following two sentences contain identical words and have identical syntaxes:

   They got married and had a baby.

> They had a baby and got married.

However, many speakers would contend that they have different meanings and connotations.

A challenge for NLU systems is that there are generally many different ways to express an idea, often with subtle differences. A set of rules constructed to extract meaning from a set of articles on a topic may work well for some expressions of the idea but fail completely for others.

For example, in formal logic the words "and" and "but" are usually considered to be equivalent. But consider the sentence "The student answered the exam questions on grammar and ignored the questions on semantics." What happens if we replace "and" with "but"? Suppose the context was a test with six questions and the instruction was to answer any three questions. If there were three of each type of question, then the word "and" may indicate that the student made a judicious choice. However, the word "but" may imply that the student exhibited a lack of knowledge regarding semantics.

There are many different semantic models, having various degrees of complexity.

4. Some more advanced systems may also incorporate logical inference within their overall framework. These can be based on various models of formal logic. Suppose that our text contains the following:

> John set out to drive from Chicago to New York.
>
> After four hours of driving, John realized that his wallet was at home on his dresser.
>
> He texted his wife who replied that she could be at a garage by the lake they could see from their living room in ten minutes.
>
> What lake was that?

There are several possible explanations. Perhaps the simplest is that John and his wife's home was in Toledo, 250 miles east of Chicago, and their house overlooked Lake Erie. It was never claimed that he began his trip at home.

How can a computer figure this out? How can a set of seemingly independent statements, some of which may be irrelevant, be combined to obtain a set of logically consistent explanations to a question which has not been asked? Which of several alternatives is most likely to be correct?

In general, different methods work best for different situations. A system that can read a novel and determine who are the principal characters and how they are related may be much different from a system that reads medical journals and attempts to figure out which papers deal with related subjects, or a system that attempts to understand the notes made by a detective investigating a crime scene. The challenge facing the Watson team was that they had to create a system that could deal with over 2,000 different categories of questions, and deal with them as quickly as the fastest humans. How they did this is described in the next two sections.

3.3 Deep Q&A

The first issue facing the Watson team was how to deal with a huge variety of clues which could be on any topic. This involved both figuring out what was being asked for and then what was the answer. The second, discussed in the next section, was how to take this capability and embed it in a system that could compete successfully in Jeopardy.

When the *Jeopardy!* Challenge project was launched, a four person team at IBM Research had been working for six years developing a QA System called Practical Intelligent Question Answering Technology (PIQUANT). This system was one of the top rated systems in the annual Text Retrieval Conference (TREC) event, co-sponsored by the National Institute of Standards and Technology (NIST) and the U.S. Department of Defense, run from 1999 to 2007. Participants in the TREC QA event were given a corpus of approximately one thousand documents and 500 questions to be answered based on this corpus. The questions were much simpler than those encountered in *Jeopardy!*, the systems were allowed to access the web and were given one week to provide answers to the questions. PIQUANT performed at the 33% accuracy range in TREC evaluations.

Note three significant differences between TREC QA and *Jeopardy!*:

1. The set of possible topics for *Jeopardy!* is (almost) completely unrestricted.

2. The answer to a question in *Jeopardy!* must be obtained within five to seven seconds if the contestant hopes to have any chance of successfully buzzing in.

3. Contestants in *Jeopardy!* are not allowed any "lifelines"; no contacts with the outside world are permitted during a game.

When evaluating human contestants as well as the system that was to become Watson, there were two fundamental measures: *accuracy* was the fraction of clues for which the contestant was sufficiently confident of the answer to buzz in; *precision* was the fraction of the time that the response was correct. The first thing the Jeopardy team did was to evaluate PIQUANT on 500 randomly sampled Jeopardy clues. On the 5% of the clues for which PIQUANT was most confident, the precision was 47%. Over all the clues in the set, the precision was 13%. In this test, speed of answering was not a factor.

Based on an analysis of 2000 Jeopardy games, a winner needed to have an accuracy of between 40% and 50% and a precision of between 85% and 95%. During Ken Jennings' winning streak, he had an accuracy of 62% and a precision of 92%. Clearly the team had work to do.

From the start it was recognized that a key to success would be accurately estimating the probability of a proposed answer to a clue being correct. This was called the *confidence level.* It was also recognized that no single approach could succeed with the variety of subjects covered by *Jeopardy!*. The system would have to effectively combine a large number of both general and specific methods.

There were four overarching principles in the DeepQA system that was developed for Watson:

1. **Massive Parallelism:** The system would use a massively parallel system which would permit simultaneous running of multiple interpretations of clues and hypotheses for answers.

2. **Many Experts:** The system would be designed to integrate and evaluate a wide range of different approaches to answering the clues in order to compute a confidence level and an answer.

3. **Pervasive Confidence Estimation:** No single approach was expected to give the answer to a clue; all components were required to produce candidate answers with associated confidence levels. A high level machine learning system would develop a proposed answer and a confidence level based on all the candidate answers and their confidence levels.

4. **Integrate shallow and deep knowledge:** Shallow knowledge is based on the natural language content and text analysis. Deep knowledge is based on material abstracted and stored in structured knowledge bases.

Building the DeepQA system that enabled Watson to compete successfully on *Jeopardy!* required integrating a number of different architectural components:

Content Acquisition: A first step in constructing a DeepQA system is to identify sources of content that will subsequently be used to determine possible answers to the clues and to validate answer hypotheses. This requires a combination of manual and automatic steps. By analyzing example questions from the problem space being considered, the kinds of questions can be identified as well as the application domains. The sources for Watson included a wide range of encyclopedias, dictionaries, thesauruses, newswire articles, literary works and so on.

Following this, an automatic corpus expansion process takes place. Starting with the identified documents, related documents are retrieved from the web and self-contained text passages are extracted from these related documents. These text passages are then scored to see whether they are informative with respect to the original seed document. If so, these passages become part of the expanded corpus.

DeepQA also leverages other curated sources of structured content which are then brought into the corpus. Examples are dbPedia, WordNet and the Yago ontology.

Because the rules for the *Jeopardy!* Challenge required Watson to be isolated from outside sources during the competition, it was critical that a sufficiently broad and comprehensive knowledge base was collected, structured and integrated.

Question Analysis: The first step in the QA process is to analyze the question to determine what is being asked for. A number of different techniques are used here. One determines what type of question is being asked. Is it a definition? a puzzle? a math question?

A second part of this analysis is to determine the *Lexical Answer Type* or LAT being asked for. This is a word or noun phrase in the question that specifies the type of the answer without attempting to understand the semantics. It is the part of the question that, if replaced by the answer, makes the question a stand-alone statement.

If the clue was

> WHEN HIT BY ELECTRONS, A PHOSPHOR GIVES OFF ELECTROMAGNETIC ENERGY IN THIS FORM.

the LAT is "THIS FORM."

If the clue was

> THIS TITLE CHARACTER WAS THE CRUSTY AND TOUGH CITY EDITOR OF THE *LOS ANGELES TRIBUNE.*

the LAT is "THIS TITLE CHARACTER."

A third component is relation detection. Most clues contain relationships between entities. In the above example, there is a relationship of "EDITOR" between "THE LOS ANGELES TRIBUNE" and the LAT "THIS TITLE CHARACTER." When relationships are discovered, it provides the opportunity to look up the answer in a curated database. However, due to the breadth of relationships in *Jeopardy!* and the variety of ways that are expressed, it turned out that this helped with less than 2% of the clues.

A fourth component is decomposition. This involves breaking up complex clues into several simpler parts, each of which can be resolved. DeepQA uses a number of different techniques to do this. Combining the answers to the parts can help discover the answer to the clue. An important additional benefit of decomposition is that it increases the confidence level of an answer.

Hypothesis Generation: After a clue has been analyzed, decomposed and relationships have been detected, a large number of candidate answers are generated. Each candidate answer then replaces the LAT in the clue, or in a part of the clue, to create a hypothesis. A confidence level is then computed for each hypothesis. The goal of this portion of the analysis is to provide a set of candidate answers which contains the correct answer. The target was for Watson to generate the correct answer as a candidate answer somewhere within the top 250 ranked candidates for 85% of the questions. If the correct answer to the clue was not generated in this stage, Watson had no chance of answering correctly. At the end of this process, Watson typically had several hundred candidate answers.

In order to deal with the speed of response required to compete on *Jeopardy!*, a lightweight filtering process was applied to these candidates to reduce their number to about 100 before proceeding with the next stage.

Hypothesis and Evidence Scoring: Scoring was a crucial part of Watson's architecture which allows it to compete at a championship level. First, it enabled ranking of the hundred candidates to determine the ones most likely to be correct. Second, Watson would only buzz in if the confidence measure produced by scoring the top ranked candidate answer passes a particular threshold. By raising or lowering this threshold, Watson can be made to play more conservatively or more aggressively.

A set of algorithms produced scores measuring how well evidence supported each of the remaining candidate answers. Watson included more than fifty scoring criteria. These ranged from formal probabilities to counts of categorical features based on a range of features. The scorers considered criteria such as the degree of match between a passage's predicate-argument structure and the question, passage source reliability, geospatial location and temporal relationships.

For example, consider the clue:

> IN 1594, HE TOOK A JOB AS A TAX COLLECTOR IN ANDALUSIA.

The two top ranked answers were "Thoreau" and "Cervantes." Temporal relationships were used to rule out Thoreau, who was not born until 1817, whereas Cervantes, the correct answer, lived from 1547 to 1616.

Each of Watson's scoring algorithms was extensively tuned and its reliability was estimated for a range of situations. In addition, interactions between different scorers were also studied. No single scoring method dominated. DeepQA's facility in adding, removing and integrating different scoring algorithms was a crucial component of its success.

At this stage, each candidate answer had a number of different scores, according to the various criteria used. These were combined in the next component to select the top candidate answer and compute the single confidence estimate that determined whether Watson should buzz in.

Final Merging and Ranking: The goal of this final component was to identify the single best supported hypothesis, given all the available evidence, and to estimate its confidence – the likelihood that it is correct. The first step was identifying equivalent candidate answers which, although they may have appeared to be quite different, corresponded to the same entity and then combining their scores appropriately. A simple example is when a person is known by several different names and several different career accomplishments. Some passages may support one of these, others may support different identifiers. If we do not successfully merge the results, we run the risk of two equivalent candidate answers competing with each other, thereby reducing each of their confidence estimates. Merging their scores can give a much more accurate score. For example, if the clue was

> THIS MOVIE ACTOR WON TWO OLYMPIC GOLD MEDALS.

then any one of these could be an answer appearing in a content source: "#23," "Owner of the Charlotte Bobcats," "Outfielder for the Birmingham Barons," "MJ" or "Michael Jordan." Different sources would support some of these choices but not others. By merging the scores, Watson could get a higher and more accurate level of confidence in the answer.

After merging, DeepQA ranked the remaining hypotheses and estimates confidence based on the merged scores. Watson handled this by adopting a machine-learning approach. This required running the system over a large set of training questions for which the correct answer was known. A model was then created which estimated a final confidence level for an answer based on the individual scoring criteria which had been computed. Watson increased the accuracy of the estimate by using different ranking models for different classes of questions.

DeepQA is a sophisticated, flexible system for obtaining answers to a broad range of clues of the sort given in *Jeopardy!*. It depends on having a flexible software architecture capable of integrating a huge variety of approaches, as well as continually improving its ability to locate candidate answers and to accurately estimate the likelihood of each candidate answer being correct.

As the different parts of this architecture were created and integrated, its quality of answer steadily improved. However there was a problem. Early versions of the DeepQA system running on a single system took approximately two hours to obtain an answer to a clue. This time had to be reduced to five to seven seconds to compete successfully on *Jeopardy!*, effectively a speed-up by a factor of 1,000. There remained work to be done.

3.4 The Anatomy of Watson

Building Watson, a self-contained computer system that could compete successfully on *Jeopardy!* against human champions, presented many challenges. The objectives were relatively straightforward:

1. **Accuracy**: be sufficiently confident to buzz in on at least 70% of the clues in a game,

2. **Precision**: be correct over 90% of the time,

3. **Speed:** find an answer and its confidence level within three to five seconds.

The hardware would have to be very fast and would need to provide the massive parallelism required to run the many algorithms comprising DeepQA independently, and also permit sharing of data and consolidation of results. It would also have to have a memory sufficiently large that it could store all the content sources and related indices in memory. Because of the speed requirement, it would not be acceptable to have to look up answers on secondary (disk) storage.

The main computational engine for Watson for the *Jeopardy!* match was a cluster of ninety IBM Power 750 servers. Each Power 750 server used a 3.5 GHz POWER7 eight core processor, with four threads per core. This enabled each server to run 32 parallel processes. The ninety servers gave a total of 2,880 POWER7 processor cores. Watson also used additional I/O, network and cluster controller nodes in 10 racks. In total, it had 16 Terabytes of RAM (random access memory). This memory was sufficient to store approximately 200 million pages of text (roughly equivalent to one million books).

Since the early 2000s, a small team at IBM Research led by David Ferrucci had been developing a software framework called UIMA – Unstructured Information Management Architecture. The goal of UIMA was to provide a framework that could unify the many diverse technologies that had been developed for text mining and processing of unstructured information. This seemed to be exactly what was needed to pull together the massive amounts of text data and the many different analysis and evaluation components that would be required by DeepQA. Apache UIMA is a framework implementation of UIMA. UIMA-AS is part of Apache UIMA which supports the parallelization of UIMA applications through asynchronous messaging. Watson's software architecture was built on UIMA-AS which successfully supported the scale-out of DeepQA onto over 2,500 compute cores. UIMA-AS handled all communication, messaging and queue management necessary for DeepQA. This software architecture running on the POWER7 cluster enabled Watson's run time to meet the three to five second target to respond to a clue. The issue of reaching the required levels of accuracy and precision still remained.

Figure 3.3 documents the progress made in improving Watson's accuracy and precision over the period 2006 to 2010. It also shows how Watson's capability compared with that of winning human players. Each red dot near the top of the chart indicates the precision and accuracy obtained by a human game winner. The purple dots to the right of these represent the precision and accuracy achieved by Ken Jennings on his remarkable winning run. The vertical axis gives the precision, the percentage of questions which the winner answered

Figure 3.2: Watson hardware - a stand-alone system.

correctly. The horizontal axis gives the accuracy, the fraction of questions that the contestant buzzed in and attempted to answer.

The dated lines on the chart show Watson's progress over time. Watson's capability was measured on each test date by giving it a blind set of more than 2000 Jeopardy questions. Watson was given the questions and required to provide both an answer and its level of confidence in the answer for each. The questions were then ordered based on these confidence levels, from highest to lowest.

For each value on the horizontal axis, the point on each dated line is the fraction of answers that Watson would have answered correctly, if it answered the corresponding fraction of the 2000 plus questions for which it had the highest confidence.

For example, by looking at the line labeled 12/07, we can see that if Watson were to have buzzed in for only the 50% of the questions for which the confidence estimate was highest, the precision would have been about 47%. If Watson had been required to achieve a precision of 60%, it could only have buzzed in on 25% of the questions.

The lines show the significant progress made over time. By 04/10, if Watson was required to (only) answer 50% of the questions, the precision would have gone up to over 90%. Answering 80% of the questions would still have maintained a precision of almost 80%.

The Baseline on the chart represents the analogous results obtained by PIQUANT, described in Section 3.3, on the same test.

Figure 3.3: Progress in accuracy and precision.

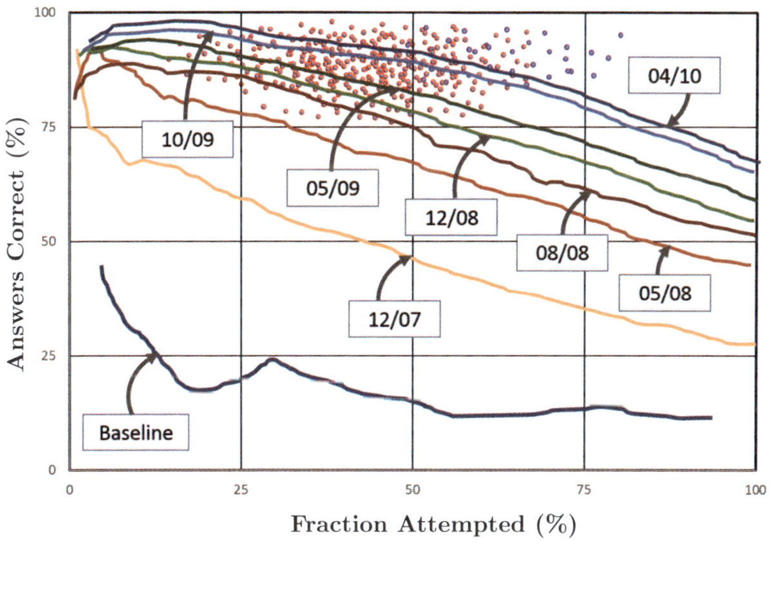

By the middle of 2010, Watson's question answering capability was reaching a level where it could compete with human winners and even with Ken Jennings on precision and accuracy. But *Jeopardy!* has a wagering component. This capability was being developed at the same time for Watson. In the case of a Double Jeopardy clue, whoever successfully buzzed in would be able to wager on their answer before seeing the clue, based only on the category and the clue's dollar value. In the case of a Final Jeopardy question, all contestants were required to wager some amount of their current winnings based only on the clue category and then give an answer to the question after seeing the clue.

The current standing of the contestants is an important factor when deciding amounts of wagers. If a player has a large lead, it makes sense to try to select the squares where the Daily Double questions are usually located (the bottom two rows of the clue table). By wagering a small amount, the player could guarantee at worst a small loss, but, more importantly, keep any opponent from landing on the Daily Double and using it to catch up. Conversely, if a player was trailing, it would be imperative to try and select Daily Double clues, wager a large amount, and try to catch up.

Similar considerations applied to Final Jeopardy. This decision making capacity also had to be incorporated in Watson.

There was also a massive preparatory process that had to be completed. This was the assembling, integrating, expansion and indexing of the content corpus for Watson as described in Section 3.3. If the answer to a clue was not there, in some form, explicitly or implicitly, then Watson had no chance. The Watson team used Hadoop to preprocess the corpus and create fast runtime indices. Hadoop distributed the content over the POWER7 cluster providing high processor utilization as well as a suite of tools for deploying, managing and monitoring the corpus analysis process.

By the end of 2010, Ferrucci and his team believed that Watson was ready. However, the best that could realistically be hoped was that Watson would compete well against Jennings and Rutter. Anything could happen in a small set of games. Watson's success would be determined, to some degree, by the categories and clues that had been selected. The team had no control over that.

The games were scheduled and, on February 16, 2011, the third show, covering the second of the two games played, was broadcast.

3.5 February 16, 2011 - Final Jeopardy

Although the games were not broadcast until mid February, 2011, both games were actually recorded on January 14, 2011 at IBM's T.J. Watson Research Center in Yorktown Heights, New York. After completion of the first game, there was a break (for the human participants) before the second game began.

Recall that the overall winner would be the contestant who had the highest winnings total over the two games of the match. At the end of the first game the score was Jennings: $4,800, Watson: $35,734, Rutter: $10,400. Watson had a lead of almost $31,000 over Jennings and more than $25,000 over Rutter. All three contestants recognized that the key in the second game would be to win control of the board by buzzing in first and correctly answering the clue and then selecting the Daily Doubles. For Jennings and Rutter, this could give them the chance to double their winnings. For Watson, this could prevent them from doing this.

Through the set of questions leading up to the first commercial break, the play was quite even. The score then in the second game was Jennings: $3,400, Watson: $4,200, Rutter: $600. After the break, Watson had control of the board. It correctly answered a $200 question and then Jennings buzzed in first on another $200 question which he answered correctly. When he selected the next clue, "Breaking News" for $600, the sirens sounded and Jennings had found a Daily Double square. He announced "I am either going to have to unplug Watson or bet it all so I am going to bet it all." He bet $3,600 on his answer.

Trebek read the clue.

> SENATOR OBAMA ATTENDED THE 2006 GROUND BREAKING FOR THIS MAN'S MEMORIAL.

Jennings paused, reflected and then gave the correct answer, "Who was Martin Luther King?" Jennings' winnings in the second game had jumped to $7,200 and he had taken the lead.

The contestants rapidly finished the Jeopardy round. At the end, the scores were Jennings: $8,600, Watson: $4,800, Rutter: $2,400. The Double Jeopardy round was next. If Jennings could land on both Daily Doubles, bet the maximum and correctly answer the clue each time and then double his winnings once more in the Final Jeopardy round, he had a chance.

The Daily Double clues are normally clues in the $1,200 or $1,600 range on Double Jeopardy. Whoever controlled the board was trying clues in this range. After four clues were gone, Watson had control and selected the category "Nonfiction" for $1,200. The siren sounded and Watson had the first Daily Double of this round. Watson wagered $2,127.

The clue was read:

> *THE NEW YORKER*'S 1959 REVIEW OF THIS SAID THAT IN ITS BREVITY AND CLARITY IT IS UNLIKE MOST SUCH MANUALS. A BOOK AS WELL AS A TOOL.

Watson answered "Let's try 'Who is Dorothy Parker?' " The correct response was "What is *The Elements of Style*?"

Watson's winnings total had dropped by $2,127, but that was unimportant. What mattered was that only one Daily Double clue remained.

The round continued. When half the clues on the board were gone, Watson landed on the last Daily Double, a $1,600 clue under the category "Legal "E"s." Watson wagered $367, not needing to increase its winnings any more to win the two game total score.

The clue was

> THIS 2 WORD PHRASE MEANS THE POWER TO TAKE PRIVATE PROPERTY FOR PUBLIC USE: IT'S OKAY AS LONG AS THERE IS JUST COMPENSATION.

This gave Watson no trouble. It replied "What is eminent domain?"

At the end of the Daily Double Round, the scores were Jennings: $18,200, Watson: $23,440, Rutter: $5,600.

The Final Jeopardy round was anticlimactic. The category was "19th Century Novelists" and the clue was

> WILLIAM WILKINSON'S "AN ACCOUNT OF THE PRINCIPALITIES OF WALLACHIA AND MOLDAVIA" INSPIRED THIS AUTHOR'S FINAL NOVEL.

All three contestants correctly identified the author of *Dracula*. Rutter and Watson answered "Who is Bram Stoker?" Jennings answered "Who is Stoker" and added the parenthetical remark "I, for one, recognize our new computer overlord."

Rutter had bet all his winnings, giving him total winnings of $11,200 in the second game. Jennings had only bet $1,000 so his total went up to $19,200. Watson had bet $17,973, raising his total to $41,413. Watson had also won the second game, and the match.

Where did Watson's bet come from? Suppose that Jennings and Rutter bet all their winnings and answered correctly. The bet of of $17,973 was the largest bet Watson could make and still guarantee to win the two game match even if his answer was wrong. Since the answer was correct, Watson had a convincing win by over $53,000 in the match.

Figure 3.4 shows the final prize money awarded. Ken Jennings is on the left, Watson is in the center and Brad Rutter is on the right. Recall that the actual prize money awarded in the match was $1,000,000 for the winner, $300,000 for the second place finisher and $200,000 for the third place winner.

Figure 3.4: The end of the match, with winnings.

Jeopardy! courtesy Jeopardy Productions, Inc.

All of Watson's winnings and 50% of Jennings and Rutters' winnings were donated to charity.

3.6 What Next?

Watson's remarkable success had similar characteristics to Deep Blue's win over Garry Kasparov in 1997. In both cases, the key to success was to develop an approach to the problem would exploit the strengths of a computer, particularly, a massively parallel computer. These were typically quite different from the way that a person would attack the problem. Both Watson and Deep Blue were remarkable feats of engineering, combining many different approaches in a seamless fashion to create a system that could play a challenging game at the level of the world's top humans.

Watson was ideally suited to answering questions which cover a broad range of material which often contains inconsistent, contradictory and incomplete information. Shortly after the match, IBM announced that a partnership with Wellpoint with the goal of applying the Watson DeepQA capability to the field of medicine. A system like Watson could be a tremendous help to a physician, both in diagnosing a patient's illness and in selecting an effective course of treatment. The initial focus was to be on cancer diagnosis and treatment. Since then, IBM has formed a business unit focusing on applications of Watson technology to a range of applications [67].

The ability of Watson to take a huge amount of unstructured information, integrate it and then use it to answer questions which may have no connection to the intentions of the original creators of the corpus gave it a broad range of applicability. This was especially true because of Watson's ability to deal with questions which are poorly formed, ambiguous and imprecise.

People ask whether Watson's astonishing capabilities make it a candidate to pass the Turing test. When interviewed on kurzweilai.net, Eric Brown, one of the lead researchers on the Watson project replied [5]:

> Whenever I get that question, my initial response is: If you were to rephrase the Turing test slightly, and couch it in terms of, if you had two players playing Jeopardy, and you couldn't tell which one was the computer and which one was the human, and that was the Turing test, then I think Watson would pass that very easily. But, of course, the Turing test is defined more broadly and open-ended, where you really have an open-ended dialogue, and Watson is not up to that task yet.

But perhaps we should give Alan Turing the last word. In his landmark 1950 paper [143], he said the following:

> We may hope that machines will eventually compete with men in all purely intellectual fields. But which are the best ones to start with? Even this is a difficult decision. Many people think that a very abstract activity, like the playing of chess, would be best. It can also be maintained that it is best to provide the machine with the best sense organs that money can buy, and then teach it to understand and speak English. This process could follow the normal teaching of a child. Things would be pointed out and named, etc. Again I do not know what the right answer is, but I think both approaches should be tried.

We may not be there yet, but Turing would probably agree that we are making progress.

3.7 Notes and Sources

Stephen Baker [9], with support from IBM, wrote an entertaining and comprehensive book describing the history of the Watson project culminating with the *Jeopardy!* match.

The Watson team at IBM has published a large number of papers describing the technology and analytics that are embodied in Watson. IBM maintains an online directory of these articles [68].

Throughout this chapter, *Jeopardy!* has been used to refer to the television show. No italics or exclamation point are used when referring to parts of the trivia game itself.

3.3. The material in this section is based on Ferrucci et al [48].

3.4. The photographs in Figures 3.1 and 3.4 were provided by *Jeopardy!* courtesy Jeopardy Productions, Inc. The photograph in Figure 3.2 was provided courtesy of International Business Machines Corporation. Figure 3.3 is based on a figure in [48].

3.5. The photograph in Figure 3.4 was provided by *Jeopardy!* courtesy Jeopardy Productions, Inc.

Part II

Sports and Games

Chapter 4

How to Evaluate Championship Players

It ain't what you don't know that hurts you, it's what you don't know you don't know.

– Mark Twain

Contents

In 1977, Bill James, a United States Army veteran who was working as a security guard at a pork-and-beans cannery, self-published an eighty-page book about statistics in baseball. While he was pleased with the 75 copies sold that year, he did not realize that he had just revolutionized the world of sports. He challenged sports fans, coaches and managers to to back up their knowledge and intuition of the game with the massive amounts of data collected about players and teams.

Over twenty years later, Billy Beane, the general manager of the Oakland Athletics, a team with one of the lowest payrolls in Major League Baseball, decided to listen to what Bill James was saying. He went against the respected and experienced scouts who worked for him, and built a team of seemingly misfit players who could actually play baseball better than most. By finding undervalued players and discovering the statistics that create runs, he took a losing team and made them the talk of baseball.

While analytics was changing the game of baseball, statisticians and data scientists started to collect and analyze data for other sports. In basketball, many new measures of player performance were introduced to objectively measure the ability of players. However, even today, players are selected as the most valuable player or inducted into the Hall of Fame from votes cast by the media or by committees, which are not necessarily based on data. These awards are often given to players based on qualitative measures instead of quantitative measures of performance.

In this chapter, we first present a few of the key ideas of the book *Moneyball* to understand the player statistics that lead to winning more games. Then, we apply some of these ideas to discover the best National Basketball Association (NBA) players of all time based on statistical performance. We rate players based on offensive and defensive ability separately, and then combine our ratings to discover the best overall players. The key message is that analytics can provide insights into the world of sports that are hard to detect by just watching the performance of players. People are often biased by losing streaks, flashy performance, or unconventional behavior. Data can reveal objective truths about player performance that can detect undervalued players.

4.1 The Story of Moneyball

More than any other sport, baseball lends itself perfectly to analytics. In the United States, there are 162 regular season games in Major League Baseball (MLB), compared to 82 in the National Basketball Association (NBA), and 16 in the National Football League (NFL). This creates a larger sample size for statistical analysis. Additionally, the average payroll of the five richest teams in Major League Baseball is almost four times the average payroll of the five poorest teams. In the NBA and the NFL, the average payroll of the richest teams is less than double that of the poorest teams. Due to the large payroll inequality in the MLB, general managers of less wealthy teams are highly motivated to find great players for lower prices.

In baseball, all teams have essentially the same goal: make the playoffs. Making the playoffs generates extra revenue from more ticket sales, an increased fan base, and more media attention. However, for the less wealthy teams to even think about gaining more revenue, they have to get to the playoffs using a much smaller budget.

This was the problem facing Billy Beane when he took over in 1998 as the general manager of the Oakland Athletics, a major league baseball team based in Oakland, California. The previous general manager, Sandy Alderson, had introduced Beane to using analytics in sports, but he knew that it would be difficult to convince anyone that statistics had a place in the game. Soon after being promoted to general manager, Beane hired Paul DePodesta, a Harvard graduate, as his assistant general manager. DePodesta had never played professional baseball, but his economics degree and interest in using analytics methods in baseball convinced Beane that DePodesta would be a valuable asset if he was going to have any luck succeeding with his plan of drafting players based on statistics alone.

Michael Lewis's bestselling book *Moneyball: The Art of Winning an Unfair Game* tells the story of how Billy Beane effectively used analytics to turn the Oakland Athletics into a winning team. In 1997, the year before Beane became the general manager, the Athletics were only winning 40% of the games they played. By 2001, they were winning 63% of the games, an impressive feat in Major League Baseball. Additionally, they were doing this with one of the smallest payrolls in Major League Baseball. Figure 4.1 shows how all teams compared from 1998 to 2001, in terms of average yearly payroll (on the x-axis) and average yearly wins (on the y-axis). The green triangle is the Oakland Athletics. They were winning a large number of games (almost 90 on average), with one of the lowest payrolls in the league (less than $30 million). For comparison, the red triangle is the Boston Red Sox, and the blue triangle is the New York Yankees, two of the richest teams in MLB.

In 2002, the Oakland Atheltics lost three of their best players, and it was generally believed that they could not continue winning. *Moneyball* follows this season, starting from the 2002 amateur draft and continuing through the regular season games.

The Athletics were the first team to heavily depend on analytics, and at the time their actions were considered very radical and actually foolish by some. But even with the third smallest payroll in major league baseball, the Oakland Athletics were able to use analytics to gain an edge. The popularity of this book started a trend of people calling the teams who use statistical analysis the "teams who play Moneyball."

Throughout this section, we use data from 1996 to 2001 to verify some of the claims made in *Moneyball*. While the Oakland A's have used analytics in many different ways to give themselves an edge over the competition, we focus in this chapter on how analytics can be used to evaluate player talent, as opposed to tactical game-time decisions. The years 1996-2001 were selected for the dataset because it was the most recent data available to the Oakland

Figure 4.1: The average number of wins for each team in Major League Baseball, plotted as a function of their average yearly payroll (from 1998 to 2001). The green triangle is the Oakland Athletics; they were winning a large number of games, with one of the lowest payrolls. For comparison, the red triangle is the Boston Red Sox, and the blue triangle is the New York Yankees, two of the richest teams in Major League Baseball.

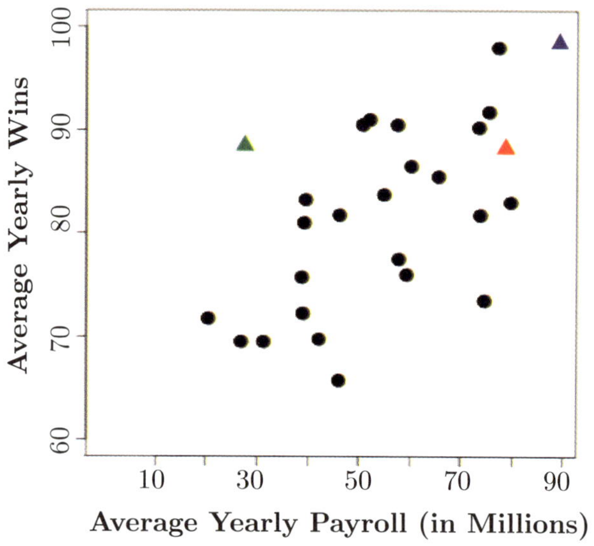

Athletics during the 2002 season. The models could easily be expanded to include more years, but due to the changing nature of baseball player abilities and the rules of the game, it might not be suitable to use all available data.

Using Analytics to Make the Playoffs

Analytics methods propose answers to objective questions about baseball, such as "which player on the Yankees contributed the most to the team's offense?" or "how well will Buster Posey play 3 years from now?" Analytics also attempts to compare teams and players statistically. As we mentioned in the introduction, Bill James, the person credited with popularizing the use of analytics in baseball, has written more than two dozen books about baseball and statistics. His most famous books are the *Baseball Abstracts*, which were some of the first books about baseball and statistics to reach a mass audience.

One of the most important questions in Major League Baseball is "what must a team do to make the playoffs?" There are two leagues, the National

League and the American League, and three divisions in each league - East, Central, and West. The team in each division with the most wins advances to the playoffs, as well as one "wild card" team from each league, which is the team with the highest number of wins out of all teams that place second in their division within that league. (This was the rule in 2002, the year *Moneyball* focuses on. In 2012, the rule changed to include two wild card teams from each league.)

Historically, about 95 wins are needed to make it to the playoffs. This is visualized in Figure 4.2. Each point corresponds to a particular team and season, from 1996 to 2001 (the six seasons before the events in *Moneyball*). The x-axis gives the number of wins in the regular season, and the y-axis just sorts the points by team. The dark blue triangles are the teams that made it to the playoffs. In the six seasons before 2002, only one team won more than 95 games and did not make it to the playoffs. So in the 2002 season, the Athletics were confident that if they won 95 or more games, they would make it to the playoffs. With this information, the Athletics set out to determine how they could select players to increase their expected number of wins.

The first step is to create an equation that predicts the number of wins that a team will have in the regular season. Once we have this equation, we can compare our predicted number of wins to the number needed to make the playoffs.

The outcome of a game depends on the number of runs that one team scored versus another. Therefore, it seems reasonable to guess that wins might be a function of the total number of runs scored by a team during the season and the total number of runs scored against a team during the season, which

Figure 4.2: The number of wins for each team and season in the MLB, from 1996 to 2001.

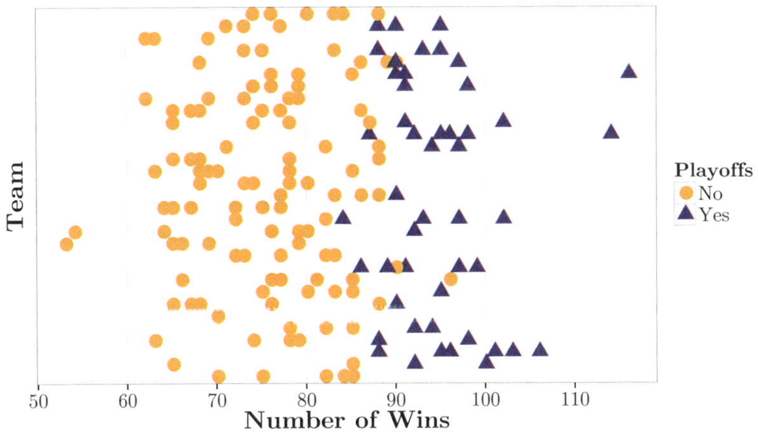

are called "runs allowed." We can use the following linear regression model to predict the number of wins for a team as a function of the "run difference," or the number of runs scored minus the number of runs allowed:

$$W = \beta_0 + \beta_1 \times (RD),$$

where W is wins, and RD is the run difference, or runs scored minus runs allowed. The coefficients of the model are β_1 and β_0, which we can estimate using known data. For more about linear regression, see Chapter 21.

If we evaluate our regression model using data from all teams and all regular seasons from 1996 to 2001, we get that $\beta_1 = 0.0965$ and $\beta_0 = 80.9375$, and both coefficients are highly significant. The R-squared of the model is 0.90, meaning that the run difference of a team explained 90% of the variation in the number of wins for this dataset. So we have a very strong model to predict wins, using the run difference of a team. Using this model, we predict that the Athletics will win at least 95 games if they have a run difference of at least 145 runs. So we need to figure out what makes the Athletics score more runs, and what makes them allow less runs.

We will build two more regression models: one to predict the number of runs scored, and one to predict the number of runs allowed. We would like these models to only depend on player statistics, since we would like to make these predictions at the beginning of a season given the players on the team. If we know the statistics that are important for predicting runs scored and runs allowed, we can assemble a team that consists of players with good values in these particular statistics.

As the assistant general manager of the Oakland Athletics, Paul DePodesta spent a lot of time trying to decide which statistics correlated closely with runs scored. He found two statistics that consistently correlated with the number of runs: *on-base percentage* and *slugging percentage.*

On-base percentage (OBP) is a measure of how often a batter reaches base, and is approximately equal to the number of times the batter gets on base on his turn, divided by the total number of times he has the opportunity to get on base. It is closely related to the more well-known statistic *batting average*, but it has one important difference: on-base percentage does not care how the player gets on base, while batting average only gives the player credit for getting on base by hitting the ball. In baseball, there are several different ways that a player can get on base (such as hitting the ball and running, or walking), and one of the key insights of Paul DePodesta was that when it comes to runs, it does not matter how a player tends to get on base, just that he got there.

The other statistic Paul DePodesta focused on was Slugging Percentage (SLG), which measures the power of a hitter, and is calculated as the total number of bases that a player has gained with hits (1 for a single, 2 for a double, 3 for a triple, and 4 for a home run), divided by the total number of times he had the opportunity to hit the ball.

Similar statistics to on-base percentage and slugging percentage are calculated for pitchers, called opponents on-base percentage (OOBP) and opponents slugging percentage (OSLG). These statistics measure how well the opposing batters hit against a pitcher.

When Paul DePodesta was trying to build an equation for runs scored, baseball fans and announcers were also starting to realize the importance of these two statistics. To merge them together, they created a new statistic, on-base plus slugging (OPS), which just added the two statistics together. However, it was still unclear what the relative importance was of these two statistics. Was one more important than the other, or should they be weighted equally?

To get some intuition for the relative importance of the two statistics, the following logic is useful. First, imagine a team that had an on-base percentage equal to 1.00. Every player that came up to bat would get to first base (or further), and the team would never get an out. So the team would score an infinite number of runs. Now, consider the ways in which a team could have a slugging percentage equal to 1.00. Every player could get to first base on his turn, and the team would again score an infinite number of runs. Or, one player could get a home run (4 bases), while the next three players didn't get on base at all. Four bases were gained for four hitters, so the slugging percentage would again be 1.00, but the team would be out with only one run scored. So according to this logic, a higher on-base percentage should mean more than a higher slugging percentage.

To compute the relative importance and to predict the number of runs scored, DePodesta used the following regression model:

$$RS = \beta_0 + \beta_1 \times (OBP) + \beta_2 \times (SLG).$$

Using this method, DePodesta computed that OBP was worth at least twice as much as SLG. This was a radical idea; most current models assumed that on-base percentage was worth at most 1.5 times slugging percentage. If we evaluate our regression model using data from 1996-2001, we get that $\beta_0 = -967.83$, $\beta_1 =$ 3,509.18, and $\beta_2 =$ 1,352.01. All coefficients are significant, and the R-squared of the model is 0.92, which can be interpreted as OBP and SLG accounting for 92% of the variation in runs scored in this dataset. So again, this is a very strong model. Additionally, in our model $\beta_1 \approx 2.5\beta_2$, which agrees with the claim that OBP is worth at least twice as much as SLG.

Similarly, we can predict the number of runs allowed with the *opponents on-base percentage* and *opponents slugging percentage*, which are measured in the same way as OBP and SLG, but they are computed using the performance of all opposing players from every game the team played. These are pitching statistics, and measure how well the opposing batters did against a team's pitchers. The regression equation is almost identical to the one above, except we are trying to predict runs allowed (RA) and OBP and SLG are instead the opponent statistics OOBP and OSLG:

$$RA = \beta_0 + \beta_1 \times (OOBP) + \beta_2 \times (OSLG).$$

If we evaluate our regression model with data from 1996-2001, we get that $\beta_0 = -837.38$, $\beta_1 =$2,913.60, and $\beta_2 =$ 1,514.29. Again, this is a very strong model, with an R-squared of 0.91.

With these regression models, we are able to predict the wins for each team before the season starts. One method would be to take all of the players on the opening day roster, and average the players statistics from the previous regular season (using hitter statistics to predict runs scored, and pitcher statistics to predict runs allowed). This is a guess as to which players will be used the most during the season, but it could be that injuries and trades change the roster as the season progresses. The predictions could be adjusted when these things happen.

Using this approach, we can estimate that the Oakland Athletics will have the following statistics in 2002: OBP = 0.339, SLG = 0.430, OOBP = 0.307, and OSLG = 0.373. These numbers were computed using the 2001 regular season statistics for all players on the 2002 opening day roster for the Athletics. Then using the models built in this section, we can predict the following for the Oakland Athletics in 2002:

$$RS = -967.83 + 3{,}509.18 \times (0.339) + 1{,}352.01 \times (0.430) = 803.15,$$

$$RA = -837.38 + 2{,}913.60 \times (0.307) + 1{,}514.29 \times (0.373) = 621.93,$$

$$W = 80.9375 + 0.0965 \times (803.15 - 621.93) = 98.4$$

.

Therefore, we predict that they will win about 98 games in 2002. Keep in mind that the models were built using data that was available before the 2002 season happened, so these are out-of-sample predictions.

Paul DePodesta also made predictions for the 2002 season, which are described in *Moneyball.* He predicted that they would score 800 - 820 runs, allow 650 - 670 runs, and win 93 - 97 games. Ultimately, the Oakland Athletics won 103 games in 2002, and set an American League record by winning 20 games in a row. They took what many considered to be a team of misfit players, and made them one of the best teams in the league.

In addition to making predictions, the models built in this section could be used to evaluate currently available players, and to make player selection decisions. Traditionally, scouts evaluated players based on five criteria: hitting on average, hitting power, speed, fielding, and throwing. Players were considered top players if they were evaluated highly on all five aspects. The Oakland Athletics challenged this approach with analytics. They were able to more accurately value players in terms of their ability to win games, by focusing on their historic OBP and SLG statistics. They found players that were undervalued by most teams, perhaps due to their lack of speed or fielding ability, and were able to get them at a bargain. A lot of teams overvalued qualities such as speed and fielding, while they should have been paying more attention to the on-base percentage and slugging percentage of the players.

What about the World Series?

Many critics point out that the Oakland Athletics have only won one playoff series since 2000. This seems to contradict the theory that analytics can help a team win. Why does this record make sense? The problem with the playoffs is that there are not enough games; they suffer from a small sample size. Over the 162 regular season games, luck has a better chance of evening out and skill is more important. But in a series of 5 or 7 games, luck can be a much larger factor. In a five game series, the baseball team with the worst overall record will beat the baseball team with the best overall record a surprising 15% of the time. Thus, analytics are very useful for getting a team to the playoffs, but they are not as helpful once the playoffs start. Billy Beane sees his job as getting the team to the playoffs, but once they get that far, luck takes over. It turns out that Billy Beane is doing a great job. The Oakland Athletics made it to the playoffs 8 times from 2000-2014. Out of the 29 other teams in Major League Baseball, only three teams have made it to the playoffs more often in this period than the Oakland Athletics (the New York Yankees, St. Louis Cardinals, and Atlanta Braves).

Additionally, the Oakland Athletics are no longer the only team that uses analytics. Around the same time that the Athletics were surprising the world of baseball with their success by using analytics, John Henry, an extremely successful futures trader, bought the Boston Red Sox. He believed in the use of analytics in baseball, and he hired Theo Epstein, a Yale University graduate, as the general manager. It is believed that this change in leadership led the Red Sox to win the World Series in 2004 and 2007, after an 86 year dry spell. Now, every major league baseball team has an analytics group and about 75% of the teams are believed to incorporate analytics methods into their major decisions. Statistics that were identified as undervalued by the Oakland Athletics in the early 2000s are no longer undervalued, and analytics now play a key role in Major League Baseball.

4.2 Introduction to the NBA

Basketball and baseball teams have one very important thing in common: the desire to win games and make the playoffs. In this section, we will show how the *Moneyball* techniques can be applied to basketball by building an equation to predict wins for basketball teams and then deciding which statistics are the most important for players and teams to possess. Instead of trying to predict the success of teams in the coming season, we will use our models to evaluate the contribution of some of the greatest basketball players of all time. While there are not as many regular season games in basketball as there are in baseball, there are enough that luck should hopefully even out over time.

We will analyze players in the National Basketball Association (NBA), which is generally regarded as the top men's professional basketball league in the world. It consists of thirty teams, twenty-nine of which are located in the United States and one in Canada.

Basketball Basics

Throughout the rest of this chapter, we will use the following basketball terms and statistics:

- A **free throw** is an unopposed attempt to score points and is generally awarded after a foul (an illegal move) on the shooter by the opposing team. Each successful free throw is worth one point.
- A **field goal** is a basket scored by any shot or tap (other than a free throw). A field goal can be worth 2 or 3 points depending on the distance of the player from the basket when he attempts the shot. To distinguish the two kinds, two point field goals are referred to as "field goals" while three point field goals are referred to as "3-point field goals."
- An **assist** is credited to a player when he passes the ball to a teammate who then scores a successful field goal.
- A **rebound** happens when a player successfully gains possession of the ball after a missed field goal or free throw. An **offensive rebound** occurs when the ball is recovered by the offensive side and does not change possession. A **defensive rebound** occurs when the ball is recovered by the defensive side and changes possession.
- A **turnover** occurs when a player from one team loses possession of the ball to a member of the other team. A high number of turnovers is generally viewed as a negative thing for a player, since this means that he frequently loses the ball. However, this can also depend on the amount of time the player is on the court and the role of the player on the team.
- A **steal** occurs when a defensive player legally causes a turnover by his positive aggressive action.

4.3 Measuring Offensive and Defensive Ability

In basketball, all players need offensive and defensive skills, but a great offensive player is not necessarily a great defensive player. We will first create two different ratings for each player, and then analyze how we can compare the two to select the best overall players. Unfortunately, it is very difficult to statistically compare players from more than 30 years ago to more recent players due to the differences in data collection and scoring. Therefore, our overall goal is to identify the best players of the last 30 years.

Model to Predict Wins

To determine the best players, it is important to know which statistics contribute the most to wins. This is very similar to our analysis in baseball. The best players are those who help their team to win games and prevent the other team from winning games. To develop the models in this section, we used team data from 1980 to 2013 for all thirty NBA teams. We used data from a longer time period to build these models because we want to evaluate the skills of players from the last thirty years. To be able to extend our models to all of these players, we need to use data from the entire time period that they played.

We have found that the number of games that a team will win in the regular season (out of 82) can be predicted by the number of points that the team scores and the number of points that they allow the other team to score throughout the regular season games. Just like we did for baseball, we used linear regression to find the following equation:

$$\text{W} = 41.00 + 0.0326 \times (\text{PD}),$$

where W is wins, and PD is "points difference," or the number of points scored minus the number of points allowed. Both coefficients in this model are significant, and the R-squared of the model is 0.94. This equation implies that if a team scores just as many points throughout the regular season as they allow, we expect them to win 41 games, or half of the games in the season. If the team scores more points, then we expect them to win more games, but if the team allows more points, we expect them to lose more games.

Model to Predict Points Scored

Now that we have a model to predict wins using points scored and points allowed, we need to find models to predict points scored and points allowed. We have to approach this differently from baseball due to the fact that we can not easily divide basketball players into offensive and defensive players. In baseball, pitching statistics could be used to predict runs allowed and batting statistics could be used to predict runs scored. Players were divided into two groups: pitchers and hitters. In basketball, all players have offensive and defensive statistics, but we do not have simple statistics for how the opponent plays like the opponent statistics for pitchers.

The model for points scored is the easier of the two since the statistics mostly capture offensive ability. Intuitively, the number of points scored should depend on the success rate of field goals and free throws as well as the number of assists. However, to score points a team or player also has to attempt more. According to historical data, the attempts of a team is positively correlated with the points of a team. This led us to use the following five variables in our model: Field Goal Attempts (FGA), 3-Point Field Goal Attempts (3PA), Free Throw Attempts (FTA), Assists (A), and Success Rate (SR). The Success Rate is a new variable that we have defined, which combines the three different types of success rates: Field Goal Success Rate (FGSR), 3-Point Success Rate (3PSR), and Free Throw Success Rate (FTSR). Each of the individual success rates is defined as the number of successful attempts divided by the number of total attempts. Using these, we compute the overall success rate as follows:

$$\text{SR} = \frac{\text{FTSR} + (2 \times \text{FGSR}) + (3 \times \text{3PSR})}{6}.$$

This weights each success rate by the number of points that are awarded for a successful shot. We divide by six to normalize the equation to a number between 0 and 1, since there are six individual terms in the numerator of the fraction.

We used linear regression to build the following equation to predict points scored (PS) using field goal attempts, 3-point field goal attempts, free throw attempts, assists, and the success rate:

$$\begin{aligned}\text{PS} = \text{-3,804} + 0.891 \times (\text{FGA}) + 1.025 \times (\text{3PA}) + 0.981 \times (\text{FTA}) \\ + 0.827 \times (\text{A}) + 4{,}898 \times (\text{SR}).\end{aligned}$$

All coefficients in this model are statistically significant, and the R-squared value is 0.90. This model has been designed to help us measure the offensive ability of a player. We could just look at how many points each player scores, but this model helps us break down offensive ability into actionable skills. An individual player might not score a lot of points overall, but they may have a lot of assists. By using this model, we will still count this as a positive offensive action.

Model to Predict Points Allowed

The model for points allowed is a little trickier since team and player statistics do not reveal much about how well the opposing team played offensively. In our points scored equation, the number of attempts is a critical variable. We would like to capture the number of times that the other team gets the ball so that we can have a variable that represents the attempts of the opposing team.

First, we know that each time one team has a successful field goal, the other team always gets the ball. Additionally, a turnover means that the other team gets the ball. We assume that the opposing team will be able to attempt to score each time one of these two things happen. The other team will also get the ball after a failed field goal unless there is an offensive rebound, in which case possession of the ball does not change. So we should also count the number of failed field goals minus the number of offensive rebounds.

We can also count the number of times that the opposing team loses the ball. This includes defensive rebounds and steals. Thus, the variables that we will use in our model to predict the number of points allowed (PA) are the number of successful field goals (SFG), the number of turnovers (T), the number of failed field goals (FFG), the number of offensive rebounds (ORB), the number of defensive rebounds (DRB), and the number of steals (S). Using linear regression, we have developed the following equation:

$$\text{PA} = 2{,}041.78 + 1.497 \times (\text{SFG} + \text{T}) + 1.308 \times (\text{FFG - ORB}) - 1.238 \times (\text{DRB} + \text{S}).$$

The independent variables used in this equation attempt to capture the times in which the opposing team gets the ball or loses the ball. However, since we do not know the other team's success rate, this model is not quite as strong as the model for points scored. The coefficients are all statistically significant, with an R-squared value of 0.85. The addition of other common defensive statistics does not improve the model.

Offensive Rating

Now that we have models for how many points a team scores and how many points a team allows, we can use these to assess the value of a player. A good player contributes many points to their team and prevents the other team from scoring points. Thus, the variables that we have found to be important to a team scoring points and allowing points should be important indicators of a player's offensive and defensive ability.

We will start by analyzing a player's offensive ability. Before we can use the equation above for a player, we need to normalize it by minutes played (MP), since a player who plays less will naturally have fewer attempts. When looking at team data, the number of minutes played did not matter since all teams play for approximately the same number of minutes throughout the regular season. Therefore, we re-built the linear regression equation for Points Scored (PS), this time using versions of the independent variables that are normalized by minutes played. The following gives the new regression equation:

$$\text{PS} = \text{-}3{,}733.1 + 17{,}499.6 \times \left(\frac{\text{FGA}}{\text{MP}}\right) + 20{,}160.1 \times \left(\frac{\text{3PA}}{\text{MP}}\right) + 19{,}431.4 \times \left(\frac{\text{FTA}}{\text{MP}}\right) + 16{,}169.6 \times \left(\frac{\text{A}}{\text{MP}}\right) + 4{,}910.2 \times (\text{SR}).$$

This is the equation that we will use for a player's offensive rating. Note that the success rate does not need to be divided by minutes played since it is given as a percentage. One interpretation of this equation for a player is that it gives the expected number of points scored during a regular season if a team was made up of five identical copies of the player, who played for every minute of every game. The average number of points scored by a team in the NBA is about 8,000. Thus, if a player's rating is higher than 8,000 it means that a team made up of that one person would do better than average, and if a player's rating is lower than 8,000 it means that a team made up of that one person would do worse than average. However, this interpretation should be used with caution. We recognize that the players on a team bring different skills to the game, and a particular player might not make a successful team using just his own skill set.

As an example, Table 4.1 gives Michael Jordan's career statistics. Using this data, we can compute that his success rate (SR) is

$$\text{SR} = \frac{0.835 + (2 \times 0.510) + (3 \times 0.327)}{6} = 0.473.$$

Given this, we can compute his offensive rating:

$$\begin{aligned}\text{Offensive Rating} =& \text{-}3{,}733.1 + 17{,}499.6 \times \left(\frac{22{,}759}{41{,}011}\right) \\ &+ 20{,}160.1 \times \left(\frac{1{,}778}{41{,}011}\right) + 19{,}431.4 \times \left(\frac{8{,}772}{41{,}011}\right) \\ &+ 16{,}169.6 \times \left(\frac{5{,}633}{41{,}011}\right) + 4{,}910.2 \times (0.473) \\ =& \ 15{,}552.\end{aligned}$$

This offensive rating tells us that Michael Jordan was an extraordinary offensive player, but the number itself is not interpretable. Therefore, when giving overall offensive ratings to players, we normalize them relative to Michael Jordan's score so that we can focus on the relative differences between players instead of the absolute numbers.

Figure 4.3 gives the career ratings of the top 20 offensive players, according to our Offensive Rating. These players were selected by first collecting career statistics (as of November 2014) for all players on the magazine SLAM's "500 Greatest NBA Players of All Time" list. Then the list was cut down to all

Table 4.1: Career statistics for Michael Jordan.

Statistic	Career Value for Michael Jordan
Minutes Played (MP)	41,011
Field Goal Attempts (FGA)	22,759
Field Goal Success Rate	0.510
3-Point Field Goal Attempts (3PA)	1,778
3-Point Success Rate	0.327
Free Throw Attempts (FTA)	8,772
Free Throw Success Rate	0.835
Assists (A)	5,633
Total Failed Field Goals (FFG)	12,345
Offensive Rebounds (ORB)	1,668
Defensive Rebounds (DRB)	5,004
Steals (S)	2,514
Turnovers (T)	2,924

Figure 4.3: Offensive Ratings for the top 20 players, according to our system.

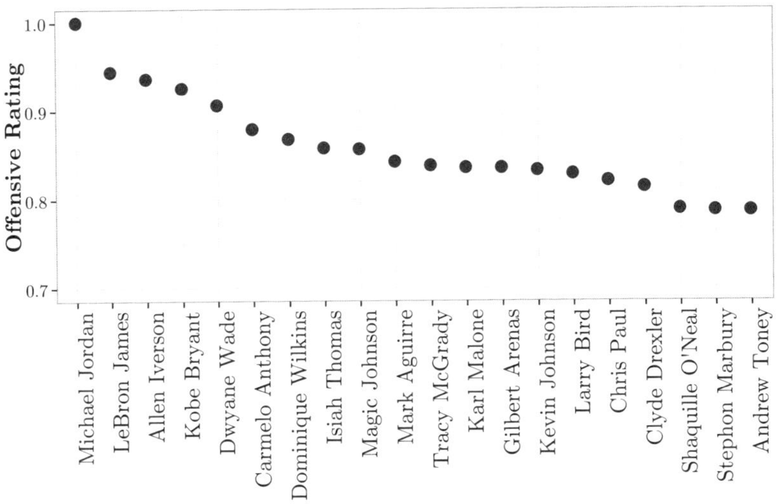

players with a start date of 1980 or later, since we are aiming to find the best players of the last 30 years. This left 279 players for which the Offensive Rating was computed.

Figure 4.3 shows that our rating is the highest for Michael Jordan, followed by LeBron James, Allen Iverson, and Kobe Bryant. Basketball rating systems generally agree that these four are some of the greatest offensive players of all time. Note that we could also give individual season ratings.

It should also be noted that the position the player plays most often does seem to make a difference here. Some point guards, shooting guards, and small forwards on this list are considered to be primary shooters on the team. There are still a few power forwards and one center on the list, but we will see more of them in the defensive rating. Keep in mind that this ranking is meant to just consider offensive skills.

Defensive Rating

Since the goal of defense is to prevent the other team from scoring points, we will use the points allowed equation for the defensive rating. This means that the lower the defensive rating is, the better the player is defensively (the opposing team scored fewer points). As in the previous section, we need to normalize the points allowed equation by minutes played before we can use it with players.

Here is the points allowed equation when we account for minutes played:

$$
\begin{aligned}
\text{PA} =& 2{,}135.0 + 29{,}494.3 \times \left(\frac{\text{SFG + T}}{\text{MP}}\right) + 25{,}779.4 \times \left(\frac{\text{FFG - ORB}}{\text{MP}}\right) \\
&\text{-}24{,}733.8 \times \left(\frac{\text{DRB + S}}{\text{MP}}\right).
\end{aligned}
$$

This equation has a similar interpretation to the one for points scored: if a team was composed of identical copies of a given player the entire game, this would predict how many points that team would allow. As mentioned above, since we are predicting the number of points that the opposing team will score, we want players with lower predicted values in this equation. But to be consistent with the offensive rating, we will invert these ratings so that higher is better and again normalize them just like we did in the previous section.

We will make one small adjustment to this equation before we start using it as a defensive rating. The equation includes the number of successful field goals. Although, following a field goal, the other team gets the ball and has the ability to score, we do not think that a player should receive a lower defensive rating because they have more successful field goals. Thus, we will take this term out of the points allowed equation when using it with players to give the following defensive rating:

$$
\begin{aligned}
\text{Defensive Rating} = 2{,}135.0 &+ 29{,}494.3 \times \left(\frac{\text{T}}{\text{MP}}\right) \\
&+ 25{,}779.4 \times \left(\frac{\text{FFG - ORB}}{\text{MP}}\right) \\
&- 24{,}733.8 \times \left(\frac{\text{DRB + S}}{\text{MP}}\right).
\end{aligned}
$$

As an example, we can compute Michael Jordan's defensive rating using his career statistics that are given in Table 4.1:

$$
\begin{aligned}
\text{Defensive Rating} = 2{,}135.0 &+ \left(29{,}494.3 \times \frac{2{,}924}{41{,}011}\right) \\
&+ \left(25{,}779.4 \times \frac{12{,}345 - 1{,}668}{41{,}011}\right) \\
&- \left(24{,}733.8 \times \frac{5{,}004 + 2{,}514}{41{,}011}\right) \\
&= 6{,}415.3.
\end{aligned}
$$

In terms of defensive ability, this is a low rating in comparison to the top defensive players. This implies that Michael Jordan was a much better offensive player than defensive player, which would agree with the assessments of many critics.

The defensive rating was computed for the same 279 players for which we computed the offensive rating. The top 20 normalized ratings are shown in Figure 4.4. Keep in mind that we flipped the defensive rating so that higher is better, to correspond to the offensive rating.

The players shown here are completely different from the players who received the top offensive ratings. This indicates that many players are either stronger offensively or stronger defensively. This makes it very hard to decide who the best players are, since both types of skills are very important for a basketball player.

4.4 The Best Players

Our goal is to determine the best overall players over the last thirty years, according to our ratings. Since we are trying to combine two different rankings, we have constructed Figure 4.5. This graph gives the offensive ratings on the horizontal axis and the defensive ratings on the vertical axis. Players who scored very well in the offensive rating, the defensive rating, or both are labeled.

Using this graph, we can find what are known as the *Pareto optimal* players. This is a concept that is often used when there are multiple measures of importance. Here, we are interested in players with high offensive ratings and high defensive ratings, but it is not obvious that one rating is more important than the other. A Pareto optimal point is defined as a point that is not *strictly*

Figure 4.4: Defensive ratings for the top 20 players, according to our system.

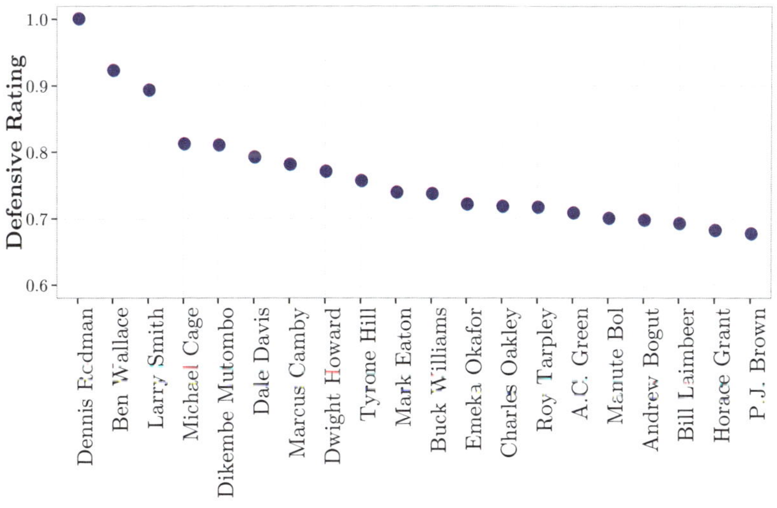

Figure 4.5: Scatterplot of offensive and defensive ratings for all players. Players that scored particular well on one or both ratings are labeled.

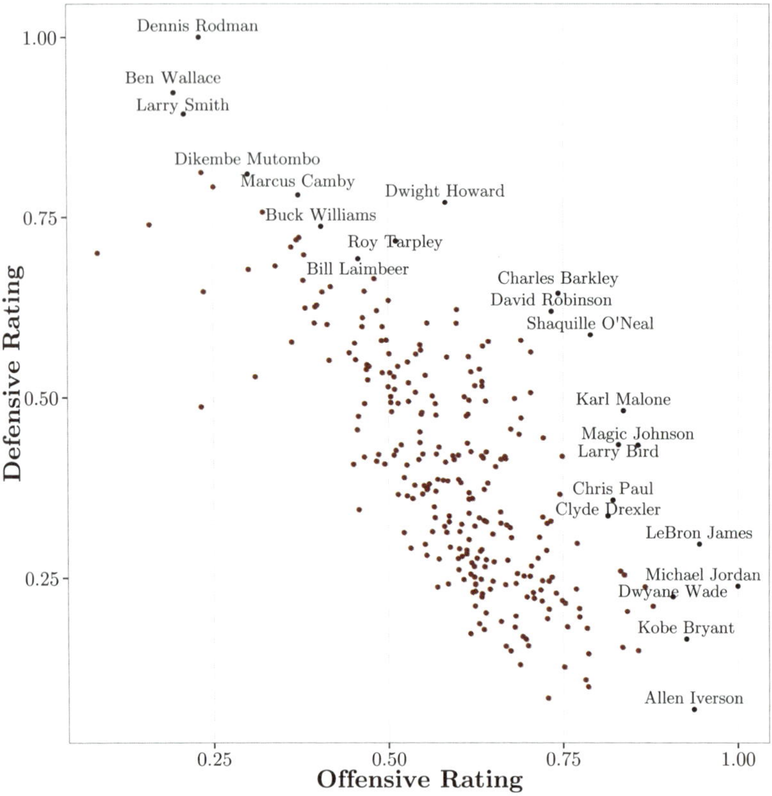

dominated by any other point; this means that there is no other point that is better in both measurements. For example, Michael Jordan is a Pareto optimal point. He is dominated by other players in the defensive rating, but no other player has a higher offensive rating. So no other player is better than him in both ratings. On the other hand, Kobe Bryant is not a Pareto optimal point. Michael Jordan is better than Kobe Bryant in both ratings, and so Michael Jordan is said to strictly dominate Kobe Bryant. This method helps us pick out a small handful of players who should be in the running for the best player. Since Michael Jordan is better than Kobe Bryant in both ratings, we should never pick Kobe Bryant over Michael Jordan.

Figure 4.6 labels only the Pareto optimal players. These players are Michael Jordan, LeBron James, Magic Johnson, Karl Malone, Shaquille O'Neal, Charles Barkley, Dwight Howard, Marcus Camby, Dikembe Mutombo, and

Figure 4.6: Scatterplot of offensive and defensive ratings for all players, with the Pareto optimal points labeled.

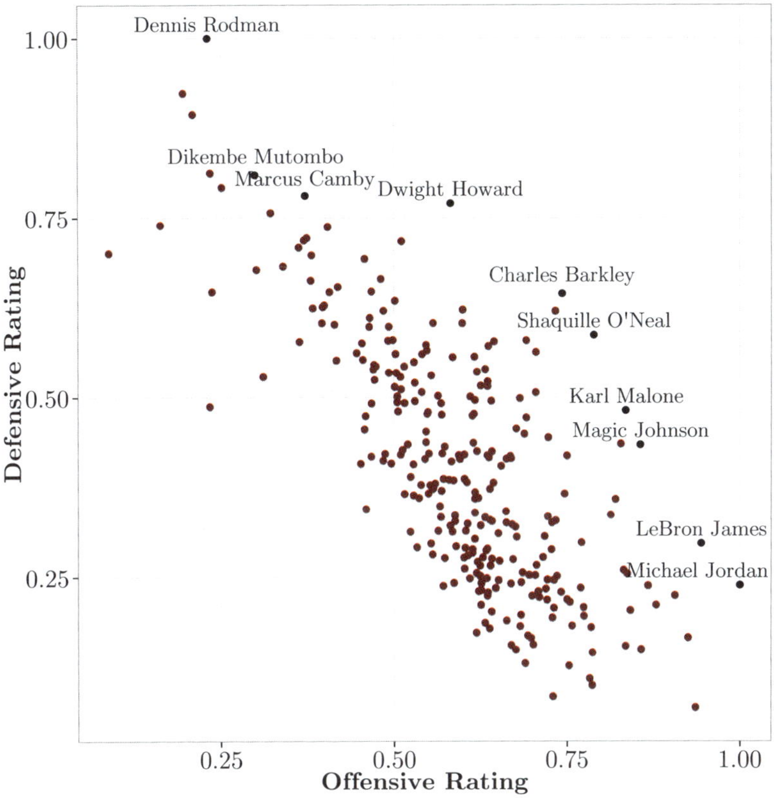

Dennis Rodman. Every other player is strictly dominated by at least one of these ten players. Therefore, we could argue that according to our ratings, these ten players are the best players of the last thirty years. Depending on the importance that is given to offensive or defensive skills, any one of these players could be said to be the best player.

Finding the Pareto optimal points as we did here is a common and useful way of understanding the trade-offs of two different measures of importance, but we could combine the two rankings in other ways. For example, we could take the maximum of the two values, or sum them to get an overall ranking.

4.5 Other Popular Rating Metrics

Many different statistical ratings have been developed to evaluate a player's overall talent in basketball. In this section, we will discuss two of the most popular rating systems and compare them with the ratings that we have computed in this chapter.

One of the most popular all-in-one ratings is the Player Efficiency Rating (PER), developed by former ESPN analyst and writer John Hollinger. It is intended to combine all of the contributions of a player into one number by adding positive statistics, such as field goals, free throws, assists, blocks, and steals, and subtracting negative ones, such as missed shots, turnovers, and personal fouls. It is adjusted on a per-minute basis, so that all players can be compared. It also adjusts for the team's pace. The league-average PER is always 15.00. PER largely measures offensive performance, and some of the best defenders in the NBA consistently receive a below-average PER rating.

The formula for PER is very detailed, and contains over fifteen different complex terms that are added or subtracted. Since the formula itself does not provide extra insight, we will not replicate it here. Instead, we will compare the top 20 players according to their career PER scores to the top players according to our ratings. Figure 4.7 shows the players with the top 20 career PER scores, out of the 279 players we are analyzing.

If we compare the PER ratings with Figure 4.6, seven out of ten of our Pareto optimal players are listed in the top twenty players in terms of PER. The three Pareto optimal players that are not in the PER top twenty list were ranked highly by our ratings due to their defensive ability. Since PER is widely believed to largely measure offensive ability, this is not surprising.

Additionally, several of the other players with high PER ratings ranked

Figure 4.7: Players with the top 20 Player Efficiency Ratings (PER).

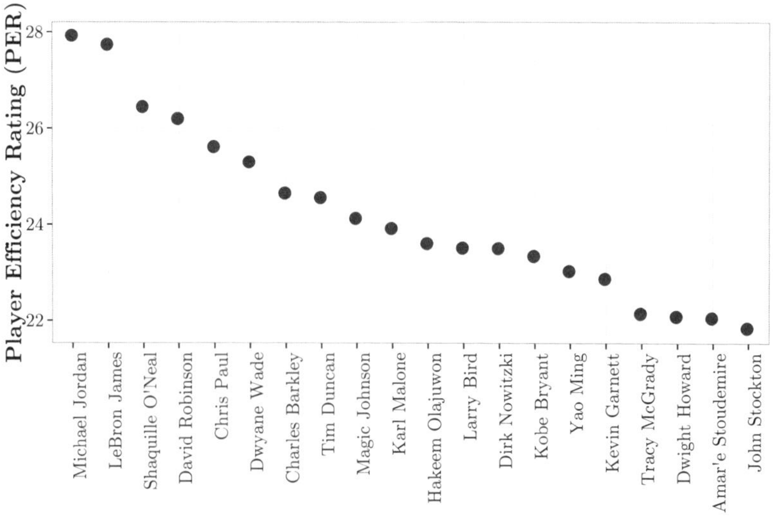

highly according to our ratings. For example, we can see in Figure 4.5 that David Robinson is very close to Charles Barkley and Shaquille O'Neal, Larry Bird is very close to Magic Johnson, and Dwayne Wade is close to Michael Jordan. Overall, our ratings and the PER ratings are similar.

Another popular set of ratings was developed by Dean Oliver, a sports author and statistician. They are referred to as "Offensive Rating" (ORtg), which measures a player's efficiency at producing points for the offense, and "Defensive Rating" (DRtg), which measures a player's efficiency at preventing the other team from scoring points. ORtg is computed as points produced (from field goals, free throws, assists, and offensive rebounds) divided by individual possessions, and then multiplied by 100. DRtg is computed as opponent's points allowed divided by opponent's possessions, and then multiplied by 100. The formulas are normalized by the number of possessions that each player has, since a player can only attempt to score when they are in possession of the ball.

Figure 4.8 shows the ORtg and DRtg for all players that we are considering. Note that here a lower DRtg is better, and so the better players are those with a high ORtg and a low DRtg (the labeled players).

If we compare these ratings with ours from Figure 4.6, we can see that many of our ten Pareto optimal players show up here as strong players. However, the very best players according to Dean Oliver's ratings are different. He rates Tim Duncan, David Robinson, and Chris Paul very highly. So while it can be seen that there are some similarities between the ratings, the two ratings are also providing different perspectives on the strength of players.

4.6 The Analytics Edge in Sports

When there are over one thousand different players to choose from, how does a team pick which players will be the most successful? Every team in baseball and basketball is faced with this question each year when drafting players. Most teams evaluate players by sending scouts to go and watch them play a few games. But can watching a few games really tell you how good a player is? Even if you were to watch several baseball games, there is a good chance that an average hitter will have more hits than a great hitter. However, when it comes to picking the better player, you clearly want the one with the better statistics across many games. But which statistics do you look at? Which ones indicate that the player will succeed? These questions are candidates for analytics models.

In this chapter, we have seen that simple models can provide insight into which statistics are the most meaningful when it comes to quantifying wins. While many more intricate models exist today to evaluate teams and players, these simple models are easily interpretable. We have given examples of how statistics can be used to predict team wins, evaluate player performance, and compare players over time. Statistical analysis provides an edge in sports that

Figure 4.8: Scatterplot of Dean Oliver's offensive and defensive ratings for all players. Players with a high ORtg, low DRtg, or both are labeled.

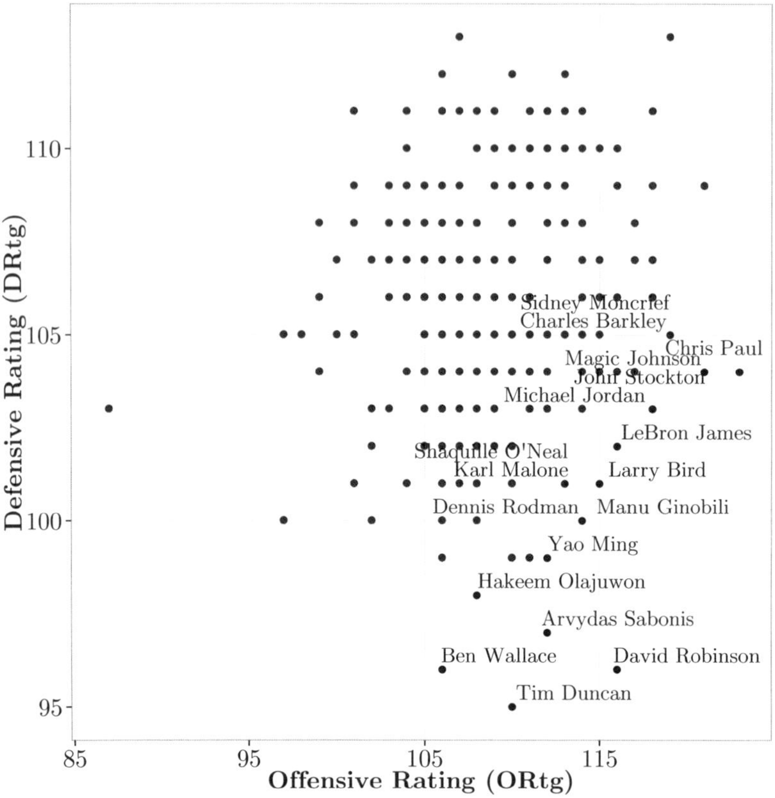

many teams now take advantage of, and those who do tend to have the stronger teams.

4.7 Notes and Sources

4.1. The information about the Oakland Athletics and their use of analytics comes from Michael Lewis's book *Moneyball: The Art of Winning an Unfair Game* [82].

4.2. The basketball definitions and data, including more information about advanced statistics like PER, can be found at Basketball-Reference.com [12].

Chapter 5

Optimizing Sports League Structures

We can't win at home. We can't win on the road. I just can't figure out where else to play.

– Pat Williams, Orlando Magic general manager,
on his team's 7-27 record in 1992.

Contents

The National Hockey League (NHL) is North America's elite level professional ice hockey league. It consists of 30 teams located in cities across the United States and Canada. Prior to 2013, the NHL was structured into two fifteen-team conferences, each subdivided into three five-team divisions.

Before the beginning of the 2011-12 season, the Atlanta Thrashers of the NHL relocated 1,289 miles north to Winnipeg, Canada where they became the resurrected Winnipeg Jets. After the move, the team remained in the Southeast division where the Atlanta Thrashers had been. This resulted in significant increases in travel for the team as well as the other teams in this division. Figure 5.1 shows the league structures both before and after the move. In this figure the teams in each division are indicated by stretching a different colored rubber band around the home cities of its teams.

The NHL recognized the need for realignment, and a new 4-division configuration, shown in Figure 5.2, was adopted beginning with the 2013-2014 season.

Designing and running a sports league is a complex problem. Each year schedulers construct a season schedule for the league which specifies when teams play each other and which team will be the home team and which team will be the visitor for each game. This schedule must satisfy a variety of different, and sometimes conflicting constraints.

Generally teams play half their games at home and half away from home. These so-called road games require travel of players, coaches and support personnel. This involves travel, usually by air for long trips or by bus for short trips, as well as hotel stays and may require the visiting team adjusting

Figure 5.1: League structure before (dotted) and after (solid) the Atlanta Thrashers moved to Winnipeg.

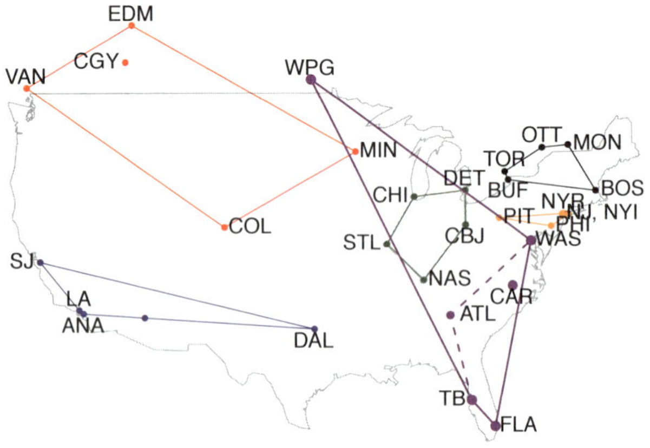

League Travel: 1,185,123 miles

Figure 5.2: League structure after realignment in 2013.

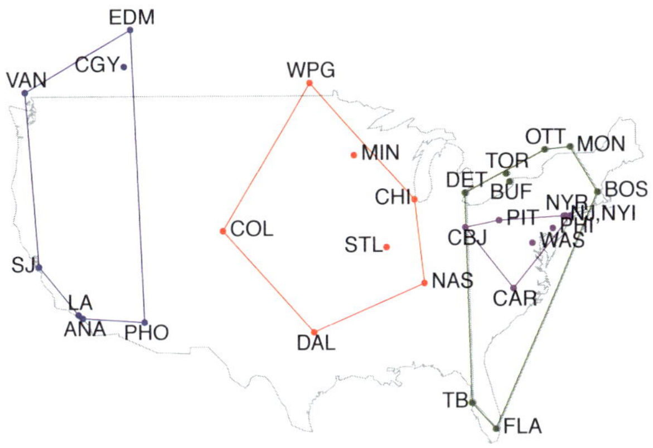

League Travel: 1,233,031 miles

to a different time zone. That is why, for example, for most sports, an eastern team rarely travels to the west coast for a single game. Rather it will play several different west coast opponents on a single road trip.

Teams in the NHL do not play each other team the same number of times each season. They play more games against teams in their division than they do against teams in other divisions in their conference. They play fewest games against teams in the other conference. Ideally the home cities of teams in the same division or conference will be geographically close to each other. The *league structure*, specifying which teams belong to which division and conference, has to be decided and then modified as teams enter the league, leave the league or change their home cities.

Creation of the league structure is a prerequisite to constructing the annual game schedule. It is hoped that there will be enough stability in the league that the structure will endure unchanged for several years. The challenge is to construct a league structure that will enable all the schedule requirements to be satisfied and which will keep travel to a minimum.

In this chapter, we describe how to create good league structures. We develop methods that create league structures that enable the construction of efficient annual travel schedules, from both the viewpoint of the league as a whole and from the viewpoints of the various teams. At times these objectives may be in conflict; minimizing total league travel over a season for all teams may require increasing the travel for some teams.

5.1 Road Trips, Travel, Leagues and Divisions

The NHL consists of thirty teams each playing eighty-two "regular season" games over the course of a season. Each team plays half of its games at home and half on the road and usually plays the same number of home and away games against other teams in the same division, and a smaller number of games against teams in other divisions and conferences. This assignment of teams to divisions and conferences, plus the specification of the number of home and away games to be played between pairs of teams in the same division and pairs of teams in different divisions is called the *league structure.*

Travel expenses form a significant part of teams' operating costs and are determined by three major factors: (1) the distance between each team and the other cities in the league, (2) the number of away games that each team plays against each of the other teams, and (3) the scheduling of the team's games.

The first factor is a function of geography – the distances between the pairs of cities in the league. The second factor, the number of home and away games played by each pair of teams, is determined by the league structure.

The third factor is the game schedule created for each season. This determines how efficiently groups of away games can be combined into multi-game road trips so as to reduce the amount of travel. Schedules are created for each playing season, taking into account a range of factors including stadium availability, holiday weekends and the length of road trips. The NHL has guidelines concerning the length of road trips and the number of games to be played. Sometimes an unusual event, like the Winter Olympics taking place in a team's home city, may necessitate a team having an unusually long road trip.

For the three seasons from 2005 to 2008, each of six divisions contained five teams. Each of two conferences contained three divisions. During the course of the season each team played eight games against teams in the same division, four games against each team in the same conference but a different division, and ten games against teams in the other conference.

From 2008 to 2012, the conference and division structure remained the same, but the number of games played by each pair of teams changed to enable each pair of teams to play each other at least once in the season. During the course of each season each team played six games against each team in the same division, four games against each team in the same conference but a different division, one game against twelve of the teams in the other conference and two games against the three other teams in the other conference. These games were split into home and away games so that each pair of teams in each conference played the same number of home and away games against each other team in the conference and nine home and away games against the fifteen teams in the other conference.

Test your understanding – can you see that each team plays forty-one home and away games each season for both of these these league structures?

Travel expenses represent a significant cost for teams. Major factors are the number of days and nights away from home and the distances traveled on road trips. Moreover, it is generally believed that long road trips can put the away team at a competitive disadvantage. For leagues with teams in both the US and Canada, crossing the US-Canada border can cause increases in travel time not reflected in travel distances. A league structure also impacts teams in ways unrelated to travel. For example, the time zone of the home team affects the starting time of the game, which in turn can impact television revenues for the away team.

A league structure normally remains unchanged for a number of years, until another team enters or leaves the league or a team moves to a different city. This happens more frequently than often realized – realignment of professional sports leagues in North America has occurred more than twenty-five times since 1967.

A big challenge in constructing a good league structure is that game schedules are created afterwards. The actual amount of travel depends on both the league structure as well as the scheduling of home and away games for each team. These determine the duration and distance traveled on road trips.

5.2 How Good is a League Structure?

The goal is to create a league structure that enables schedule creators to construct good schedules. We define a measure for the goodness of a league structure which can be computed efficiently. This measure is used to estimate the actual amounts of league travel over several seasons and found a very high correlation between it and the actual distance that each team traveled. In later sections, we describe how to create league structures which optimize this measure.

Let S be a league structure. The measure $D(S)$ is defined to be the sum, over all pairs (u, v) of teams in the league, of the travel distance between the home cities of teams u and v multiplied by the number of away games team u plays at the home of team v in the course of a season.

For example, the home city of the Florida Panthers (FLA) is 180 miles away from Tampa Bay Lightning (TB), and TB plays three away games there, so the weighted distance from would be $3 \times 180 = 540$. Similarly, the weighted TB-FLA distance would also be 540. The Boston Bruins (BOS) are 1,184 miles from TB, and TB plays there twice, which gives $2 \times 1{,}184 = 2{,}368$. The "cost" of a league structure is the sum of these weighted distances over all pairs of teams.

Formally, this is defined as follows: For each pair (u, v) of cities, let $d(u, v)$ denote the distance between u and v and let $g(u, v)$ be the number of games that team u plays in v's city. These depend only on the league structure, not on the actual season game schedule. The measure is defined as

$$D(S) = \sum_{(u,v)}{}' d(u,v)\, g(u,v). \tag{5.1}$$

How well does this measure represent the actual distance traveled by all teams over the course of a season? Teams rarely play single game road trips and when they do, they travel to and from the opponent's city not just to the city. When schedule builders put a road trip in the schedule, they try to visit cities that are located relatively close to each other and which, hopefully, permit an "efficient" trip through the cities and back home. Building a league structure which minimizes $D(S)$ will tend to put teams located in cities close to each other in the same division and conference, but we need an estimate of how good our measure is at predicting league travel.

Leagues publish past schedules and this data was used to see how well our measure for a given league structure compares with actual distances traveled in previous seasons. The measure makes no use of actual travel data from previous seasons. The total league travel only changes a small amount each year, so we evaluate the measure by comparing it to the average travel distances for 2008-09 through 2011-12 seasons.

Table 5.1 gives the results comparing the average travel with the measure. Figure 5.3 shows the actual vs. the predicted travel for individual teams over the last four years. Note the correlation coefficient is 0.92. The measure is within 0.5% of the actual travel both for the league and for the individual teams. We also checked before the Atlanta Thrashers (ATL) moved ($2008 - 09$ thru $2010 - 11$) and after ATL moved ($2011 - 12$) separately, and it was equally good in both cases.

Note that the measure does not itself directly predict total league travel, but because its value is so highly correlated with observed total league travel, we can rescale the measure and get a very good prediction.

For the last several years, the NHL has begun its season with two teams playing a pair of games in Europe. These trips were removed from our calculations, but that did not significantly affect the results.

Table 5.1: Actual NHL Travel from 2008-09 through 2011-12 compared with measure estimate.

	Miles
Actual	4,696,275
Estimate	4,673,053
Difference	23,222
% Difference	0.5%

Figure 5.3: Actual vs. estimated team travel.

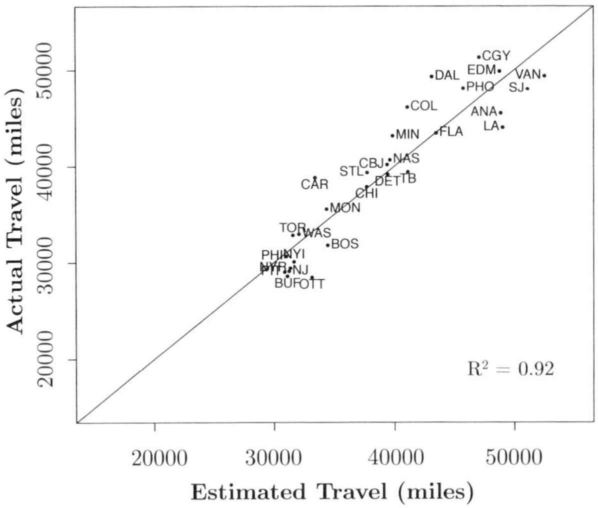

5.3 A Fast Structure Construction Heuristic

A *heuristic* is a method which is not guaranteed to produce an optimal solution to a problem in a reasonable amount of time but which, hopefully, does pretty well. In this section, we describe a heuristic for the optimal league structure problem based on viewing the problem geometrically.

In Section 5.4, we describe an exact method which is guaranteed to find an optimal solution but which can take much longer than the heuristic. In every case, the solution found by the heuristic was the same as the solution found by the exact method.

Suppose we have divided the thirty NHL teams into divisions and conferences. Take a map of North America and put a nail in the map at the location of the home city of every team in a given division or conference. Stretch a rubber bound around all the nails and let it snap tight. The region of the map inside the rubber band is called the *convex hull* of the set of cities.

Geometrically, a set in the plane is *convex* if, for every pair of points in the set, the entire line joining the points lies within the set. The convex hull of a set of points in the plane is the smallest convex set that contains them. See Figures 5.1 or 5.2, for examples.

If the convex hulls of two sets are disjoint, we say that the two sets are *non-overlapping*. Intuitively, from the standpoint of minimizing distance, it seems advantageous to have the convex hulls of the cities of the teams in the divisions be non-overlapping. We call such a league structure a *non-overlapping structure*. In this section, we describe an efficient method for finding a good non-overlapping league structure. However, note that the current NHL structure shown in Figure 5.2 does have two overlapping divisions.

A fundamental theorem of geometry states that two convex sets in the plane are non-overlapping if and only if a straight line can be drawn in the plane which separates the sets. By adjusting such lines, we can assume that each such line passes through a pair of cities. This really speeds things up. If we had to consider every possible way to split thirty cities into two sets of fifteen cities, we would have to consider 155,117,520 possibilities. If we wanted to evaluate all ways to split them into a sixteen team conference and a fourteen team conference, we would have to consider 145,422,675 possibilities. But by limiting ourselves to splits defined by lines passing through pairs of cities, we have much fewer cases. The number of pairs of cities from the set of thirty NHL cities is only 435, so that is the maximum number of splits that we would need to consider if we limit ourselves to non-overlapping conferences.

The heuristic algorithm could consider all such lines. However, in fact, most such lines need not be considered. In the case of the current structure of the NHL, we only need consider separating lines that split the teams into two sets, one consisting of 16 teams, and the other consisting of 14 cities. The line between Los Angeles (LA) and Vancouver (VAN), for example, does not split the league evenly and does not need to be considered. By limiting ourselves to lines that do split the league evenly, we are left with the lines shown in Figure 5.4.

Some remaining lines would still be undesirable for splitting the league into conferences. Lines that are close to horizontal would split the league into a northern half and a southern half. These splits would result in west coast teams being in the same conference as east coast teams, and the conferences

Figure 5.4: Lines that divide the league into equal halves.

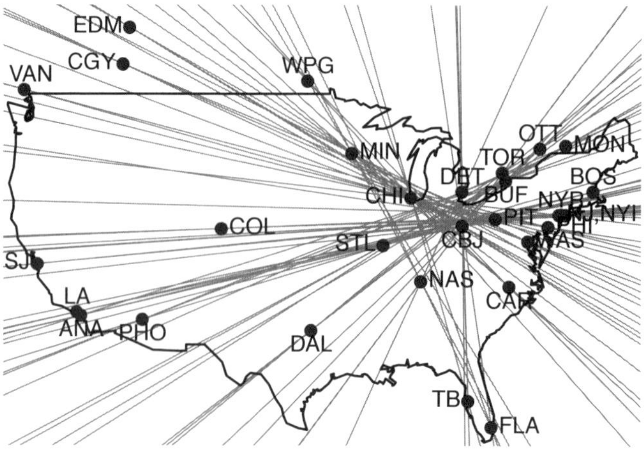

would span four time zones. Even if we did not care about time zones and included these lines, the resulting solutions would not be near the top of the list of the best solutions based on total travel. So we choose to remove many of these near-horizontal lines. We are left with about 20 lines, which are shown in Figure 5.5.

With each of these remaining lines, we can form two conferences, grouping the cities that are on the same side of the line into the same conference. Figure 5.6 shows the convex hulls of the two conferences that result from using one of these lines.

We then repeat this process and split each conference into two divisions.

Figure 5.5: Non-horizontal lines that divide the league into equal halves.

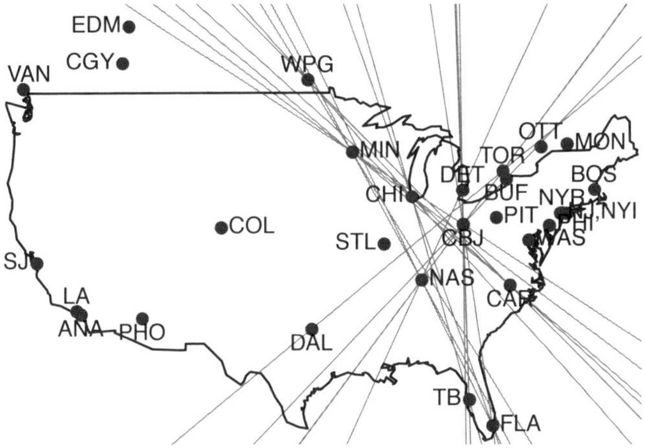

Figure 5.6: Convex hulls of two conferences defined by one of these lines.

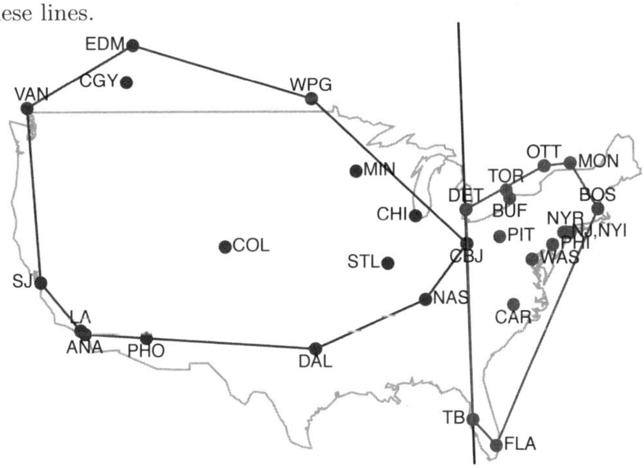

For the 16-team conference, we try all lines that split the conference into two eight-team subgroups. For the 14-team conference, we try all lines that split the conference into two seven team subgroups. The main difference between generating the divisions and generating the conferences is that we do not eliminate horizontal lines while generating divisions.

Tens of thousands of possible league structures were created using this method. For example, in optimally structuring the NHL with the current two conference, four division league structure, we generated over $45,000$ different candidates. For each, we computed the estimated travel using the measure $D(S)$ described in the previous section. We then sorted the list of solutions based on this estimated travel.

When we ran this algorithm on a laptop computer it took approximately two minutes to compute all the candidate league structures, about ten minutes to compute the estimated travel for each and to choose the one with lowest estimated travel distance.

Including additional constraints

This approach has another benefit in addition to its speed. When creating a league structure, other factors besides travel distance are important. There may be traditional rivalries that we want to maintain, for example, Montreal-Toronto or Pittsburgh-Philadelphia in the NHL. We may wish to sacrifice overall league distance travel in order to reduce travel for Florida and West Coast teams. We may want to keep each division within at most two time zones. The heuristic deals with this very easily. The complete set of solutions can be filtered based on relevant, possibly complex, criteria and then sorted based on estimated travel. This can produce several alternative structures with similar estimated travel costs, and decision-makers can choose among them based on other "soft" criteria.

Quality of Solutions

The league structures produced by this heuristic satisfy two properties: First, the divisions are non-overlapping as are the conferences. Second, the divisions and conferences are constructed by a sequence of straight line cuts. Such cuts are called *guillotine cuts*. How much do we lose by only considering such structures?

A best possible non-overlapping structure may not be optimal in some situations, for example, see Figure 5.7(a). A fictitious league consists of six cities, three of which form the vertices of a large triangle and three of which are very close to each other and located in the center of the triangle. Suppose we wish to construct a league with two 3-team divisions. The optimal structure has the three vertices of the triangle in one division and the three central cities in another division. The best possible non-overlapping structure would have one division consisting of two teams from the triangle and one from the center and the other of two teams from the center and one from the triangle. Figure 5.7(b) gives an example of a set of nine cities and a partition into three non-overlapping 3-city divisions which cannot be found if we are limited to guillotine cuts.

In practice, however, it seems that very little is lost with these restrictions when applied to real data. Optimal structures were obtained using the mixed-integer optimization (MIO) approach described in the next section to a number of the cases discussed here. In every case tried, this established that the best solution produced by the heuristic was not just the best of the solutions we generated, but was in fact optimal among *all* solutions.

5.4 Using Integer Optimization to Optimize League Structure*

The problem of finding a league structure for which the measure $D(S)$ is minimized can be formulated as an MIO problem. We have a set T of n teams/cities and a set M of m divisions. For any two teams $u, v \in T$ recall that $d(u, v) = d(v, u)$ is the travel distance between the home cities of u and v. The input data consists of the following:

- $D = (D_{uv} = d(u, v) : u, v \in T)$ is the $n \times n$ (symmetric) inter-city distance matrix. There may be situations where travel times are not symmetric. For example, in North America, west-bound flights between two cities typically take 20% longer than east-bound flights, because of prevailing winds. Our formulation works whether or not D is symmetric.

- G is the $m \times m$ away game matrix. For each pair (i, j) of divisions, G_{ij} specifies the number of away games to be played by teams in division i against teams in division j. In the case that this number is not the same for all pairs of teams in these divisions, we let G_{ij} be the average number of away games between each pair of teams in

Figure 5.7: Divisions not constructible by heuristic.

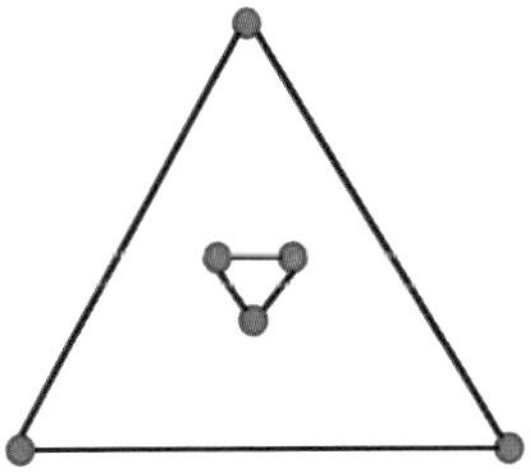

(a)

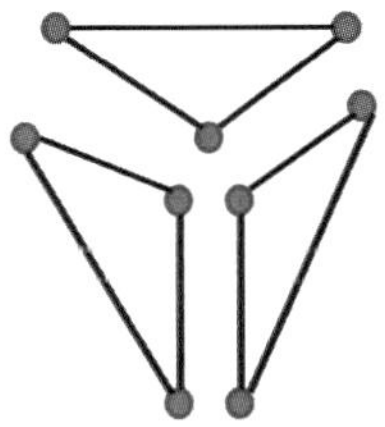

(b)

the two divisions. When considering intra-divisional games, that is, when $i = j$, we only consider pairs of distinct teams.

- b is an m element vector with b_i equal to the number of teams required in division i. Note that $\sum_{i=1}^{m} b_i = n$.

In the case of the 2008 to 2012 NHL, $n = 30$, $m = 6$, $b = [\ 5\ \ 5\ \ 5\ \ 5\ \ 5\ \ 5\ ]$. The away game matrix G is given by

$$G = \begin{bmatrix} 3.0 & 2.0 & 2.0 & 0.6 & 0.6 & 0.6 \\ 2.0 & 3.0 & 2.0 & 0.6 & 0.6 & 0.6 \\ 2.0 & 2.0 & 3.0 & 0.6 & 0.6 & 0.6 \\ 0.6 & 0.6 & 0.6 & 3.0 & 2.0 & 2.0 \\ 0.6 & 0.6 & 0.6 & 2.0 & 3.0 & 2.0 \\ 0.6 & 0.6 & 0.6 & 2.0 & 2.0 & 3.0 \end{bmatrix}.$$

For the current 4-division league structure, adopted by the NHL at the start of the 2013-14 season, $n = 30$, $m = 4$, $b = [\ 8\ \ 8\ \ 7\ \ 7\ ]$ and the away game matrix G is given by

$$G = \begin{bmatrix} 2.14 & 1.5 & 1 & 1 \\ 1.5 & 2.14 & 1 & 1 \\ 1 & 1 & 2.42 & 1.5 \\ 1 & 1 & 1.5 & 2.42 \end{bmatrix}.$$

- For each team v and each division i, we have a real decision variable x_{vi} satisfying $x_{vi} \geq 0$. Our formulation will ensure that in an optimal solution x_{vi} will be $\{0, 1\}$-valued. It will have the interpretation $x_{vi} = 1$, if team v is in division i, and $x_{vi} = 0$, if not.

In order to compute the measure $D(S)$, we create a set of $(m \times n)^2$ $\{0, 1\}$-valued decision variables y_{uvij} as follows:

- For each pair (u, v) of teams and for each pair (i, j) of divisions, we want these to take on the values $y_{uvij} = 1$, if team u is assigned to division i and team v is assigned to division j, and $y_{uvij} = 0$, if not.

- The cost c_{uvij} of y_{uvij} is defined to be $c_{uvij} = D_{uv} \cdot G_{ij}$.

In our example, we have $30 \times 6 = 180$ variables x_{vi} and $180^2 = 32,400$ variables y_{uvij}.

There are three sets of constraints on our variables. The first set ensures that we have the correct number of teams in each division and that each team belongs to a division:

$$\sum_{v \in T} x_{vi} = b_i \text{ for each division } i \in M;$$

$$\sum_{i \in M} x_{vi} = 1 \text{ for each team } v \in T.$$

The second ensures that each pair of teams play in exactly one pair of divisions.

$$\text{For each pair } u, v \text{ of cities, } \sum_{i,j \in M} y_{uvij} = 1;$$

$$\text{For each pair } i, j \text{ of divisions, } \sum_{u,v \in T} y_{uvij} = b_i \cdot b_j.$$

The third set of constraints forces the x and y variables to behave consistently. We want to have $y_{uvij} = 1$ only if $x_{ui} = 1$ and $x_{vj} = 1$ and $y_{uvij} = 0$ otherwise. We create the inequalities

$$y_{uvij} \leq 0.5(x_{ui} + x_{vj}) \text{ for all } u, v \in T, i, j \in S. \tag{5.2}$$

Because we constrain y_{uvij} to be a $0 - 1$ variable for all u, v, i, j, we will have $y_{uvij} = 0$ unless both $x_{ui} = 1$ and $x_{vj} = 1$. We will modify the objective function so that in this case we will have $y_{uvij} = 1$. We define a new cost function c' by letting $c'_{uvij} = K - c_{uvij}$ for all $u, v \in T$ and $i, j \in S$, where K is a constant larger than any cost c_{uvij}. Then, minimizing c is equivalent to maximizing c' and all c'_{uvij} are strictly positive.

Each variable y_{uvij} occurs in a single inequality (5.2) and has a positive cost coefficient. Therefore, if we maximize our objective, every y_{uvij} can take on its largest possible value 1 if and only if both $x_{ui} = 1$ and $x_{vj} = 1$, as we desire and it would be suboptimal for y_{uvij} to take on a smaller value. Otherwise, y_{uvij} will have value 0.

Summarizing, the mixed integer optimization problem that we solve to obtain an optimal league structure is

$$\begin{aligned}
\text{maximize} \quad & \sum_{u,v \in T, i,j \in M} y_{uvij} \cdot c'_{uvij} \\
\text{subject to} \quad & \sum_{v \in T} x_{vi} = b_i \text{ for each division } i \in M; \\
& \sum_{i \in M} x_{vi} = 1 \text{ for each team } v \in T; \\
& \sum_{i,j \in M} y_{uvij} = 1 \text{ for each pair } u, v \text{ of cities }; \\
& \sum_{u,v \in T} y_{uvij} = b_i \cdot b_j \text{ for each pair } i, j \text{ of divisions}; \\
& y_{uvij} \leq 0.5(x_{ui} + x_{vj}) \text{ for all } u, v \in T, i, j \in M; \\
& x_{uv} \geq 0 \text{ for all } u, v \in T;
\end{aligned}$$

$$y_{ij} \in \{0, 1\}, \text{ for all } i, j \in M.$$

It is straightforward to add extra constraints to this model to require certain teams, or combinations of teams to be in specified divisions. In all cases, the optimal solution to the MIO was identical to the best solution found by the heuristic!

In general, the solution time required to solve these league structure problems ranged from several hours to tens of hours on a moderately powerful workstation. We were able to reduce solution time by providing the MIO solver with a starting solution equal to the best solution found by the heuristic for the problem. Also, requiring selected pairs of cities on opposite sides of the continent to be in different divisions generally improved solution times.

Solving the MIO produced a single, provably optimal, structure. The set of optimal and near optimal solutions provided by the heuristic of the previous section provided many more options, some of which may have been preferable to league planners who wish to consider "soft" constraints.

5.5 Results

Figure 5.8 shows the best league structure for the 2008-2012 NHL alignment of two conferences, each divided into three divisions, each consisting of five teams. This were obtained by both of the methods of the previous two sections.

Surprisingly, the two Florida teams, the Florida Panthers (FLA) and Tampa Bay Lightning (TB), are *not* in the same division. In fact, they are not even in the same conference, as Tampa Bay is in the Western Conference

Figure 5.8: The best 6-division structure.

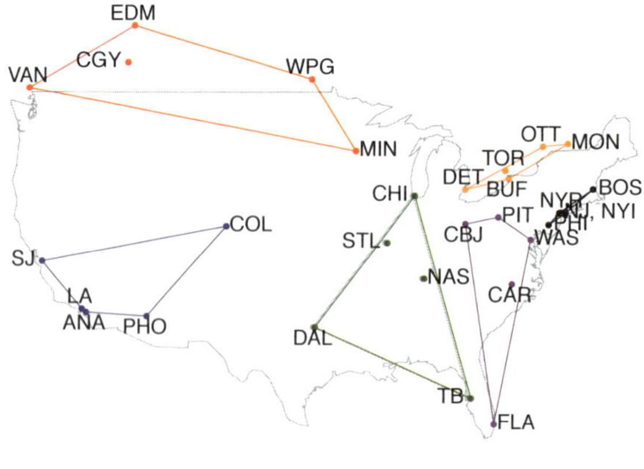

League Travel: 1,155,391 miles

and the Florida Panthers are in the Eastern Conference. So, although this is a structure that minimizes total league travel, it would probably be unacceptable. In addition, it could be preferable to have a league structure that reduces travel for the teams that have the greatest amount of travel, the west coast and Florida teams, if this can be done with only a small increase in total league travel.

We can add constraints on acceptable league structures by filtering violating structures from the list of possibilities created by the heuristic. When all structures in which FLA and TB are in different divisions were eliminated, the league structure shown in Figure 5.9 is the best solution keeping FLA and TB in the same division. This only increases the estimated overall league travel by a 578 travel miles (out of 1,155,391 miles), probably a small price to pay for keeping those teams together. This solution also had the effect of reducing travel for the west coast and Florida teams.

Best 4-division configurations The NHL adopted the 4-division structure shown in Figure 5.2 in March of 2013 and has used it since the 2013-14 season. This structure had two eastern divisions, each with eight teams, and two western divisions each with seven teams. The game schedules to be created were required to satisfy the following:

- Each eastern team plays four games against each of five other teams in its division and plays five games against each of the other two teams in its conference.
- Each western team plays five games against each of five other teams in its divisions and plays four games against the other team in its conference.

Figure 5.9: Best structure with TB and FLA in same division.

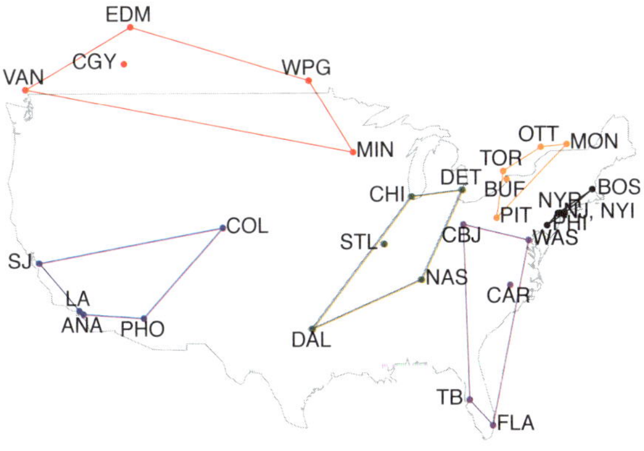

League Travel: 1,155,969 miles

- Each eastern team plays three games against each team in the other eastern division.

- Each western team plays three games against each team in the other western division.

- Each eastern team and each western team play each other twice, once away and once at home.

- Each team plays forty-one home games and forty-one away games. The number of home and away games played between each pair of teams is within 1 of being equal.

The "best" such solution is shown in Figure 5.10.

The difference in team travel under the new alignment and our best solution is given in Figure 5.11. Only Eastern Conference teams are shown since the two proposals have the same Western Conference divisions. TB and FLA are expected to have much more travel than all of the other teams, but optimizing total league travel would only reduce their travel by about 700 miles.

Both the heuristic in Section 5.3 and the MIO formulation in Section 5.4 can be easily modified to handle the 4-division structure. For the heuristic, first split the thirty teams into an eastern set of sixteen teams and a western set of fourteen teams. Then, each of these sets is split into two equal sized conferences. For the integer optimization formulation, it is straight forward to adapt the model described in Section 5.4.

Figure 5.10: The best 4-division structure with 16 teams in the east and 14 teams in the west.

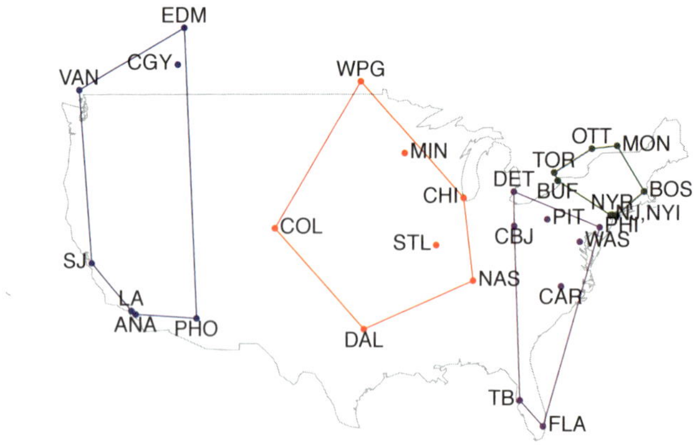

League Travel: 1,230,102 miles

Figure 5.11: Difference in Eastern Conference team travel between new NHL structure and optimum 4-division solution (Figure 5.10).

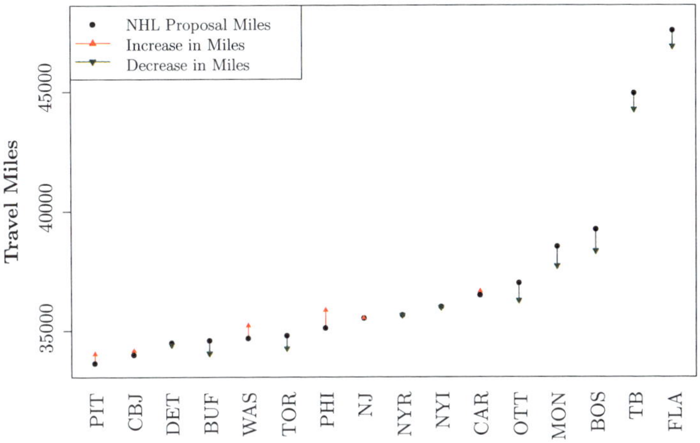

Finally, Figure 5.12 shows the best 4-division structure if we do not insist that the Eastern Conference have sixteen teams and the Western Conference have fourteen teams.

Figure 5.12: The "best" configuration for a 4-division structure with two 7 team divisions and two 8 team divisions.

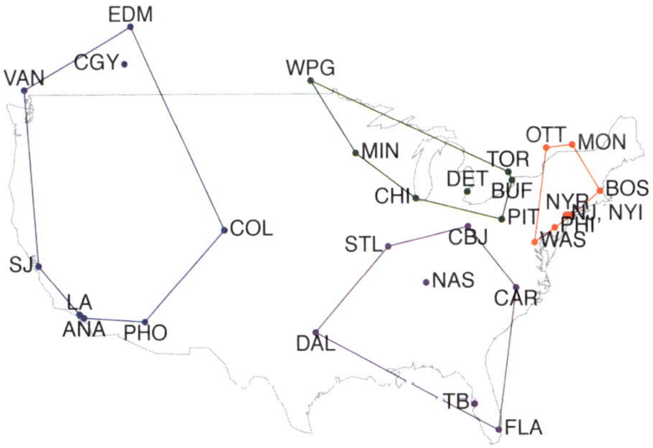

League Travel: 1,203,918 miles

The travel required by 4-division structures is typically much greater than the current 6-division structure. The best 4-division solutions are about 85,000 miles worse than the best 6-division solutions. Much of this difference is due to the more balanced schedule that was proposed along with this realignment which requires all teams to travel more.

5.6 Conclusions

The material presented in this chapter demonstrates a phenomenon that occurs frequently when using analytics. Solving a real world problem requires a combination of analytic methods, human insights and ways of integrating these two aspects. The problem we considered, constructing a "good" league structure, is poorly defined. There are many so-called hard constraints – constraints that must be satisfied like having every team play the same number of home and away games – and many so-called soft constraints – constraints that are desirable to satisfy but may be violated but not by too much. Examples of these are the constraints requiring teams from the same state play in the same division or that road trips should not be too long.

The heuristic approach outlined here can be applied to a variety of problems. First, create a method capable of creating all, or at least a large number, of feasible solutions. Second, evaluate these solutions for quality and select those that satisfy soft constraints sufficiently well. Third, present these to a user responsible for selecting the solution to be implemented. Human decision makers generally prefer to be presented with a set of solutions plus some measure of the quality of each from which one can be selected. (In our case, this was a set of league structures plus the estimate of the total travel for each.)

Integer optimization provides a powerful method for obtaining a provably optimal solution to a variety of problem. However, the long computation time required may make this impractical, but it can give us confidence in the quality of heuristically generated solutions. It also has the weakness that it is difficult to obtain a variety of good candidate solutions which can be given to a human decision maker.

Table 5.2 summarizes the NHL restructuring results obtained. The first two rows give the measure of the "old" NHL both before and after the Atlanta Thrashers moved to Winnipeg. The next two rows give the measure of the best possible six division two conference league structure, allowing Florida and Tampa Bay to be in different divisions and requiring them to be in the same division. The difference in total league travel is only 578 miles.

The last three rows provide the measures for the current NHL four division structure as well as two variations. The first variation matches the current NHL structure by requiring there be a two division fourteen team Western Conference and a two division sixteen team Eastern Conference. The total league travel estimate for the best four division structure with these constraints is about

Table 5.2: Comparison of Estimated Travel with Different League Structures.

League Structure	# Conf.	# Div.	Travel (miles)	Travel over min.
NHL Prior to 2011	2	6	1,147,543	
NHL 2011-12 and 2012-13 (after ATL → WPG)	2	6	1,185,123	29,732
Best six division (after ATL → WPG)	2	6	1,155,391	0
Best six division (after ATL → WPG, FL and TB in same div.)	2	6	1,155,969	578
NHL post 2013-14	2	4	1,233,031	29,113
Best four division (16 teams in East.)	2	4	1,230,078	26,160
Best four division (Div. sizes 7, 7, 8, 8)	2	4	1,203,918	0

3,000 miles lower than for the current NHL. The last row estimates travel for a best possible four division conference with two seven team divisions and two eight team divisions. This requires teams in two divisions to be in two different time zones, which is viewed as undesirable. Although the total league travel for four division league structures is greater than for six division structures, a part of this increase is due to teams playing fewer intra-division games and more games against teams in other divisions and conferences. The benefit of a more balanced schedule may offset the disadvantage of additional travel.

5.7 Notes and Sources

5.1. The primary source for this chapter is Macdonald and Pulleyblank [88]. In this paper, similar analysis is also performed for each of Major League Baseball, the National Basketball Association and the National Football League. A web site with a variety of related material is [87]. This includes an animation depicting the two conferences that result from using each of the lines remaining in Figure 5.5.

5.2. The problem of constructing a league structure S for which $D(S)$ is minimized can be formulated as a Quadratic Assignment Problem (QAP). See Pardalos et al. [112] for an overview of solution methods for QAPs and computational comparisons of their effectiveness.

5.3. A similar QAP based approach was studied in Mitchell [97] in the context of NFL realignment. There the objective was to minimize intra-divisional travel distance whereas ours is to minimize total league travel. These two problems are similar, but our objective supports multi-level (divisions and conferences) league structures.

Chapter 6

The MIT Blackjack Team

The count was perfect because card counting is a perfectly mathematical exercise. It is based solely on numbers and data contained in the cards and, as such, represents a perfect application of analytics.

– Jeffrey Ma

Contents

In the 1960s, Edward Thorp, an applied mathematics professor, published a landmark book titled "Beat the Dealer," which describes how blackjack players can use card counting to turn the advantage against the casinos and in favor of the player. Thorp confirmed his claims by using probability theory, computer simulations, and experiments in casinos. News spread quickly throughout the gambling community, and Thorp became an instant celebrity among blackjack players.

Almost two decades later, a group of students at MIT used the insights of Thorp to teach themselves card counting, and began traveling to Atlantic City and Las Vegas to start collecting their fortune. By 1984, the team consisted of more than 35 players and by the 1990s, the team had over 80 players all over the country. They relied on a basic strategy, card counting, team play, and a million dollar bank to win as much as \$400,000 in a single weekend.

This chapter tells the story of how analytics were used to turn the odds in favor of the player and, ultimately, to drive casinos to change the rules of blackjack for the first time in history. While using card counting requires a significant amount of concentration and a good memory, the techniques developed by Thorp just relied on probability theory and the results of computer simulations.

The foundation of the MIT team's strategy was a huge amount of data. The team collected data on everything, from the timing of the game to the moves of the other players. This data not only influenced their next moves, but also the salaries of the players and the locations they would play. Every decision was based on analytics, and without it, they would have needed an extraordinary streak of good luck to have amassed an equivalent fortune in winnings.

6.1 The Game of Blackjack

Today, blackjack is one of the most widely played casino games in the world. Over 100 different versions of the game have been documented. In this section, we describe a common, but not universal, set of rules that we will assume throughout the rest of this chapter. Throughout this section, we will refer to Figure 6.1 as an example game.

In blackjack, one to eight decks of cards are used. (Casinos actually started increasing the number of decks used in response to card counting, since more decks makes card counting harder for players.) The cards are shuffled by the dealer, and "cut" by one of the players, meaning that the player picks a point in the deck for the dealer to start the deal from. A number of deals are then dealt out to all the players. When the number of cards remaining is less than a certain percentage of the total cards, the deck is reshuffled (this percentage is set by the casino). Before each round of cards is dealt, the players place their bets, with minimum and maximum bets typically set by the casino.

(The amount of a player's bet typically represents how confident the player is that he or she can beat the dealer on that hand.)

The dealer then deals two cards to himself and two cards to each of the players. (Note that the cards are dealt one at a time, so each player gets one card and then each player gets their second card.) The players' cards are dealt face up, while the dealer has one card face up and the other face down. In Figure 6.1, the top half of the figure shows the initial deal. The dealer has an

Figure 6.1: An example of the game of blackjack, with four players.

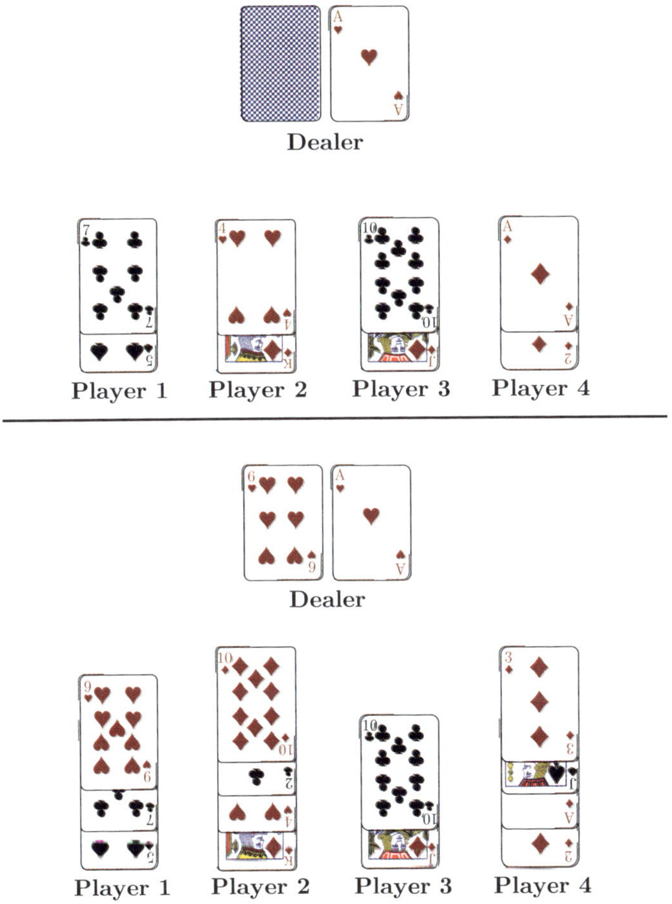

Ace as his face up card, the player on the far left (we will refer to this player as Player 1) has a five and a seven, the next player (Player 2) has a King and a four, the third player (Player 3) has a Jack and a ten, and the last player (Player 4) has a two and an Ace. A variation of the game deals the players' cards face down, but dealing the cards face up is actually an advantage for card counting, since the counter can see all of the cards that the other players have.

In blackjack, points are counted by adding up the cards in a player's hand. Face cards (King, Queen, or Jack) are worth 10 points, Aces are worth either 1 or 11 points (whichever is better for the hand), and the other cards are all worth their actual number. A hand in which the Ace can still be counted as 11 points without going over 21 is called a "soft" hand. If the Ace can only be counted as one point without going over 21, the hand is called a "hard" hand. Any hand without an Ace is referred to as a "hard" hand as well (a hard hand is one that has no flexibility). In the top half of Figure 6.1, Player 4's hand is worth 3 or 13 points, so it is considered a "soft" hand worth 13 points. Player 1's hand is worth 12 points, Player 2's hand is worth 14 points, and Player 3's hand is worth 20 points.

The play of each deal of the game (or "round") starts by checking if any of the players or the dealer got a *blackjack*, which means that as their first two cards, they have an Ace and a card worth ten points. If a player gets a blackjack and the dealer does not, then the player receives 1.5 times their initial bet from their dealer. (So if the player bet \$10, they would get \$15 from the dealer, in addition to getting their initial bet back.) This is the first way that a player can win the game. None of the players in Figure 6.1 have a blackjack. If the dealer has a blackjack but the player does not, the player loses their bet. The bottom image in Figure 6.1 shows that the dealer's facedown card was a 6, so the dealer did not have a blackjack. If both the player and the dealer have a blackjack, then no money changes hands. (In general, if the player and dealer have the same score, the player keeps his bet, so no money changes hands.)

If neither the player nor the dealer is dealt a blackjack, the game continues with each player deciding whether or not they want to take additional cards (called a "hit") or just keep the cards they have (called a "stand"). Players who take additional cards and "bust," meaning that the addition of another card made their hand exceed 21, lose their bet to the dealer before the dealer even plays. In Figure 6.1 this happened to Player 2, which is shown in the bottom image. He decided to take a third card, which ended up being a 2, increasing his total from 14 to 16. He then took a fourth card, which was a 10, making him bust with a total of 26. He would lose his bet to the dealer at this point, and be out of the game (if he bet \$10, he would lose \$10).

Player 4 also decided to take additional cards, but he did not exceed 21. Player 4's third card ended up being a Jack. Counting the Ace as 1, he had a new total of 13. Note that he now has a "hard" 13, since he can no longer count the Ace as 11 without going over 21. Player 4 then took a fourth card, for a total of 16, and then decided to stand.

Player 3 decided to "stand" from the beginning with a total of 20. Player

1 took one additional card, and it ended up being a nine. This gave him a total of 21.

After each player busts or decides to stand, the dealer also has to play. Most casinos require the dealer to draw a card until he busts or achieves a value of 17 or higher. In Figure 6.1, the dealer has a 17 with his first two cards, so he does not need to draw an additional card. If the six had instead been a five, he would have drawn an additional card. This predictable behavior of the dealer is critical for defining and analyzing basic strategy, which will be discussed in the next section.

At this point, the dealer's score is compared to the score of each of the players. Player 4 would lose his bet to the dealer, since his total of 16 is lower than the dealer's total of 17. Players 1 and 3 would both win their respective bets, since they have scores higher than the dealers score, with scores of 20 and 21. In most casinos, winning with a higher point total (but not a blackjack) means that the player wins their original bet from the dealer. So in this case, if Players 1 and 3 each bet \$10, they would each win \$10 from the dealer, for a total of \$20. Note that even though Player 1 got a total of 21, this is not considered a blackjack since he had to draw more than two cards. So Player 1 would just win his original bet, not 1.5 times his original bet.

Once all players and the dealer have played, the hand is over, and another round is dealt. Note that the dealer has a clear advantage in blackjack, because the player always goes first. If the player busts, the round is over for the player and the dealer wins, even though the dealer might have also busted if they had played. But with basic strategy and card counting, which we will discuss in the next section, the player can overcome this advantage of the dealer, and turn the odds in his favor.

So ultimately, a player wins a hand by "beating the dealer," which as we saw here, can be done in multiple ways. The player can get a blackjack (without the dealer getting a blackjack), reach a final score higher than the dealer without exceeding 21, or the dealer can bust. Note that the player is only competing against the dealer in blackjack – it does not matter how well or how poorly the other players do. In summary, the player wants to get as close to 21 as possible, without exceeding 21.

While this section explained the basic rules of blackjack, there are a few other more elaborate things that the player can do, such as splitting, doubling down and taking insurance. For a player to consistently win at blackjack, they need to be very familiar with all of these concepts. However, in this chapter, we will skip these additional possibilities and just stick to the basics. To learn more about the game of blackjack, see the references in Section 6.5.

6.2 A Beatable Game

Edward Thorp started thinking about gambling when he was a high school student. One of his teachers returned from a trip to Las Vegas claiming that it was impossible to beat the casinos. But Thorp was not so sure about this. He started by thinking about roulette as a graduate student at UCLA, with the goal of developing a mathematical system to consistently win at roulette. Unfortunately, roulette is a game of pure chance and the probability of winning is slightly higher for the house, and so Thorp was struggling to create a strategy to beat the game. It has been proven, using probability theory, that for most of the standard gambling games (like roulette and craps) no betting scheme can ever be devised that will overcome the casino's long-run advantage.

While Thorp was on a trip to Las Vegas, trying in vain to beat roulette, he decided to try out a blackjack strategy he recently came across, called "basic strategy." This strategy was from a recently published article in the Journal of the American Statistical Association by a U.S. Army mathematician Roger Baldwin and three of his colleagues. While Thorp was not able to win a fortune using basic strategy that time (he lost $8.50 of the $10 he was using), he believed that the strategy could be improved and requested the data used by Baldwin. In 1959, Thorp spent many hours feeding this data into a computer, and ultimately discovered how to overcome the house advantage. The main idea was to use an aspect of the game that the player has more control over: how much to bet on each hand. By discovering this advantage, Thorp changed the game forever.

Basic Strategy

In this section, we will describe the key idea of basic strategy. There are many nuances to the rules presented here based on various components of the game (such as splitting and doubling down). To successfully win in a casino, these components are critical and should be studied carefully. However, we will just focus on the main strategy in this chapter. For more information, see the references in Section 6.5.

Basic strategy refers to the optimal moves a player can make to increase his odds of beating the dealer (without counting cards). By following a set of simple rules, a player can make it so that he is at just a small disadvantage to the casino, about 2% per hand. This means that, on average, the player should expect to lose about 2% of the total amount of money he bets while playing the game. (In any particular hand, the player could of course be winning or losing, but if a player plays long enough, this is what he should expect to happen.) Basic strategy can be defined for any casino game, and it does not rely on anything special about blackjack. However, a player can do even better in blackjack because of a property called *conditional probability*, which can be used to the player's advantage by counting cards (we will discuss this further in the next section). The combination of basic strategy and card counting can give the player a 2% *advantage* over the casino. We will describe basic strategy first, and then see how card counting can be incorporated.

The only information used in basic strategy is the player's own total count, and the dealer's up card. Table 6.1 shows what the player should do given his total and the dealers up card, given that he has a "hard" hand, meaning that if he has an Ace, the Ace can only be counted as an 11.

The possible totals of the player are listed on the left in the table, and the possible up-cards of the dealer are listed on the top of the table. Players' totals less than 12 are not shown in the table, because basic strategy says that the player should always draw another card if their total is less than or equal to 11. Similarly, players' totals greater than 17 are not shown in the table, since the player should always stand with a total of 18 or more, given that they have a "hard" hand.

These rules were developed analytically with the help of probability theory, and then verified with computer simulations. For example, let us consider the case where the player has a hard 16, and the dealer is showing a nine. Should the player draw or stand? The basic strategy table tells us that the player should draw, but why? At first thought, this might seem like a strange thing to do, because the player is going to bust if they draw a card worth 6, 7, 8, 9, or 10 points, cards which account for 32 of the 52 cards in a full deck, or 61.5% of the cards. But let us think about what the dealer has. With a nine, there is a higher chance that the dealer has a good hand (higher than a 16). So if the player stands, the dealer will probably win most of the time. Let us investigate in more detail by using simulations.

We will simulate what happens in different scenarios with a 52 card deck. Table 6.2 shows the percentage of times the player wins if they stand, out of 10,000 hands, versus the percentage of times the player wins if they draw, for each of the possible combinations of two cards that the player could have (to give a hard total of 16). These simulations were run by first removing the player's two cards and the dealer's 9 from a "deck of cards," simulated on a

Table 6.1: Basic strategy guidelines. The combinations for which the player should draw another card are shaded and marked with a D. The combinations for which the player should stand are marked with an S. There can be some exceptions based on the number of decks used and the specific casino rules.

	Dealer's Up Card									
Player's Total	**2**	**3**	**4**	**5**	**6**	**7**	**8**	**9**	**10**	**Ace**
17	S	S	S	S	S	S	S	S	S	S
16	S	S	S	S	S	D	D	D	D	D
15	S	S	S	S	S	D	D	D	D	D
14	S	S	S	S	S	D	D	D	D	D
13	S	S	S	S	S	D	D	D	D	D
12	D	D	S	S	S	D	D	D	D	D

computer. Then, the cards were randomly sorted (shuffled) and the first card in the deck was given to the dealer as his second card. The player either took the next card from the deck (if the player decided to draw) or the player did not take any additional cards. The dealer then took cards until his total exceeded 16, which the dealer is almost always required to do according to the casino's rules.

If the player busts, the hand is marked as being won by the dealer. If the dealer busts, the hand is marked as being won by the player. If neither the player nor the dealer busts, the hand is won by the person with the higher total. This was repeated 10,000 times for each combination of cards that the player could have, first with the player standing and then with the player drawing a card.

Table 6.2 shows us that regardless of which exact cards the player is holding, they have a higher chance of winning if they draw instead of stand. Unfortunately, the player does not have great odds of winning in this situation no matter what they do, but at least by drawing, they increase their odds a little bit. If the dealer has an Ace, King, Queen, Jack, 10, 9, or 8 to go with their 9, then the dealer will definitely win if the player stands, since the dealer will have a higher point total than the player. But if the player draws, then the player has a chance of winning. So in any of these situations, it is definitely better for the player to draw. This contributes to the higher odds of the player winning if they draw instead of stand.

Table 6.3 shows the results of the simulations when the player still has a hard sixteen, but the dealer has a 6. The basic strategy table tells us that the player should stand, which is confirmed with these simulation results. The player has a significantly higher chance of winning in this situation if they stand instead of draw. Unfortunately, the player again still has less than a 50% chance of winning, but by choosing to stand they are definitely making the right choice (a 16 is an unfortunate hand for the player in general, because it is easy to bust if another card is drawn, but it is also likely that the dealer will beat a 16).

Every entry in Table 6.1 can be confirmed by repeating this experiment. The basic strategy for what to do if the player has a soft hand or a pair is also detailed in the book "Beat the Dealer" by Edward Thorp, but we won't go into detail about it here. The main idea of basic strategy is that by memorizing a

Table 6.2: The percentage of times the player wins blackjack when they draw or stand on a hard 16 when the dealer shows a nine.

Player	**Dealer**	**% Hands Won if Draw**	**% Hands Won if Stand**
10, 6	9, ?	30.9%	24.9%
9, 7	9, ?	30.5%	25.3%
8, 8	9, ?	28.8%	26.0%

Table 6.3: Simulations of the percentage of times players win blackjack when they draw or stand on a hard 16 when the dealer shows a six.

Player	Dealer	% Hands Won if Draw	% Hands Won if Stand
10, 6	6, ?	32.6%	44.3%
9, 7	6, ?	32.2%	44.2%
8, 8	6, ?	32.0%	44.0%

few small tables with some basic rules, the player knows what to do when faced with any situation.

Card Counting

The key difference in blackjack compared to other casino games is that it is subject to *conditional probability*, meaning that what is seen in each hand affects what can be seen in subsequent hands. In games like craps or roulette, what is seen in the past does not change the odds of winning or losing at all. Rolling a six last time tells a player nothing about what they will roll this time. However, when playing blackjack, having an Ace in a hand this time says that there is one less Ace in the deck. So the odds of getting an Ace in the next hand are lower than they would have been if the Ace had not appeared. If a player can keep track of the cards that have already been seen, there are times when they can give themselves an advantage over the house.

Thorp developed what is referred to as the "Hi-Lo Method," a simple card counting methodology that could turn the odds against the casinos in favor of the players. Thorp developed this method by simulating the effect that each card had on the player's chance of winning the game. He used a technique called *Monte Carlo Simulation*, which is used to understand events that have unknown random behavior. The name actually comes from the act of playing and recording results in a real casino. Monte Carlo Simulation repeats an experiment that has a random aspect to it (like drawing a card from a deck) over and over to analyze what happens in the long-run. Thorp used an IBM 704 computer, and simulated hands of blackjack with all the twos removed from the deck, then all the threes removed from the deck, and so on. He found that two through six were "bad" cards, since removing these cards from the deck would increase the players chances of winning (the presence of these cards is bad for the player). Tens, Jacks, Queens, Kings, and Aces were deemed "good" cards, since removing these cards from the deck decreased the player's chances of winning the game (the presence of these cards is good for the player). The remaining cards were found to be "neutral" cards, since removing them from the deck did not have a noticeable effect on the odds of the game.

Table 6.4 gives the results of running these simulations 10,000 times with six decks each time. This leads to about 500,000 hands of blackjack, although the exact number of hands played depends on which card was removed (more cards are needed on average per hand if there are fewer high cards). The first row of the table shows that with a normal deck of cards, the player wins about 43.14% of the hands (the player used basic strategy in these simulations, but did not do any splitting). Then each of the other rows shows how this percentage changes with different cards removed from the deck. In these simulations, two through seven were found to be bad cards, since when they were removed, the player's winning percentage increased, and eight through Ace were found to be good cards, since when they were removed, the player's winning percentage decreased. These results are very similar to what Thorp discovered in the 1960s.

These observations about good and bad cards make sense because of the rules of the game. The dealer is typically forced to take another card when their total is sixteen or less. So if there are a lot of high cards in the deck, the dealer has a higher chance of busting, which is good for the player. But if there are a lot of low cards left in the deck, then the dealer has a higher chance of not busting, and beating the player.

The differences in the winning percentage are very small, but when a lot of money is on the table, or when a player can play for a long time (betting

Table 6.4: Simulations of the percentage of time the player wins blackjack when each of the cards is removed. Six decks were used in each simulation, and the simulations were run 10,000 times. The dashed line indicates the point when the removal of the card starts to decrease the player's winning percentage. So the cards 2-7 are bad cards for the player (their removal increases the player's chances of winning), and the cards 8-Ace are good cards for the player (their removal decreases the player's chances of winning).

Card Removed	Percentage of Hands Player Wins
None	43.14%
2	43.25%
3	43.65%
4	43.55%
5	43.84%
6	43.35%
7	43.72%
8	43.06%
9	42.43%
10	42.31%
Jack	42.24%
Queen	42.31%
King	42.39%
Ace	42.90%

more when his odds of winning are greater and less when they are worse), this difference can lead to a significant enough edge for the player. Jeffrey Ma, a former player on the MIT Blackjack Team, said that the lesson in blackjack, as well as in business, is that "you need to have a long-term perspective and the corresponding financial commitment to make analytics pay off."

So how were these observations used to count cards? The Hi-Lo Method was developed to keep a rough count of how good the remaining cards were. Players only had to keep track of a single number, called the *running count*. The number was added to every time a low card (two through six) came out of the deck, and subtracted from every time a high card (10, Jack, Queen, King, or Ace) came out of the deck. The more positive the running count is, the more high cards are left in the deck, and the higher the player's chances of winning. If a player could keep track of the running count, they could increase their bet when the count is positive, and lower their bet when the count went negative.

Unfortunately, this technique had a couple of major flaws. One was that the player needed to have access to an enormous about of money to make any money, since the advantage of the player is only about $2-3\%$ against the casino (the player should expect to win about $52-53\%$ of the time). Another flaw was that the technique was too easy to spot. Even in the 1960s, when Thorp invented the method, casinos had a significant security team trying to spot card counting techniques. By the time the MIT Blackjack Team was playing in the 1980s and 1990s, casino security had significantly increased. While card counting in general is a legal practice, casinos have the right to ban individual players from entering the casino for any reason. They tend to do this if they suspect a player of being a card counter.

Team Play

To overcome the detectability of the Hi-Lo Method, the MIT Blackjack Team relied on *team play*, which divides a team of players into three types: spotters, gorillas, and big players. This system was invented by Ken Uston, a legend of the game of blackjack, who describes the strategy in a book called *The Big Player*. He made tens of millions of dollars using the strategy he invented. This system was so elaborate, that the MIT Blackjack Team did not even consider it card counting. They believed that anyone can learn how to count cards, but what they did was an art form.

The *spotter's* job was to find a blackjack table with a "hot" deck, that is, a deck with a high positive count. They would do this by playing the minimum bet at a table. The spotter would not use any sophisticated techniques to win money, they would just play like an average player would. When the count was high enough, they would signal to either the *gorilla* or the *big player* to join the table.

A gorilla player is a big better. He would put on a show, stumbling over to the table like a drunk rich kid, and throwing down big money. On the other hand, a big player would play intelligently, counting the cards, placing intelligent bets, and tracking the cards in the deck. Both the gorilla and the big player would leave the table when the spotter signaled to them that the deck had gone bad.

Gorilla players served as distractions – they did not really attract the attention of the casino personnel since they did not seem to be playing intelligently at all. They just seemed like a careless rich kid who liked to throw away money. But the big player would definitely draw the attention of the casino security, since they appeared to be playing intelligently, by varying their bet and frequently winning a large amount of money. The casino security is often referred to as the "eyes in the sky," since they watch the player's every move, and seem to have eyes everywhere. But perhaps even more threatening were the private detectives hired by casinos to detect card counters or other suspicious players. In Las Vegas, someone is always watching.

More Advanced Techniques

The techniques used by the MIT Blackjack Team did not stop at card counting and team play. Some of the best players used significantly more advanced techniques, that required precise knowledge of the placement of the cards in the deck.

Many of the techniques they used involved getting a glimpse of the bottom card in the deck. They would then cut the deck to a precise location so that they knew where the bottom card moved to in the deck. This required the bottom card in the deck to be exposed when the dealer picked up the cards, which was more likely if the team selected a dealer with small hands! (Now, a *cut card* is often used to prevent the bottom card of the deck, or shoe, from being exposed during play.) Whether or not they could get a glimpse of the bottom card was pure luck, but then it took significant skill to cut the deck to a precise location. It took months of practice, but they were able to know exactly where in the deck the bottom card moved to.

When the bottom card was an Ace, it gave the team a 51% advantage over the house for the hand with the Ace. This advantage was huge, and practically undetectable by casino security. To successfully pull off this technique, the players had to keep track of the number of cards that had been seen, and they had to play intelligently to make sure that the Ace was dealt to one of them. But when they did pull it off, the odds of winning skyrocketed.

Another technique increased their odds of winning even more, by giving them a 30% advantage over the casino on every single hand they played. This was done when it could be detected that a 10 card was at the bottom of the deck, and then playing strategically so that the 10 card was dealt to the dealer, significantly increasing the odds of the dealer busting. By doing this, they could gain an unheard of advantage against the casino, since the dealer busting caused them to win all of their hands. (Of course, they had to be the only players sitting at the table.) This technique was so hard to detect, that it was impossible for the casino personnel to figure out what they were doing.

They were not changing the outcome of the game; they were just using the information in front of them to their advantage.

There are many other strategies that have been devised to win at blackjack, including ones that use knowledge of the exact cards remaining in the deck. We will not discuss all of them here, but for more information see the references in Section 6.5.

6.3 Data Collection

While basic strategy and card counting are methods that were developed using probability theory and computer simulations, implementing the methods flawlessly was done by collecting vast amounts of data. Semyon Dukach, a former member of the MIT Blackjack Team, said that "after a trip to Vegas, we would enter all the information about what happened into the computers." The MIT players did not play an emotional game that relied on intuition; they knew exactly what to do in any situation because they had carefully analyzed vast amounts of data.

The MIT Blackjack Team was initially founded by Bill Kaplan, who was a student at Harvard Business School. While he was running the team, he would insist that the players carry around print-outs of spreadsheets to collect data. The players would then meet every six hours to give the data to Kaplan by calling an 800 number (the casinos all recognized Kaplan by 1984, and his presence would alert the casino security that his team was there, so Kaplan could not set foot in the casinos). Kaplan would then determine whether the teams should change their bets based on the data he received from the players.

The amount of data collected was huge. They recorded everything, from how much they varied their bets, to how much they won and lost each hour. Kaplan would check the data collected in the casinos against his computer-generated projections of how much he expected each player to win or lose. Not only did this data help him determine how they should play in the future, but it tipped him off if one of the players was not playing correctly or was stealing some of the team's winnings. This data was also provided to investors and players to better understand how the team was operating.

6.4 Blackjack Today

The MIT Blackjack Team influenced the game of blackjack at casinos, and the game of blackjack also influenced the MIT Blackjack Team players. As far as casinos are concerned, the security in casinos today is significantly more advanced than it was when the MIT Blackjack Team was at their prime. While card counting is a legal strategy to use while playing blackjack, casinos are private establishments, and are allowed to take measures to prevent card counters from playing successfully. Modern casino security is a multi-million dollar investment that consists of a physical security force and a special surveillance department, known as the "eye in the sky." This existed when the MIT Blackjack Team was playing in the 1990s, but the technology is getting increasingly complex. Casinos now use facial recognition programs built into the surveillance camera equipment to spot people on a nationwide list of suspected or known card counters. This technology can help assist the security personnel comb through the database of suspected counters faster. And as technology is improving, these programs are getting better at recognizing people, even in disguise.

Casino dealers can also take measures to distract suspected card counters, like re-shuffling the cards midway through the deck, or distracting the player with conversation. Devices that track the count on the dealers side have also been developed, which will alert the dealer when the odds are in the player's favor so that they can shuffle the cards. Many of these measures would not be so important if there were not so many card counters out there, including very successful card counters like the MIT Blackjack Team.

Blackjack also had a lasting impact on the players. Jeffrey Ma has written a book detailing how he has applied many of the lessons he learned playing blackjack to start a company in sports analytics. He says that one of the biggest takeaways from playing blackjack is being able to withstand variance, since "in blackjack and in business, it is necessary to maintain a long term perspective and to ride out the inevitable downward swings." He believes that many people have difficulty applying analytics to fields where human behavior can change the rules of the game, and that he was able to use his experience on the MIT Blackjack Team to start a successful sports analytics company.

Jeffrey Ma is not the only former member of the MIT Blackjack Team who became an entrepreneur; many of the students who played on the team found careers in entrepreneurship. Semyon Dukach, another player on the MIT Blackjack Team in the 1990s, is now the Managing Director of Techstars in Boston, a startup accelerator. Playing on the MIT Blackjack Team helped these students to value teamwork, gain confidence, evaluate and understand risk, and take a long-term view. These are critical skills in starting companies, and gaining these skills significantly influenced the lives of the MIT blackjack players. Card counting is a technique used to minimize risk and to optimize the use of available data to predict outcomes, making it a winning example of the analytics edge.

6.5 Notes and Sources

The information in this chapter about the MIT Blackjack Team and team play comes from books written by Ben Mezrich, Jeffrey Ma, and Ken Uston [86, 95, 96, 147].

6.1. The rules about blackjack come from the book "Beat the Dealer," by Edward O. Thorp [139].

6.2. The information about basic strategy and the Hi-Lo Method comes from [139]. The paper referenced about basic strategy is titled "The Optimum Strategy in Blackjack" and is written by Roger R. Baldwin, Wilbert E. Cantey, Herbert Maisel, and James P. McDermott [10]. For another classic reference about strategy in gambling, we direct you to "Scarne's New Complete Guide to Gambling" [121].

Part III

Healthcare

Chapter 7

The Framingham Heart Study

You can observe a lot just by watchin'.

– Yogi Berra

Contents

In 1948, Americans were ready for a time of luxury and indulgence after surviving the Great Depression and World War II. Refrigerators were full of whole milk, steaks, and cream. One million households owned televisions, compared to just 5,000 households in 1945. The first McDonald's was opened in San Bernardino, California, and almost half of all Americans smoked.

But amidst all this luxury and indulgence, heart disease had emerged as an epidemic. One in three deaths in the United States was caused by heart disease, more than four times the rate in 1900. Physicians were puzzled as to what was causing heart attacks and strokes, but even worse, there was nothing to be done if heart disease was discovered. High blood pressure and heart disease were being accepted as inevitable consequences of aging.

This chapter is about the Framingham Heart Study, and how all of this changed with the help of analytics. The Framingham Heart Study started in 1948, with the goal of observing a large population of healthy adults over time to better understand the factors that led to heart disease. It was a study that revolved around data. Over 80 variables were collected about 5,209 people at a time when computers did not exist and everything had to be recorded on paper. This data has now been used in more than 2,400 studies, and the *Texas Heart Institute Journal* declared the Framingham Heart Study one of the top 10 cardiology advances of the twentieth century, alongside the electrocardiogram and open-heart surgery.

7.1 Early Misconceptions

In 1948, physicians were trained to believe that high blood pressure was a natural part of aging. Blood pressure measures the amount of pressure exerted by circulating blood on the walls of the arteries, and is measured in two numbers, like 120/80. The first number is systolic blood pressure, which measures the pressure when the heart beats, pushing blood through the arteries. The second number is diastolic blood pressure, which measures the pressure between beats, when the heart is at rest. In 1948, physicians believed that a systolic blood pressure of 100 plus one's age was healthy. Today, a systolic blood pressure of 140 is considered high, and medication is prescribed to lower blood pressure and thereby reduce the stress on artery walls.

In 1945, three years before the Framingham Heart Study started, President Franklin Delano Roosevelt, the 32nd President of the United States, died from heart disease at age 63. This stunned the American people, and surprised the President's closest friends and family. Little did they know that while President Roosevelt was leading the country through the Great Depression and World War II, his blood pressure was steadily increasing to alarming levels. In 1931, his blood pressure was already 140/100. Today, a healthy blood pressure is less than 120/80, so by today's standards this is already considered high blood pressure. One year before President Roosevelt's death, his blood pressure was 210/120, which is today called hypertensive crisis, and emergency care is needed. At the time, the President's personal physician said that this was "a moderate degree of arteriosclerosis, although no more than normal for a man of his age." Two months before his death, his blood pressure was 260/150, and the day he died his blood pressure was 300/190. These numbers are very rarely even seen today, and if they are, it is considered a crisis and treatment is immediately given.

The President's personal doctor hid Roosevelt's deteriorating health from his family and the public. It's unclear if this deception was medical ignorance or a deliberate cover-up, but even if the President was properly diagnosed, there was no treatment at the time to give. The death of the President of the United States due to heart disease served as a wake-up call, bringing together physicians and politicians behind a massive research effort to understand the causes of heart disease.

7.2 The Beginning of the Study

When the Framingham Heart Study began in 1948, it was unlike anything that had ever been conducted before. The plan was to track a large cohort of initially healthy patients over time, and the city of Framingham, Massachusetts was selected. This particular town was selected for several reasons: it was of an appropriate size; the population was very stable, and they expected the participants to be around to observe for many years; the doctors and residents of the town were willing to participate; and the town was close to Boston, a city that had several prestigious medical schools and research institutions.

In total, 5,209 men and women between the ages of 30 and 59 volunteered to participate in the study. The inclusion of women is surprising for a study that began in 1948, and therefore many people believe that the study was ahead of its time in recruiting men and women. However, the reason for including women in the study was because medical science believed at the time that women were immune to heart disease, and they wanted to discover what was protecting women. Researchers later discovered that women were not immune to heart disease, they just acquired it at a lower rate than men (one in three women will develop heart disease in their lifetime, compared to one in two men). In addition to discovering if men were truly more susceptible than women, the leaders of the heart study hoped to discover if family history played a role in heart disease, and if smoking, drinking, obesity, inadequate sleep, high blood pressure, or high cholesterol had anything to do with the development of heart disease.

The Data

The 5,209 volunteers were given a questionnaire and an exam every 2 years, starting in 1948. In the beginning, the physicians collected data on 80 different variables, all recorded on paper. The variables collected included: family and personal history of disease; present conditions, complaints, and drugs taken; height, weight, temperature, respiratory rate, and mental state; an x-ray of the heart; electrical activity traced on an electrocardiogram; samples of urine and blood; examination of the pupils, retinas, thyroid, and liver; and body type measurements (like body-mass index, or BMI). The exams and questions expanded over time to include additional risk factors, such as physical activity and genomic information.

The Framingham Heart Study is now in its seventh decade of collecting and analyzing this data. In 1971, the Framingham Offspring Study was started, which follows 5,124 sons and daughters of the original Framingham Heart Study volunteers. In 2002, the Third Generation Study was started, which follows 3,500 grandchildren of the original Framingham Heart Study volunteers.

First Findings

The first paper of key findings of the Framingham Heart Study, "Coronary Heart Disease in the Framingham Study," was published in 1957, almost ten years after the study began [41]. The paper published results that were surprising at the time, including the unexpected rate of heart disease in women, and evidence that both high blood pressure and high cholesterol are risk factors for heart disease. In 1961, the researchers leading the Framingham Heart Study published a groundbreaking paper showing that by detecting and treating certain *risk factors*, like high blood pressure and high cholesterol, heart disease could be prevented [74].

7.3 The Framingham Risk Score

Dealing with the large amount of data collected in the Framingham Heart Study was a huge hurdle for statisticians working on the project. They responded by developing *multivariate analysis*, a method that is at the core of virtually every epidemiology study done today. Multivariate, or multiple variable, models are used to capture the effects of multiple risk factors on a single outcome. In this particular application, the researchers were trying to understand how risk factors such as age, blood pressure, cholesterol, smoking, and diabetes affect a person's risk of developing heart disease.

In 1998, a landmark paper describing the Framingham Risk Score was published [152]. The Framingham Risk Score is computed using a simple prediction algorithm involving a few key risk factor categories that allows physicians to predict coronary heart disease risk in patients. It has been adjusted several times since the original publication, and in 2004 a paper was published that developed a "points system" to make the models more useful to practitioners [135]. Today, individuals can go online and predict their 10-year risk of having a heart attack (http://cvdrisk.nhlbi.nih.gov/) using a simple online form.

In this section, we describe a multiple logistic regression model to predict an individual's ten year risk of developing coronary heart disease (CHD) that we developed using the Teaching Dataset provided by the National Heart, Lung, and Blood Institute. This dataset is an anonymized version of a large subset of the original Framingham Heart Study data. This data can be downloaded from the online companion for this book and can be used to build the models described in this chapter (www.dynamic-ideas.com/analytics-edge).

After building and evaluating the model, we will describe how the model translates into a points system. The Framingham Risk Score is calculated using a related method, called *Cox proportional hazards*, but we focus here on a logistic regression model because it is simpler and is commonly used in the medical literature. To learn more about logistic regression, see Chapter 21.

The Data, Variables, and Model

The data used to develop this model is an anonymized sample of 4,240 participants from the original Framingham Heart Study. The dataset includes exam results and questionnaire data from the examination in 1956, and whether or not each participant developed heart disease in the ten year period from 1956 to 1966. The participants were between the ages of 32 and 70 and free of heart disease at the start of the time period.

When building the Framingham Risk Score models, researchers only used a limited number of the available risk factors, due to correlations between the risk factors and because some variables (like obesity, family history, or physical activity) can be difficult to quantify. They also wanted to make sure that all of the risk factors used were readily available in clinical practice. Likewise, we use a few simple risk factors in the model built in this chapter: age, male (1 if the participant is male, 0 otherwise), systolic blood pressure, diabetes diagnosis (1 if the participant has diabetes, 0 otherwise), and current smoking status (1 if the participant smokes, 0 otherwise). We will denote these variables by Age, Male, SystolicBP, Diabetes, and Smoker.

Our ultimate goal is to predict an individual's 10-year risk of developing coronary heart disease (CHD), which is indicated by a heart attack or coronary death. A total of 644 participants developed CHD in the 10-year period (15% of all participants in our dataset).

To build the model, we first randomly split the data into two pieces: 70% of the data to train the model (the training set), and 30% of the data to test the model out-of-sample (the testing set). This is important to evaluate how the model performs on new patients. All patients in the test set will not be used to construct the model, so when we make predictions on these patients, we are able to estimate how good the model will do at predicting the 10-year risk of new patients.

Using the training set, the following logistic regression model was developed to predict the probability of a participant developing CHD:

$$\text{Logit(CHD)} = -7.7013 + 0.0524 \times (\text{Age}) + 0.6555 \times (\text{Male})$$

$$+ 0.0205 \times (\text{SystolicBP}) + 0.6723 \times (\text{Diabetes})$$
$$+ 0.2991 \times (\text{Smoker})$$

All of the five independent variables are significant in the model. This equation describes the "logit" of the logistic regression model, and can be translated to a probability of developing CHD with the following equation:

$$\text{Probability of CHD} = \frac{1}{1 + \exp(\text{-Logit(CHD)})}$$

For example, suppose that we have a patient who is 65 years old, male, has a systolic blood pressure of 145, has diabetes, and is not a smoker. We can use these equations as follows:

$$\begin{aligned}\text{Logit(CHD)} = & -7.7013 + (0.0524 \times 65) + (0.6555 \times 1) \\ & + (0.0205 \times 145) + (0.6723 \times 1) + (0.2991 \times 0) = 0.005,\end{aligned}$$

$$\text{Probability of CHD} = \frac{1}{1 + \exp(-0.005)} = 0.501.$$

So, according to our model, this patient has a 50.1% chance of developing CHD in the next 10 years. As another example, suppose we have a patient who is 40 years old, female, has a systolic blood pressure of 155, does not have diabetes, and is a smoker. Then we can calculate for her that Logit(CHD) = -2.1287, and her probability of developing CHD in the next 10 years is 0.106. The treatment guidelines indicate that a 10-year risk above 20% should be handled with aggressive treatment, while a 10-year risk between 10% and 20% indicates that more moderate treatment is needed.

How good is this model? The Receiver Operator Characteristic (ROC) curve for the model is shown in Figure 7.1. An ROC curve gives the false positive rate (the percentage of patients that *did not* develop CHD that the model predicted *incorrectly*) and the true positive rate (the percentage of patients that *did* develop CHD that the model predicted *correctly*) for varying threshold values on the predicted probabilities. If we select a higher threshold, we can achieve a lower false positive rate, but we also have a lower true positive rate. For this data, we can select a threshold value that gives us a true positive rate of about 60%, while only having a false positive rate of about 25%. This means that we will make correct predictions for 60% of the patients that do end up developing CHD, while incorrectly flagging 25% of the patients who do not actually end up developing CHD. If we want a higher true positive rate, we can select a lower threshold value. The ROC curve tells us that we can select a threshold value that will yield a true positive rate of about 85%, with a false positive rate of about 60%. In this case, we would make correct predictions for

85% of the patients that end up developing CHD, but we also incorrectly flag 60% of the patients who do not end up developing CHD.

The area under the curve (AUC) of the model is 0.72. The AUC captures the model's ability to distinguish between the two outcomes. So while the model does make mistakes, the AUC tells us that the model can correctly distinguish between a randomly selected patient who will develop heart disease in 10 years and one who will not develop heart disease in ten years 72% of the time. For clinical prediction models, which are often very challenging to develop, this is a promising result. For more about ROC curves and AUC, see Chapter 21.

In this particular situation, there is an important tradeoff between false positives and false negatives. Remember that a false positive prediction means that for a person who actually *did not* develop CHD in the next ten years, the model predicted that they *would*. This prediction might unnecessarily alarm the patient, and unnecessary treatment might be applied. However, the patient remains healthy. A false negative prediction means that, for a person who actually *did* develop CHD in the next ten years, the model predicted that they

Figure 7.1: The Receiver Operator Characteristic (ROC) Curve for the model on the training set.

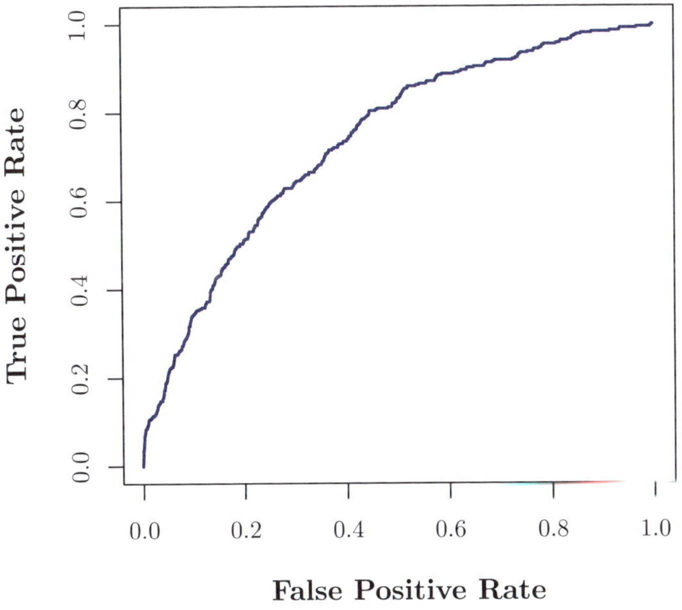

Table 7.1: Classification matrix for the logistic regression model on the training set. A threshold of 0.25 is used. The columns are labeled with the predicted outcome, and the rows are labeled with the actual outcome.

	Predicted No CHD	Predicted CHD
Actual No CHD	2,204	313
Actual CHD	289	162

would not. This prediction could result in no preventative action being taken with the patient, and so the model did not help this patient improve their health. For this reason, false negatives are often seen as more costly long-term than false positives in this application. While the immediate cost of a false positive might be higher due to the unnecessary treatment, the long-term cost of a false negative prediction can be drastic due to the expense of treating CHD (not to mention the emotional cost to the patient). Therefore, we are more inclined to select a lower threshold.

Table 7.1 shows the classification matrix on the training set with a threshold of 0.25. We predict that 475 participants will develop heart disease in the next 10 years - these patients would receive preventative treatment according to our model. If clinicians had used this model in 1948, they would have unnecessarily treated 313 people who did not develop CHD (or 12.4% of the "no CHD" patients), but they would have correctly treated 162 people who did develop CHD (or 35.9% of the "CHD" patients). If we want to decrease our false negative rate even further, we could lower the threshold more.

On the test set, again using a threshold of 0.25, we correctly predict CHD for 68 out of the 193 patients who develop CHD, and we incorrectly predict CHD for 130 out of the 1,079 patients who did not develop CHD. Our AUC on the test set is also 0.72. Overall, this model can give physicians an edge in deciding which patients to prioritize for treatment. Using even more advanced methods and more detailed data, the model can be improved further.

A Points System

The equations developed here make predictions possible. However, a points system was developed to make the calculation even easier for physicians and patients. To implement the points system, each of the risk factors is first organized into meaningful categories and assigned a reference value, which is just the mid-point of values in that category. These numbers are given in Table 7.2.

The categories for age and blood pressure are meaningful because they are designed to mirror clinically meaningful states. In particular, the blood pressure categories are defined by using the Joint National Committee's blood pressure

Table 7.2: Variable categories and reference values.

Variable	Category	Reference Value
Age	30-39	34.5
	40-49	44.5
	50-59	54.5
	60-69	64.5
	70-79	74.5
Sex	Female	0
	Male	1
Systolic Blood Pressure	< 120	107
	120-129	125
	130-139	135
	140-159	150
	≥ 160	175
Diabetes	No	0
	Yes	1
Current Smoker	No	0
	Yes	1

categories. Note that the age categories only include values that were in the original data. More validation would be necessary if we wanted to extrapolate the model beyond the values seen in the training set.

The next step to develop the points system is to make a "base" computation, by adding up all of the reference values that represent low risk, according to the risk prediction model. If we look at the logistic regression equation, we can see that the lowest risk is for a person in the age category 30-39, who is female, has a systolic blood pressure of less than 120, does not have diabetes, and is not a current smoker. We will actually use the blood pressure category 120-129 for the base model, and give "bonus points" to people who have an even lower blood pressure.

Table 7.3 adds two new columns to Table 7.2: the difference in reference value from the base value for each variable (Base Diff), and the Base Diff column multiplied by the corresponding logistic regression coefficient for that variable (Logit Units).

The next step is to scale and round the "Logit Units" column to produce an integer number of points. We will use a five year increase in age as the scaling factor, or $5 \times 0.0524 = 0.262$, so each number in the Logit Units column of Table 7.3 is divided by 0.262, and rounded to the nearest integer (recall that

0.0524 is the coefficient for the variable "Age" in our logistic regression model). This produces the points values given in Table 7.4.

Now given these point values, each value can be assigned a risk estimate. The point value represents the value of the Logit (relative to the baseline) divided by 0.262. So we can compute an estimate of the Logit for a given points value P by using the Logit equation for a "baseline" person, and adding $0.262 \times P$:

$$\begin{aligned}\text{Logit(CHD)} \approx & -7.7013 + (0.0524 \times 34.5) + (0.6555 \times 0) \\ & + (0.0205 \times 125) + (0.6723 \times 0) + (0.2991 \times 0) \\ & + (0.262 \times P) \\ & = -3.331 + (0.262 \times P)\end{aligned}$$

So for each possible point value (a person can have a minimum point value of -1 and a maximum of 18) we can compute the probability of developing CHD, or the risk estimate, by using the following equation:

Table 7.3: Variable categories and reference values, with the difference from the base category and the logistic regression model units.

Variable	Category	Reference	Base Diff	Logit Units
Age	30-39	34.5	0	0
	40-49	44.5	10	0.5240
	50-59	54.5	20	1.0480
	60-69	64.5	30	1.5720
	70-79	74.5	40	2.0960
Sex	Female	0	0	0
	Male	1	1	0.6555
Systolic BP	< 120	107	-18	-0.3690
	120-129	125	0	0
	130-139	135	10	0.2050
	140-159	150	25	0.5125
	≥ 160	175	35	0.7175
Diabetes	No	0	0	0
	Yes	1	1	0.6723
Current Smoker	No	0	0	0
	Yes	1	1	0.2991

$$\text{Probability of CHD} \approx \frac{1}{1 + \exp(3.331 - 0.262 \times P)}$$

These values are given in Table 7.5.

While slightly complicated to develop, this points system significantly simplifies the process for a patient or physician to compute a risk of CHD. They only need to use Table 7.4 to compute the number of points for an individual patient given the variable categories, and Table 7.5 to match that point value with a risk estimate. The risk estimates in the table are just estimates, but they correspond well with the estimates made by the exact equation.

Alternatively, individuals can go online and predict their 10-year risk of having a heart attack (http://cvdrisk.nhlbi.nih.gov/) using a simple online form. The individual inputs their personal data, and then the form gives a prediction of CHD. This website might be just as simple to use as the points system, but the points system adds an extra level of transparency to the model that can be insightful since patients can easily see what they can do to reduce their risk in terms of blood pressure and smoking. For example, suppose a 65 year old male has a systolic blood pressure of 145, does not have diabetes, and is a current smoker. He would have a points total of 12, and a risk estimate

Table 7.4: Variable categories and points values.

Variable	Category	Points
Age	30-39	0
	40-49	2
	50-59	4
	60-69	6
	70-79	8
Sex	Female	0
	Male	3
Systolic Blood Pressure	< 120	-1
	120-129	0
	130-139	1
	140-159	2
	≥ 160	3
Diabetes	No	0
	Yes	3
Current Smoker	No	0
	Yes	1

of 0.4534. But if he was able to reduce his systolic blood pressure from 145 to 128, he could reduce his points total to 10, and reduce his risk to 0.3294. If he also quit smoking, his risk would further decrease to 0.2743. The points system allows the patient to understand how much each action reduces his risk.

The points system is an example of how analytics models can be simplified to become more useful to people who do not necessarily understand the mathematics behind the model. Providing patients and physicians with logistic regression equations would not be feasible, but two tables of results are much easier to understand and use.

Validating the Model on Other Populations

The Framingham Risk Score was shown to be predictive for the Framingham Heart Study population. However, there were concerns about whether or not the results could be extended to other populations. The Framingham Heart Study population was mostly white and middle-class. In 1999, researchers set out to better test the validity of the Framingham Risk Score in ethnically and racially diverse populations. Studies were performed on Native Americans

Table 7.5: Point values and risk estimates.

Points	Risk Estimate
-1	0.0268
0	0.0345
1	0.0444
2	0.0569
3	0.0728
4	0.0925
5	0.1170
6	0.1469
7	0.1829
8	0.2253
9	0.2743
10	0.3294
11	0.3896
12	0.4534
13	0.5187
14	0.5835
15	0.6454
16	0.7029
17	0.7545
18	0.7998

(The Strong Heart Study), Japanese American men (The Honolulu Heart Program), whites and blacks (The Atherosclerosis Risk in Communities Study), and Hispanic men (The Puerto Rico Heart Health Program).

In each study, the Framingham Risk Score was used to predict CHD risk, and the predictions were compared to actual outcomes. The model performed well in whites and blacks. Black participants had a higher diabetes rate, but the predictions handled it very well. Only minor recalibration was needed for other groups. For example, Japanese men had a much lower CHD rate, so the predictions needed to be scaled down to be accurate for this population. These studies provided strong evidence that the Framingham Risk Score could be used in other settings.

7.4 Other Impacts of the Study

In addition to the Framingham Risk Score, the Framingham Heart Study had a very significant impact in other ways. More than 2,400 studies have used the Framingham Heart Study data, and the number of publications is increasing substantially (see Figure 7.2). In particular, the study was key to the development of drugs to lower blood pressure and hypertension, and it also paved the way for clinical decision rules in other areas of medicine.

Development of Medication

In 1948, drugs to lower blood pressure were too toxic for practical use. The side effects of the drugs were severe – one caused projectile vomiting, another blocked the whole autonomic nervous system, and a third turned the patient blue. But in the 1950s, the drug chlorothiazide was developed. Chlorothiazide belongs to a class of drugs called diuretics, drugs that are still used today to treat high blood pressure. The Framingham Heart Study gave Ed Freis, a leading researcher at the time on the treatment of hypertension, the evidence he needed to argue for testing the effects of blood pressure drugs in clinical trials. Since most physicians believed that hypertension was benign, he needed the justification provided by the Framingham Heart Study to pursue a clinical trial testing whether or not lowering blood pressure would reduce a patient's risk for cardiovascular disease. He started the Veterans Administration Trial, which ultimately established that lowering blood pressure can be used to decrease risk of heart disease. Now, there is a billion dollar market for diuretics worldwide, and there are dozens of drugs available to treat blood pressure.

In addition to drugs for lowering blood pressure, the Framingham Heart Study was instrumental in the development of drugs to lower cholesterol. The study published evidence that high cholesterol was a risk factor for heart disease in the early 1960s, but it was not until the 1970s that the first cholesterol lowering drug was developed. This drug was the first statin, a class of drugs for which there is now a $20 billion market. Patients now have a choice between more than a dozen cholesterol-lowering drugs.

Figure 7.2: Number of studies using the Framingham Heart Study data published each year, from 1960 - 2012.

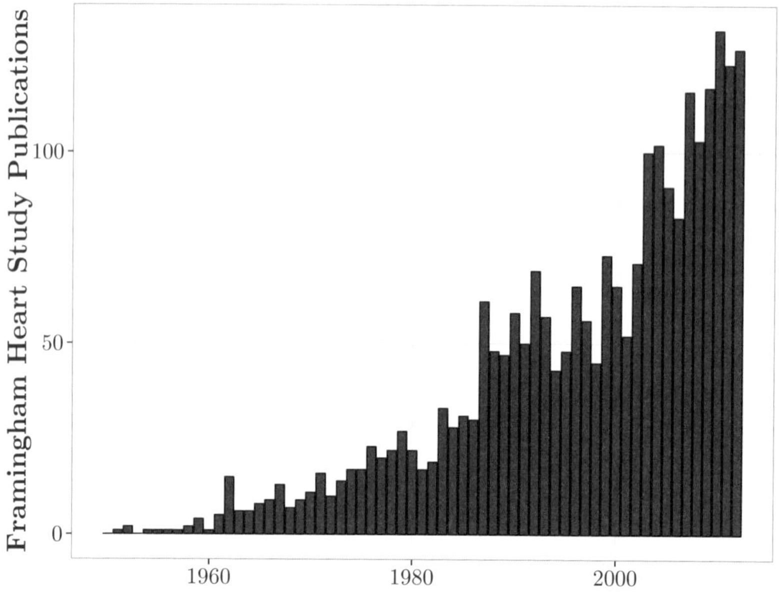

Clinical Decision Rules

The Framingham Heart Study also paved the way for clinical decision rules in many different areas of medicine. Clinical decision rules are models that predict clinical outcomes using data such as patient characteristics and test results. More than 75,000 papers have been published across medicine regarding clinical decision rules, and the rate is still increasing. Figure 7.3 shows the number of clinical decision rules that have been published by year, since 1960. Today, over 7,000 clinical decision rules are published every year.

Some popular clinical decision rules predict the likelihood of strep, predict whether or not a patient with joint pain will develop Rheumatoid Arthritis in one year, and whether or not a knee injury requires the use of an x-ray to assess a fracture. These models are able to incorporate many different risk factors, and are unbiased and unemotional. One of the key arguments for the use of clinical prediction rules is that they can assist new physicians with little experience to draw from when making decisions.

While thousands of clinical prediction rules exist, they are not used as much in practice as they could be. One reason is the fact that most of these prediction rules are not presented in a user-friendly way. With approaches like the points system presented here, researchers hope to increase the use of clinical prediction rules.

7.5 A Different World

Since its peak in 1963, the death rate from coronary heart disease has fallen 60% and the death rate from stroke has fallen 66%. While heart disease is still the leading cause of death in the United States, we have made tremendous progress in understanding and treating this disease. The Framingham Heart Study and the studies that have followed from it have led to a better understanding of the risk factors involved in heart disease, and the hope is that more discoveries will occur in the coming years.

Sandra Merloni, one of the original volunteers for the heart study said that "it's amazing what the whole country has learned from this study. It's not just benefiting Framingham or Massachusetts. It's benefiting the whole world, really." With the continuation of the Framingham Heart Study and the analytical decision rules that it has inspired, the data collected has greatly influenced the way heart disease is treated today.

Figure 7.3: Number of clinical decision rules published each year, from 1960 - 2012.

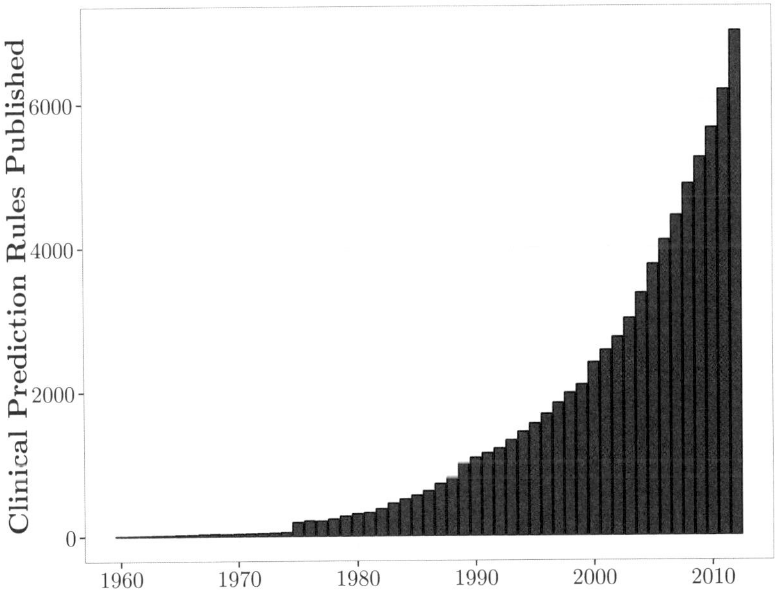

7.6 Notes and Sources

Information about the history of the Framingham Heart Study in this chapter comes from the book *A Change of Heart: Unraveling the Mysteries of Cardiovascular Disease* by Levy and Brink [81].

7.3. The Framingham Risk Score information comes from the papers Sullivan et al. [135] and Wilson et al. [152].

Chapter 8

Predicting Healthcare Costs

The only relevant test of the validity of a hypothesis is comparison of its predictions with experience.

– Milton Friedman

Contents

In late 2008, in the middle of one of the most severe financial crises in United States history, Chris Kryder, the founder and CEO of D2Hawkeye, received a very significant offer to sell the company. The offer was from Verisk Analytics, a $6 billion public company. Chris, a former MIT physician, had grown D2Hawkeye from a six-person start-up into a leading developer and provider of medical analytics in the United States. In 2008, D2Hawkeye was processing data from approximately 20 million individuals every month, about 7% of the United States population. Using analytics, D2Hawkeye summarized financial information, estimated future health care costs and predicted the quality of care received for individual patients.

The vision of the company was that by intervening in the care of individual patients when predicted costs are high and estimated quality of care is low, both future costs can decrease and medical outcomes for patients can improve significantly. With millions of lives being monitored every month, manual detection of the individuals who will benefit from medical intervention is simply infeasible, and an analytics approach capable of quickly processing tens of millions of claims per month is essential.

This chapter describes the advantages that analytics can create for health care as well as opportunities for discovering new medical knowledge through analytics. Since the 1850s, medical knowledge has been developed primarily using clinical trials involving tens or hundreds of patients. The availability of digital data involving millions of individuals provides an opportunity to systematically discover new medical knowledge using analytics, an idea we explore in Section 8.4.

8.1 Dealing with Claims Data

In this chapter, we illustrate the process of using analytics to develop accurate predictions of health care costs with data from D2Hawkeye. Every month, D2Hawkeye received claims data from several thousand employers involving tens of millions of individuals. Claims data is generated when hospitals and other health care providers send claims to third party payers to receive reimbursement for their services. The data came in different formats, often with missing items, and sometimes with errors. An important challenge was to clean the data and to put it in a unified format. While this seems a simple task, the size and diversity of the data made it challenging. D2Hawkeye was the largest employer in Katmandu, Nepal, employing a team of over 500 engineers to accomplish this task.

We discuss an analytics approach that uses a training set, builds prediction models on the training set and reports results on a test set. The data consisted of claims from 8/1/2004 – 7/31/2007, split up into a 24 month long observation period (training set) from 8/1/2004 – 7/31/2006 and a 12 month results period (test set) from 8/1/2006 – 7/31/2007. Models were built using information from the observation period to predict outcomes in the results period. The data set included medical claims data for 838,242 individuals, from 2,866 different employers and employer groups across the United States. The data set includes both medical and pharmaceutical claims, as well as information on the period an individual (and his or her family) was covered by the insurance policy. The data also contains basic demographic information such as age and gender. All patients have eligibility starting no later than 8/1/2005 and ending no sooner than 8/1/2006, and all employers had continuous coverage starting no later than 8/1/2005 and ending no sooner than 8/1/2007. This ensures that every employee (and his or her family) had at least 12 months of data in the observation period and that big populations do not drop out during the results period due to a change in an employer's insurance carrier.

The observation data set is split, by random assignment, into equally sized parts: a training sample and a validation sample. The training sample is used to build prediction models, while the validation sample is used to evaluate the performance of the various models. The results period was set aside while building and calibrating the models, and only used at the very end of the experiment to report results of the finalized models.

Aggregation of the Claims Data

Claims data included diagnosis, procedure and drug information. The diagnosis data was coded using the ICD-9-CM (International Classification of Diseases, Ninth Revision, Clinical Modification) codes, the universal codes for medical diagnoses and procedures at the time. The procedures were coded under various coding schemes generating over 22,000 codes. Furthermore, the data included pharmacy claims, giving information about which, if any, prescription drugs a patient was taking, coded in terms of 45,972 drug codes.

Claims data relies on health care professionals to encode their diagnoses and procedures in terms of the standard codes. Although coding for medical claims starts with a clinician, it is most often completed and submitted by a separate dedicated billing operator. Because of the inevitable variations in interpretations introduced by these practices, and to reduce the data to a more manageable size, individual codes were aggregated into coding groups and included in the model. Over 13,000 individual diagnoses were reduced to 218 diagnosis groups, over 22,000 individual procedures were classified into 180 procedure groups, and over 45,000 individual prescription drugs were classified into 336 therapeutic groups. Also included in the analysis were over 700 medically developed quality and risk measures which designate hazardous clinical situations (for example, patients with a pattern of emergency room care without office visits, or diabetics with foot ulcers). The number of diagnoses, procedures, drugs, and risk factors that each patient had were also used as variables for the models. In summary, the medical variables used included the diagnosis groups, the procedure groups, the drug groups, the medical risk factors, and the overall counts, for a total of about 1,500 possible medical variables.

Cost and Demographic Data

In addition to the medical variables, 22 cost variables, age and gender were used. In order to capture the trajectory of medical costs (as a proxy of the overall medical condition of an individual), D2Hawkeye used monthly costs for the last twelve months of the observation period, the total drug cost, the total medical cost over the entire observation period, and the overall cost in the last six months and the last three months of the observation period. Furthermore, in order to capture the pattern of costs, a new indicator variable was developed, one that captures whether or not a patient's cost pattern exhibits a "spike" pattern, i.e., a sudden increase followed by a sudden decrease in cost. To demonstrate this idea, Figure 8.1 depicts the monthly cost of two patients in the last twelve months of the observation period. While both patients have around $98,000 in paid claims, patient A has relatively high, but constant, medical costs (a typical pattern for a patient with a chronic condition), while patient B has a spike in her cost profile (a typical pattern for a patient with an "acute" condition). The key idea here is that while constant high medical costs have a strong tendency to repeat in the future, a cost pattern that exhibits a spike might have a low risk of high future health care costs, for example in the case of pregnancy complications, accidents, or acute medical conditions like pneumonia or appendicitis.

Table 8.1 summarizes all the variables used when building predictive models. In total, over 1,500 variables were defined to help D2Hawkeye predict future medical cost.

Table 8.1: Summary of the variables used.

Variable	Description
1 - 218	Diagnosis Groups
219 - 398	Procedure Groups
399 - 734	Drug Groups
735 - 1485	Medically defined risk factors
1486 - 1489	Count of diagnoses, procedures, drugs and risk factors
1490 - 1521	Cost variables, including overall medical and pharmacy costs
1522 - 1523	Gender and age

Figure 8.1: Twelve months of health care costs for two patients, with an overall cost of $97,500 for patient A and $98,100 for patient B. The cost profile for patient A has the characteristics of a chronic illness, while the characteristics of patient B's profile is "acute." The diagnoses behind the most expensive claims of patient A are lymphedema and respiratory failure. The reasons behind the highest claims of patient B reflect childbirth complications.

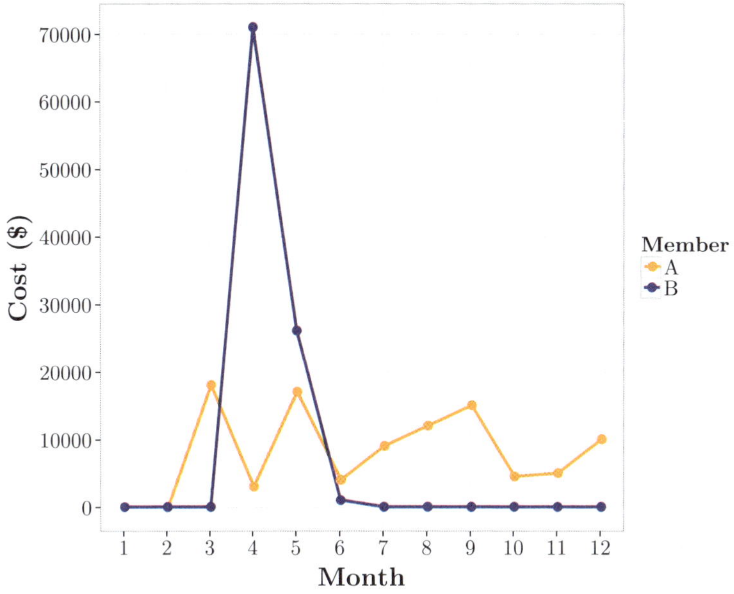

Cost Bucketing

In many healthcare contexts, the range of costs and medical needs from patient to patient is significant. In this dataset, some patients had $0 in annual healthcare expenses, while others had $710,000 in annual healthcare expenses. Moreover, 80% of the overall cost of the population originates from only 20% of the patients. Figure 8.2 shows the cost characteristics of the population in the training set. We note that for our sample, around 8% of the population contributes 70% of the total health care costs.

In order to reduce noise in the data and at the same time reduce the effects of extremely expensive patients (who can be considered outliers), the patients' costs are partitioned into five different cost buckets in such a way that the sum of all patients' costs in each bucket are approximately equal (approximately $117 million per cost bucket). Table 8.2 shows the range of each bucket and the percentage of patients that are in each bucket. Naturally, cost bucket 1 has significantly more patients, since their costs are very low. This division into

Figure 8.2: Cumulative health care costs in the training set.

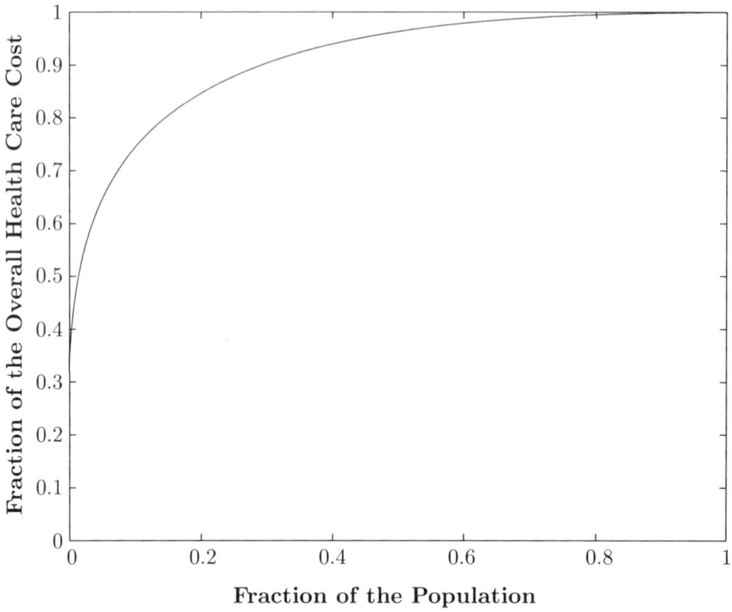

Table 8.2: Cost bucket information.

Bucket	Cost Range	Percentage of Patients
1	< \$3,000	83.9%
2	\$3,000-\$8,000	9.7%
3	\$8,000-\$18,000	4.2%
4	\$18,000-\$50,000	1.7%
5	> \$50,000	0.5%

cost buckets balanced the total cost in each bucket.

D2Hawkeye was interested in predicting the cost bucket a patient will be in the following year. This knowledge is valuable to health care management professionals for case management. Buckets 1 through 5 can be interpreted as representing low, emerging, moderate, high and very high risk of medical complications. Patients predicted to be in Buckets 2 and 3 are candidates for wellness programs, patients predicted to be in Bucket 4 are candidates for disease management programs, and patients forecasted to be in the most expensive bucket are candidates for case management programs, the most intense type of patient care program.

8.2 Methods to Predict Costs

D2Hawkeye used two different methods to predict healthcare costs: classification trees and clustering. In this section, we will first discuss how the methods were evaluated, both in terms of metrics used and a baseline method to compare against. Then we will discuss the analytics that were used to build the predictive models.

Performance Measures

The performance of the models was measured with three different metrics: the overall accuracy, the penalty error and the absolute prediction error (APE).

The Overall Accuracy
The overall accuracy is the percentage of patients for whom we forecast the correct cost bucket.

The Penalty Error
The penalty error is motivated by opportunities for medical intervention and is therefore asymmetric. There is greater penalty for underestimating higher costs, consistent with the greater medical and financial risk in missing these individuals. The penalty of misidentifying an individual as high risk, when their actual costs are low, is smaller, as little harm or cost ensues in this instance. Therefore, the penalties for underestimating a cost bucket are set as twice those for overestimating it. Table 8.3 shows the penalty table for the five cost buckets. The numbers are shaded according to how high the penalty is for that particular type of error. We define the penalty error measure to be the average forecast penalty per patient of a given sample.

Table 8.3: The penalty error measure for the five cost buckets.

		Forecast				
		1	2	3	4	5
Outcome	1	0	1	2	3	4
	2	2	0	1	2	3
	3	4	2	0	1	2
	4	6	4	2	0	1
	5	8	6	4	2	0

The Absolute Prediction Error
We define the absolute prediction error to be the average absolute difference between the forecasted and the realized annual dollar amounts. As an example, if we forecast a patient's health care cost to be \$500 in the results period, but in reality the patient has an overall health care cost of \$2,000, then the absolute prediction error for the patient is $|\$500 - \$2,000| = \$1,500$. We define the absolute prediction error (APE) for an entire sample to be the average absolute prediction error over the given sample. An advantage of APE is that it does not square the prediction errors like some standard metrics, which makes it less sensitive to outliers (patients with extreme health care cost). This is of special concern due to the nature of health care cost data, as there are a few individual patients with very unpredictably high costs.

The Baseline Method

In order to make meaningful comparisons, we define a baseline method against which we can compare the results of the prediction models. As our baseline method, we use the health care cost of the last twelve months of the observation period for an individual as the forecast of the overall health care cost in the results period for that individual. Since current health care cost is a strong indicator of a person's health, this baseline is a strong method, and mirrors the industry standard. Table 8.4 shows how the population transitions from a bucket in the observation period to a bucket in the results period. As an example, over 75% of the population are in Bucket 1 in both periods. The sum of the diagonal elements gives the total overall accuracy of this method.

We further note that for patients that fell into Buckets 1 through 4 in the observation period, the most common bucket in the results period is Bucket 1. On the other hand, for patients who fell into Bucket 5 in the observation period, the most common results period bucket is Bucket 5. A possible interpretation is that most patients who are experiencing moderate cost usually get better, while those in the most expensive bucket have a greater tendency to incur high medical costs in the future.

Table 8.5 summarizes the baseline performance for all error measures. The baseline prediction model has an overall accuracy of 80.0%, the average penalty error is 0.43 and the absolute prediction error is \$2,677. In order to get a deeper understanding of the baseline method, we examine the effectiveness of the baseline method with respect to each of the buckets in the observation period. From Table 8.5 we observe, for example, that for Bucket 1 patients the accuracy is 90.1%, the penalty error is 0.29 and the absolute prediction error is \$1,279. Note that the performance measures worsen with each increasing cost bucket, which alludes to the fact that the higher cost buckets are harder to predict.

Table 8.4: The cost bucket distribution from the observation period to the results period.

Cost Bucket in Results Period	Cost Bucket in Observation Period 1	2	3	4	5
1	75.63%	5.03%	1.81%	0.51%	0.10%
2	5.54%	2.98%	1.01%	0.38%	0.08%
3	1.88%	1.19%	0.91%	0.34%	0.08%
4	0.66%	0.39%	0.39%	0.38%	0.10%
5	0.20%	0.11%	0.08%	0.11%	0.13%

Table 8.5: Performance measures of the baseline method.

Bucket	Accuracy (%)	Penalty Error	APE ($)
all	80.0	0.43	2,677
1	90.1	0.29	1,279
2	52.3	0.99	4,850
3	41.7	1.36	9,549
4	30.5	1.67	21,759
5	19.3	1.83	75,808

Classification Trees

The first analytics method used by D2Hawkeye to predict health care cost was classification trees, or CART. For more about this method, see Chapter 21. Classification trees are easily interpretable and therefore these models can be medically verified easily. Tables 8.6 and 8.7 describe characteristics of subgroups predicted to be in Buckets 4 and 5, respectively. These scenarios demonstrate how the trees use both cost and medical information along with age to identify the risky patients of the population.

Clustering Methods

Clustering algorithms organize objects so that similar objects are in the same cluster while dissimilar objects belong to different clusters. For more about the method of clustering, see Chapter 21.

First, patients were clustered using only their cost data, resulting in patients with similar cost-characteristics being placed in the same cluster. Then, for each cost-similar cluster, we ran the clustering algorithm on the medical data to create subclusters whose patients both have similar cost characteristics as well as medical conditions. We have found that this two-tiered approach gave stronger results than alternatives. The intuition for this is that cost trajectory provides a global summary of the health of the person. We then assigned a

Table 8.6: Examples of patients for whom the CART model predicted Bucket 4.

- Patients in Buckets 2 through 5 during the observation period, and who have taken more than 34 drug classes during the observation period.
- Patients in Bucket 1 during the observation period who have been in a hospital in the last three months with around $1,300 in health care costs in the last 3 months.
- Women in Bucket 1 during the observation period who have between $1,300 and $1,500 in costs in the last 6 months of the observation period, who do not have renal failure, but have taken Arava (a disease-modifying anti-rheumatic drug) within 180 days prior to delivery and do not have prescribed prenatal vitamins during pregnancy.
- Patients in Bucket 1 during the observation period who have more than $1,700 in health care costs in the last 6 months of the observation period, have non-acute cost profiles, and have hypertension but no lab test in the observation period.
- Patients with more than $24,500 in health care costs in the observation period, but less than $3,200 in pharmacy costs and on fewer than 14 different therapeutic drug classes during the observation period. They also have a non-chronic cost profile, do not have a diagnosis of secondary malignancy, but have more than nine office visits in the last 3 months of the observation period.

forecast for a particular cluster based on the known results period costs of the training sample.

To illustrate, let us give an example. We start with a cluster, found by the algorithm using cost characteristics only. The cost profiles of the patients are shown in Figure 8.3. Each box plot shows the distribution of cost in a single month across all 57 patients in this cluster. We note that all patients have relatively low cost in the first eight months of the observation period, but a greater average cost in the last four months of the period.

However, there were several different medical conditions leading to this cost, and therefore when using cost information only we are not able to distinguish between the patients in the cluster. The clustering algorithm

Table 8.7: Examples of patients for whom the CART model predicted Bucket 5.

- Patients with acute cost profiles and overall costs between $12,300 and $16,000 in the last 12 months of the observation period. They take no more than 14 different therapeutic drug classes during the observation period, and have not had a heart blockage followed by dose(s) of amiodarone hcl. They have more than 15 individual diagnoses and at least one of the following conditions: a) admitted to the ICU because of Congestive Heart Failure, b) has Chronic Obstructive Pulmonary Disease with more than one prescription for Macrolides or Floxins, c) has Renal Failure with more than one hospitalization in the observation period, or d) has both Coronary Artery Disease and Depression.
- Patients with more than $24,500 in costs in the observation period, an acute cost profile and a diagnosis of cancer.
- Patients in Bucket 2 during the observation period, with a non-acute cost profile, costs between $2,700 and $6,100 in the last 6 months of the observation period, and with either: a) Coronary Artery Disease and Hypertension receiving antihypertensive drugs or b) Peripheral Vascular Disease but without taking medication for it.
- Patients in Bucket 2 during the observation period and taking between 15 and 34 different therapeutic drug classes during the observation period, with a non-acute cost profile, costs between $1,200 and $4,000 in the last 6 months of the observation period, and have a Hepatitis C related hospitalization during the observation period.
- Patients in Buckets 2 and 3 during the observation period with non-acute cost profiles, less than $2,400 in pharmacy costs and on fewer than 13 therapeutic drug classes, but have received Zyban (prescription medication designed to help smokers quit) after a seizure.

then uses medical information to identify subgroups within the cost cluster and partitions the patients into two subclusters. Table 8.8 shows some of the medical characteristics with the greatest difference in prevalence between the two groups. By creating these sub clusters, we can better predict future

Figure 8.3: Distribution of the monthly costs during the last 12 months of the observation period for all patients of a cost similar cluster. Each box plot shows the distribution of monthly cost across all 57 patients in this cluster. The thick dark blue line shows the median value, and the box gives the first and third quartile values. The points represent outliers.

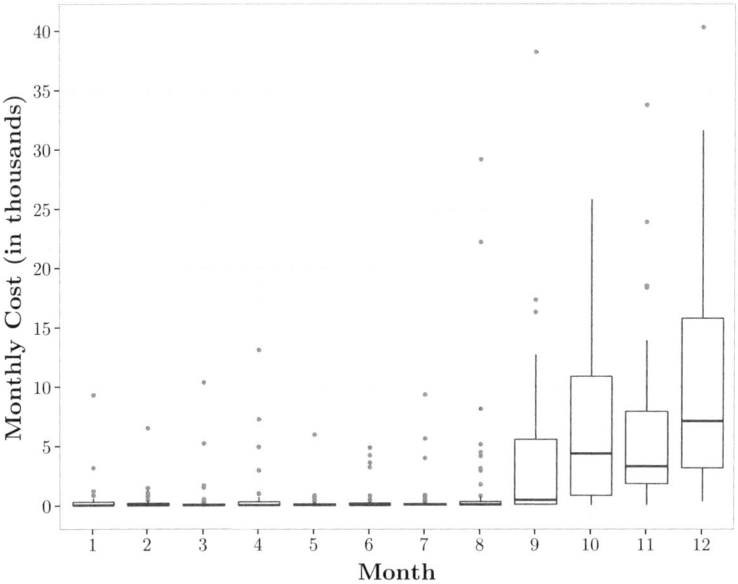

healthcare cost.

The first cluster consists of patients that have pathology, cytopathology, infusions and other indicators of cancer indicating a potentially serious health problem that is likely to lead to higher health care costs in the future. The second cluster consists predominantly of patients who are in physical therapy and have had orthopedic surgery and with other musculoskeletal characteristics and we can expect that these patients will be getting better, and thus have lower health care costs in the following year.

8.3 The Results

Both the classification tree and clustering algorithms were run using the training sample and were calibrated using the validation sample. There were three distinct classification trees built, one designed to optimize each of the three performance measures. We report in Table 8.9 the overall accuracy of the tree built for predicting the overall accuracy, the penalty error of the tree built for

Table 8.8: Distinguishing features of medical clusters.

Frequency in Cluster 1	Frequency in Cluster 2	Description
18%	**72%**	Physical therapy
29%	**83%**	Durable medical equipment
14%	**66%**	Orthopedic surgery
4%	**48%**	Osteoarthritis
39%	3%	>$4,000 paid for injectables
71%	38%	Pathology
32%	0%	Hematology/oncology infusions
7%	**38%**	Rehab
21%	**52%**	Musculoskeletal disorders
25%	3%	Emetics
25%	3%	Blood products/transfusions
18%	0%	Cancer therapies

predicting the penalty error, and the absolute prediction error for the tree built for predicting the absolute prediction error, all in the testing sample. Both algorithms lead to considerable improvement in all the performance measures over the baseline method. For the classification tree algorithm, the improvement in absolute prediction error is over 16%, the reduction in the penalty error is 10.5% and a 5% improvement in the overall accuracy. The results are comparable for the clustering algorithm but it has an edge in the absolute prediction error.

For both algorithms, the improvements are most significant for the high cost buckets. For the classification tree algorithm and high cost bucket, the overall accuracy almost doubles, the decrease in the penalty error is 23% and the decrease in the absolute prediction error is over 50%. The clustering algorithm similarly more than doubles the overall accuracy, decreases the penalty error by more than 35%, and decreases the average absolute prediction error by over 58%. The classification tree algorithm does a bit better on the lowest cost buckets for the overall ratio and penalty error, but the clustering algorithm works better on the higher cost buckets.

In Table 8.10 we report performance measures for models that use only cost information. In general, the classification trees do not benefit from adding the medical variables, but the clustering algorithm does benefit from using medical information, especially on APE. The clustering algorithm continues to have an edge for Buckets 4 and 5. However, given that the key objective of cost prediction is medical intervention through patient contact, the tree models with interpretable medical details are preferred. In other cases, the simpler models that achieve good results using only 22 cost variables, as opposed to almost 1500 medical variables, may be preferred.

Overall, both algorithms improved predictions over the baseline method

Table 8.9: The performance measures in the results period.

	Method	All	Bucket 1	Bucket 2	Bucket 3	Bucket 4	Bucket 5
Overall Acc. %	Trees	84.6	90.2	60.2	51.9	43.3	36.9
	Clustering	84.3	89.9	58.7	52.7	44.4	42.7
	Baseline	80.0	90.1	52.3	41.7	30.5	19.3
Penalty Error	Trees	0.39	0.28	0.86	1.04	1.24	1.41
	Clustering	0.37	0.26	0.88	1.07	1.18	1.17
	Baseline	0.43	0.29	0.99	1.36	1.67	1.83
APE($)	Trees	2,243	1,398	4,158	6,598	12,665	36,541
	Clustering	1,977	1,152	4,051	6,585	11,116	31,613
	Baseline	2,677	1,279	4,850	9,549	21,759	75,808

Table 8.10: The performance measures using cost information only.

	Method	All	Bucket 1	Bucket 2	Bucket 3	Bucket 4	Bucket 5
Overall Acc. %	Trees	84.6	90.1	60.3	52.3	42.7	35.2
	Clustering	84.2	90.1	57.5	49.9	41.7	40.5
	Baseline	80.0	90.1	52.3	41.7	30.5	19.3
Penalty Error	Trees	0.39	0.28	0.87	1.03	1.26	1.37
	Clustering	0.40	0.28	0.92	1.09	1.27	1.22
	Baseline	0.43	0.29	0.99	1.36	1.67	1.83
APE($)	Trees	2,214	1,395	4,033	6,462	12,310	35,875
	Clustering	2,116	1,269	4,146	6,580	12,412	33,907
	Baseline	2,677	1,279	4,850	9,549	21,759	75,808

for all performance measures, and the improvement was more significant for more costly patients. The clustering method resulted in better predictions for high cost bucket patients and consistently better absolute prediction error, while the classification tree algorithm had an edge on lower cost patients when we look at the overall accuracy and the penalty error. The doctors of D2Hawkeye had a clear preference to use the CART models, because they were more interpretable.

Using the CART model, D2Hawkeye selected patients in Buckets 4 and 5 to intervene. The tree provided intuition on why a patient was classified into Bucket 4 or Bucket 5, which helped the nurses in their communications with the patients.

8.4 Autonomous Discovery of Medical Knowledge

Since the 1850s, medical knowledge was primarily developed using clinical trials involving tens or hundreds of patients. The availability of claims data involving millions of individuals in electronic form provides an opportunity to systematically discover new medical knowledge based on the algorithms developed in this chapter. In this section, we explore the idea that we can obtain new medical insights from the data.

Association of Estrogens with Antidepressants

The clustering algorithm applied to data for female patients between 45 and 65 years of age discovered an interesting cluster consisting of 26,651 patients. The top distinguishing characteristics of this cluster are shown in Table 8.11. The top two characteristics were estrogen and antidepressants, which suggests a strong association between estrogens and antidepressants.

After noting this relationship, we analyzed the dataset and found that the probability of a patient being on an antidepressant goes up by 166% if they are also on an estrogen and we found the difference to be statistically significant. This observation was consistent with reports of a relationship

Table 8.11: The top ten most distinguishing features of the antidepressants and estrogen cluster. This pattern of estrogen coupled with antidepressants (and in some cases depression) was repeated throughout the clustering.

Prevalence	Description
50%	Estrogens & comb.
32%	Antidepressants
28%	Antihyperlipidemic drugs
27%	Hypertension
22%	Ace inhibitors & comb.
20%	Beta blockers & comb.
20%	Thyroid agents / hormones
16%	Gastrointestinal drugs
14%	Calcium channel blockers & comb.
11%	Cardiac drugs

between osteoporosis and depression, as estrogens are the most common treatment for osteoporosis.

Discovering the Averse Affects of Vioxx

Table 8.12 shows information on two additional clusters that both contain cardiac patients. This clustering was done using claims data from 2002-2004. The patients of the first cluster have significantly higher health care costs (Bucket 4) in the results period, while patients of the second cluster have significantly lower health care costs (Bucket 2). Comparing the characteristics of each cluster, we observed that they are very similar except for the fact that non-steroidal anti-inflammatory agents are present in Cluster 1 but not in Cluster 2. The clustering algorithm discovered autonomously that cardiac patients taking nonsteroidal anti-inflammatory agents had higher costs in the following year. Based on this discovery, one could develop more rigorous statistical testing to examine this hypothesis further.

Non-steroidal anti-inflammatory drugs have been used to target an enzyme responsible for inflammation and pain. One such drug, commonly known as Vioxx, was marketed by Merck & Co. to treat osteoarthritis, acute pain conditions, and dysmenorrhoea. Vioxx was approved by the Food and Drug Administration (FDA) on May 20, 1999. Vioxx gained widespread acceptance among physicians treating patients with arthritis and other conditions causing chronic or acute pain. Worldwide, over 80 million people were prescribed Vioxx at some time. On September 30, 2004, Merck voluntarily withdrew Vioxx from the market because of concerns about increased risk of heart attack and stroke associated with long-term, high-dosage use. Merck withdrew the drug after disclosures that it withheld information about Vioxx's risks from doctors and patients for over five years, resulting in

Table 8.12: The distinguishing features of two clusters of cardiac patients. Cluster 1 contains patients that have significantly higher health care costs in the results period, while Cluster 2's patients have significantly lower health care costs in the results period.

Frequency in Cluster 1	Frequency in Cluster 2	Description
41%	44%	Antihyperlipidemic drugs
38%	33%	Ace inhibitors & comb.
33%	37%	Hypertension
34%	23%	Calcium channel blockers & comb.
24%	31%	Beta blockers & comb.
13%	15%	Cardiac drugs
25%	0%	Nonsteroidal /Anti-Inflam. agent

between 88,000 and 140,000 cases of serious heart disease. Vioxx was one of the most widely used drugs ever to be withdrawn from the market. In the year before withdrawal, Merck had sales of $2.5 billion from Vioxx.

The two examples we presented suggest that the clustering algorithm may reveal unexpected associations amongst diagnoses, procedures and drugs and may identify potential safety issues with drugs in common use, which can be useful for drug surveillance.

8.5 Conclusions

The board of D2Hawkeye decided to sell the company to Verisk Analytics in late 2008. Why was D2Hawkeye an attractive acquisition for Verisk Analytics? D2Hawkeye used both descriptive analytics to give intuition on health care costs and predictive analytics (the CART method we described in this chapter) to predict future costs and identify high cost patients. In seven years, D2Hawkeye developed a considerable edge in its industry and became a leading medical analytics company. The acquisition was a verification of the edge.

8.6 Notes and Sources

Dimitris Bertsimas was a member of the board of directors of D2Hawkeye from 2002 until the company was sold in 2008. He was able to experience first-hand the transformation of the company from a small start-up into a leading provider of medical analytics. He was able to observe the challenges and successes, and contributed to the development of the analytics core engine of the company. The material in this chapter is from Bertsimas et al. [16].

Chapter 9

Medical Monitoring and Predictive Diagnosing

Declare the past, diagnose the present, foretell the future.

– Hippocrates of Cos

Contents

In the neonatal intensive care unit (NICU) at Toronto's Hospital for Sick Children, eight infants are being monitored with the standard intensive care unit (ICU) devices: electrocardiograms (ECGs) and blood pressure monitors, temperature monitors, IV pumps, and feeding tubes. At first glance, the equipment in the room seems very similar to that in most intensive care units. However, there is a small box located in the unit that is transmitting all of the data and information collected from the infants to a remote computer lab. The data is being analyzed in real-time by an advanced algorithmic environment called Artemis, which is able to detect signs of complications and conditions before they are visible to the human eye. These infants are part of a first-of-a-kind pilot effort to use analytics to reduce mortality and morbidity rates in premature and ill newborns around the world.

In a different environment over 500 miles away, researchers at the Massachusetts Institute of Technology (MIT) have developed methods to predict and help prevent heart attacks, a growing concern in the United States. The researchers have used insurance claims data from thousands of patients to detect diagnostic patterns in people who have experienced heart attacks. Using these patterns, they can predict the occurrence of a heart attack based on past medical history. These algorithms can identify patients at high-risk for a heart attack and assist physicians in providing appropriate preventative care.

In both of these examples, analytics tools are used to improve medical monitoring and predictive diagnosing. In this chapter, we will first discuss the example of detecting patterns of heart attacks, which uses a stored dataset and tries to detect patterns in different groups of patients. The dataset is updated over time, and predictions and observations can be made at any point. Then, we will discuss the example of Artemis in the NICU, which is a system that analyzes data and detects abnormalities in real-time. The dataset is not stored in one place, but rather there is a continuous stream of data that needs to be collected, cleaned and analyzed as quickly as possible. This chapter shows how analytics can assist medical staff in both of these situations to utilize every piece of data available to ultimately make more accurate diagnoses as quickly as possible.

9.1 Detecting Patterns of Heart Attacks

In a research project conducted at the Massachusetts Institute of Technology, medical claims data from over 47,000 patients was used to find temporal diagnostic patterns and predictive models associated with a higher incidence of myocardial infarction (heart attack). This work was a joint effort between the Operations Research Center at MIT and Draper Laboratory.

A myocardial infarction, also known as an MI or a heart attack, results from the interruption of blood supply to part of the heart, causing heart cells to die. MI is most commonly due to a complication of coronary heart disease, and it is a growing concern in the United States. According to the Centers for

Disease Control and Prevention, heart disease is the leading cause of death in the United States, responsible for more than one in every four deaths. In 2010, heart disease was estimated to cost the United States $316.4 billion. This included the cost of healthcare services, medications, and lost productivity. If we could predict future MIs, more rigorous preventative measures could hopefully be taken to alter the health of high-risk patients.

The nature of an MI makes it hard to predict, prevent and even diagnose. There are many well known symptoms of a heart attack, like chest pain (angina), shortness of breath, heartburn, arm pain, jaw pain, toothache, headache, nausea, and upper back pain. However, approximately 25% of all heart attacks are silent, meaning that no obvious symptoms are observed. It is a current research problem to discover clinical characteristics of the patients who had an MI event and who may have exhibited earlier symptoms. These unexpected heart attacks call for an increased understanding of the patterns in a patient's diagnostic history that are linked to MI. One way to achieve this is through analytics.

The Data

Like many data-driven studies in healthcare, the researchers here used insurance claims data to study the patterns in a patient's medical history. (We also saw examples of using claims data in Chapters 1 and 8.) Insurance claims are coded bills that healthcare providers send to insurance companies to receive payment for their services. There are many advantages to using insurance claims data for analysis, including a large population of patients, geographically diverse data, many records for the same patients over a wide time range, and a lower cost of acquiring the data.

The dataset contained health insurance claims filed for 47,763 members from a commercially insured population. The members were located throughout the United States, and data was collected from January 2000 through November 2007. Rather than using the entire dataset, the researchers wanted to analyze a subpopulation of patients with a reasonably long medical history, and who might be at higher risk of having a heart attack. Therefore, the researchers concentrated their analysis on patients who were diagnosed with Coronary Artery Disease (CAD), had at least five claims with CAD diagnostic codes and five with hypertension diagnostic codes, had data for at least five years, had at least 100 total medical claims, and had at least five pharmacy claims.

To reduce the number of diagnosis codes, procedure codes, and drug codes, clinicians combined codes into similar groups for analysis purposes. To analyze changes over time, the observation period was split into 21 periods, each 90 days in length. With this data, the researchers were ready to build a predictive model.

Building a Predictive Model

The goal of this study was to build a model to find patterns leading up to a heart attack. Therefore, the dataset needed to consist of some patients who experienced a heart attack, and some patients who did not. For the rest of this chapter, we will refer to the patients with MI as "Group A" and the patients without MI as "Group B." Group A was constructed by selecting patients who had both an MI diagnostic code and an indication of a visit to an emergency room or hospital. Both conditions were necessary in selecting patients with an MI event because the MI diagnostic group code also accounts for follow-up events to the heart attack. For each patient, only the first occurrence of a heart attack was considered. To have enough data to find patterns in events leading up to the heart attack, nine months of data before the time of the heart attack was used. If the patient did not have nine months of data before the MI incident in the database, that patient was not included in Group A.

In order to balance the dataset with an equal number of patients in Group B, a patient without an MI diagnostic code was selected to "match" each of the patients in Group A. This was done by finding a patient in the database who did not have an MI recorded in their entire available diagnostic history, and whose data was from the same time period as each of the selected patients in Group A. As an example, suppose the first patient in Group A had available data from January 2002 through December 2005. To find a matching patient for inclusion in Group B, we would look through all of the patients in the database, and find one who did not have a heart attack and who also had data from January 2002 through December 2005. We would then add this patient to our dataset with a "no MI" event at the same time as the corresponding Group A member's "MI event" and move on to the next patient in Group A. The population of patients not having an MI was much larger than those with an MI, so it was possible to select an appropriate match for each MI patient.

Since the order of the events leading up to the MI or no MI occurrence is more important than the actual date the events occurred, the nine month periods for all selected patients were aligned so that they started and ended simultaneously, preserving the order of the events. Finally, the data was divided into two parts: a training set to build the model, and a test set to evaluate the model's performance. All of the predictive results reported later are for the test set, which was not used to build the model.

In this situation, the target variable that we want to predict is binary: whether the patient did or did not have a heart attack (Group A or Group B). The variables available to predict this target variable included gender, diagnoses, and healthcare cost.

Healthcare cost often provides a good indicator of a person's overall health. For this reason, the researchers decided to first divide the patient population into three different cost buckets, according to their healthcare cost: one for below-average to average cost, one for average to above-average cost, and one for high cost. Table 9.1 gives the cost ranges for the three buckets and the amount of data that was collected in each.

Note that the amount of data in each cost bucket decreases significantly as the cost increases. However, the percentage of patients with MI stays fairly constant. By dividing the patients into cost buckets, the researchers were hoping they could build different and more appropriate predictive models for each of the smaller groups. We will discuss the mathematical models used in each of the cost buckets in the next section.

Analytics Methods

A combination of two different analytics methods was used to increase the predictability of the model. The first method used was the *random forest algorithm*, which builds a large collection of classification trees. Each classification tree "votes" on the predicted outcome for every observation (heart attack or no heart attack), and the final vote is taken to be the majority vote. An important aspect of the random forest algorithm is that the trees are built so that they are uncorrelated. The algorithm builds the trees with different subsets of the available data, and also uses different predictive variables. The random forest algorithm can be thought of as "asking" many classification trees to vote on the prediction, instead of just one. For this reason, it will sometimes outperform basic classification tree algorithms. Here, the parameters of the random forest model were selected by using cross-validation. For more about random forests, see Chapter 21.

The second method used was *clustering*, which is typically employed to find relationships among different input variables (like diagnoses, age, and gender). Its goal is to divide the data into meaningful groups such that records in the same group are similar and those in different groups are dissimilar. Common clustering methods include *K-means clustering* and *spectral clustering*. Both of these clustering methods require that the number of clusters be specified ahead of time. After testing with different numbers of clusters, the researchers decided to use ten different clusters. For more technical details about these methods, see Section 9.4 and Chapter 21.

The random forest algorithm and clustering were combined by first clustering the patients into similar groups, and then using random forests to make predictions about future heart attacks within each of the groups. The

Table 9.1: Summary of cost bucket partitioning.

Bucket	Cost Range	% of Data	# Members	% with MI
1	$< \$2,000$	67.56%	4,416	36.14%
2	\$2,000 - \$10,000	21.56%	1,409	43.22%
3	$\geq \$10,000$	10.88%	711	38.12%

Table 9.2: Classification results on the test set from using random forests and clustering.

Cost Bucket	Prediction Accuracy
1	68.25%
2	71.55%
3	79.15%

clustering and random forest models were built using the training set, and then applied to the test set. So, these results are *out-of-sample*, meaning that the model never saw the test data before having to make predictions.

Table 9.2 shows the prediction accuracy on the test set (the percentage of patients accurately predicted to have or not have a heart attack) obtained by using cost buckets, spectral clustering (which slightly outperformed k-means clustering for this application), and random forests. The prediction accuracy is given as a weighted average of the accuracy in each of the clusters, weighted by the number of patients in the cluster.

Without using cost buckets or clustering, the prediction accuracy of random forests was 51.8%. The division into cost buckets helped to improve the prediction accuracy, but most of the improvement was due to clustering the data. Prediction improvement from clustering can often occur when there are very different types of observations in the dataset, as is the case in this application.

Diagnostic Patterns that Lead to Heart Attacks

By using clustering, the researchers were able to detect some interesting trends in the diagnostic trajectories of the patients. These trends were discovered by first running the clustering algorithm, and then analyzing the patients that were grouped together in each cluster. Since the clusters form similar groups of patients, each cluster tended to have very different diagnostic characteristics.

We will focus on some of the trends, or patterns, seen in clusters in cost bucket 2 (average to above-average risk). Table 9.3 gives the number of patients in each cluster of cost bucket 2, the number of patients with MI, the number of patients without MI, and the prediction accuracy rate for each cluster.

Many of the diagnostic patterns in the clusters are known or have been confirmed by other studies, such as gradually increasing chronic obstructive pulmonary disease (COPD), overall deteriorating health, or chest pain in the three month period before the heart attack. This was the case for the cluster shown in Figure 9.1. This figure shows the average number of doctor visits by patients in one specific cluster (cluster 7) in cost bucket 2 (average risk), for different diagnoses and at different times. The x-axis shows the three different time periods leading up to the possible MI event, and each line gives the number of visits for a different diagnosis. The patients in this cluster had a clear increasing trend in the number of times they visited a doctor for chronic obstructive pulmonary disease (COPD). We can compare these numbers to cost bucket 2 in general, for which patients had an average of 0.5 visits for COPD in any time period. The patients in cluster 7 were clearly grouped together because of their unusual trend in COPD visits. Keep in mind that this cluster contains patients that had an MI, and patients who did not have an MI. So while this is a clear diagnostic pattern for patients in our dataset, it does not necessarily lead to a heart attack.

Another interesting pattern detected by the clustering was a drastic increase in visits for chest pain in the 3-6 month period before the heart attack, but very few visits for chest pain in the 3 months leading up to the heart attack. While chest pain is a well-known symptom of a heart attack, the timing of chest pain in this example is unusual. Figure 9.2 shows the average number of visits in this cluster (cluster 8 of cost bucket 2) for various diagnoses. Compared to the average number of visits for cost bucket 2 as a whole, these patients had about 17 more visits (on average) for chest pain in the 3-6 month period before a possible MI event. In the other time periods, these patients had about the same number of visits for chest pain as patients in cost bucket 2 overall. In this cluster, over two-thirds of the patients had an MI.

There were also interesting patterns in clusters that mostly contained patients who did not experience a heart attack. Figure 9.3 shows the average number of visits for various diagnoses of patients in cluster 3 of cost bucket 2. Over half of the patients in this cluster did not have a heart attack. These patients had a large number of visits for chest pain 6-9 months before the

Table 9.3: Patient distribution and prediction accuracy for each cluster in cost bucket 2.

Cluster	Total Number of Patients	Total with MI	Total without MI	Prediction Accuracy
1	51	32	19	72.41%
2	227	111	116	62.58%
3	35	14	21	70.59%
4	57	21	36	82.93%
5	111	61	50	70.97%
6	57	30	27	65.31%
7	55	30	25	73.17%
8	45	31	14	72.00%
9	63	25	38	73.91%
10	99	45	54	69.32%

Figure 9.1: Average number of visits for patients in cluster 7 of cost bucket 2. The x-axis gives the time periods leading up to a possible MI event, and the y-axis gives the average number of visits for patients in cluster 7. Each line corresponds to a different diagnosis: chronic obstructive pulmonary disease (COPD), anemia, congestive heart failure (CHF), chest pain, coronary artery disease (CAD), diabetes, and hypertension.

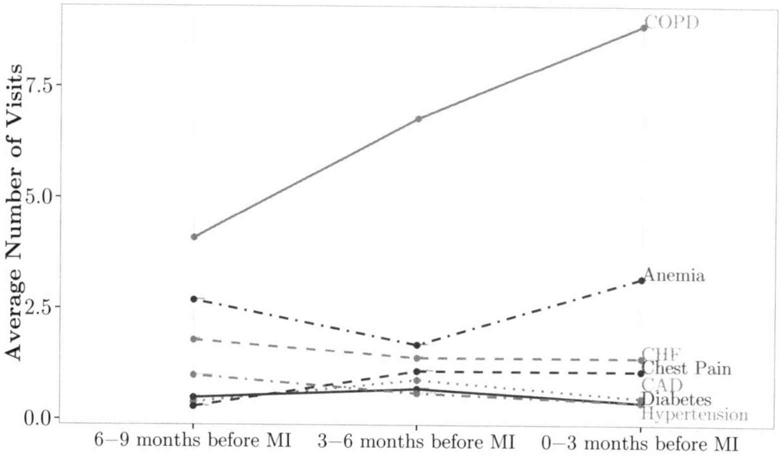

expected time of the heart attack, but no more than an average number of visits for chest pain at later dates (compared to the patients in cost bucket 2 as a whole). Thus the methods detected that immediate chest pain or chest pain up to 6 months before the heart attack is predictive of an MI incident, but if the chest pain is more than 6 months ago, a heart attack is not expected.

The predictability of the models developed in this work and the observations that can be seen in the different clusters indicate that there is potential to detect patients who are at high risk for a heart attack before the heart attack occurs. By closely monitoring these patients and taking appropriate preventative measures, the number of heart attacks and complications could be greatly reduced.

9.2 The Artemis Project: Real-Time Analysis in the NICU

The Artemis Project, named after the Greek goddess associated with protecting child-bearing women and young children, is a collaborative research effort between IBM Canada, the University of Ontario Institute of Technology

Figure 9.2: Average number of visits for patients in cluster 8 of cost bucket 2. The x-axis gives the time periods leading up to a possible MI event, and the y-axis gives the average number of visits for patients in cluster 8. Each line corresponds to a different diagnosis: chest pain, diabetes, coronary artery disease (CAD), congestive heart failure (CHF), and hypertension.

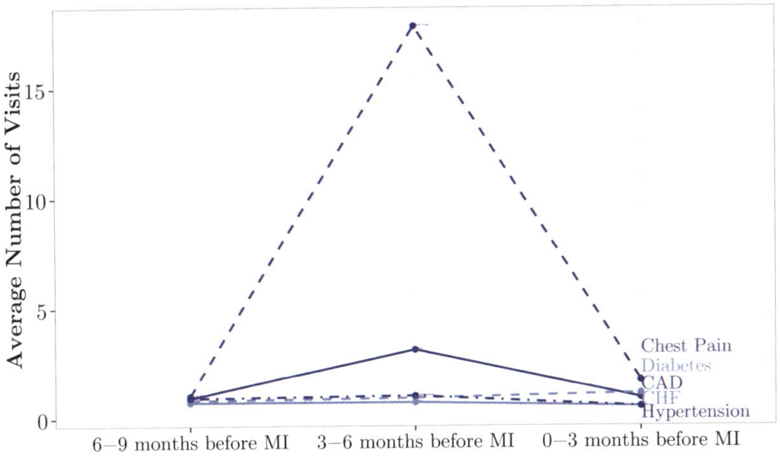

(UOIT), the Hospital for Sick Children (SickKids) and the Department of Pediatrics at the University of Toronto. The project is led by Dr. Carolyn McGregor, a UOIT associate professor and Canada Research Chair in Health Informatics.

Artemis is designed to improve the care of newborn infants in neonatal intensive care units (NICU), specialized departments in hospitals for ill or premature newborns. According to the Centers for Disease Control and Prevention (CDC), more than 500,000 newborns in the United States are born premature each year (about one in every eight births), meaning that the newborn is born at least three weeks before the expected due date. Common conditions affecting patients in the NICU include respiratory disorders, infection, congenital malformations, and birth asphyxia (oxygen deprivation). Some babies spend up to four months in the NICU, and can have lifelong chronic medical conditions as a result. Additionally, the cost of care in the NICU is significant; one infant's stay in the NICU can easily cost over $100,000.

In many NICUs, information and data is recorded on paper by the nursing staff, typically in sixty minute intervals. This is very time-intensive for the nursing staff, and a lot of data is lost in the process. Additionally, as many as 16 different streams of physiological data, including respiratory rate, heart rate,

Figure 9.3: Average number of visits for patients in cluster 3 of cost bucket 2. The x-axis gives the time periods leading up to a possible MI event, and the y-axis gives the average number of visits for patients in cluster 3. Each line corresponds to a different diagnosis: chest pain, diabetes, hypertension, and coronary artery disease (CAD).

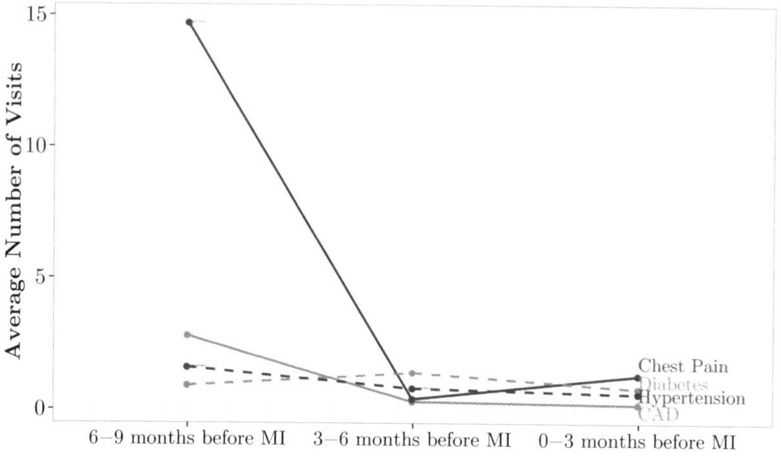

and blood pressure, are displayed for a single infant, with rates ranging from one to 512 readings per second. Figure 9.4 shows a diagram of the standard equipment used on an infant in the NICU.

Recent medical research has reported that many of the most common conditions affecting babies in the NICU exhibit early indicators in physiological data. However, it is hard for human observers to detect all of the abnormal variations in the mass amounts of data being collected. The Artemis environment provides NICUs with a tool to detect subtle changes in physiological data that can enable the earlier use of appropriate interventions, minimize the severity of the detected condition, and thus significantly reduce neonatal morbidity and mortality. The system has been in use at the NICU of the SickKids in Toronto since early August 2009.

The Artemis System

Artemis is an environment designed to detect medically significant conditions that precede the onset of medical complications. Unlike many other software systems that are designed to analyze a fixed and well-organized dataset, Artemis uses advanced stream computing software developed by IBM Research, which

Figure 9.4: Diagram of standard equipment used on an infant in the NICU.

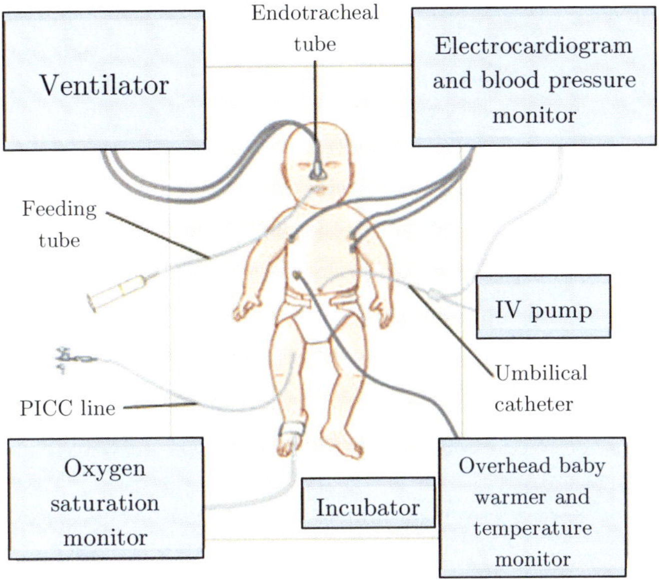

allows it to rapidly process data arriving very quickly and from many different sources.

The Artemis system is composed of many different hardware and software elements that allow it to connect and interact with the medical devices used in intensive care environments. Figure 9.5 shows a simple diagram of the system architecture.

Artemis is able to collect data from all of the different medical devices in the NICU and process this data in a computer lab. To limit the additional equipment needed in the crowded NICU, the system is configured so that only a small terminal unit is placed in the NICU, and the data is forwarded to a computer lab elsewhere. Many of the software and hardware elements used in Artemis are from Capsule Tech, Inc., a company that provides solutions for medical device data integration based in Andover, Massachusetts. Artemis also has a device to interface with the hospital's clinical information management system, which contains all of the patient data that is not collected from the medical devices but might also be used in treatment (such as age or weight). This part of the system is depicted as the data acquisition step of Figure 9.5.

The core of Artemis is a stream computing software developed by IBM, called the InfoSphere Stream Computing System. It is able to process multiple streams of high-volume and high-rate data and analyze the data in real time, as opposed to most systems that store the data first and then process it later.

The streams of data include heart rate (HR), oxygen saturation (SpO2), and blood pressure (BP), which are collected and processed simultaneously to give alerts for different medical conditions. This part of the system is depicted as the real-time analysis step of Figure 9.5. The data is then sent to the user interface to present real-time results to the medical staff, and to the computer lab to extract more information from the data.

The knowledge extraction component of Artemis uses innovative machine learning techniques to enable new clinical research with the data that is collected. It suggests and runs clinical rules, which are specifications of clinical guidelines, such as "notify me when an hourly systolic blood pressure (BP) reading exceeds 140." If a condition defined by a clinical rule is found to be present, it predicts an impending clinical event and should be reported to a nurse or physician. As shown in Figure 9.5, the data is sent to the knowledge extraction component after real-time analysis, but then the information found in the knowledge extraction step is sent back to the real-time analysis step to enhance the process.

Running and discovering clinical rules is one of the major goals of the Artemis project. Some of the clinical rules that Artemis implements are already known, but others are discovered by analyzing all of the data that is collected. The goal is to determine combinations of symptoms that provide early warning of an impending condition. These rules are developed by analysts, and then programmed into the system to raise alarms when a rule is triggered. This allows for real-time tracking of patients; when a rule applies, an alarm is raised.

In addition to developing new rules, Artemis can easily raise flags for clinical rules that are known but require second-to-second observations. Without Artemis, these rules are impractical and sometimes impossible for people to monitor.

Figure 9.5: Diagram of the Artemis system architecture.

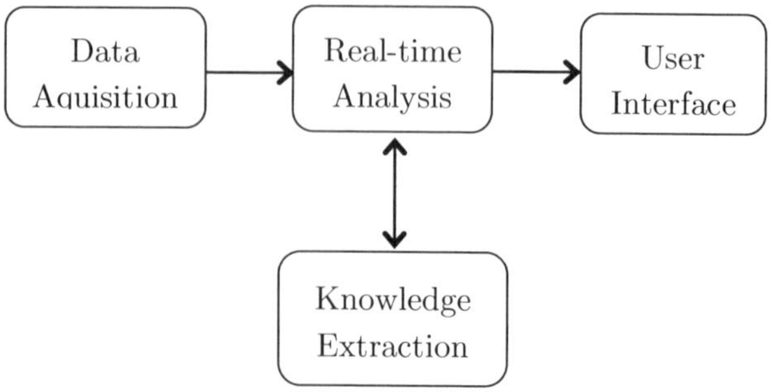

Detecting Apnea and Infections

Apnea is a temporary cessation of breathing, and is the most common problem of ventilatory control in premature infants. It frequently prolongs hospitalization and the need for cardiopulmonary monitoring. In most NICUs, a nurse will record an event of apnea if it is perceived to be of significance, but manual recording is often limited in its degree of detail. Artemis is able to collect all of the clinical data, and researchers are also currently using the data to see if there are patterns in multiple data streams (such as respiratory rate, heart rate, and blood oxygen saturation) during apnea episodes. Previous clinical evidence suggests that it may be the case that clinical rules for apnea should involve multiple events occurring in parallel or sequentially, but these rules are often too involved to detect quickly in current manual systems. One example is: "A lapse in breathing (respiratory rate) of a neonate (of 35 weeks gestation) for greater than 15 seconds is of clinical relevance. At all neonatal gestational ages a fall in peripheral oxygen saturation less than 85% for greater than 20 seconds combined with a HR of less than 100 bpm is also of clinical relevance." In Artemis, all of these data streams are processed and analyzed together and produce clinical alerts if necessary.

Another serious problem in the NICU is nosocomial infections, also called hospital-acquired infections. These are infections that are secondary to the original cause for admission into the NICU. Almost 30% of infants born at 25-28 weeks gestation and more than 45% of infants born prior to 25 weeks gestation experience a serious nosocomial infection while in the NICU. These infections can be life threatening to premature infants, who are some of the most fragile patients in the hospital. Early diagnosis is difficult, since the clinical signs are usually subtle and vague until the infection is well established. However, it has been observed that changes in heart rate variability may occur up to 24 hours prior to the clinical presentation of the infection. These changes are almost undetectable; the infant's pulse is within acceptable limits, but it is not varying as it should. Heart rates normally rise and fall throughout the day, but in an infant with an infection, this does not happen as much and the heart rate is too regular over time. This change can be subtle and happen over a long period of time, so it is hard for nurses to detect in a busy NICU environment. This type of medical monitoring is perfectly suited to Artemis, and the early indications of its success are promising.

Currently, Artemis is collecting data from up to eight neonatal patients in the Hospital for Sick Children in Toronto. Clinical research is being done with this collected data to develop new clinical rules that Artemis is able to apply. The system is currently being extended to all of the patients in the Hospital for Sick Children NICU, and data from two other hospitals is also being collected. One of the goals of the project is to continue expanding the technology that is used in Artemis to other ICUs beyond the neonatal unit.

9.3 A New Type of Physician's Assistant

In this chapter, we have given two different examples of how analytics can be used to improve medical monitoring and predictive diagnosing. The methods here have the ability to provide warning signs and detect abnormalities and patterns in mass amounts of data before they are visible to clinical staff. The methods bring together human knowledge and expertise with data-driven analytics to produce better results than manual monitoring. The physicians, nurses, and other medical staff are critical to the process, but the algorithms and analytics systems can improve patient outcomes.

The systems discussed here are preliminary steps to integrate healthcare and analytics, and they show that there is a place for analytics in medicine. The patterns found to lead to heart attacks in claims data could be extended to other conditions, and the real-time monitoring of Artemis has the potential to be used to monitor patients in all ICUs, in other areas of the hospital, and even outside of the hospital. Healthcare is an area full of data and decisions, and analytics is perfectly suited to aid medical staff to improve patient care.

9.4 Notes and Sources

9.1. The material in this section is from Bertsimas, Markuzon, and Shenk [24]. The data used to develop the models was provided by Verisk Health.

For more technical details about spectral clustering, we direct the reader to the tutorial by von Luxburg [148].

9.2. The Artemis system is described in more detail in the journal papers by Blount et al. [29] and Catley et al. [34], and in two news articles [65, 130].

Chapter 10

Analytics for Kidney Allocation

The purpose of models is not to fit the data but to sharpen the questions.

– Samuel Karlin

Contents

Renal or kidney transplantation and maintenance dialysis are the only treatments for end-stage renal disease, a terminal disease currently affecting over 500,000 people in the United States. Despite being a major surgical procedure, transplantation is the treatment of choice for such patients, as a successful transplantation improves their quality of life. On the other hand, dialysis treatment requires that the patient visits a dialysis center for at least 12 hours each week, preventing the patient from having regular life activities. Furthermore, a multitude of research and clinical studies have statistically demonstrated that transplantation also reduces the mortality risk for patients. Thus, a kidney transplant is considered by many as a potentially life-saving gift.

The two sources of kidneys for transplantation are living donors (usually family members or friends of the patient) and deceased or cadaveric donors. The majority of patients are unsuccessful in finding living donors, and thus join a pool of patients waiting for a deceased donor organ. In the case of a living donor, the donation is typically made to a specific patient. However, in the deceased donor case, an important allocation problem arises: once an organ is procured from a deceased donor, there can be thousands of medically compatible recipients in need of the organ. The problem becomes even more significant if one accounts for the organ shortage and the size of the pool of waiting patients in the United States. At any one time, about 90,000 patients are waiting for a kidney transplant. In 2009, there were 33,671 new additions to the list of patients waiting for a kidney, but only 16,829 transplantations were performed, from which 10,442 transplants were from deceased donors.

In this chapter, we use analytics to design a national policy for kidney allocation. In particular, we present a method for designing allocation policies based on point systems in a systematic, data-driven way. This method offers flexibility to the policymaker to select the fairness constraints to be applied, as well as the prioritization criteria on which the point system will be based. The method then outputs a conforming point system policy that approximately maximizes medical efficiency, while satisfying the fairness constraints. This chapter uses a variety of methods to achieve its objectives: linear optimization, linear regression and simulation. See Chapter 21 for more about these methods. The use of analytics in this chapter is unusual in that, rather than solving a tactical problem, we use analytics to design strategic policies for a problem of national importance.

10.1 Distribution and Allocation Policies

In recognition of the kidney allocation problem and the growing difficulty of matching supply and demand, the United States Congress passed the *National Organ Transplant Act* (NOTA) in 1984. According to this legislation, deceased donor organs are viewed as national resources in the United States, and as such, their allocation has to be based on fair and equitable policies. Moreover, the sale of organs or money transfers of any nature in the acquisition of organs are strictly prohibited. Instead, the policy for allocating the organs should utilize waiting lists and have the form of a *priority method.* This means that patients in need of a transplant register on waiting lists. Then, once an organ is procured, all medically compatible patients are ranked according to some priority rules and the organ is successively offered to the patients according to their ranking, until it is accepted. Subsequent to the NOTA, the United States Congress also established in 1984 the *Organ Procurement and Transplantation Network* (OPTN) to maintain a national registry for organ matching and develop allocation policies. NOTA called for OPTN to be operated by a private, non-profit organization under federal contract, called United Network for Organ Sharing (UNOS). People use the terms UNOS/OPTN interchangeably, although, UNOS is a "contract" and OPTN is the "contractor." The custodian of OPTN is the Department of Health and Human Services (HHS), specifically, the Health Resources and Services Administration (HRSA, which belongs to HHS). For OPTN-proposed policies to become implemented, they need to be approved by HHS. In particular, there is a series of steps outlined in the OPTN Bylaws. First, the proposal is run by the OPTN Board of Directors. Then, there is a public comment period so that external feedback is solicited. After that, the proposal is brought back to the OPTN Board of Directors. If approved by the Board, non-mandatory policies are implemented straight away. For mandatory policies to be enforced, they are forwarded to the Secretary of HHS for review, comment and final approval.

Naturally, the allocation policies are of central importance and have to accomplish major objectives in alleviating human suffering, prolonging life and providing nondiscriminatory, fair and equal access to organs for all patients, independent of their race, age, blood group or other physiological characteristics. Some of the main challenges in designing a kidney allocation policy are the following:

- **Fairness constraints**: What does fair and equal access to organs mean? Due to the subjective nature of fairness, there is no single fairness criterion that is universally accepted by policymakers and academics alike. As such, a great challenge lies in identifying the appropriate fairness constraints that the allocation outcomes of a policy should ideally satisfy. An example of such a constraint could be a lower bound on the percentage of organs allocated to a particular group of patients – say, requiring that at least 47% of all transplants are received by recipients of blood type O. In the absence of such a constraint, these groups could otherwise be at a disadvantage and not have enough access to organs because of their physiological characteristics.

- **Efficiency**: Since a successful transplantation typically prolongs the life of a patient while also improving his quality of life, the policy needs to ensure that the number of quality adjusted life years (QALY) garnered by transplantation activities is as high as possible. The QALY is a measure of disease burden, including both the quality and the quantity of life lived. It is based on the number of years of life that would be added by a medical intervention. Each year in perfect health is assigned the value of 1, and smaller values (with a minimum value of 0) represent a lower-quality of life. If the extra years would not be lived in full health, for example if the patient would lose a limb, be blind or have to use a wheelchair, then the extra life-years are given a value closer to 0.

- **Prioritization criteria**: Prioritization needs to be based on medically justified criteria and physiological characteristics of patients and organs in order to rank potential patients both on the basis of need and of expected benefit. However, ethical rules disallow the use of criteria that can be deemed as discriminatory (e.g. race and gender).

- **Simplicity**: Patients need to make important decisions about their treatment options, together with their physicians. To this end, they need to be able to estimate the probability of receiving an organ, or at least understand the allocation mechanism. For this reason, the priority method that is used needs to be simple and easy to communicate.

- **Implementation**: After selecting transparent and desired fairness constraints, prioritization criteria and a simple priority method, what emphasis should be put on the different criteria, so as to design a policy whose allocation outcomes would maximize efficiency, while satisfying the fairness constraints?

All the above challenges were faced by the OPTN policymakers in 2004, when they initiated the development of a new national allocation policy that will eventually replace the current one. In 2008, the OPTN released a concrete proposal that is currently under consideration by the United States Department of Health and Human Services.

The Distribution Process

In the United States, the non-profit *Organ Procurement Organizations* (OPOs) are directly responsible for evaluating, procuring and allocating donated organs within their respective designated service area. All OPOs have to follow all mandatory OPTN policies. There are a few non-mandatory policies that OPOs have the autonomy of adopting or not. Once consent is obtained and an organ is procured by an OPO, the OPTN computerized national registry automatically generates a list of patients who are medically compatible with the procured organ. Medical compatibility of patients is determined by their physiological characteristics and those of the procured organ (e.g. accounting for ABO incompatibility[1], weight and size, and unacceptable antigens). Subsequently, the priority method used by the OPO determines the order in which the organ will be offered to patients. Once a kidney is procured, it can typically be preserved for up to 36-48 hours, after which the organ can no longer be used for transplantation. For that reason, priority is usually given to local patients, although there are rules that determine when priority should be given to non-local patients. After an offer is made to a patient, the patient and his medical team must decide whether to accept it within a limited amount of time (typically 2-3 hours). The typical reason a patient might not accept an organ is that he believes a higher quality organ might be available in the future. In case of non-acceptance, the organ is offered to the next patient according to the specified order and so on. If no patient accepts the organ within 36-48 hours, the organ is discarded.

In addition to using the OPTN national registry, the activities of the OPOs, and their allocation policies in particular, are coordinated and regulated by the OPTN. That is, the OPTN provides general guidelines and lays out a national allocation policy. The allocation policy of every OPO then needs to be consistent with the national policy, although minor alterations are possible subject to approval by the OPTN.

National Allocation Policies

National policies for the allocation of deceased donor kidneys are developed by the OPTN *Kidney Transplantation Committee* (KTC), and are approved by the United States Department of Health & Human Services. Policies need to account for numerous legal, economic, institutional, ethical, and other societal factors; the requirements for an allocation policy are included in the OPTN Final Rule. Below we summarize the most important guidelines that policies have to conform to as per the OPTN Final Rule. In particular, the allocation:

1. Shall seek to achieve the best use of donated organs, and avoid organ wastage;

2. Shall set priority rankings based on sound medical judgment;

3. Shall balance medical efficiency (extra life years) and equity (waiting time), without discriminating against patients based on their race, age and blood type;

4. Shall be reviewed periodically and revised as appropriate.

Additionally, the priority method in place needs to be simple and easy to communicate, as discussed earlier in the chapter. As such, the ranking of

[1] ABO incompatibility is a reaction of the immune system that occurs if two different and not compatible blood types are mixed together. The Acronym ABO comes from the fact that A, B, AB, and O are the four major blood types. See http://www.nlm.nih.gov/medlineplus/ency/article/001306.htm for more information.

patients is typically achieved by means of a *point system* or *scoring rule*. All national allocation policies that have been used in practice have been based on scoring rules. In this section, we formally define the notion of a scoring rule policy and then discuss the current national policy and suggested revisions.

Scoring Rule Policies

Under a policy based on a scoring rule, patients are ranked according to a calculated score, commonly referred to in this context as the *Kidney Allocation Score* (KAS). Specifically, for a particular patient and a particular organ, a scoring rule is a weighted combination of score components that include the number of years the patient has been registered on the waiting list, the life expectancy of the patient in case he remained on dialysis, and the life expectancy in case he received the procured organ.

One can think of a scoring rule based policy as a priority method that awards points to patients based on different criteria (the score components). Patients are also potentially awarded different amounts of points per criterion, based on the score weights. The ranking is then calculated based on the number of points collected by each patient. The current policy in use and the one recently proposed by United States policymakers are both examples of scoring rule based policies and are discussed next.

Current Allocation Policy

The policy in effect in 2014 that all OPOs use was put into place more than twenty years earlier. It is based on a scoring rule that utilizes waiting time, a measure of the patient's sensitization[2], and tissue matching[3] of the organ and the patient as score components. The rationale behind this rule is as follows. Points are given for waiting time and sensitization in order to serve the fairness objective of the allocation and to provide equal access to organs to all patients (note that highly sensitized patients have reduced medical compatibility with donors). On the other hand, since tissue matching is an indication for a successful transplantation, the points given to matched patients serve the medical efficiency objective of the allocation.

Recent advances in medicine and changes in patients' needs have rendered the current policy inappropriate. More specifically, these changes have rendered the current policy inconsistent with the objectives of the OPTN Final Rule.

[2]Potential recipients are "sensitized" if their immune system makes antibodies against potential donors. Sensitization usually occurs as a consequence of pregnancy, blood transfusions, or previous transplantation. Highly sensitized patients are more likely to reject an organ transplant than are unsensitized patients. For more information, see http://www.ustransplant.org/

[3]When two people share the same human leukocyte antigens (abbreviated as HLA), they are said to be a "match," that is, their tissues are immunologically compatible with each other. HLA are proteins that are located on the surface of the white blood cells and other tissues in the body. For more information, see http://www.stanford.edu/dept/HPS/transplant/html/hla.html

The long waiting times experienced by the patients, coupled with advances in medicine that have prolonged the survivability of patients on dialysis, have resulted in the accumulation of patients with a high number of points due to long waiting times. This accumulation of points has then created an imbalance between the efficiency and fairness objectives of the allocation. In response to that, and in line with the requirement of the OPTN Final Rule for periodic review of the policy, the KTC has been reviewing the policy for the past few years and is currently in the process of developing a new policy.

Development of a New Policy

The OPTN has set the primary objective of the new policy to be the design of a scoring rule that strikes the right balance between fairness and medical efficiency. As mentioned above, the design of a scoring rule involves the identification of the appropriate score components, and the corresponding score weights that form the Kidney Allocation Score. The KTC has decided to base the score components on the following criteria for a patient p and an organ o:

1. *Life years from transplant* $\mathrm{LYFT}(p, o)$, which is equal to the expected incremental quality-adjusted life years gained of patient p from receiving organ o, compared to remaining on dialysis;

2. *Dialysis time* $\mathrm{DT}(p)$, which is equal to the years the patient has already spent on dialysis;

3. *Donor profile index* $\mathrm{DPI}(o)$, which is a number between 0 and 1, indicating the quality of the donated organ (0 corresponds to an organ of highest quality);

4. *Calculated panel reactive antibody* $\mathrm{CPRA}(p)$, which is a number between 0 and 100, measuring the sensitization of the patient (0 corresponds to the lowest sensitization level).

The KTC considered more than 28 different scoring rules based on the above criteria, and utilized simulation to evaluate their performance and identify the appropriate weights. The dominant proposal up to this point entails the following formula for the Kidney Allocation Score:

$$\begin{aligned} \mathrm{KAS}(p, o) = \; & 0.8\,\mathrm{LYFT}(p, o) \times (1 - \mathrm{DPI}(o)) + 0.8\,\mathrm{DT}(p) \times \mathrm{DPI}(o) \\ & + 0.2\,\mathrm{DT}(p) + 0.04\,\mathrm{CPRA}(p). \end{aligned}$$

The rule is comprised of four components. The first two components are the life years from transplant and dialysis time, scaled by the donor profile index. The scaling ensures that in the case of a high quality organ (DPI close to 0), emphasis is given on life years from transplant, whereas in the case of a low quality organ (DPI close to 1), emphasis is given on dialysis time. The last two components are the dialysis time and calculated panel reactive antibody score of the patient.

As an example, consider two organs, G (for good) and B (for bad), with $\text{DPI}(G) = 0.25$ and $\text{DPI}(B) = 0.75$. Recall that DPI takes values between 0 and 1, with 0 corresponding to an organ of highest quality. There are two patients, a "healthier" patient H who has been waiting for 1 year, and a "sicker" patient S who has been waiting for 5 years. Therefore, $\text{DT}(H) = 1$ and $\text{DT}(S) = 5$, where DT is dialysis time. Suppose that the life benefit (LYFT) for the healthy patient is 8 years if assigned the good organ and 5 years if assigned the bad. Suppose that the life benefit for the sick patient is 2 years if assigned the good organ and 1 year if assigned the bad. That is, $\text{LYFT}(H, G) = 8$, $\text{LYFT}(\text{H}, \text{B}) = 5$, $\text{LYFT}(\text{S}, \text{G}) = 2$, and $\text{LYFT}(S, B) = 1$. Suppose also that both patients are 60% sensitized (i.e., they are incompatible with 60% of donors), and are both compatible with the organs we consider here. That is, $\text{CPRA}(H) = \text{CPRA}(S) = 60$.
We can now calculate the scores. Allocating the good organ to the healthier patient leads to a score of

$$0.8 \times 8 \times (1 - 0.25) + 0.8 \times 1 \times 0.25 + 0.2 \times 1 + 0.04 \times 60 = 7.6,$$

while allocating the good organ to the sicker patient leads to a score of

$$0.8 \times 2 \times (1 - 0.25) + 0.8 \times 5 \times 0.25 + 0.2 \times 5 + 0.04 \times 60 = 5.6.$$

Therefore, it is preferable to allocate the good organ to the healthier patient. Additionally, allocating the bad organ to the healthier patient leads to a score of

$$0.8 \times 5 \times (1 - 0.75) + 0.8 \times 1 \times 0.75 + 0.2 \times 1 + 0.04 \times 60 = 4.2,$$

while allocating the bad organ to the sicker patient leads to a score of

$$0.8 \times 1 \times (1 - 0.75) + 0.8 \times 5 \times 0.75 + 0.2 \times 5 + 0.04 \times 60 = 6.6.$$

Therefore, it is preferable to allocate the bad organ to the sicker patient. In other words, the KAS scoring rule directs the good organ to the patient that will live longer from it, and the bad organ to the patient who has been waiting a lot.

10.2 Designing Allocation Policies

In this section, we develop a method for designing scoring rule based policies for the allocation of deceased donor kidneys to patients. Specifically, we explain a data-driven method that computes, in a systematic way, score weights associated with pre-specified score components, so that the resulting policy achieves a near-optimal medical utility (measured by life years from transplant gains). In other words, after one has decided upon the components to include in a scoring rule, the method utilizes historical data to efficiently compute associated weights, so as to maximize the efficiency of the policy. In addition, the method can also take as input fairness constraints on the allocation outcomes. By doing this, the method captures a multitude of important and commonly studied constraints of interest to policymakers. Then, the method computes the score weights, so that the resulting policy is as efficient as possible, and the fairness constraints are approximately satisfied.

Typically, policymakers select the desired score components and constraints that the allocation outcomes need to satisfy. Given these selections, this method provides an efficient, scalable and systematic way of striking the right balance between the selected score components by designing a policy that approximately maximizes medical efficiency, subject to the selected constraints.

Methodology

Given a list of n score components, historical data of patients, donated organs' characteristics, and constraints on the allocation outcomes (precisely defined below), we calculate score weights $w_1, \ldots, w_n$, such that the resulting scoring rule policy satisfies the constraints approximately, while maximizing estimated life years from transplant.

Consider a fixed time period over which we have complete information about all patients registered on the waitlist (pre-existing and arriving) in that time period. In particular, we know their physiological characteristics, the time of their initial registration, as well as the evolution of their medical status and availability for a transplant during that time period. Suppose we also have complete information about the organs that are procured during the period, that is, the time at which they are procured and their physiological characteristics. We index the patients by $p = 1, \ldots, P$ and the organs by $o = 1, \ldots, O$. We say that patient p is *eligible* to receive organ o, or equivalently that the patient-organ pair (p, o) is eligible for transplantation, if at the time of the organ procurement all conditions below are met:

1. The patient is registered on the waitlist for a transplant;

2. The patient is actively waiting for a transplant and his medical status is appropriate for transplantation;

3. The patient is medically compatible with the organ.

Let $\mathcal{C}$ be the set of patient-organ pairs eligible for transplantation, i.e.,

$$\mathcal{C} = \{(p, o) : \text{ patient } p \text{ is eligible to receive organ } o\}.$$

Note that one can construct $\mathcal{C}$ simply by using the arrival information and characteristics of the organs and the patients, and the evolution of the availability and medical status of the patients.

We then compute the score components for each eligible patient-organ pair, as well as the estimated life years from transplant. Let $f_{j,(p,o)}$ be the value of the jth component score, $j = 1, \ldots, n$. For example, the first component might be the estimated life years from transplant LYFT(p, o), the second component might be the dialysis time DT(p), the third might be the donor profile index DPI(o) and the fourth might be the calculated panel reactive antibody CPRA(p).

We next construct an optimization model that will help us design an allocation policy using the following binary decision variables. Let $x_{(p,o)}$ be defined for every eligible patient-organ pair (p, o) as

$$x_{(p,o)} = \begin{cases} 1, & \text{if organ } o \text{ is assigned to patient } p, \\ 0, & \text{otherwise.} \end{cases}$$

We next define the constraints on the allocation outcomes. We will only use constraints that are linear in the decision variables x. The class of constraints that can be modeled in this way is very broad, and captures the majority of constraints a social planner might wish to incorporate; for instance, one can impose lower bounds for a specific group of patients on:

- the probability of receiving a transplant,
- the average expected life years from transplant gained among the actual transplant recipients,
- the average time spent on dialysis among the actual transplant recipients.

As an example, consider a group of four patients $\{p_1, p_2, p_3, p_4\}$ with a particular characteristic (for instance patients of blood type O) and a set of three organs $\{o_1, o_2, o_3\}$, such that patient p_1 is eligible to receive organs o_1 and o_2, patient p_2 is eligible to receive organs o_1 and o_3, patient p_3 is eligible to receive all organs o_1, o_2, o_3 and patient p_4 is only eligible to receive organ o_2. The constraint that at least two organs should be allocated to this group of patients can be written as:

$$x_{(p_1,o_1)} + x_{(p_1,o_2)} + x_{(p_2,o_1)} + x_{(p_2,o_3)} + x_{(p_3,o_1)} + x_{(p_3,o_2)} + x_{(p_3,o_3)} + x_{(p_4,o_2)} \geq 2.$$

More generally, given a group of patients $\mathcal{G}$ and a set of available organs, the requirement that at least L organs should be allocated to a group of patients $\mathcal{G}$ can be expressed as

$$\sum_{p \in \mathcal{G}} \sum_{o:(p,o) \in \mathcal{C}} x_{(p,o)} \geq L.$$

This constraint means that among all eligible allocations of patients to organs, there should be at least L organs that are allocated to group $\mathcal{G}$. By adding a constraint for each group $\mathcal{G}$, we obtain a set of constraints that we call "fairness" constraints.

We now present the proposed method. Consider a social planner with foresight who has knowledge of the set of all eligible pairs $\mathcal{C}$ and the life years from transplant score for every pair in the set. Suppose also that patients accept all organs offered to them. In this setup, the problem of allocating organs to patients so as to maximize medical efficiency, i.e., life years from transplant, subject to the fairness constraints we described, can be formulated as a linear optimization problem:

$$
\begin{aligned}
\text{maximize} \quad & \sum_{(p,o)\in\mathcal{C}} \text{LYFT}(p,o)x_{(p,o)} \\
\text{subject to} \quad & \sum_{o:(p,o)\in\mathcal{C}} x_{(p,o)} \leq 1, \quad \text{for each patient } p \\
& \sum_{p:(p,o)\in\mathcal{C}} x_{(p,o)} \leq 1, \quad \text{for each organ } o \\
& \sum_{p\in\mathcal{G}} \sum_{o:(p,o)\in\mathcal{C}} x_{(p,o)} \geq L_{\mathcal{G}}, \quad \text{for each group } \mathcal{G} \text{ and bound } L \\
& 0 \leq x_{(p,o)} \leq 1.
\end{aligned}
$$

In this optimization model, we maximize the expected life years from transplant. The first set of constraints means that each patient is allocated to at most one organ. The second set of constraints means that each organ is offered to at most one patient. The last set of constraints means that every group of patients we have selected receives at least $L_{\mathcal{G}}$ eligible organs (the fairness constraints). Note that instead of imposing the requirement that the variables $x_{(p,o)}$ are binary, we require that they take values between 0 and 1 with the interpretation that $x_{(p,o)}$ is the probability of assigning organ o to patient p in a randomized policy.

For every fairness constraint corresponding to a group $\mathcal{G}$ in the linear optimization model, there is an associated shadow price that we denote by $y_{\mathcal{G}}$. See Chapter 21 for more information about shadow prices. If we increase $x_{(p,o)}$ by θ, we increase the objective function value by $\theta \times \text{LYFT}(p,o)$, but we decrease the required organs for group $\mathcal{G}$ by θ, and thus the objective function decreases by $\theta \times y_{\mathcal{G}}$. Thus, the contribution to the objective function value associated with a unit increase ($\theta = 1$) of $x_{(p,o)}$ is

$$
c_{(p,o)} = \text{LYFT}(p,o) - \sum_{\mathcal{G}:\ p\in\mathcal{G}} y_{\mathcal{G}},
$$

that is, we subtract from the benefit $\text{LYFT}(p,o)$ all the shadow prices associated with all groups patient p belongs to.

Our goal is to construct a scoring mechanism for allocating organ o to patient p based on the factors $f_{1,(p,o)}, \ldots, f_{n,(p,o)}$. In other words, we seek to find weights $w_1, \ldots, w_n$ corresponding to the factors $f_{1,(p,o)}, \ldots, f_{n,(p,o)}$, so that

$$
c_{(p,o)} \approx w_0 + w_1 f_{1,(p,o)} + \ldots + w_n f_{n,(p,o)}.
$$

This would ensure that the score of allocating organ o to patient p is approximately the sum of the weights times the corresponding factors.

Having solved the linear optimization model, we can calculate the scores

$$c_{(p,o)} = \text{LYFT}(p,o) - \sum_{\mathcal{G}:\ p\in\mathcal{G}} y_{\mathcal{G}}.$$

In order to find how to weigh the various factors, we can use linear regression to find weights $w_0, w_1, \ldots, w_n$ such that for every eligible patient-organ pair

$$c_{(p,o)} \approx w_0 + w_1 f_{1,(p,o)} + \ldots + w_n f_{n,(p,o)}.$$

See Chapter 21 for more about linear regression.

Overall, the method can be summarized as follows:

Input: List of n score components, data for the fairness constraints associated with all groups $\mathcal{G}$, set of eligible patient-organ pairs $\mathcal{C}$, life years from transplant LYFT(p,o) and values of score components, $f_{1,(p,o)}, \ldots, f_{n,(p,o)}$ for every eligible pair (p,o).

Output: Weights for the scoring rule, $w_1, \ldots, w_n$.

Algorithm:

1. Solve the linear optimization problem.

2. Compute the shadow prices associated with every group $\mathcal{G}$.

3. Calculate the benefit of allocating organ o to patient p that takes into account the shadow prices:

$$c_{(p,o)} = \text{LYFT}(p,o) - \sum_{\mathcal{G}:\ p\in\mathcal{G}} y_{\mathcal{G}}, \quad \text{for all } (p,o) \in \mathcal{C}.$$

4. Use linear regression to find $w_0, w_1, \ldots, w_n$, such that for all $(p,o) \in \mathcal{C}$

$$c_{(p,o)} \approx w_0 + w_1 f_{1,(p,o)} + \ldots + w_n f_{n,(p,o)}.$$

In the next section, we provide numerical evidence of the strength of the policy derived in this way.

10.3 Numerical Evidence and the Design of a New Allocation Policy

We utilize the method described in the previous section to design a new scoring rule based allocation policy. We compare its results with those of the benchmark method, which is the dominant proposal of the OPTN Kidney Transplantation Committee (referred to also as the KTC policy), presented in the Request for Information document in 2008. Our new policy uses the same criteria and achieves an 8% increase in life years from transplant, while exhibiting similar fairness properties. To ensure a fair comparison, we evaluate the performance of the policies by using the same statistical models and tools, as well as the same datasets used by the OPTN KTC policymakers. We first provide details about the data and models, and then present the methodology and results.

Data, Statistical Models and Tools

This work uses highly detailed historical data from the Scientific Registry of Transplant Recipients (SRTR). The SRTR data system includes data on all donors, wait-listed candidates, and transplant recipients in the United States, submitted by the members of OPTN. The datasets include all the various physiological and demographic characteristics of wait-listed patients and donors that are needed for our study, as well as the evolution of the medical status of the patients, and the arrival process of the donated organs.

In addition, the SRTR has developed sophisticated survivability models for end-stage renal disease patients using historical survival rates. The models provide an estimate for the anticipated lifespan of a patient in case he remained on dialysis, or in case he received a particular kidney, based on a plethora of physiological attributes (the patient's age, body mass index, diagnosis, as well as tissue matching, the donor's age, cause of death, etc.). The SRTR has also developed an acceptance model that predicts the probability of a particular patient accepting a particular organ offered to him, based on the physiological characteristics of the patient and the donor, the distance, etc.

The above datasets and statistical models have also been utilized by the SRTR in the development of an event-driven simulator that simulates the entire allocation process using historical data, for different allocation policies. It was developed in order to support studies of alternative policies. The simulator is the platform that the OPTN KTC is utilizing to evaluate the performance of their proposed policies. The simulator has been extensively tested and is widely considered as very accurate. It outputs the expected life years from transplant and the race, age, dialysis time, blood type, diagnosis type and sensitization type distributions for recipients. For the purposes of this study, we obtained the simulator and utilized its simulation engine in order to obtain realistic allocation outcomes of the policies we consider. The life years from transplant gains are estimated using the aforementioned survivability models, embedded in the simulator.

Methodology

Using the simulator, we simulate the KTC policy for the 2008 dataset. We record the number of transplantations occurring and the net life years from transplant. To explore the fairness properties of the policy, we record the percentage distribution of transplant recipients across different races, age groups, blood types, sensitization groups, as well as diagnosis types, years spent on dialysis and geographical regions. Note that this practice is in line with the comparison criteria studied by the OPTN policymakers.

To design a new policy based on the algorithm described in Section 10.2, we use the following as input:

- Historical data: We use the first 6 months of data of the 2008 dataset as input to our method (training data). The data pertaining to the remaining 6 months is used to evaluate performance.

- Score components: We use the estimated life years from transplant (LYFT), dialysis time (DT)[4] and calculated panel reactive antibody (CPRA) as the score components. Note that the components are based on exactly the same criteria as in the KTC policy[5]. In summary, the scoring rule rewards the patient with w_1 points per life year from transplant gained, w_2 points per year on dialysis for the first 5 years, w_3 points per year on dialysis for years 5-10, w_4 points per year on dialysis beyond the 10th year, and w_5 points per percentage point of CPRA.

- Fairness constraints: To ensure that the fairness properties are similar to the KTC policy, we use the recorded percentage distributions for the KTC policy as input constraints. We use lower bound constraints on the percentage of organs allocated to the following groups: Caucasian, African-American, Hispanic, or patients of another race; patients aged between 18-34, 34-49, 49-64, or above 64 years; patients who have spent less than 5 years, 5-10 years, 10-15 years, or more than 15 years on dialysis; blood type O, A, B, or AB patients; patients diagnosed with nephritis, hypertension, polycystic kidney disease, diabetes, or another disease; patients with a sensitization level (CPRA) of 0-10, 10-80, or 80-100; and patients registered at each of the 11 distinct geographical regions[6] in the U.S. in which UNOS operates. For instance, consider the fairness constraints pertaining to dialysis time. The recorded percentage distribution of recipients for the KTC policy is as follows: 55.4% of the recipients have spent less than 5 years on dialysis, 28.8% between 5-10 years, 10.2% between 10-15 years and 5.6% more than 15 years. The constraints we add then as input to our method are:

$$\sum_{p:\,0\leq \mathrm{DT}(p)\leq 5}\ \sum_{o:(p,o)\in\mathcal{C}} x_{(p,o)} \geq \frac{55.4}{100}\sum_{(p,o)\in\mathcal{C}} x_{(p,o)},$$
$$\sum_{p:\,5\leq \mathrm{DT}(p)\leq 10}\ \sum_{o:(p,o)\in\mathcal{C}} x_{(p,o)} \geq \frac{28.8}{100}\sum_{(p,o)\in\mathcal{C}} x_{(p,o)},$$
$$\sum_{p:\,10\leq \mathrm{DT}(p)\leq 15}\ \sum_{o:(p,o)\in\mathcal{C}} x_{(p,o)} \geq \frac{10.2}{100}\sum_{(p,o)\in\mathcal{C}} x_{(p,o)},$$
$$\sum_{p:\,\mathrm{DT}(p)\geq 15}\ \sum_{o:(p,o)\in\mathcal{C}} x_{(p,o)} \geq \frac{5.6}{100}\sum_{(p,o)\in\mathcal{C}} x_{(p,o)}.$$

[4]Our scoring rule is piece-wise linear in this component.

[5]The Donor Profile Index (DPI) component proves superfluous.

[6]For its own operational purposes, UNOS has divided the U.S. into 11 distinct geographical regions. Region 1 for instance includes all the states in New England. For more information, see http://www.unos.org/docs/Article_IX.pdf.

To evaluate the performance of the method, we use the simulator to simulate the output policy for the 6 months of 2008 that were not used as input. We record the number of transplantations occurring and the net life years from transplant. To compare the fairness properties of the policy, we also record the same percentage distributions of transplant recipients as for the KTC policy.

Results

The output of the method is the scoring rule assigning the Kidney Allocation Score to a patient-organ pair (p, o) of

$$\mathrm{KAS}(p, o) = \mathrm{LYFT}(p, o) + g\,(\mathrm{DT}(p)) + 0.12\,\mathrm{CPRA}(p),$$

where

$$g\,(\mathrm{DT}) = \begin{cases} 0.55\,\mathrm{DT}, & 0 \leq \mathrm{DT} \leq 5, \\ 2.75 + \mathrm{DT}, & 5 \leq \mathrm{DT} \leq 10, \\ 7.75 + 0.25\,\mathrm{DT}, & 10 \leq \mathrm{DT}. \end{cases}$$

According to the above scoring rule, patients are awarded 1 point for every life year from transplant gain, 0.12 points per point of their sensitization score and points based on their dialysis time as follows: 0.55 points for the first 5 years, 1 point for every additional year up to 10 years and 0.25 points for every additional year beyond that. The simulation results are presented in Table 10.1.

Compared to the KTC proposed policy, the one designed by the proposed method delivers an almost identical performance in terms of percentage distributions of transplant recipients, but results in an important 8.2% increase in life years from transplant. Both policies appear to have the same performance in number of transplantations. Figure 10.1 illustrates the distribution of recipients under the two policies across the 11 distinct geographical regions that UNOS has divided the U.S. into. Again, in comparison with the KTC policy, the designed policy has an almost identical performance in terms of percentage distributions of transplant recipients across all regions.

10.4 The Power of Analytics

In this section, we summarize the essential characteristics of the method and comment on the edge of the the analytics-based approach we presented in this section.

1. The proposed method uses detailed historical medical data to extract near optimal score weights in an efficient manner. In particular, the method is highly scalable and can learn the parameters from potentially highly detailed and complicated historical datasets, with no need for clustering or grouping of patients' and/or organs' characteristics.

2. The method offers flexibility and allows policymakers to focus only on identifying score components and desired fairness properties of

Table 10.1: Simulation results of the KTC policy and the policy designed in Section 10.3, for an out-of-sample period of 6 months in 2008.

	KTC Policy	Designed Policy
Transplantations and Efficiency		
Number of transplantations	5,746	5,796
Net life years from transplant	34,290	37,092
Average life years from transplant	5.95	6.4
Racial Distribution		
Caucasian	41.8%	43.5%
African-American	35.7%	33.3%
Hispanic	13.9%	14.5%
Other	8.6%	8.7%
Age Distribution		
18-34 years	5%	4.2%
34-49 years	26.4%	24.8%
49-64 years	50.6%	52.8%
64+ years	18%	18.2%
Dialysis Time Distribution		
0-5 years	55.4%	56%
5-10 years	28.8%	28%
10-15 years	10.2%	10.1%
15+ years	5.6%	5.9%
Blood Type Distribution		
O	47.9%	47.7%
A	37.9%	37.6%
B	11.7%	12%
AB	2.5%	2.7%
Diagnosis Type Distribution		
Nephritis	19.5%	18.9%
Hypertension	21.6%	19.2%
Polycystic	9.9%	11.8%
Other	23%	25%
Diabetes	26%	25.1%
Sensitization Level Distribution		
CPRA 0-10	55.4%	54.9%
CPRA 10-80	24.7%	24.9%
CPRA 80+	19.9%	20.2%

Figure 10.1: Simulated percentage distribution of transplant recipients across the 11 distinct geographical regions that UNOS has divided the U.S. into, under the KTC policy (white) and the policy designed in Section 10.3 (blue), for an out-of-sample period of 6 months in 2008.

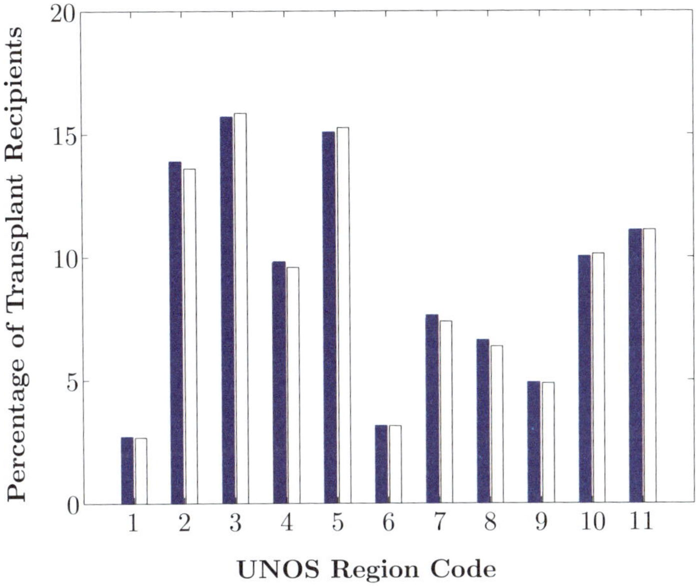

allocation outcomes in the design of a new policy. The method undertakes the more involved part of finding appropriate weights and balancing score components. Although medical intuition can help in making educated guesses for the weights, there is little guarantee that a policy designed in such way would yield the desired results. Furthermore, even if a set of weights yields a policy with the desired outcomes, there can be another policy delivering a superior performance. Due to the computational intensity of simulations, one simply cannot explore all possible combinations of weights. The proposed method uses analytical tools to automatically extract near-optimal weights from historical data.

3. While the proposed method is in the context of kidney allocation, the same procedure can be generalized in a straightforward manner for other organs as well. Thus, the methodology is applicable for any organ allocation policy one wishes to design based on scoring rules.

4. The current OPTN kidney allocation policy fails to keep up with

advances in medicine and the changes in patients' needs over time. In such a dynamic and complex environment, revisions to policies are likely to be required in the future as well, a fact that is also recognized by the OPTN Final Rule. Furthermore, even in the current process of developing a new policy, there is no guarantee that the Office of Civil Rights will approve the criteria of life years from transplant, dialysis time, etc., suggested by the OPTN policymakers. In both cases, the proposed method will expedite the development of a new policy, as it would require only an updated list of score components and fairness properties to be specified.

5. The method allows for sensitivity analysis; specifically, one can efficiently evaluate the outcomes of relaxing some or introducing new fairness constraints. In the previous section, we provided such an analysis that reveals the dependence of medical efficiency on fairness concepts, and illustrated how it can be used in practice by policymakers. In particular, note that one of the main goals that the OPTN policymakers have set for a new national policy is to deemphasize the role of waiting time and increase medical efficiency.

Overall the analytics edge of the proposed approach is that it uses detailed historical data, works within the policymakers' suggestions, provides a general method for all organ allocations and can easily be updated, adjusted and re-run.

10.5 Notes and Sources

The material in this chapter comes from Bertsimas, Farias, and Trichakis [20].

10.1. Information about kindey transplantation and maintenance dialysis can be found in the U.S. Renal Data System Annual Data Report [146] and on the UNOS website [145]. The references [136], [124], [114], and [107] have statistically demonstrated that transplantation reduces the mortality risk for patients.

The current national kidney allocation policy is described in [106]. For a precise definition of life years from transplant (LYFT) we refer the reader to Wolfe et al. [153].

10.2. A discussion of some of the main challenges in designing a kidney allocation policy can be found in UNOS reports [108, 109, 115] and an update on the new kidney transplant allocation system [105]. The requirements for a national kidney allocation policy are included in the OPTN Final Rule [42].

Part IV

The Internet

Chapter 11

The Heart of Google's Search Engine

I think Google should be like a Swiss Army knife: clean, simple, the tool you want to take everywhere.

– Marissa Mayer

Contents

In 1996, Sergei Brin and Larry Page, two graduate students in the computer science department at Stanford University, started a research project that would revolutionize the internet. They were developing an algorithm that used properties of the internet to measure the importance of any webpage. Observing that this algorithm would make a better search engine than those currently in use, they started the search engine Google. (The name was selected as a play on googol, the word for the number 10^{100}.) Brin and Page initially used their dorm rooms and a friend's garage for their new business. When it started to take off, they took a leave of absence from Stanford, and by the end of 1998, Google had a database of about 60 million webpages and was already being recognized for returning extremely relevant results.

This chapter tells the story of Google and PageRank, the algorithm that has been fundamental to the development and success of Google. This algorithm remains one of the key tools that Google uses to determine which webpages are ranked at the top of the list of search results. The use of analytics provided Google with a significant edge over other companies. Google returns such relevant search results that "google" is now commonly used in place of the word "search" when it comes to the internet. In fact, the word google has become so pervasive in the English language that it has even entered the Oxford dictionary!

11.1 The Growth of Google

Google grew out of an interesting observation by Sergei Brin and Larry Page: the internet is a gigantic network of webpages connected with hyperlinks, links on webpages that readers can directly follow to other webpages. Using these hyperlinks, the internet can be viewed as a graph, a common mathematical structure that illustrates the relationship between several entities (vertices) by showing the various connections between them (arcs). With this observation, Brin and Page set out to explore the properties of the internet from a mathematical perspective.

Given a certain search string, they developed an algorithm that could return results that not only measured the number of times the search string appeared on a page, but also the importance of each page. It was this algorithm, which they called PageRank, that inspired Brin and Page to start Google as a new type of search engine. While many other search engines only ranked results based on the number of times a search string appeared on the webpage, Google was designed to also use the PageRank algorithm to show the most reliable and important results first.

This idea clearly intrigued many investors as well. The first funding for Google was $100,000, given in 1998 by Andy Bechtolsheim, a co-founder of Sun Microsystems. By 1999, a $25 million round of funding was announced. Five years later, Google's initial public offering (IPO) took place, when they offered 19,605,052 shares for $85 per share.

In 2001, Eric Schmidt, former CEO of Novell, became the CEO of Google. Since then, Google has acquired many companies, mainly small technology

Table 11.1: Financial growth of Google.

Year	Revenue (millions)	Net Income (millions)
2002	440	100
2003	1,466	106
2004	3,189	399
2005	6,138	1,465
2006	10,604	3,078
2007	16,593	4,204
2008	21,795	4,227
2009	23,651	6,521
2010	29,321	8,505
2011	37,905	9,737
2012	46,039	10,737
2013	55,519	12,920
2014	66,001	14,444

companies. Many of these companies have turned into Google applications, including Google Earth and Google Voice. Google also acquired the popular online video site YouTube in 2007. Along the way, Google has partnered with many other companies on various projects, including NASA, Sun Microsystems, NBC, and Amazon.

Presently, Google is the most widely used search engine in the United States. It is estimated that Google indexes trillions of webpages and receives over one billion search queries each day. Additionally, Google has consistently ranked highly as one of the best places to work, attributed to their informal corporate culture.

Since the use of a search engine is free and unlimited for any consumer with internet access, search engine companies must use various ways to make money. Some search engines charge webpages a fee to index their webpage faster. Most search engines sell user data to various companies, such as popular query words or types of searches. They can also sell their searching capabilities to other webpages. But the most common and profitable source of income is online advertising, of which Google is a key player. We discuss online advertising more in Chapter 12.

In 2000, Google started selling advertisements associated with search keywords. This allowed Google to not only gain respect as a search engine, but generate revenue as well. The vast majority of Google's revenue is derived from its advertising programs. Table 11.1 lists the revenue and net income of Google from 2002 to 2014, and Figure 11.1 graphs the annual revenue.

At the beginning of 1999, Google had 8 employees. By 2004, Google had over 2,000 employees, and it has been growing ever since. The company now

Figure 11.1: Financial growth of Google, in terms of annual revenue.

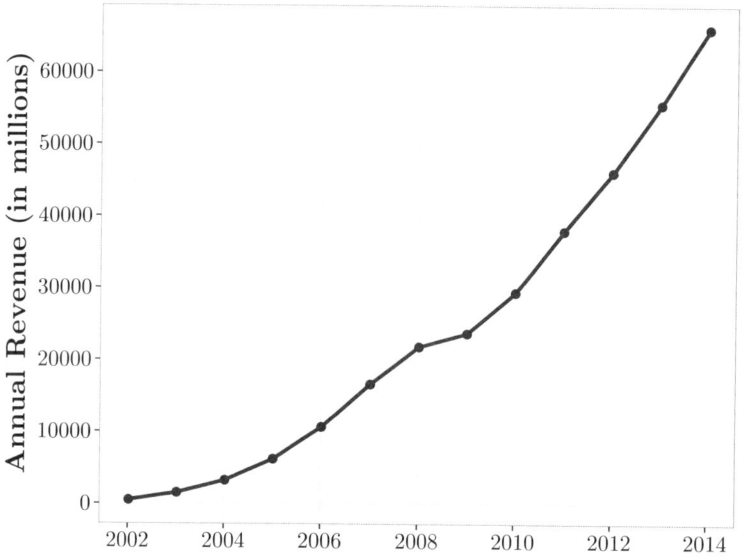

has over 50,000 employees worldwide, and the two founders of Google continue to play active roles in the company.

11.2 The PageRank Algorithm

A web search for a particular topic can easily result in hundreds of thousands, or even millions, of pages. The results are typically provided to users in the form of websites and summaries. Since it would be impractical for the user to search through all of these webpages to find what they are looking for, the results are typically shown ten to a page. How does Google select the pages that the user will consider the most relevant?

This question was not new, and many other companies were trying to sufficiently address it before Google entered the scene. LexisNexis is a company that pioneered information search. Lexis was for legal references, and Nexis was for news articles. These two offerings had very different goals. Lexis was expected to be comprehensive; lawyers using the site wanted to be aware of all relevant cases, so they were not surprised in court. Nexis, on the other hand, wanted to be efficient and not provide multiple references to nearly identical items. LexisNexis is still a widely used search engine today, but Google was able to rapidly produce relevant search results with a new type of algorithm.

Google has a patented algorithm called PageRank which they use to rank webpages that match a given search string. The algorithm analyzes human-generated links, with the reasoning that webpages linking from many important pages are likely to also be important. In this sense, a hyperlink is viewed as a recommendation or an endorsement of the webpage. However, a good recommendation has two qualities: the recommender is both popular and respected simultaneously, and he or she is not very generous in giving out recommendations. For example, an endorsement from Warren Buffett probably does more to strengthen a job application than 20 endorsements from 20 unknown teachers and colleagues. However, if the interviewer knows that Warren Buffett is very generous with his praise and has written 20,000 recommendations, then the endorsement drops in weight. In the context of webpages, if there is a link to your webpage from a very popular site that does not have very many links on it, that is a heavily weighted endorsement. Given the hyperlinks, each webpage is given a score based on the weighted sum of the PageRanks of the pages linking to it.

The Google search engine is so popular that people now hire consultants with knowledge of PageRank to help them increase the rank of their webpages. (This practice of changing a website to increase search visibility is called *search engine optimization, or SEO.*) There are many papers and books written on the details of the PageRank algorithm, and the algorithm has been applied to a wide range of applications.

Google also uses other confidential criteria to improve the quality of search results, but PageRank is the main idea behind the creation of Google. According to the Google website, "the heart of Google's software is PageRank . . . which continues to provide the basis for all of our web search tools."

The Web as a Directed Graph

A *directed graph* is a mathematical representation of any set of objects that are connected by one-way links. The objects are called vertices (which are usually represented by numbered circles), and the links are called arcs (which are usually represented as arrows connecting the objects). The direction of the arcs, or the way in which the arcs are pointing, shows the direction of the connection. (Keep in mind that two vertices can potentially have two arcs between them, each arc pointing from one vertex to the other.)

The PageRank system views the web as a massive directed graph: the webpages are vertices, and the hyperlinks are arcs that connect the webpages. As an example, an arc from Wikipedia to YouTube means that Wikipedia has a link to YouTube, so Wikipedia is said to "endorse" YouTube. Figure 11.2 is an example showing a six page network. In comparison to the actual web, which has a very complicated structure with billions of vertices and arcs, this example gives a very clean and clear graph. To relate this figure to the actual internet network, say page 4 is your personal blog. If you write an entry about the MIT Sloan School of Management, page 5 could be the MIT homepage, and

Figure 11.2: An example network with six vertices, representing six webpages.

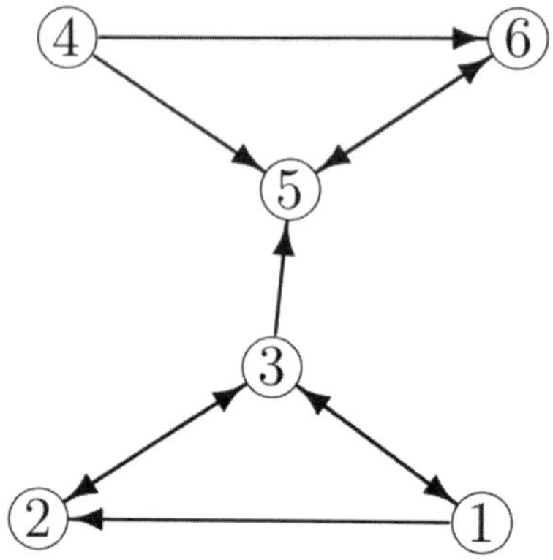

page 6 could be the MIT Sloan School of Management homepage. However, neither of these webpages links back to your blog, so these are one way links. Pages 5 and 6 also link to each other, so there is a two-way link between these pages. Continuing in this way, each numbered vertex can represent a particular webpage.

The Mathematics of PageRank

Consider the network in Figure 11.2. To assess the popularity of a webpage, we could try the following approach. Each time we arrive at a webpage, we randomly click on one of the hyperlinks on that webpage, where each hyperlink has equal probability of being selected. Furthermore, we are equally likely to follow any link, so the hyperlinks all have the same probability of being chosen. Looking at Figure 11.2, if we are at page 3, we can click on a link to page 1, page 2, or page 5. But if we are at page 5, there is only a link to page 6.

So that we do not get stuck in this process, if we ever arrive at a page that has no hyperlinks, we randomly go to any page in the network. To make the process fair, we add this option to every webpage. Thus, a web surfer is more likely to follow a hyperlink if one is present, but there is a small probability that they will go to any page in the network. (Think of this as the surfer getting bored and abandoning their web surfing by going to a random page.) So if we are at page 5, there is a small probability of going to any of the other webpages, and a much larger probability of going to page 6 (the only link on page 5). We will use the standard probabilities historically used by Google: a hyperlink is used with probability 0.85, and a new page is randomly chosen with probability

0.15. Thus, about 85% of the time a link is followed, and about 15% of the time the links are ignored and a different page is randomly selected in the network.

Viewing the network in this way, the PageRank of a webpage is defined as the probability of being at that page after a large number of clicks. As an example, a PageRank of 0.5 for Wikipedia means that there is a 50% chance that you will be at Wikipedia at any moment in time after you have been surfing the web for a while. The PageRanks can be computed with an iterative procedure, where each webpage starts with the same PageRank. Note that while the PageRanks reported by Google are rescaled to be 1-10 (using a logarithmic rescaling), we will use numbers 0-1 (the probabilities) for simplification. We will show part of the iterative computation for our example in Figure 11.2. Note that although we will not present it in full generality here, it can be extended to any size graph.

At the first iteration, we can set all of the PageRanks to 1/6 for the pages in Figure 11.2, since they need to sum to 1 (you must be somewhere), and we have 6 pages. (Any starting point can be selected for the PageRank values, but this is a natural choice when no prior knowledge exists about the PageRanks.) We will start by computing the PageRank for page 1 at the first iteration. We need to account for randomly selecting a new page in the network and for using a hyperlink. If we randomly select a new page (this happens with probability 0.15), page 1 is selected with probability 1/6, since each page is selected with equal probability. Thus, the probability that we select page 1 when randomly selecting a new page is $0.15 \times (1/6)$. According to the graph, the only way that page 1 can be selected using a hyperlink (which happens with probability 0.85) is if you are at page 3. But since page 3 has three hyperlinks on it (to pages 1, 2, and 5), we only give page 1 a third of the PageRank of page 3. Therefore, we add $0.85 \times (1/3) \times (1/6)$ to the PageRank for page 1. So the computation of the PageRank for page 1, denoted $r(P_1)$, is

$$r(P_1) = 0.15 \times \left(\frac{1}{6}\right) + 0.85 \times \left(\frac{1}{6} \times \frac{1}{3}\right) = 0.0722.$$

Similarly, we can compute the PageRank of page 5 at iteration 1. The first term is the same as that for page 1. For the second term, we now have 3 pages with hyperlinks to page 5. Page 3 links to page 5, but it has 3 hyperlinks on it, so we get one third of the PageRank of page 3. Page 6 links to page 5 and has no other hyperlinks, so we get all of the PageRank of page 6. And page 4 links to page 5, but has two links on it, so we get one half of the PageRank of page 4. Thus, the PageRank for page 5 at iteration 1 is

$$r(P_5) = 0.15 \times \left(\frac{1}{6}\right) + 0.85 \times \left[\left(\frac{1}{6} \times \frac{1}{3}\right) + \left(\frac{1}{6} \times 1\right) + \left(\frac{1}{6} \times \frac{1}{2}\right)\right] = 0.2847.$$

After we compute the PageRank for each page for the first iteration, we can use these new values to repeat the process for the second iteration. We will not go through the computation for each one, but the values for some of the iterations are displayed in Table 11.2. One of the properties of the PageRank algorithm with random re-starts (randomly selecting a new page) is that the PageRanks will eventually stabilize, for all graphs. So if the iterative process is repeated enough times, the PageRanks will no longer change, and a steady state will be reached. Furthermore, this is true regardless of the starting point. So starting from any initial PageRank values that sum to 1, the same solution will eventually be reached. Table 11.3 shows the iterative process with a different starting point (different values for Iteration 0).

Note that while the final solution has not yet been reached at iteration 10 for either starting solution, the pages are ranked in the correct order as early as iteration 2 (if ordered in terms of $r(P)$). This is not always the case, but typically relatively few iterations are needed to reach the final ranking, and many advanced methods have been proposed to speed up the process. The final column in Tables 11.2 and 11.3 is the solution.

From this computation, we can make several observations to gain some intuition about the algorithm. First, we note that the PageRank of page 4 immediately goes to 0.0250 and then does not change. This is because page 4 has no hyperlinks to it. No webpage "endorses" page 4, and thus the only way to reach page 4 is by randomly picking it at any page, which happens with this small probability. Additionally, we observe that the pages with the highest PageRanks are page 5 and page 6. If we look at Figure 11.2, we can see that page 5 has the most endorsements, and page 6 is endorsed by page 5. Hence, we can expect page 5 to be ranked higher than page 6.

Finally, note that the values at iteration 10 are not too far off from the solution. This tells us that after a relatively small number of iterations, we are fairly close to the solution.

Instead of running the iterative procedure, more advanced mathematical techniques can be used to solve for the PageRank values. For more information about the mathematics of PageRank, we refer you to the sources in Section 11.5.

Table 11.2: The PageRank values $r(P)$ for Figure 11.2, shown at iterations 0, 1, 2, 10, and the final solution.

Page	Iter. 0	Iter. 1	Iter. 2	Iter. 10	Solution
P_1	0.1667	0.0722	0.0923	0.0614	0.0598
P_2	0.1667	0.1431	0.1230	0.0878	0.0852
P_3	0.1667	0.2375	0.1773	0.1269	0.1229
P_4	0.1667	0.0250	0.0250	0.0250	0.0250
P_5	0.1667	0.2847	0.3048	0.3592	0.3629
P_6	0.1667	0.2375	0.2776	0.3396	0.3441

Table 11.3: The PageRank values $r(P)$ for Figure 11.2, computed from a different starting point (Iteration 0 values) than in Table 11.2.

Page	Iter. 0	Iter. 1	Iter. 2	Iter. 10	Solution
P_1	0.1	0.0817	0.0923	0.0613	0.0598
P_2	0.2	0.1242	0.1270	0.0877	0.0852
P_3	0.2	0.2375	0.1653	0.1267	0.1229
P_4	0.0	0.0250	0.0250	0.0250	0.0250
P_5	0.3	0.2517	0.3409	0.3692	0.3629
P_6	0.2	0.2800	0.2495	0.3300	0.3441

11.3 Applications of the PageRank Algorithm

The PageRank algorithm is not exclusive to the internet - it can be applied to any collection of entities with reciprocal quotations and references. In this section, we first give an example of how the PageRank algorithm can be used to rank graduate programs. Then, we discuss how the PageRank algorithm could be used in another area, and provide some thought exercises for the reader to dive deeper into the topic.

In addition to these applications, the PageRank algorithm has been used in biology to analyze genes, in sports to rank teams and players, and in literature to rank novels. It is also used in general network analysis to give a measure of importance to a node, regardless of the application considered.

Ranking Graduate Programs

One example uses the PageRank algorithm to rank political science graduate programs by placement of students after graduation into academic positions. Traditionally, the most influential ranking systems for graduate programs have used surveys given to prominent members in the field asking them to rank all programs. However, such a system is flawed for multiple reasons: there is a bias towards large schools with a large number of faculty, great programs at small schools might be overlooked, and rankers are asked to evaluate programs with which they may have no prior experience.

A PageRank-based algorithm could focus on a graduate programs' history of placing graduates into faculty positions. This may be a superior method, since it measures both the quality of the students and the value that the program adds to the students. Additionally, since well over half of political science graduates are seeking academic positions, it is applicable to most students.

In this example, the vertices of the graph are colleges, and the arcs show the paths of graduates to tenure-track positions. For example, an arc would point from Stanford to MIT if at least one graduate of Stanford holds a tenure-track position at MIT. Now instead of making each arc equivalent, we could weight each arc by the number of graduates that followed the arc. Thus, if more graduates from Stanford go to MIT than Harvard, it will be more likely that we take the arc from Stanford to MIT instead of the arc from Stanford to Harvard.

Furthermore, in this situation, we have something similar to randomly picking any webpage. Here, we want to make sure that any program that has placed at least one graduate has a higher PageRank than a program that does not have a placement record at all. Thus, any program that is participating in the network has a ranking larger than 0.

Using this method, the values can also be normalized to eliminate the bias given to the larger schools. This is called the weighted ranking, since we are weighting each school based on the number of graduates it produces. Normalization allows smaller schools with smaller programs to compete with the larger schools who naturally have more graduates.

A New Election Process

Suppose that the members of the executive board of an American public corporation were facing the daunting task of electing a new CEO after the resignation of their current CEO. A reasonable first step would be for the executive board members to conduct a preliminary vote for internal candidates. Votes would be collected from all of the members, with the assumption that each would vote for at least one and no more than five members (not including themselves).

Given this data, what is the best strategy to rank the board members? Although the new CEO should not necessarily be the highest ranking member, a small group of high ranking people could become candidates for the position. Google's PageRank algorithm could be a good solution to rank the candidates. The votes could be viewed as a directed graph, in which a vote from board member A for board member B would point from A to B.

To analyze this situation in more detail, resources have been provided in the Online Companion of this book (www.dynamic-ideas.com/analytics-edge). After understanding the available materials, consider the following questions:

- Just looking at the voting graph and/or the list of votes, can you make any intuitive guesses about the rankings? Who would you expect to be ranked the highest? Why?

- Compute the PageRanks for this graph. How do the PageRanks compare with your intuitive guess? How do they compare with a simple ranking system of ranking people by the number of votes they received?

- Who would you recommend as candidates for CEO?

- Suppose that you are one of the board members, and you know ahead of time that the PageRank algorithm will be used. Assuming that none of the other board members have this knowledge, how could you manipulate the system? What are the best actions to increase your PageRank?

- Now suppose that other board members also have knowledge of the system, and that they are also trying to raise their PageRanks. What would you do now to increase your PageRank? How would your behavior change?

- How would you present the use of this ranking to the board, in a concise and intuitive way?

This example illustrates that even in a small graph, the PageRank computation can be sophisticated. However, its use can add a significant edge to many different applications.

11.4 The Edge of Simplicity

The simplicity, generality, and accuracy of the PageRank algorithm are a few of the key reasons why it has not only given Google an edge over the competition, but why it is now used in a variety of applications. When Google started in the late 1990s, it was not the only search engine that existed. They entered a space with a lot of competition, but they were confident that they had a better way of returning search results. At the heart of Google's strategy is the use of analytics, a strategy that successfully made them the most used search engine on the web.

11.5 Notes and Sources

11.1. Information about the history of Google is from Langville and Meyer [78] and the Wikipedia page titled "History of Google" [60]. Financial information is from Google's investor relations site [56].

11.2. For more mathematical details of the PageRank algorithm, we refer you to the original academic paper written by the founders of Google, Page and Brin [111]. When the probabilities of transitions between pages are represented in matrix form (with the rows and columns representing the web pages), it can be seen that the PageRank process is actually a Markov chain process, a more general random process with many interesting properties and applications. For a nice introduction to Markov Chains, see Bertsekas and Tsitsiklis [15].

11.3. The application of PageRank to rank graduate programs is from an academic paper published in 2007 by Schmidt and Chingos [122]. For an interesting example of using PageRank to rank sports teams, see Lazova and Basnarkov [79]. For a more in-depth discussion of the applications of PageRank, see the paper written by Gleich [50].

Chapter 12

How Online Advertising Changed the Internet

Advertising is totally unnecessary. Unless you hope to make money.

– Jef I. Richards

Contents

In 1994, the first advertisement appeared on the internet: a simple banner ad. Soon after, the first interactive ad with an embedded video game was created. By the late 1990s, websites were charging up to $100 for a single banner ad. When the dot-com bubble burst in 2000, online advertising started declining. However, search engines such as Google were still very popular due to their proven efficiency and dependability. Just in time to bring online advertising back to life, Google introduced Adwords and the idea of text ads instead of banner ads. Google understood the importance of isolating the ads from the search results and sorting them in terms of relevance.

This chapter is about online advertising and how Google introduced a revolutionary way to advertise on the internet. Google's advertising product Adwords uses many different ideas to produce a successful and interesting advertising campaign for many companies. We will discuss how both the advertisers and Google can maximize revenue using optimization techniques. Online advertising has not only allowed internet companies to generate revenue, it has changed the dynamics of the internet.

12.1 Introduction and History of Google Advertising

Internet advertising is the main method used by search engine companies to generate revenue. Companies such as Google, Yahoo!, and MSN are all large providers of search advertising, from which they receive most of their revenue. They allow advertisers to advertise based on search queries posted by users. Traditionally, advertising had been offered at a fixed price. Advertisers bought TV and newspaper ads based on what they could afford. However, it was difficult to put a fixed price on search advertisements because the types of search queries that will occur each day is unpredictable. Therefore, search companies use auctions to determine the prices.

Google is a popular search engine, and therefore, it is a popular site for advertisers to place their ads. An advertisement on Google attracts the largest group of potential buyers. AdWords, the main advertising product for Google, was launched in 2000 in an attempt to increase Google's revenue. They envisioned a new kind of online advertising that was simple and effective. Their opening pitch was, "Have a credit card and 5 minutes? Get your ad on Google today." AdWords allows advertisers to place bids for search keywords and then selects some of the ads to place on the search page. The original idea was invented by Bill Gross from Idealab, who had borrowed the idea from Yellow Pages. The similarities in the two systems led to some legal action, but the dispute was settled out of court, and AdWords continued unharmed.

When a user searches on Google, advertisements may be shown as "sponsored links" at the top of the search results, or on the right hand side of each page. Originally, advertisers paid a monthly amount and Google handled the advertising campaign. Now, AdWords is a self-service product, and many companies hire a third-party service provider to assist them with their campaign. While the original AdWords product was fairly simple, Google now uses an intricate system to determine the order of the ads. AdWords has been very successful for Google, and has historically provided Google with over 90% of their annual revenue. Table 12.1 shows the total advertising revenue in millions and as a percentage of the total revenue from 2001 through 2014. Note that these numbers are for the gross revenue before subtracting related costs.

12.2 AdWords

AdWords allows text, banner, and media ads, and includes local, national, and international distribution. Text ads are limited to one headline and two additional text lines, while image ads can be one of several different standard sizes. There are several aspects of AdWords that distinguish it and make it more popular than other online advertising programs. One is that the ads are clearly distinguished from the search results; a viewer can easily tell which are results and which are ads. Another is that they enforce guidelines on the style of the ads to keep the clean and clear tone of the search results page. Yet another is that they make it easy for anyone to join in and advertise on Google. AdWords is not just for big companies, but also for small local businesses.

Table 12.1: Advertising revenues of Google from 2001-2014.

Year	Advertising Revenue (millions)	Percent of Total Revenue
2001	67	77%
2002	411	93%
2003	1,421	97%
2004	3,143	99%
2005	6,065	99%
2006	10,493	99%
2007	16,413	99%
2008	21,129	97%
2009	22,889	97%
2010	28,236	96%
2011	36,531	96%
2012	43,686	95%
2013	50,547	91%
2014	59,056	89%

Pay-Per-Click Advertising

In AdWords, the advertisers only pay if a user clicks on their link, so we define what is known as a *price-per-click (PPC)*. This is the amount that an advertiser will pay if a user clicks on their link. For example, if the PPC is $5 and 3 people click on the ad, the advertiser would pay $15. Advertisers select words to potentially trigger their ad as well as the maximum amount they are willing to pay to have their ad appear on the results page for those words. The success rate of an advertisement is measured by its *click-through rate (CTR)*, which is defined as the number of users who clicked on an ad divided by the number of times the ad was delivered. For example, if an ad appeared 20 times and 5 people clicked on the ad, the CTR would be $5/20 = 0.25$ or 25%. The CTR values are estimated to be equal to the percentages given in Table 12.2. We will assume here that the CTR for an ad higher on the page is always larger than that for an ad lower on the page.

A search results page contains a fixed number of possible positions for advertisements. The order of the ads is determined by two factors: the advertiser's bid, and the advertiser's quality score. The quality score is determined by Google, and takes into account the historical CTR of the ad, the relevance of an advertiser's text to the search, the advertiser's account history, and other factors that Google chooses not to reveal. This secrecy makes it harder to manipulate the quality score.

Generalized Second-Price Auctions

The auction mechanism that AdWords uses to determine the order of the ads is based on a generalized second-price auction (GSP auction). A GSP auction is a specific way of allocating the ad slots and selecting prices when there are multiple bidders. The terminology *second-price* is used because of the way in which the prices are selected (explained below), and *generalized* means that there is more than one spot that the bidders are bidding for. This is the same type of mechanism that is used in most online advertising, including the advertising at Yahoo!. One of the interesting properties of a GSP auction is that participants do not necessarily fare best when they bid truthfully. For

Table 12.2: Estimated Click-Through-Rates (CTRs).

Position on Page	CTR
First	8.0%
Second	5.0%
Third	2.5%
Fourth	1.0%
Fifth	0.5%

example, they might actually still receive the top spot on the results page if they do not bid the maximum amount that they are willing to pay for this top spot. Note that while the actual algorithm that Google uses is not publicly known, we do know that the method is based on a GSP auction.

The simplest GSP auction starts with advertisers submitting bids for a specific keyword. These bids give the maximum willingness to pay for a click. When a user enters this keyword, the ads appear in order of decreasing bid. Then, if the user clicks on the ad in position 1, the advertiser in position 1 pays the bid of the advertiser in position 2. Similarly, if the user clicks on the ad in position 2, the advertiser in position 2 pays the bid of the advertiser in position 3, etc. Therefore, the advertiser is charged an amount equal to the next highest bid, hence "second-price" auctions. As an example, suppose there are 5 advertisers who submit bids for the query "computer." Dell submits a bid of $10, Gateway submits a bid of $5, HP submits a bid of $12, Toshiba submits a bid of $8, and Apple submits a bid of $15. On the results page, the ads would appear in the following order: Apple, HP, Dell, Toshiba, Gateway. If the user clicks on Apple's ad, Apple pays Google $12, which is the bid of HP (the next highest bidder). If the user clicks on HP's ad, then HP pays Google $10, which is the bid of Dell. Note that Apple could have bid $13 ($2 less than the maximum amount Apple is willing to pay) and still kept the top spot. In this scenario, the order of the ads is solely determined by the bids of the advertisers. When we also take the quality score into account, the ordering and cost changes, but the concept that the amount paid depends on the next position remains the same.

12.3 Using Optimization to Create an Edge

Viewing AdWords as an optimization problem creates an edge for both Google and the advertiser. However, depending on whether we are viewing the problem from Google's perspective or from the advertiser's perspective, the objective and decisions are different. We will explain this problem through a small example, where the bidders are all hotels near the Massachusetts Institute of Technology (MIT). Since the bidders are all selling a similar product, they are likely to be bidding on similar queries. We will first set up the notation in this section, and then discuss the two different perspectives: that of Google (in Section 12.4) and that of an advertiser (in Section 12.5). For more about optimization in general, see Chapter 21.

Assume that we are interested in finding the optimal solution for a time horizon of one day. In reality, the time horizon is normally much longer, such as a month. The advertiser would then change their daily decisions based on what has happened so far, making this a *dynamic optimization problem*. To simplify the problem, we will use discrete optimization to find the solution for a single day.

Our set of bidders (advertisers) are the Kendall Hotel, the Marriott, Royal Sonesta, and Hotel Marlowe. The Kendall Hotel and the Marriott are both located in Kendall Square (the area of Cambridge where MIT is located), while Royal Sonesta and Hotel Marlowe are located a little further away, but still in Cambridge. Suppose that the queries that these four hotels bid on during this day are "hotel near MIT," "MIT hotel," and "Cambridge hotel." Note that although the queries seem to be different phrasing of the same question, they could lead to different search results. So although the first two queries are similar, they are not the same. Table 12.3 summarizes the bids and budgets for each hotel.

We can see from this table that the Kendall Hotel bid \$8 for the first query, \$12 for the second query, and did not bid for the third query. Note that the sum of their bids can be higher than their daily budget of \$10 since this is a generalized second price auction. The amount that they actually pay per click is not equal to their bid; it is determined by the bids and quality scores of all bidders involved. Since the Kendall Hotel is a small hotel, they have a small daily budget, and thus chose not to bid on the "Cambridge hotel" query, because they would prefer to target MIT guests due to their proximity to the MIT campus. On the other hand, the Marriott is a very large hotel, and therefore has a much bigger budget. While Royal Sonesta is also a large hotel, it does not have as much funding for their Adwords campaign. And finally, Hotel Marlowe is an upscale hotel, and thus can afford to spend a little more on advertising. From historical data, Google knows that on average, the number of times each query occurs during the day are as listed in Table 12.4. Thus, we will say that on average, the query "hotel near MIT" occurs 15 times during one day, query "MIT hotel" occurs 20 times during one day, and query "Cambridge hotel" occurs 25 times during the day.

For each hotel and query we also have a quality score (QS) assigned by Google. Recall that the quality score takes into account the historical click-through rate, account history, relevance of the ad, and quality of the webpage. We do not have a way of knowing the actual quality scores, but suppose they are as listed in Table 12.5. Note that there is a different quality score for each

Table 12.3: Bids and budgets for the hotels and each of the queries (in dollars).

		Hotel			
		Kendall	**Marriott**	**Sonesta**	**Marlowe**
Query	**"hotel near MIT"**	\$8	\$25	\$15	\$15
	"MIT hotel"	\$12	\$15	–	\$20
	"Cambridge hotel"	–	\$25	\$15	\$10
	Daily Budget	\$10	\$50	\$20	\$30

Table 12.4: Average number of times each query occurs during the day.

Query	Number of Times Asked
"hotel near MIT"	15
"MIT hotel"	20
"Cambridge hotel"	25

query because an ad and webpage can be deemed more appropriate for one query over another. For example, an advertisement for the MIT Sloan School of Management probably has a very high quality score for the query "business school" and a very low quality score for the query "medical school." The quality of the advertisement and webpage itself is the same in both queries, but the appropriateness is different. In this example, quality scores are given on a $1 - 10$ scale, where any QS below 7 is below average, and any QS above 7 is above average. A quality score of 7 is "neutral," so if Google does not have any information about the ad with the query, it is assigned a QS of 7.

We can now define what is known as the *bidding landscape* for each query, which is an ordered set of all bidders who bid on that query. They are ordered by bid multiplied by the quality score, so the first bidder in the bidding landscape has the highest bid times QS, the second bidder in the bidding landscape has the second highest bid times QS, etc. For the query "hotel near MIT," the bidding landscape is {Marriott, Marlowe, Sonesta, Kendall}. Marriott is ranked the highest since its bid times QS is $25 \times 5 = 125$, whereas Kendall is ranked the lowest since its bid times QS is $8 \times 9 = 72$. Similarly, the bidding landscape for "MIT hotel" is {Marlowe, Kendall, Marriott} and the bidding landscape for "Cambridge hotel" is {Marriott, Sonesta, Marlowe}. Note that the hotels that do not bid on a query are not included in the bidding landscape at all.

For our small example, suppose that there are only two available advertisement spots per search. Then, since all of the ads will not fit in the results for each query, Google not only has to decide the order to place the ads, but also which ads to include. To simplify the number of variables we will need for our optimization problem, we will use what are commonly referred to as

Table 12.5: Quality scores for the hotels and queries.

Query	Kendall	Marriott	Sonesta	Marlowe
"hotel near MIT"	9	5	6	8
"MIT hotel"	9	5	7	8
"Cambridge hotel"	7	7	8	10

Table 12.6: All possible slates (22 in total).

Query	Slate	Decision Variable
"hotel near MIT"	{Marriott, Marlowe}	x_{10}
	{Marriott, Sonesta}	x_{11}
	{Marriott, Kendall}	x_{12}
	{Marlowe, Sonesta}	x_{13}
	{Marlowe, Kendall}	x_{14}
	{Sonesta, Kendall}	x_{15}
	{Marriott}	x_{16}
	{Marlowe}	x_{17}
	{Sonesta}	x_{18}
	{Kendall}	x_{19}
"MIT hotel"	{Marlowe, Kendall}	x_{20}
	{Marlowe, Marriott}	x_{21}
	{Kendall, Marriott}	x_{22}
	{Marlowe}	x_{23}
	{Kendall}	x_{24}
	{Marriott}	x_{25}
"Cambridge hotel"	{Marriott, Sonesta}	x_{30}
	{Marriott, Marlowe}	x_{31}
	{Sonesta, Marlowe}	x_{32}
	{Marriott}	x_{33}
	{Sonesta}	x_{34}
	{Marlowe}	x_{35}

slates. A slate lists the advertisements that will appear on the results page in the order that they will appear. As an example, a possible slate for the query "MIT hotel" is {Marlowe, Kendall}, meaning that the advertisement for Marlowe will appear first on the results page, followed by the advertisement for Kendall. Another possible slate is {Marlowe}, meaning that only the advertisement for Marlowe will appear on the results page. The ads are always listed in the same order as in the bidding landscape, and can be seen as ordered subsets of the bidding landscape. By using slates, we take into account the ads that appear along with the order that they appear in. Each slate can have at most two bidders, since there are only two available spots. Table 12.6 lists all of the possible slates for each query, as well as the corresponding variable that we will use for our optimization problem. Note that in all of the slates, the order of the bidding landscape is maintained. It is important to include the slates with just single bidders since we will want to use them if all of the other bidder's budgets are gone; it is better to just display one ad than to not display any.

We now want to define the click-through rate (CTR) and the price-per-click (PPC) for this example. The actual CTRs, the rates at which the ads are

Table 12.7: Price-per-click (PPC) amounts for each hotel and query (in dollars).

Query	Kendall	Marriott	Sonesta	Marlowe
"hotel near MIT"	\$0.01	\$24.01	\$12.01	\$11.26
"MIT hotel"	\$8.34	\$0.01	–	\$13.51
"Cambridge hotel"	–	\$17.15	\$12.51	\$0.01

clicked on per showing of a slate, are calculated using historical data. However, for this example we will assume that the CTRs are as listed in Table 12.2, regardless of the query or the ad itself. The PPC, the amount a bidder pays each time a user clicks on their ad, is defined as the minimum amount a bidder must pay to retain their current position in the bidding landscape. To illustrate this, consider the query "hotel near MIT." The Marriott has the top spot with a bid of 25 and a QS of 5. Hotel Marlowe is in the second position with a bid of 15 and a QS of 8. To keep the top spot, Marriott needs $25 \times 5 > 15 \times 8$. So as long as Marriott's bid is greater than $\frac{15 \times 8}{5} = 24$, they will keep the top spot (note that a bid of 24 would technically tie the two hotels, but we will ignore ties to simplify matters). So the PPC for Marriott for the query "hotel near MIT" is \$24.01. Note that this makes sense in a GSP auction, since the amount the bidder pays heavily depends on the bid and quality of the bid ranked right below him. All of the PPCs are listed in Table 12.7. Note that if an ad is last in the bidding landscape, they pay \$0.01 since they should pay more than someone who does not bid at all.

With these definitions, we can compute the expected cost for a bidder for a single query. This is the cost of a click multiplied by the probability that the user will click on the ad, which is just $PPC \times CTR$. Note that we are talking about *expected cost*; this is what we expect to happen in the long run, not what will happen every time the ad appears.

12.4 The Problem from Google's Perspective

From Google's perspective, the challenge is to decide which ads to display in order to maximize revenue. Since this is a pay-per-click situation, Google wants to display relevant and interesting ads so that the user will click on them. This is why Google uses a quality rating in addition to the auction mechanism. If they display an ad that is not relevant to the search or an ad that has a low CTR, then they will not receive as much revenue from that ad, regardless of how much the advertiser bids for the spot. If they just used an auction, the highest bidder would receive the top spot regardless of the quality or historical CTR of the ad.

To state the optimization problem in this setting, we need to define the revenue. The expected revenue to Google for the showing of one slate is the sum over all positions of the expected costs to the bidders. Since we only have two positions in this case, it is the sum of the expected cost to the bidder in position 1, $CTR_1 \times PPC_1$, and the expected cost to the bidder in position 2, $CTR_2 \times PPC_2$. We will define the expected revenue for query i ($i = 1$, 2, or 3) and slate k by R_{ik}. By looking at Table 12.6, we can see that if $i = 1$, then there are 10 possible slates, numbered from 0 to 9. If $i = 2$ then there are 6 possible slates, numbered from 0 to 5, and if $i = 3$ there are also 6 possible slates, numbered from 0 to 5. Then, we have $R_{ik} = (CTR_1 \times PPC_1) + (CTR_2 \times PPC_2) = (0.08 \times PPC_1) + (0.05 \times PPC_2)$ by definition of the click-through-rates in Table 12.2.

We define our decision variables as follows. For each query i and slate k, define the decision variable x_{ik} to be equal to the number of times slate k appears for query i. These decision variables are shown in Table 12.6. The total expected revenue is

$$\sum_{i=1}^{3} \sum_{k} R_{ik} x_{ik},$$

which sums over all three queries and all 22 slates that are listed in Table 12.6. For this example, we can expand this sum as follows. For the first query, "hotel near MIT," there are 10 different slates listed in Table 12.6. The expected revenue for the first slate is $R_{10} = CTR_1 \times PPC_1 + CTR_2 \times PPC_2 = (0.08 \times \$24.01) + (0.05 \times \$11.26) = \$2.4838$, which corresponds to variable x_{10} (note that we start numbering the slates from 0). Thus, we have the term $2.4838x_{10}$ in our sum. The expected revenue for the second slate is $(0.08 \times \$24.01) + (0.05 \times \$12.01) = \$2.5213$, which corresponds to variable x_{11}. Thus, we have the term $2.5213x_{11}$ in our sum. We can repeat this for all of the other slates and all of the other queries. This sum will be our objective function since we are trying to maximize revenue. Note that the revenue from the second slate is actually higher than the revenue from the first slate. This illustrates that since the Royal Sonesta has such a low quality score, they are having to pay more per click than Hotel Marlowe, even though they are ranked below Hotel Marlowe.

We have two different types of constraints. The first type is what we will refer to as the budget constraints. Since each hotel has a specified budget, we have to make sure that we do not violate the budget during the day. This amounts to making sure that the sum over all queries and slates of the expected cost times the number of times the slate is shown does not exceed the budget. For each hotel, we only have to consider the slates containing the hotel, since if they are not in a slate, their expected cost is zero. The following is the constraint for the Kendall Hotel:

$$0.01[0.05x_{12} + 0.05x_{14} + 0.05x_{15} + 0.08x_{19}] + 8.34[0.05x_{20} + 0.08x_{22} + 0.08x_{24}] \leq 10.$$

The first four terms are multiplied by 0.01 since 0.01 is the PPC for the Kendall Hotel for the first query, and all of these terms correspond to the first query. The remaining terms are multiplied by 8.34 since 8.34 is the PPC for the

Kendall Hotel for the second query, and these terms correspond to the second query. Note that there are no terms for the third query since the Kendall Hotel did not bid on the third query. Additionally, each term is multiplied by the corresponding CTR, depending on the position of the Kendall Hotel in that slate (as noted in Table 12.6). There is one budget constraint for each hotel.

The second type of constraints are what we will call query constraints. They insure that we do not show more slates than the expected number of times the query happens. As stated before, we expect the first query to happen 15 times during the day, the second query to happen 20 times during the day, and the third query to happen 25 times during the day. The sum of all of the decision variables for each query must be less than or equal to these expected values. For the first query, this amounts to the following constraint:

$$x_{10} + x_{11} + x_{12} + x_{13} + x_{14} + x_{15} + x_{16} + x_{17} + x_{18} + x_{19} \leq 15$$

There is one query constraint for each query.

Now that we have described the objective function and constraints, we can state the overall optimization problem (in words) as follows:

maximize: Total Expected Revenue

subject to:

Kendall's Expected Cost $\leq$ 10

Marriott's Expected Cost $\leq$ 50

Sonesta's Expected Cost $\leq$ 20

Marlowe's Expected Cost $\leq$ 30

Number of Slates Appearing for Query "hotel near MIT" $\leq$ 15

Number of Slates Appearing for Query "MIT hotel" $\leq$ 20

Number of Slates Appearing for Query "Cambridge hotel" $\leq$ 25

All Decision Variables take Integer Values

This is an integer optimization problem with 22 variables and 7 constraints, and can be solved using Excel Solver, or any other integer optimization software. The optimal solution has $x_{10} = 10, x_{12} = 1, x_{13} = 3, x_{15} = 1, x_{20} = 20, x_{30} = 21, x_{32} = 4$, and all other variables equal to 0 (the optimal solution is shown in Table 12.8). This gives an objective function value of \$108.13. You can see from the optimal solution that for the first query we will show the slate $\{Marriott, Marlowe\}$ ten times, the slate $\{Marriott, Kendall\}$ once, the slate $\{Marlowe, Sonesta\}$ three times, and the slate $\{Sonesta, Kendall\}$ once. Note that the optimal values of the decision variables inform Google how many times they should display each slate to maximize their revenue.

To show the potential gain from using optimization in this setting, let us consider solving this problem using a myopic method (also known as a "greedy" approach), where we display as many slates as possible for those with the largest objective function coefficients. The decision variable x_{11} has the largest

Table 12.8: The optimal solution to Google's optimization problem.

Query	Slate	Decision Variable	Optimal Solution
"hotel near MIT"	{Marriott, Marlowe}	x_{10}	10
	{Marriott, Sonesta}	x_{11}	0
	{Marriott, Kendall}	x_{12}	1
	{Marlowe, Sonesta}	x_{13}	3
	{Marlowe, Kendall}	x_{14}	0
	{Sonesta, Kendall}	x_{15}	1
	{Marriott}	x_{16}	0
	{Marlowe}	x_{17}	0
	{Sonesta}	x_{18}	0
	{Kendall}	x_{19}	0
"MIT hotel"	{Marlowe, Kendall}	x_{20}	20
	{Marlowe, Marriott}	x_{21}	0
	{Kendall, Marriott}	x_{22}	0
	{Marlowe}	x_{23}	0
	{Kendall}	x_{24}	0
	{Marriott}	x_{25}	0
"Cambridge hotel"	{Marriott, Sonesta}	x_{30}	21
	{Marriott, Marlowe}	x_{31}	0
	{Sonesta, Marlowe}	x_{32}	4
	{Marriott}	x_{33}	0
	{Sonesta}	x_{34}	0
	{Marlowe}	x_{35}	0

objective coefficient, \$2.5213, so we will make x_{11} as large as possible first. This decision variable is in the second constraint (Marriott's budget constraint), the third constraint (Sonesta's budget constraint), and the fifth constraint (the query constraint for "hotel near MIT"). If all of the other decision variables are zero, x_{11} can be no more than 15 without violating one of these constraints, so we set $x_{11} = 15$. (Note that we also have to make sure it equals an integer value.) If we repeat this for each of the decision variables in order of decreasing objective function coefficient values, we get the following solution:

$$x_{11} = 15, x_{20} = 20, x_{30} = 15, x_{32} = 1, x_{35} = 9,$$

which has an objective function value of \$98.7465. By just setting up the optimization problem, it is easy to use a simple greedy method and get a decent solution. However, compared to the optimal objective function value of \$108.1332, we are losing about \$10 by not solving the optimization problem.

Thus, this shows that an advertiser using optimization would have an edge over an advertiser just selecting what seems to be a good solution.

12.5 The Problem from the Advertiser's Perspective*

From the viewpoint of advertisers, the challenge is to optimally take advantage of this auction mechanism. The goal is to maximize the exposure of the ad and the traffic to their webpage, so a common objective for advertisers is to maximize the number of clicks. When advertisers decide to participate in AdWords, they are faced with three decisions: the set of keywords to bid on, the bids for each keyword, and a daily budget. Here we assume that the keywords and daily budgets are already chosen, and we are trying to decide the bids for each query.

If we are the Kendall Hotel, we have three decisions to make: the amount to bid for the query "hotel near MIT," the amount to bid for the query "MIT hotel," and the amount to bid for the query "Cambridge hotel." We will denote these as $b_1, b_2,$ and b_3. Let us assume that all other bidders have already placed their bids, and that these values are as in Table 12.3. Note that it is not usually the case that we know what our competitors are bidding, but suppose that we have estimated these values through observation of past history. We can look at their historical placements on the results pages and make estimates as to what their bids were. Similarly, we will use the quality scores listed in Table 12.5. In this case, we will assume that there are four positions on the results page for advertisements, with click-through-rates as shown in Table 12.2. This simplifies the problem; we no longer have to deal with slates since all of the ads with positive bids will appear on the results page. Since there are only four different advertisers for these queries, the maximum number of ads that we will need to display is four. Since we have four available spots, we do not need to select a subset of the bidding landscape; we can display the entire bidding landscape. As illustrated in the section on Google's perspective, we could also solve the problem when there are less positions for ads in the results.

Note that the amount we pay and our click-through rate (as the Kendall Hotel) depends on our position in the bidding landscape, which depends on the bid that we make. For the first query, our quality score is 9, so our bid times quality score is $9 \times b_1$. The bid times quality score is 125 for the Marriott, 90 for the Royal Sonesta, and 120 for Hotel Marlowe. We will either be in position 1, 2, 3, or 4 (or no position if we do not bid on this query). If $9b_1 > 125$, then we will be in the first position. This will happen if $b_1 > \frac{125}{9} = \$13.89$. If $125 \geq 9b_1 > 120$, then we will be in the second position. This will happen if $\$13.89 = \frac{125}{9} \geq b_1 > \frac{120}{9} = \$13.33$. If $120 \geq 9b_1 > 90$, then we will be in the third position. This will happen if $\$13.33 = \frac{120}{9} \geq b_1 > \frac{90}{9} = \$10.00$. And if $\$10.00 = \frac{90}{9} \geq b_1 > 0$, we will be in the last position. We can do the same thing for the other queries. The following are the CTRs for each of the queries

($CTR_1(b_1)$ corresponds to the query "hotel near MIT," $CTR_2(b_2)$ corresponds to the query "MIT hotel," and $CTR_3(b_3)$ corresponds to the query "Cambridge hotel"):

$$CTR_1(b_1) = \begin{cases} 0, & \text{if } b_1 = 0, \\ 0.01, & \text{if } 0 < b_1 \leq \frac{90}{9}, \\ 0.025, & \text{if } \frac{90}{9} < b_1 \leq \frac{120}{9}, \\ 0.05, & \text{if } \frac{120}{9} < b_1 \leq \frac{125}{9}, \\ 0.08, & \text{if } \frac{125}{9} < b_1, \end{cases}$$

$$CTR_2(b_2) = \begin{cases} 0, & \text{if } b_2 = 0, \\ 0.025, & \text{if } 0 < b_2 \leq \frac{75}{9}, \\ 0.05, & \text{if } \frac{75}{9} < b_2 \leq \frac{160}{9}, \\ 0.08, & \text{if } \frac{160}{9} < b_2, \end{cases}$$

$$CTR_3(b_3) = \begin{cases} 0, & \text{if } b_3 = 0, \\ 0.01, & \text{if } 0 < b_3 \leq \frac{100}{7}, \\ 0.025, & \text{if } \frac{100}{7} < b_3 \leq \frac{120}{7}, \\ 0.05, & \text{if } \frac{120}{7} < b_3 \leq \frac{175}{7}, \\ 0.08, & \text{if } \frac{175}{7} < b_3. \end{cases}$$

Note that $CTR_2(b_2)$ only has 4 possible values because the Royal Sonesta did not bid on query 2. The CTR for each query is a *piecewise constant* function of the bid. The values of CTR_1 as a function of b_1 are shown in Figure 12.1. The other CTRs can be plotted similarly. Note that they are called piecewise constant functions since they are divided into pieces, where each piece is constant over its respective interval.

The PPC is defined as the minimum amount required to maintain the position. Thus, for each of these intervals, the PPC is the lower endpoint, rounded up to the nearest penny. In our case, this becomes:

$$PPC_1(b_1) = \begin{cases} 0, & \text{if } b_1 = 0, \\ 0.01, & \text{if } 0 < b_1 \leq \frac{90}{9}, \\ 10.01, & \text{if } \frac{90}{9} < b_1 \leq \frac{120}{9}, \\ 13.34, & \text{if } \frac{120}{9} < b_1 \leq \frac{125}{9}, \\ 13.89, & \text{if } \frac{125}{9} < b_1, \end{cases}$$

$$PPC_2(b_2) = \begin{cases} 0, & \text{if } b_2 = 0, \\ 0.01, & \text{if } 0 < b_2 \leq \frac{75}{9}, \\ 8.34, & \text{if } \frac{75}{9} < b_2 \leq \frac{160}{9}, \\ 17.78, & \text{if } \frac{160}{9} < b_2, \end{cases}$$

$$PPC_3(b_3) = \begin{cases} 0, & \text{if } b_3 = 0, \\ 0.01, & \text{if } 0 < b_3 \leq \frac{100}{7}, \\ 14.29, & \text{if } \frac{100}{7} < b_3 \leq \frac{120}{7}, \\ 17.14, & \text{if } \frac{120}{7} < b_3 \leq \frac{175}{7}, \\ 25.01, & \text{if } \frac{175}{7} < b_3. \end{cases}$$

Now we can compute the cost, which as before is just the CTR times the PPC. If we denote the cost for query i by c_i, we have that $c_1(b_1) = CTR_1(b_1) \times PPC_1(b_1)$, $c_2(b_2) = CTR_2(b_2) \times PPC_2(b_2)$, and $c_3(b_3) = CTR_3(b_3) \times PPC_3(b_3)$. We can also state the cost as piecewise constant functions:

$$c_1(b_1) = \begin{cases} 0, & \text{if } b_1 = 0, \\ 0.0001, & \text{if } 0 < b_1 \leq \frac{90}{9}, \\ 0.25025, & \text{if } \frac{90}{9} < b_1 \leq \frac{120}{9}, \\ 0.667, & \text{if } \frac{120}{9} < b_1 \leq \frac{125}{9}, \\ 1.1112, & \text{if } \frac{125}{9} < b_1, \end{cases}$$

Figure 12.1: Graph of $CTR_1(b_1)$ as a function of b_1.

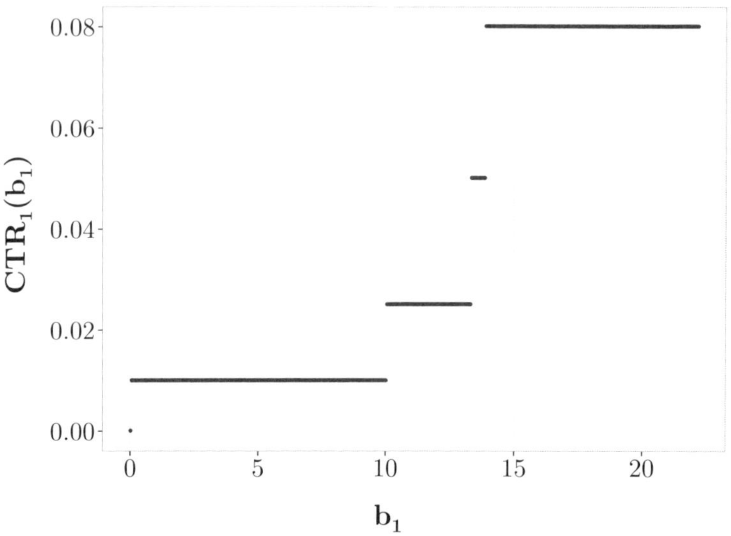

$$c_2(b_2) = \begin{cases} 0, & \text{if } b_2 = 0, \\ 0.00025, & \text{if } 0 < b_2 \leq \frac{75}{9}, \\ 0.417, & \text{if } \frac{75}{9} < b_2 \leq \frac{160}{9}, \\ 1.4224, & \text{if } \frac{160}{9} < b_2, \end{cases}$$

$$c_3(b_3) = \begin{cases} 0, & \text{if } b_3 = 0, \\ 0.0001, & \text{if } 0 < b_3 \leq \frac{100}{7}, \\ 0.35725, & \text{if } \frac{100}{7} < b_3 \leq \frac{120}{7}, \\ 0.8575, & \text{if } \frac{120}{7} < b_3 \leq \frac{175}{7}, \\ 2.0008, & \text{if } \frac{175}{7} < b_3. \end{cases}$$

In this case, our objective is to maximize the number of clicks, so we want to maximize the sum of the number of times each query appears times our CTR for that query. Recall that the expected number of times that each query appears is listed in Table 12.4. Our constraints consist of our budget constraint and nonnegative constraints for the bids. The optimization problem in this case can be stated as follows:

$$\begin{aligned}
\text{maximize} \quad & 15CTR_1(b_1) + 20CTR_2(b_2) + 25CTR_3(b_3) \\
\text{subject to} \quad & 15c_1(b_1) + 20c_2(b_2) + 25c_3(b_3) \leq 10 \\
& b_1, b_2, b_3 \geq 0.
\end{aligned}$$

In this form, it may not seem obvious how we should solve this problem. It is a nonlinear optimization problem involving six different piecewise constant functions of the decision variables. To solve this problem, we use an indirect formulation where we re-write the optimization problem without the piecewise constant functions. We can do this by assigning a variable to each of the "pieces." But before we start assigning variables, we can simplify our problem by making a few key observations. If $c_1(b_1)$ is equal to either 1.1112 or 0.667, the budget constraint will be infeasible. Thus, there are actually only three possible values for $c_1(b_1)$. Similarly, $c_2(b_2)$ cannot be equal to 1.4224 and $c_3(b_3)$ cannot be equal to 2.0008 or 0.8575. This greatly reduces the number of variables we need for the pieces.

Let s_{11} correspond to $c_1 = 0.25025$, s_{12} correspond to $c_1 = 0.0001$, s_{13} correspond to $c_1 = 0$, s_{21} correspond to $c_2 = 0.417$, s_{22} correspond to $c_2 = 0.00025$, s_{23} correspond to $c_2 = 0$, s_{31} correspond to $c_3 = 0.35725$, s_{32} correspond to $c_3 = 0.0001$, and s_{33} correspond to $c_3 = 0$. So s_{11} will be equal to 1 if $c_1 = 0.25025$, s_{12} will be equal to 1 if $c_1 = 0.0001$, and so on. Each s variable corresponds to one of the pieces of the cost functions. We enforce the following constraints on these variables:

$$\begin{aligned}
s_{11} + s_{12} + s_{13} &= 1 \\
s_{21} + s_{22} + s_{23} &= 1 \\
s_{31} + s_{32} + s_{33} &= 1 \\
s_{11}, s_{12}, s_{13}, s_{21}, s_{22}, s_{23}, s_{31}, s_{32}, s_{33} &\in \{0, 1\}.
\end{aligned}$$

These constraints model the fact that one s variable for each query should be equal to 1, and all others should be equal to 0, since we can only pick a bid in one of the possible pieces. We can define the CTRs and the c's in terms of the s variables as follows:

$$\begin{aligned}
CTR_1 &= 0.025s_{11} + 0.01s_{12} \\
CTR_2 &= 0.05s_{21} + 0.025s_{22} \\
CTR_3 &= 0.025s_{31} + 0.01s_{32} \\
c_1 &= 0.25025s_{11} + 0.0001s_{12} \\
c_2 &= 0.417s_{21} + 0.00025s_{22} \\
c_3 &= 0.35725s_{31} + 0.0001s_{32}.
\end{aligned}$$

Note that the s variables corresponding to the zero values are not needed in these constraints. Now we can rewrite our optimization problem by substituting these equations for the corresponding functions in the original formulation, and including the constraints on the s variables shown above:

$$\begin{aligned}
&\text{maximize:}\\
&\quad 15CTR_1 + 20CTR_2 + 25CTR_3\\
&\text{subject to:}\\
&\quad 15c_1 + 20c_2 + 25c_3 \leq 10\\
&\quad s_{11} + s_{12} + s_{13} = 1\\
&\quad s_{21} + s_{22} + s_{23} = 1\\
&\quad s_{31} + s_{32} + s_{33} = 1\\
&\quad s_{11}, s_{12}, s_{13}, s_{21}, s_{22}, s_{23}, s_{31}, s_{32}, s_{33} \in \{0, 1\},
\end{aligned}$$

where CTR_1, CTR_2, CTR_3, c_1, c_2, and c_3 are defined in terms of the s variables, as stated above.

This problem can be solved using an integer optimization software, like Excel Solver. The optimal solution is $s_{12} = 1$, $s_{21} = 1$, and $s_{32} = 1$. Thus, the optimal decision is to be in the fourth position for the first query, the second position for the second query, and the fourth position for the third query. This implies that our optimal bids are $b_1 \in (0, 10]$, $b_2 \in (\frac{75}{9}, \frac{160}{9}] \approx (8.33, 17.78]$, and $b_3 \in (0, \frac{100}{7}] \approx (0, 14.29]$. Note that the optimal solution to this problem gives us an optimal range for each of the bids. This means that the Kendall Hotel could select bids anywhere in these ranges and they would get the optimal solution.

12.6 Online Advertising in Practice

Online advertising is used by many different websites in addition to search engines. For example, social media sites often target advertisements to individuals based on their personal data and behavior. Internet advertising revenues in the United States were over $40 billion in 2013, surpassing that of cable television.

While the optimization problems presented in this chapter can assist Google and an advertiser in making better decisions, different heuristics and estimation approaches are typically used in practice due to the large size of the problems that need to be solved. However, the optimization problems presented here can help us better understand how the system works, and general strategies that can lead to higher revenue, both for the search engine and for the advertiser.

12.7 Notes and Sources

12.1. The financial information about Google is from Google's Investor Relations page [56].

12.2. Information about Google Adwords is from the Google Adwords page [55] and from the Wikipedia page on Adwords [2]. The information about GSP auctions is from [45].

12.3. The ideas about using optimization in online advertising are from Abrams et al. [1] and Feldman et al. [47].

Chapter 13

Recommendations Worth a Million

"Data! Data! Data!" he cried impatiently. "I can't make bricks without clay."

– Sir Arthur Conan Doyle in *The Adventures of Sherlock Holmes*

Contents

In October 2006, Netflix announced that they would award a one million dollar prize to the first developer of a recommendation algorithm that could do a better job than their current system at recommending movies to users. The executives at Netflix believed in the value of great recommendations so much that they were willing to award a large sum of money for a better algorithm. Three years after the prize was announced, a seven person team of statisticians, machine-learning experts, and computer engineers were finally awarded the prize.

The Netflix contest was closely followed by researchers around the world because recommendation systems are used for much more than suggesting movies. Amazon, the world's largest online retailer, uses an intricate recommendation system for almost any item imaginable. eHarmony, an online dating site, uses a recommendation system to recommend compatible matches to single men and women. With the large number of choices available, recommendation systems help users to quickly find what they might be interested in.

In this chapter, we discuss how three popular companies – Netflix, Amazon, and eHarmony – have implemented recommendation systems to accurately predict their users' interests. An effective recommendation system provides an edge over competitors by increasing sales and improving the satisfaction of customers. The best recommendation systems use massive datasets efficiently and appropriately.

13.1 Getting Advice from Data

When a customer walks into a store, a sales representative often asks, "Can I help you find something?" This question is targeted toward customers who know what they want; they have come into the store looking for a specific item, and they just need to locate it. Similarly, almost every online store has a search tool that can be used to find specific items in the store. But what about the customer who has just come to the store to browse? They are interested in buying something, but they do not have a specific item in mind. Ideally, a worker at a store could instantly make recommendations for someone based on their previous purchases and the previous purchases of similar customers. This is hard to do without the help of a computer, since it requires massive amounts of knowledge about customers, their previous purchases, and purchases by other customers with similar interests.

Online recommendation systems develop recommendations by utilizing massive datasets, which many online retailers or service providers now have at their disposal. A recommendation system uses an information filtering device to recommend items or other services to users. This allows companies to search through large databases of items or options to pick out the ones that a user will most likely be interested in. This is beneficial to the company and to customers; the company is able to identify potential customers for its products, and customers can more easily find items that they may find sufficiently interesting to buy.

Creating a good recommendation system has many challenges in addition to collecting the huge amount of data needed. Often, the recommendations have to be available in real-time. This means that if a user gives a rating or preference for an item, the system should be able to immediately use that information to select other candidates which are of interest to a buyer. The system must produce recommendations that the user will find helpful. If a user is constantly getting recommendations for things that they are not interested in, they might get frustrated and the company could lose a customer. Additionally, different customers have different amounts of information available. The system should work with users for whom the system has very little information on ratings or purchases, as well as high activity users.

13.2 Types of Recommendation Systems

There are two main types of recommendation systems: collaborative filtering and content-based filtering. Collaborative filtering systems make recommendations based on the attributes of users, while content-based filtering systems make recommendations based on the attributes of items. While some recommendation systems are one type or the other, there are also many systems that combine these approaches to improve functionality. In this section, we will discuss basic collaborative filtering and content-based filtering systems as an introduction to later sections, where we will discuss some of the most successful recommendation algorithms in use today.

Collaborative Filtering

In collaborative filtering systems, each user is represented by a vector of items. The length of the vector is the number of distinct items that can be offered to, rated by, or purchased by the user. Each entry in the vector gives the customer's rating for the item, if the customer has rated the item. This means that the vectors often have many empty entries; most customers will have rated only a small fraction of the total number of items available.

Collaborative filtering uses a measure of similarity between users to make rating predictions. There are many different ways of measuring similarity, but one popular method is to use the correlation between the item vectors of the users. The similarities are used as weights in predicting ratings for a user. If we predict that a user will like an item, we will recommend it to him or her.

As an example, suppose we have five different customers (Amy, Bob, Carl, Dan, and Eva) and we are looking at their ratings (out of 5) for four different movies. Table 13.1 gives the ratings, where users and movies are denoted by letters. The blank entries indicate that the person has not rated the movie.

Let $r_{i,j}$ be the rating that user i gives to movie j. Thus, $r_{A,F} = 5$ since Amy (A) gave a rating of 5 to the movie *Forrest Gump* (F). Let μ_i be the average rating of user i, and σ_i be the standard deviation of the ratings of customer i. In our example, the average rating for Amy would be

Table 13.1: Example user ratings.

User	Forrest Gump (F)	Godfather (G)	Inception (I)	Jaws (J)
Amy (A)	5		4	3
Bob (B)	3	5	2	5
Carl (C)		3	5	4
Dan (D)	4	5	4	
Eva (E)	4	4		3

Table 13.2: User means and standard deviations for ratings.

User	Mean Rating	Std Dev Rating
Amy (A)	4.00	0.82
Bob (B)	3.75	1.30
Carl (C)	4.00	0.82
Dan (D)	4.33	0.47
Eva (E)	3.67	0.47

$$\mu_A = \frac{5+4+3}{3} = 4,$$

and the standard deviation for Amy would be

$$\sigma_A = \sqrt{\frac{(5-4)^2+(4-4)^2+(3-4)^2}{3}} = 0.82.$$

Table 13.2 gives the mean and standard deviation of the ratings for each of the five users. (Note that, for simplicity, we are dividing by n in the computation of standard deviation, instead of $(n-1)$ as is done when computing an unbiased estimate of the population standard deviation.[1])

We now want to compute the similarity between any two users. In this example, we will use correlation as a measure of similarity, but different recommendation systems use different measures of similarity. Using the definition of correlation, we define the similarity between users A and B as:

$$s_{A,B} = \frac{\frac{1}{n}\sum_{i=1}^{n}(r_{A,i} - \mu_A)(r_{B,i} - \mu_B)}{\sigma_A \sigma_B},$$

[1]When calculating the standard deviation of a sample, $(n-1)$ is often used in the denominator instead of n, to produce what is called an "unbiased estimate of the population standard deviation." For this application, either approach is valid. Note that the choice of n or $(n-1)$ in the denominator will only make a material difference when n is small.

where n is the number of items (in this case, n = 4). We have to adjust this definition slightly to only average over the items that both users have rated, since the rating for an item that a user has never rated is undefined. Thus, we will just replace n with number of items that both users have rated. Note that this may lead to similarities between users that are larger than 1 or smaller than -1 (unlike standard correlation). However, the interpretation remains the same. Two users with a similarity close to 1 have positively correlated (similar) preferences, two users with a similarity close to -1 have negatively correlated (opposite) preferences, and two users with a similarity close to zero do not have very correlated preferences at all.

As an example, the similarity between Amy (A) and Bob (B) in our example case is:

$$s_{A,B} = \frac{\frac{1}{3}[(5-4)(3-3.75)+(4-4)(2-3.75)+(3-4)(5-3.75)]}{0.82 \times 1.30} = -0.63.$$

Note that there are only three terms in the numerator since Amy has never rated *The Godfather*, and so they have both rated only three movies.

Table 13.3 gives the similarities between all pairs of users. Each entry in the table is the similarity between the user corresponding to the row and the user corresponding to the column. Note that each user has a similarity of one with themselves.

Once we know the similarities between all users, we can predict a rating for a user. The prediction for user A and item i is given by:

$$p_{A,i} = \mu_A + \frac{\sum\limits_{u \in U_i} s_{A,u}(r_{u,i} - \mu_u)}{\sum\limits_{u \in U_i} s_{A,u}},$$

where each sum is over all other users u who have rated item i (denoted by the set U_i). This takes the average rating for user A, and adjusts it based on the ratings of similar users. The numerator of the fraction adds up the ratings of all other users for item i (relative to their average rating), weighted by their similarity with user A. Thus, if a similar user liked the movie more than their average rating or if a dissimilar user liked the movie less than their average rating, we would add a positive factor to user A's rating. On the other hand, if a similar user liked the movie less than their average rating or if a dissimilar user liked the movie more than their average rating, we would add a negative factor to user A's rating. The denominator of the fraction normalizes this sum by the total similarity between user A and all other users who have rated item i. So the prediction for a selected user can be thought of as an average of other user's ratings, weighted by the similarities of these users to the selected user.

As an example, we will predict Eva's rating for *Inception*:

$$p_{E,I} = 3.67 + \frac{1.30\times(4-4)-0.37\times(2-3.75)-0.43\times(5-4)+0.25\times(4-4.33)}{1.3-0.37-0.43+0.25} = 3.85.$$

Table 13.3: Similarities between all users.

	Amy (A)	Bob (B)	Carl (C)	Dan (D)	Eva (E)
Amy (A)	1	-0.63	0.00	-0.43	1.30
Bob (B)	-0.63	1	-0.94	0.91	-0.37
Carl (C)	0.00	-0.94	1	-1.30	-0.43
Dan (D)	-0.43	0.91	-1.30	1	0.25
Eva (E)	1.30	-0.37	-0.43	0.25	1

Therefore, we predict that Eva will like *Inception* more than her average rating, but not by much. Depending on our criteria for recommending movies, we may or may not recommend *Inception* to Eva.

This method works very well, but involves a significant amount of computation when there are many users and items. Different ways of addressing this problem exist, such as randomly sampling users, ignoring unpopular items, and clustering the items by type first.

It can also be challenging to get accurate results with collaborative filtering when the number of items is significantly larger than the number of users, due to the fact that it is highly unlikely that multiple users will have rated the same items. More generally, this is referred to as a *sparsity* problem. When the available data is very sparse, content-based filtering, which we discuss next, often performs better.

Content-based Filtering

Just as collaborative filtering made recommendations by finding similar users, content-based filtering works by finding "similar" items; given a pair of similar items, if the user likes one of the items, then the other item should be recommended to that user. Similarity can be defined in different ways, but it is typically determined by analyzing attributes of the items, such as the genre of a movie, keywords on a webpage, or harmony of a song. This differs from collaborative filtering methods since we are not looking at whether or not other users like these items; we only consider the information about the items themselves and the user we are making recommendations to. For example, if a customer buys the book *Moneyball* by Michael Lewis, the recommendation system might suggest other books by Michael Lewis or other books about statistics and sports.

Computing similarity between items is often very similar to how we computed the similarity between users in the previous section, but the vectors are of item attributes instead of user ratings. If we are trying to find the similarity between two movies, we might define a vector for each of them that describes things like the genre, director, main actors and actresses, year, etc.

This requires someone to define the attributes for each item, which could be subject to human judgment.

Once the similarity between the items is computed, an item is recommended to a user if it is similar to an item that they indicated they liked. For example, if content-based filtering is used for a movie system, it might recommended *Toy Story 2* to someone who indicated that they liked *Toy Story*.

Content-based filtering often works better than collaborative filtering when the user has not purchased or rated very many items. In content-based filtering, items can be recommended as soon as the user indicates that they like a single item, whereas in collaborative filtering, the user needs to be linked to other similar users, which requires significantly more data. But when the user has rated or purchased thousands of items, content-based filtering has a hard time making recommendations that use all of the known information. This is because each item that the user likes has many similar items, and it becomes difficult to know which ones to recommended at a given time. Additionally, it is difficult to make recommendations in an area not present in the user's previous history. In collaborative filtering, we could recommend an item to someone that might be very different from what they have previously purchased or rated because a similar user liked it. But in content-based filtering, the users themselves have to purchase or rate similar items for an item to ever get recommended. This limits the extent to which the recommendation algorithm could get customers interested in buying items that they might not think to purchase on their own.

13.3 Netflix

Being able to rent movies is a nice luxury. You can watch the entire movie in the comfort of your own home at a fraction of the price of buying the movie or going to the movie theater. Before Netflix was founded in 1997, the only places to rent movies were rental stores. A customer could rent the movie for a fixed number of days, usually somewhere between 1 day and 5 days. If they returned the movie late, they would be charged late fees. The founders of Netflix, Reed Hastings and Marc Randolph, felt that this business model was flawed. DVDs are easily lost under stacks of magazines, piles of mail, or even forgotten in the DVD player. Before long, late fees have accumulated and the cost of the rental has become more than the cost of just buying the DVD in the first place. This inspired Hastings and Randolph to create a new business model, and a new way of renting movies.

The website netflix.com was launched in April 1998 and started as an online version of the traditional pay-per-rental model used in movie rental stores. In September 1999, they introduced the monthly subscription concept still in use today; for a flat monthly fee, customers could get unlimited rentals without due dates, late fees, or shipping and handling fees. As soon as a customer mailed back the movie he currently had, he would be sent a new one.

Table 13.4: Financial Growth of Netflix.

Year	Revenue (in mil. $)	Net Income (in mil. $)	Market Cap (in mil. $)
2002	153	-22	267
2003	272	7	741
2004	506	22	1,260
2005	682	42	996
2006	997	49	1,770
2007	1,210	67	1,420
2008	1,360	83	1,590
2009	1,670	116	1,940
2010	2,160	161	3,060
2011	3,200	226	10,430
2012	3,610	17	5,280
2013	4,370	112	6,290
2014	5,505	267	22,340

Netflix now offers on-demand internet streaming of many titles, as well as over 100,000 titles on DVD.

In September 2002, four years after launching their website, Netflix had 670,000 subscribers. By September 2006, they had reached 5.6 million subscribers, and in July 2014 they announced over 50 million subscribers in 40 different countries. Table 13.4 lists the revenue, net income, and market capitalization of Netflix for the years 2002-2014. After taking a hit to Net Income in 2012 (attributed to a change in the subscription policy), Netflix is on the rise again.

Cinematch

Netflix introduced its recommendation system, called Cinematch, in 2000. Users of Netflix are asked to give a rating, from one to five stars, for any movie they have watched. These ratings are used to power the recommendations.

The recommendation system helps to keep more of the movie library in circulation since people receive recommendations from the entire library of movie titles, not just recent or mainstream movies. This gives independent films and movies that were not very successful in the theaters a wider distribution. Netflix has reported that 60% of subscribers add recommended movies to their list of movies to watch.

According to Netflix, the original Cinematch algorithm used "straightforward statistical linear models with a lot of data conditioning." They claimed that the predictions from Cinematch were accurate within half a star 75% of the time, and half of Netflix users gave five stars (the best possible rating) to movies that they rented after a recommendation.

The Netflix Prize

In October 2006, Netflix announced that it would award a one-million-dollar prize to the first developer of a recommendation algorithm that could beat Cinematch at predicting customer ratings by more than 10% (in terms of root mean squared error) on a data set. Netflix provided the competitors with a training set of over 100 million ratings that 480,189 customers gave to 17,770 different movies. Each entry included the user ID, movie ID, date of the rating, and the rating (from one to five stars). This data set was much larger than previous recommendation data sets that had been made available to researchers in the field of collaborative filtering and recommendation systems.

The contestants had to improve the predictive accuracy on a qualifying set of over two million ratings, for which the true results were only known to the judges of the competition. This contest was intriguing to both Netflix and recommendation system researchers; if someone claimed the prize, Netflix would have a much improved recommendation system and increased publicity, and the winner would win one million dollars and become well known in the field of recommendation algorithms.

Six days after the contest went live, a team had already submitted an algorithm that beat Cinematch. By June 2007, eight months after the contest started, over 20,000 teams had registered from over 150 different countries. At this point, teams started joining forces to improve their algorithms even more.

On June 26, 2009, almost three years after the competition started, the team "BellKor's Pragmatic Chaos" submitted a 10.05% improvement over Cinematch, signaling the end of the contest. However, Netflix decided to announce a "last call," which meant that teams had 30 days to make additional submissions. With one day left, the team "The Ensemble" submitted a 10.09% improvement, and by the time the competition officially ended, "BellKor's Pragmatic Chaos" had also submitted a 10.09% improvement. Netflix then tested the algorithms on a private test set, which the competitors had never seen before.

On September 18, 2009 the million dollar prize was awarded to "BellKor's Pragmatic Chaos." This team was composed of two researchers from AT&T labs, two Austrian researchers from Commendo Research & Consulting, one researcher from Yahoo!, and two Canadian researchers from Pragmatic Theory. This team combined many different recommendation strategies in their final algorithm, including nearest neighbors and matrix factorization, which we will focus on here. They also discovered unusual characteristics of users, including the fact that people tend to rate movies differently on Fridays versus Mondays, and that ratings can be very different depending on how long ago the user saw the movie.

It was the combination of many different ideas that made the winning algorithm successful. This is a general principle of analytics: successful systems often use sophisticated infrastructure to combine a variety of approaches.

Nearest Neighbors

The Nearest Neighbors method is similar to content-based filtering in that ratings are predicted based on the similarity between items.

We can again define the rating of user A for item i by $r_{A,i}$ and the similarity between items i and j by $s_{i,j}$. The similarity between items can be computed in many different ways, and typically depends on the type of item. For example, if we are rating movies, then two movies would probably have a higher similarity score if they are in the same genre, or have the same director.

Of all of the items that a user has rated, a certain number of the most similar items are selected and used to predict the user's rating for a new item. The group of items that are considered the most similar to an item are called the *neighborhood* of that item. Thus, predicted ratings do not consider other users, just similar items that a particular user has rated. Using this approach, the predicted rating for user A and item k is:

$$r_{A,k} = \frac{\sum\limits_{j \in N(A;k)} s_{j,k} r_{A,j}}{\sum\limits_{j \in N(A;k)} s_{j,k}},$$

where $N(A;k)$ is the set of neighbors of item k that have been rated by user A. The neighbors depend on the particular recommendation system. For example, the neighbors of the movie *The Shawshank Redemption* probably would include other movies based on books by Stephen King, other movies directed by Frank Darabont, or other movies starring Morgan Freeman.

As in collaborative filtering, there are various methods that can be used to define the similarity between two items. There are also variations of this method that weight the neighbors differently. If two neighbors of an item are very similar themselves, it is almost like the same movie is being counted twice. For example, the three movies in *The Lord of the Rings* trilogy are all considered similar to *The Chronicles of Narnia: The Lion, The Witch, and The Wardrobe*, and would probably all be considered neighbors with very similar similarity ratings. Additionally, most people probably give similar ratings to the three movies in the trilogy (when compared to all other movies in the database), and so it is like there are three identical terms in the numerator for the predicted rating of *The Chronicles of Narnia* movie. This gives the trilogy a weight that is three times larger than the weight of any other neighbor. Since there are three movies, some people could argue that this is accurate, but since the movies all belong together, other people could argue that it is unfairly weighted. Situations like this produce different variations of the Nearest Neighbors method.

Matrix Factorization

Many submissions for the Netflix Prize used the method of *matrix factorization*, including the team that ultimately won the million dollar prize. This method represents both items and users by vectors of a fixed length. The length of these vectors is much smaller than either the number of items (like in collaborative filtering) or the number of users. Instead, each entry of the vector represents some possible characteristic of the item, like in content-based filtering. For a movie, the entries in the vector might be whether the movie is a drama or comedy, the amount of violence, the rating, etc. The values in the vectors for users are weights that represent how much they like high values in that component of the vector. Assume for now that the user's weights are numbers between 0 and 1, where 0 means that they do not like movies with high numbers in that entry at all, and 1 means that they love movies with high numbers in that entry.

As a small example, suppose our items are movies and we have vectors with three entries: the amount of violence on a scale of one to five, whether the movie is a drama or comedy (a value between 0 and 1 with 0 representing a dramatic movie with no comedy, and 1 representing a funny movie without drama), and the popularity/experience of the cast (on a scale of 1 to 10, with 1 being a movie with an unknown cast, and 10 being a movie with a very well-known cast). A possible vector for *The King's Speech* could be $(1, 0.1, 8)$, since it had very little violence, was mostly a drama, and mostly had a very well-known cast. The movie *Pulp Fiction* could have a vector $(5, 0.5, 9)$ since it is a violent movie with comedy and drama, and also had a very popular cast. Similarly, we can imagine different vectors for users. A person who likes violent dramatic movies and thinks a better cast indicates a good movie might have a vector $(0.9, 0.1, 0.75)$, whereas a person who prefers comedies and doesn't really care about the cast might have a vector $(0.2, 0.9, 0.2)$.

The amount a user might like an item is predicted by taking the sum of the corresponding terms of the vectors multiplied together (the inner product of the vectors). Thus, we predict that a person with vector $(0.9, 0.1, 0.75)$ will give a rating of $(0.9 \times 1) + (0.1 \times 0.1) + (0.75 \times 8) = 6.91$ to *The King's Speech* and a rating of $(0.9 \times 5) + (0.1 \times 0.5) + (0.75 \times 9) = 11.3$ to *Pulp Fiction*. However, these ratings don't necessarily match on the scale of the ratings that users are giving to movies. If this was for Netflix, the predicted ratings should be between one and five, since a user gives a one to five star rating for a movie. To fix this, we estimate the item and user vectors using ratings that we already know.

Suppose we have a user who gave a rating of 5 to *The King's Speech*, 4 to *Pulp Fiction*, and 3 to *The Godfather*. We need to find the user's vector (u_1, u_2, u_3), the movie vector for *The King's Speech*, (a_1, a_2, a_3), the movie vector for *Pulp Fiction*, (b_1, b_2, b_3), and the movie vector for *The Godfather*, (c_1, c_2, c_3). From the ratings, we know that

$$(u_1 \times a_1) + (u_2 \times a_2) + (u_3 \times a_3) = 5$$

$$(u_1 \times b_1) + (u_2 \times b_2) + (u_3 \times b_3) = 4$$
$$(u_1 \times c_1) + (u_2 \times c_2) + (u_3 \times c_3) = 3.$$

Using all known ratings by users for items, we would like to estimate the item and user vectors. This can be done using one of several different matrix computation methods (for more details, see the references in Section 13.7). This technique gives us vectors for all items that have ever been rated and for all users that have ever rated an item. This allows us to predict ratings for users and items that we did not originally have a rating for.

Several extensions of the matrix factorization technique have been implemented. One idea used by the winners of the Netflix prize is that users often select which items to rate, and so missing ratings can also provide information. It could be that a user tends to rate movies that they love or hate, and so we can assume that if a user watched a movie and didn't rate it, they probably neither loved nor hated it.

13.4 Amazon

Named after the largest river in the world, Amazon.com has become the world's largest online retailer. The company was founded in 1994 by Jeff Bezos and is headquartered in Seattle, Washington. It started as an online bookstore, but now sells almost any item imaginable, including electronics, furniture, food, and toys. It has an established presence in over ten countries in addition to the United States.

Amazon.com, Inc. issued its initial public offering of stock in May of 1997. The initial business plan was to not expect a profit for four to five years, which provoked stockholder complaints. But when the dot-com bubble burst, Amazon did not go out of business like many of its competitors, and finally turned its first profit in the fourth quarter of 2001, seven years after the company was launched. Table 13.5 gives the revenue, net income, and market capitalization of Amazon for the years 2001-2014.

Amazon's Recommendation System

In 1998, Amazon developed a recommendation system called "item-to-item collaborative filtering," which is still in use today. The basic idea of item-to-item collaborative filtering is to use the methods of collaborative filtering on the items themselves. Unlike content-based systems where similarity is only defined based on attributes of the items, this method also considers items to be similar if customers tend to purchase them together. Thus, the attributes of the items themselves and the behavior of the entire customer population are taken into account. One of the benefits of this approach is that there is no need for the customers to rate items to receive good recommendations.

This method uses a mapping between items and similar items. Occasionally, the previous purchases of customers are analyzed and items are deemed similar if enough customers purchased them together. For example, if many customers purchased an Origami book together with extra Origami paper, these items would be considered very similar. The higher the number of customers who purchased the items together, the more similar the items are considered to be. Note that this method does not require all pairs of items to be considered; only those that customers actually purchased together. So if an Origami book and Calcium supplements are never purchased together, the algorithm doesn't even need to compute the similarity between these two items. Items can also be considered similar based on their attributes, as in content-based systems, to enhance the accuracy of this method. So the Origami book and the extra Origami paper might be considered similar, even without a customer having purchased them together.

To generate a set of recommendations for the user, the system retrieves the items that were considered similar to the items that we know the user likes (either by the user giving a high rating to the item, or by the user putting the item in their online shopping cart). These similar items are combined into a list that is shown to the user. Based on how similar the items are, they might be shown in a particular order, such as the most similar to the least similar, or the similar items to the customer's most recent purchases might be shown before the similar items to older purchases. These strategies are meant to increase the likelihood that the customer will actually purchase items in the

Table 13.5: Financial Growth of Amazon.com. Note that the net income of Amazon in 2012 and 2014 was negative, partly due to an increasing trend of spending by Amazon on digital content.

Year	Revenue (in mil. $)	Net Income (in mil. $)	Market Cap (in mil. $)
2001	3,120	-567	4,550
2002	3,930	-149	6,390
2003	5,260	35	15,220
2004	6,920	588	17,850
2005	8,490	359	16,600
2006	10,710	190	14,870
2007	14,840	476	27,970
2008	19,170	645	29,910
2009	24,510	902	27,360
2010	34,200	1,150	58,760
2011	48,080	631	82,580
2012	61,090	-39	83,880
2013	74,450	274	123,190
2014	88,990	-241	179,720

recommendation list.

One of the advantages of item-to-item collaborative filtering is that by analyzing the recent purchases of customers, it can detect buying trends of customers. The method also is able to compute recommendations on the spot since the similarity mapping is previously calculated.

In 2010, the online video sharing website YouTube revealed that it is using a new system that is a variation on Amazon's item-to-item collaborative filtering technique. Even though Amazon's recommendation method was developed over ten years ago, Google still considered it to be so effective that they wanted to implement a version of it themselves.

13.5 eHarmony

Founded in 2000, eHarmony is an online dating site that matches single men and women for long-term relationships. The company is privately-held, and has over 20 million registered online users. In 2009, it exceeded one billion dollars in cumulative revenue over its ten years of existence.

It was started by Dr. Neil Clark Warren, a clinical psychologist, who used his 35 years of experience counseling married couples to define the traits that often lead to relationship success. According to Dr. Warren, "opposites attract, then they attack." Their strategy seems to be working, since an average of 542 eHarmony members marry every day in the United States as a result of being matched on the site, and nearly 4% of marriages in the United States in 2012 were a result of eHarmony.

Prospective eHarmony members complete a questionnaire with over 400 different questions about their characteristics, beliefs, values, emotional health, and skills. They are then matched by eHarmony using algorithms that the company has developed and refined. While the details of these algorithms are not publicly known, the idea is very similar to recommendation systems used by Netflix and Amazon. However, because of the two-way nature of dating recommendation systems, the process can be much trickier. For both Netflix and Amazon, the customer just has to like the movie or item. But in online dating, not only does the customer have to like the match, but the match has to like the customer back. It is not enough to make recommendations to a user of other people that they might be interested in. The system has to recommend people that the user is *compatible* with; people who the user is interested in and who are also interested in the user. Using information on known successful matches, the previous history of users can be used to find other matches that are predicted to be successful.

Unlike many other online dating sites, the users at eHarmony are not allowed to browse photos and profiles of all members, only the ones that the algorithms match them with. This system serves two purposes: it tries to increase the number of long-term relationships resulting from the site, and it reduces the number of profiles that users have to search through. With over 20 million members on eHarmony, it can be very useful for the site to provide recommendations. Other online dating sites are also increasingly using recommendation systems. Since there are many different online dating sites to choose from, companies are looking for ways to make their recommendations more complex and personalized. This leads to more and more systems like those resulting from the Netflix prize.

Chief Technology Officer of eHarmony Joseph Essas, previously at Yahoo!, developed matching algorithms that are based on Yahoo's system for targeting advertising based on specific users' preferences and behaviors. These algorithms have been shown to be very useful in online dating, because what people say they want and what they actually want are often two different things. These new algorithms not only take questionnaire responses into account, but also how people behave and communicate. Software innovation has become a key priority for eHarmony, and they have already seen a 10% increase in users communicating with their matches due to more sophisticated recommendation systems.

13.6 The Edge of Recommendation Systems

This chapter has shown that many companies are willing to invest large amounts of resources into creating strong recommendation systems, since helpful recommendations lead to satisfied customers and increased sales. While recommendation systems are very appealing, they also need to be efficient and appropriate. We have seen through the examples in this chapter that there are many factors that contribute to a successful recommendation system:

1. Depending on the specific business, the appropriate type of recommendation system needs to be used. The recommendation system that was constructed as a result of the Netflix prize was designed to predict movie ratings and help customers find interesting movies. Similarly, Amazon's recommendation system is designed to perform well on many different types of items, while eHarmony's recommendation algorithm is built to recommend compatible matches.

2. A successful recommendation system often needs large amounts of data. Without a large database of customers and previous purchases or ratings, it is challenging to find appropriate recommendations.

3. The recommendation system should provide fast and accurate results. Customers need the recommendations to appear as soon as the webpage loads. Additionally, customers will become impatient if the recommendation system is not providing recommendations that they are interested in.

Recommendation systems can be used in a variety of fields, including commerce, science, and politics. There are companies that use recommendation algorithms to suggest employers to job seekers and investors to companies seeking capital. Recommendation systems efficiently use massive datasets on customers and purchases to improve the experience of the customer and increase the sales of the company.

13.7 Notes and Sources

The financial information in this chapter is provided by Wikiinvest [151] and Ycharts [155].

13.3. The details about Netflix are from the press and investor pages of netflix.com [101, 100], and the information on the Netflix Prize is from a paper written by the winners of the prize [13].

13.4. The information about Amazon is from amazon.com and from a paper about their recommendation system [85].

13.5. The information about eHarmony is from eHarmony.com and from several news articles [127, 63].

Part V

Combating Crime

Chapter 14

Fraud Detection

Corruption, embezzlement, fraud, these are all characteristics which exist everywhere. It is regrettably the way human nature functions, whether we like it or not. What successful economies do is keep it to a minimum. No one has ever eliminated any of that stuff.

– Alan Greenspan

Contents

On July 18, 2005, the New York Times ran a story with the headline "New York Medicaid Fraud May Reach Into Billions" [80]. The authors, Clifford J. Levy and Michael Luo, reported that "New York State's Medicaid program had become a $44.5 billion target for the unscrupulous and the opportunistic."

Medicaid is a federal program that was adopted in New York State in the 1960s to provide medical coverage for residents who were not covered by any other medical insurance program and whose income was below a prescribed threshold. The annual cost of this program for New York State had grown to $44.5 billion by 2005. Private medical insurance companies had already found that consistently 10% to 20% of their claims should not have been paid because they were either fraudulent or because the procedures were of no value. (The latter situation often occurred when prescribed tests and procedures were rendered obsolete by new medical developments.) Based on this, it was recognized that the annual loss to New York State due to fraud and abuse was many billions of dollars.

Levy and Luo used the state Freedom of Information Law to access information on payments made to physicians by Medicaid. They discovered extraordinarily large payments made to some providers; over one million dollars of these were deemed to be fraudulent. These included a dentist operating out of a Brooklyn storefront who claimed to have performed as many as 991 procedures one day in 2003. Her dental practice had grown to become the state's biggest Medicaid dental practice within one year. The New York Times investigation also discovered abuses in speech therapy, nursing home operations and in the diverting of drugs intended for AIDS patients to bodybuilders.

On July 19, 2005, Governor George Pataki of New York ordered a broad overhaul of state agencies that protect Medicaid from fraud and abuse, creating an independent inspector general's office and bringing in a former federal prosecutor to help reorganize the policing of the problem.

In this chapter, we discuss how a computer based analytics system can work with a trained human auditor to identify claims that should not be paid. We also describe experiences encountered when IBM's Center for Business Optimization used this system working with New York State to combat Medicaid fraud.

14.1 Reducing Health Care Fraud

There are many issues encountered when trying to reduce losses due to fraud and abuse in health care. A first challenge is detection: discovering which claims are likely to be fraudulent and which providers should be investigated. In some cases, such as a dentist claiming to have performed 991 procedures in a single day, this is not difficult. However, in other cases which are not as blatant, it becomes much more difficult to identify which claims and claimants are suspicious. Fraudsters often will try to hide spurious claims by inserting them with large groups of valid claims. It is often only by examining large numbers of transactions in the context of other claims that investigators can detect those that seem suspicious.

A second challenge is deciding which cases should be pursued and which of these cases should be taken to court. Investigations themselves are expensive and take time. The overall goal is to reduce unnecessary costs incurred by the program. If the savings resulting from an investigation are less than the cost of the investigation, then the process may be deemed counterproductive.

A third challenge is recovering payments which should not have been made. The traditional approach has been termed "chase and pay." This consists of detecting an improper payment after the fact and then attempting to recover the money. However, in many cases, it can be difficult or impossible to recover such payments. A more appealing solution is to detect fraudulent claims before payments are made and deny them. However, this has to be reconciled with the requirement that legitimate health care provider claims should be paid promptly.

A fourth challenge is that the world is constantly changing. Any system developed to detect fraudulent claims will need to adapt as quickly as fraudsters can invent new ways to cheat the system.

In general, there are two main ways of abusing a program. One is by unauthorized persons masquerading as legitimate claimants to a system and submitting claims that would be legitimate if they were submitted by a valid claimant. For example, a person who is not a medical doctor (MD) should not be able to be paid for claims that can only come from MDs.

The second occurs when a legitimate claimant makes a claim that should be rejected for any of several reasons. This can be a complex issue for Medicaid fraud prevention, because there are so many types of legitimate claims. As an example of this type of fraud, Levy and Luo reported that ambulettes (specially equipped vans for transporting patients unable to walk unaided in nonemergency circumstances) cost taxpayers up to $200 million per year. They regularly submitted claims for transporting scores of people who walked quite easily while being observed by a reporter. Moreover, in some cases, the rides that the state paid for may have never taken place.

The first problem, identifying a claimant and determining whether they are entitled to make a claim, is covered by a range of biometrics and knowledge based identifiers and we do not address it in this chapter. Our focus is on the second form of abuse: How can we tell whether a claim submitted by a legitimate claimant is itself valid and should be paid? Can we identify which legitimate claimants are submitting invalid claims?

14.2 Detection and Prevention of Medical Fraud and Abuse

Three main parties are involved in the providing of health care to insured patients: These are (a) *service providers*, which includes doctors, hospitals, ambulance companies, and laboratories; (b) *insurance subscribers*, which includes patients and patients' employers; and (c) *insurance carriers*, who receive regular premiums from their subscribers and pay health care costs on behalf of their subscribers. This last group may include governmental health departments as well as private insurance companies.

Li et al [83] report that the largest source of fraud is due to service providers. This is primarily due to billing for items, such as services not delivered or for procedures such as lab tests not actually obtained. This may place patients at risk and is recognized as the most urgent problem for improving the quality and safety of a health care system.

An insurance carrier receives tens of thousands of claims daily from providers. Most of these are legitimate but some are not, and should be rejected. If a claim is legitimate, it is important that it is paid promptly. If not, service providers may decide to stop accepting that company's coverage. If it has been paid, and subsequent analysis indicated that this was a mistake, then it may or may not be possible to recover the funds, but in either case, this may be difficult and very costly.

It is not expected that an analytic system will be able to correctly classify all claims. The goal of these systems is to quickly identify claims that are sufficiently suspicious that they warrant investigation by a human expert. An ideal system will keep the number of *false positives* – valid claims flagged for investigation – and *false negatives* – invalid claims approved for payment – below acceptable thresholds. Every false positive incurs an investigative cost, with no resulting recovery, and has a negative impact on the claimant's satisfaction with the company. Every false negative results in an invalid payment being made and which may be difficult or impossible to recover. It is easy to create a system that guarantees zero false positives by simply rejecting all claims, or zero false negatives by simply paying all claims. The difficulty is designing a system which maintains an acceptable balance between the two.

Determining an acceptable balance between false positives and false negatives depends mainly on the consequences of each type of error. Recovering from a false negative may require collecting invalid payments that were made. A false positive may be difficult to recover from if it results in service providers leaving the network.

In addition, claims selected for investigation should be prioritized based on the expected amount of funds recoverable. This depends on both the potential recovery from a paid fraudulent claim and the probability of a successful recovery of the funds.

The financial importance of reducing fraud and abuse can be significant. A major insurance carrier reported a net income from continuing operations of $1.3 billion in 2011. The total adjusted claims they paid was $0.75 billion. If 20% of these claims should not have been paid, this would have moved $0.15 billion from the cost line to the net income line in the annual report, an increase of approximately 3%.

A successful fraud prevention and recovery program should have the following characteristics:

- Claims are analyzed quickly enough to avoid unacceptable delays in payment of valid claims.
- The numbers of false positives and false negatives are kept below acceptable limits.
- Claims identified as suspect and passed on to investigators have sufficient value to justify the cost of investigation.
- Investigators are provided with data-based justification for rejecting the suspected fraudulent claims.
- The system is adaptable and able to respond quickly to new types of fraudulent claims.

The simplest types of fraud detection systems are *rule based systems*. In this case human domain experts create sets of rules that they expect valid claims to satisfy. For example, a dentist should not see more than twenty-five patients per day. A person living in a certain town should not live in a multi-million dollar home. A patient receiving treatment for hypertension should not require x-rays. A patient being treated for high cholesterol should not see a doctor more than twice per month.

Violating these rules may or may not indicate fraud or abuse. In some cases there may be a valid reason. For example, the person receiving treatment for hypertension may, at the same time, be diagnosed for another condition.

Claims are then processed by verifying that all or most of the rules defining acceptability are satisfied. If they are, the claim is paid. If not, the claim is rejected.

There are several difficulties with such a system. First, it is difficult to define effective sets of rules, especially for a rapidly evolving field such as medicine, where new processes, treatments and norms require the rule sets to be continually revised and updated. Second, the rules generally try to encapsulate the intuition of human experts. Often fraud is carried out in ways that avoid extreme exceptions to normal behavior. For example, a small number of fraudulent claims per month may pass through undetected. Third, it is difficult to detect new approaches to fraud.

Instead, data based fraud detection systems operate by assembling large collections of provider, insurer and patient data. They take as input records giving detailed information on all claims, healthcare providers and other medical factors. Domain experts then work interactively with the system to identify clusters of records, called *peer groups*, that should have similar characteristics. For example, cardiologists working in clinics of comparable sizes serving patients in the same communities could form a peer group.

After peer groups have been identified, a range of statistical measurements can be applied to the data in each group to determine normal behavior and identify statistical outliers. These become potential candidates for investigation.

Finding peer groups is an example of *unsupervised learning*. Unsupervised learning refers to approaches which do not depend on experts carrying out a prior classification of all claims in the training set as either valid or fraudulent before acceptance criteria are developed. Rather, they propose peer groups in the unclassified data and look for statistical outliers.

Targets for investigation are differentiated based on whether they are identified before or after payment of the claim has been made. *Forensic analysis* applies to claims which have already been paid. *Preventative analysis* reviews claims submitted but not yet paid. For the latter class of claims, speed of analysis is critical. For the former, not only must we take into account the probability of a claim in the cluster being fraudulent or improper for reimbursement, but also the size of the claim and the probability of a successful recovery.

14.3 Defining Peer Groups

The identification of peer groups uses *clustering*, an important class of analytics methods falling under the category of *unsupervised learning*. The input is normally a large database of records and the objective is to partition the records into smaller sets called *clusters* or *peer groups* all of which are "similar" and such that records in different clusters are "dissimilar." There are many different ways of clustering records, depending primarily on the choice and relative importance of attributes considered when determining the difference between two records. We provide general information on clustering in Chapter 21.

Records related to medical claims could contain the following data elements:

- Provider ID
- Provider Specialty Code
- Provider Address
- ZIP code of Provider
- Patient ID
- Patient ZIP Code
- Code for Service Provided
- Usual time claimed for service provided
- Date and time of service
- Charge for service

- Lab tests prescribed
- Pharmaceuticals prescribed

Suppose that we had data available for all medical claims received by an insurance company over a year. We could cluster the data in many different ways, based on (a) the provider ID or the Patient ID, (b) the provider address or the patient address, (c) the provider specialty, or (d) the month when the service was provided.

However, more useful clusters are often obtained by combining criteria. Suppose we clustered based on the combination of Provider Specialty Code, Code of Service Provided and Patient ZIP Code. This would enable us to consider data corresponding to patients living in different geographic areas who had certain services provided by different types of specialists. After clustering, we could try to identify "normal" behavior. For example, we might discover that in ZIP code 10589, patients seeing a certain specialty provider have certain types of services provided more frequently than those in a neighboring ZIP code.

When clustering criteria are chosen, we are then able to characterize common and unusual characteristics within each cluster. In the above example, if the number of bills with procedure code BX23 was, on average, three per month and provider 2642 billed for twenty-four per month, this would be detected as unusual behavior. This does not necessarily mean that there is fraud, but it does indicate that this could be a case worth investigating.

A key to success is choosing suitable clusters. If the clusters are too large, then it may be difficult to identify outliers for investigation. If, in the above example, we had grouped all specialties of providers together, then we might have found that within this larger group, twenty-four billings of procedure BX23 is normal, but when restricted based on the providers' specialty, it stands out.

There are many different ways to define clusters on a set of data. Usually, a first step is to decide which attributes are likely to be relevant for the subsequent analysis to be performed. For example, the number of doctor visits per year by a particular patient could be important but the patient's middle initial could be deemed to be irrelevant. Clustering is an iterative process and frequently, based on results obtained, the selected attributes will be changed and clustering will be redone.

It may also be advantageous to define new attributes which are composites of attributes coming in the raw data. Domain experts may know that a certain type of lab test is normally applied to specific types of condition and so may define a new attribute combing the test and the condition.

We define a *distance* or *dissimilarity index* between each pair of data records, based on the attributes that we wish to consider. In the above example, the distance between records s and t could be defined as follows:

Let $Specialty(s,t) = 0$ if s and t have identical Provider Specialty Codes and 10 if they are different.

Let $Service(s,t) = 0$ if s and t have identical Codes of Services Provided, 1 if the services are different but similar and 5 if they are completely different.

Let $ZIP(s,t) = 0$ if the ZIP codes are identical, 5 if they are different but in the same state and 10 if they are in different states.

The distance between records s and t could then be defined as

$$d(s,t) = Specialty(s,t) + Service(s,t) + ZIP(s,t).$$

More generally, we would define $d(s,t)$ to be a weighted sum of the attribute distance values, where the weights are determined by combining the assessments of domain experts and data analysts.

The goals are (1) for the members of each cluster to be sufficiently similar in the selected attributes that we could expect them to have similar billing characteristics, and (2) for the members of different clusters to be sufficiently different in their billing characteristics. These goals are often contradictory.

There are many different approaches to clustering; different methods may work better on different data sets. In practice a data analyst will often work together with a domain expert to find a combination of distance measure and clustering method which works well for the particular application.

Figures 14.1 and 14.2 illustrate some of the issues encountered with clustering. We have represented fifteen records by points where the measure $d(s,t)$ of the distance between records s and t is proportional to the Euclidean distance between the points representing the records.

Here are two trivial clusterings. One consists of a single cluster containing all the points. The other consists of fifteen clusters, each containing a single point. A possibly more useful clustering, shown in Figure 14.1, divides the points into four clusters containing five, one, six and three points.

In practice, we often want a clustering to satisfy additional properties. These could include upper and/or lower bounds on the number of points in each cluster or the total number of clusters.

Figure 14.1: Set of points representing 15 records and a "natural" clustering.

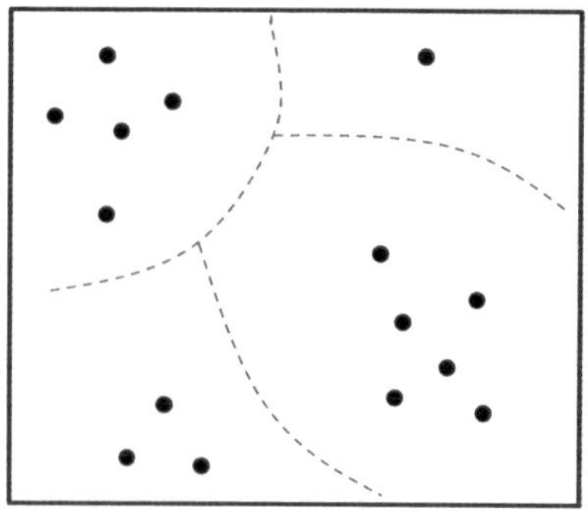

In Figure 14.2 we show a clustering satisfying the constraint that each set should contain at least four points. This constraint results in a clustering that looks less natural.

When we are using clustering to construct peer groups for fraud analysis, we generally do not have rigid size criteria. However, we do want the groups to be of a sufficient size to permit valid statistical analysis but still small enough to permit detection of a reasonable number of outliers across the entire population.

After a distance $d(s,t)$ between individual records s and t has been defined, we can extend the definition of d to a distance D between sets S and T of records in several ways. For example, the distance between two sets could be defined as the distance between the nearest pair of points in the two sets, the distance between the most distant pair of points in the two sets or the average distance between all pairs of points in the two sets.

The *diameter* of a cluster S is the maximum value of $d(s,t)$ for all $s, t \in S$.

The overall goal in clustering is to find a collection of clusters for which

1. the diameters are small;
2. the distances between clusters is large;
3. the sets satisfy any required size constraints;
4. the number of sets in the cluster is acceptable.

There are several general approaches. One is a "bottom-up" approach called *agglomerative hierarchical clustering*. Initially each point is a one element cluster. Then two existing clusters S and T, for which the selected distance measure is minimum, are repeatedly combined to create a larger cluster.

Another approach, called *divisive hierarchical clustering*, is "top-down." Start with a single cluster that contains all the points. Repeat the following operation until done: For each existing cluster which is too large, find a way to split the cluster into two smaller clusters S and T so that you maximize

Figure 14.2: Clustering with all sets containing at least 4 points.

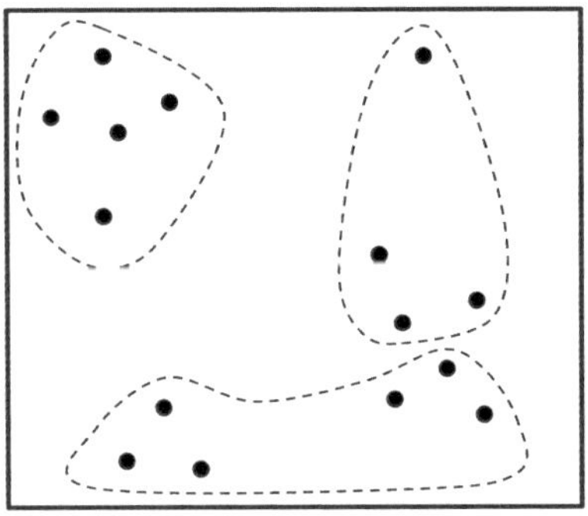

the distance between them. See Chapter 21 for further discussion of these approaches.

The use of clustering in fraud detection applications is to partition the data records into clusters for which the records have a high degree of similarity for a selected set of attributes. We can then apply statistical analysis to each cluster to understand typical behavior. In the Specialty/Service/Zip example, we could determine the average amounts of billings. We could also determine the average number of patients seen per day or the most common prescriptions associated with these services. Or, we could discover the extent to which these values are correlated with where a patient lives.

For fraud detection, the goal of clustering is to create clusters for which statistical outliers in the clusters are suitable targets for investigation. For example, these outliers could be healthcare providers seeing an unusually large number of patients per day or those who bill for an unusually large number of services, compared to other members of their peer group. In the next section, we describe the method of clustering that was the most effective in practice in creating peer groups which enabled identification of "interesting" outliers.

14.4 The Condorcet Method

In this section, we describe a clustering technique developed by Pierre Michaud and Jean-François Marcotorchino of IBM France [89]. It has been referred to by various names: *The Condorcet Method*, *Similarity Aggregation*, or *Relational Clustering*. It has been found to be very effective for performing clustering which enables detection of suspicious claims.

Suppose we are given a set R of n records. Each record contains the same sequence of m attributes (fields). An analyst typically begins by selecting a subset A of the attributes as the basis for the clustering. Let v be the number of attributes selected.

If the data is presented as a spreadsheet, then the records correspond to the rows, the attributes correspond to the columns and A is the set of v columns selected as the basis for the clustering. Let A_j be the set of all possible values for the jth attribute that can occur in the records.

Recall that a clustering is a partition of all records R into a number of pairwise disjoint sets called clusters. For *categorical* attributes the set of possible values in A_j is discrete and hopefully of a manageable size for each j. These contrast with *continuous* attributes which are allowed to take any value within a prescribed range. If A_j is categorical with a large number of categories, or continuous, we can perform a preliminary process called *bucketing*. We partition A_j into some manageable number of subsets and replace the original attribute with the index of the subset to which it belongs.

We can define a trivial clustering based on any single attribute. For each record r, we let r_j denote the value of its jth attribute. We put records r and s in the same cluster if $r_j = s_j$ and in different clusters if $r_j \neq s_j$. This defines a clustering consisting of at most $|A_j|$ clusters based solely on the value of the jth attribute but which completely ignores all other attributes. It is generally not of much use.

The Condorcet Method has two goals: The first is to define a distance measure that provides a "reasonable" combination of these trivial clusterings. The second is to develop an effective method of constructing a "good" clustering.

Distance and Optimal Clusterings

For each pair (r, s) of records, we let $d(r, s)$ be the number of attributes for which r and s *disagree*. We then have $0 \leq d(r, s) \leq v$ for every pair (r, s) of records, $d(r, s) = 0$ if r and s agree for all attributes in A and $d(r, s) = v$ if they disagree for all attributes in A.

We specify a target L satisfying $0 \leq L \leq v$. The goal is to create clusters satisfying the following conditions:

$$\text{If } d(r, s) \leq L, \text{ then } r \text{ and } s \text{ are in the same cluster;} \tag{14.1}$$

$$\text{If } d(r, s) > L, \text{ then } r \text{ and } s \text{ are in different clusters.} \tag{14.2}$$

In general, it is not possible to simultaneously satisfy these conditions for all pairs of records. Our goal is to efficiently find a clustering for which the amount of violation of (14.1) and (14.2) is small, ideally as close to the minimum as possible. This we do by computing a penalty $p(r, s)$ for each pair of records which violate (14.1) and (14.2) equal to $d(r, s) - L$ if r and s are in the same cluster and $d(r, s) > L$, or equal to $L - d(r, s)$ if $d(r, s) \leq L$ and r and s are in different clusters. We then try to construct a clustering which minimizes the sums of these penalties over all pairs $\{r, s\}$ of records.

For example, in Figure 14.3, the nodes represent four records r_1, r_2, r_3 and r_4. The values on the edge joining each pair of nodes $\{r_i, r_j\}$ represent the disagreement $d(r_i, r_j)$ between r_i and r_j. Suppose $L = 5$. The low disagreement on the edges r_1r_2, r_2r_3 and r_3r_4 indicates that we should have a single cluster consisting of all the records. The high disagreement on the edges r_1r_3, r_2r_4 and r_1r_4 indicates that we do not want a single cluster containing any of these pairs of records. Any way we cluster these records, we will either have two records with disagreement less than 5 in different clusters or two nodes with disagreement greater than 5 in the same cluster.

We blend the two conditions (14.1) and (14.2) by defining an aggregate measure:

$$D(\mathcal{C}) = \sum(d(r, s) - L : r, s \text{ are in the same cluster of } \mathcal{C} \text{ and } d(r, s) > L)$$

$$+ \sum(L - d(r, s) : r, s \text{ are in different clusters of } \mathcal{C} \text{ and } d(r, s) \leq L). \tag{14.3}$$

Note how (14.3) takes into account both disagreement between pairs of records in the same cluster and agreement between pairs of records in different clusters.

Our objective then is to find a clustering $\mathcal{C}$ for which $D(\mathcal{C})$ is as small as possible.

In the example of Figure 14.3, if $L = 5$, then the optimum clustering is $\mathcal{C} = \{\{r_1, r_2\}, \{r_3, r_4\}\}$ and $D(\mathcal{C}) = 2$. If $L = 8$, then the cost of this clustering would become $8 = (8 - 3) + (8 - 6) + (8 - 7)$. An optimal clustering $\mathcal{C}$ for this case would be a single cluster containing all the records and $D(\mathcal{C}) = 2$.

The second requirement for Condorcet clustering is an effective method of constructing a clustering $\mathcal{C}$ which minimizes, or comes close to minimizing, $D(\mathcal{C})$. Michaud and Marcotorchino proposed two approaches. The first is an exact optimization method which computes a clustering which minimizes $D(\mathcal{C})$. The second method is a heuristic which works well in practice but cannot be guaranteed to find a cluster $\mathcal{C}$ which actually minimizes $D(\mathcal{C})$.

The first method has the disadvantage that the time required can increase significantly as the number of records grows. This presents a problem because typically we have very large sets of records for fraud analysis because there is one for each transaction. We outline this method at the end of this section.

We focus here on the second, heuristic, method. It works well in practice, is relatively fast and is the method used in the software systems we describe in Section 14.6.

Condorcet Clustering Heuristic

We defined the distance $d(r, s)$ between records r and s as the number of attributes we are using for clustering for which the records have different values. We now define the distance $d(r, K)$ of record r from a cluster K as

$$d(r, K) = \sum(d(r, s) - L : s \in K \text{ and } d(r, s) > L)$$

$$+ \sum(L - d(r, s) : s \notin K \text{ and } d(r, s) \leq L). \tag{14.4}$$

Figure 14.3: Conflicting values of $d(r_i, r_j)$.

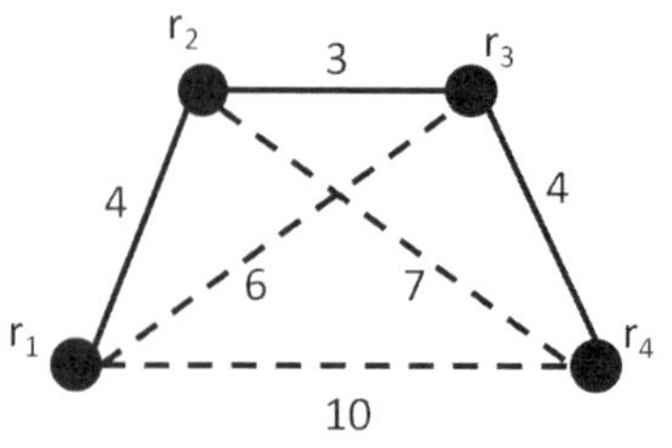

This captures the fact that if we add r to K, we incur a cost of $d(r, s) - L$ for each $s \in K$ such that $d(r, s) > L$, and incur a cost of $L - d(r, s)$ for each s such that $s \notin K$ and $d(r, s) \leq L$.

The Condorcet clustering heuristic has two phases. In the first phase it constructs a starting clustering $\mathcal{C}$ in a greedy fashion. In the second phase it repeatedly performs an improvement process wherein it makes local improvements to the current clustering $\mathcal{C}$ which reduce $D(\mathcal{C})$.

Initialize: Let $\mathcal{C} = \emptyset$ be the empty clustering.

Process each record $r \in R$ in turn.

If there exists a cluster K in $\mathcal{C}$ for which $d(r, K) \leq L$, then choose such a K for which $d(r, K)$ is minimum. Add r to K.

If there is no cluster $K \in \mathcal{C}$ for which $d(r, K) \leq L$, then we form a new cluster $K' = \{r\}$ and let $\mathcal{C} := \mathcal{C} \cup \{K'\}$.

Local Improvement: Process each record r in turn.

See whether $D(\mathcal{C})$ would be reduced by removing r from the set K containing it and adding it to a different set $K' \in \mathcal{C}$ or letting r be a new (singleton) cluster in the clustering.

If so, choose the best such option. If not, do nothing.

Repeat the Local Improvement step: Until no sufficiently large reduction in $D'(\mathcal{C})$ is obtained.

In practice, usually after a small number of repetitions (four or five) of the Local Improvement cycle, the reduction in $D(\mathcal{C})$ at each subsequent step becomes very small. At this point, we consider the clustering step to be complete and terminate this part of the process.

There are several possible variations to this method. Instead of simply defining d_{st} to be the number of attributes for which r_s and r_t differ, we could let d_{st} be the sum of measures of the differences between the attribute values using some suitable scale. We could also make d_{st} a weighted sum of the measures of these differences.

We could modify the Condorcet clustering algorithm local improvement step by "parking" any records that the algorithm selects to start a new singleton cluster. Then perform a second pass on these parked records after all other records have been processed. This can have the effect of delaying difficult decisions until many straightforward decisions have been made.

However, there are a couple of caveats: First, different variations may work better on some data and worse on other data. The best way to evaluate variations is to try them on real datasets and compare the outcomes. Second, the purpose of the clustering is to enable us to find outliers as described in the next section. Sometimes a clustering can be worse when evaluated by the clustering criterion, but still may enable us to find more interesting outliers.

Optimal Clustering*

The Condorcet clustering problem can be solved as a mixed integer optimization problem [89]. Recall that we are given a set R of n records and for each pair $\{r, s\}$ of records we have defined a distance $d(r, s)$ between the two records based on our selection of attributes, relative weightings of the attributes and the costs we assign to a difference in the values of each attributes for the two records.

We want to create a clustering of a set of the records in R based on $d(r, s)$. We can represent a clustering by a $n \times n$ (0,1)-matrix $X = (x_{rs} : r, s \in R)$ with the interpretation that $x_{rs} = 1$, if r and s are in the same cluster, and $x_{rs} = 0$, otherwise. We impose the following constraints on X:

- Reflexivity: (Each point is in the same cluster as itself.)
$$x_{ss} = 1 \text{ for all } s \in R, \tag{14.5}$$
- Symmetry: (If records r and s are in the same cluster, then both x_{rs} and x_{sr} have value 1.)
$$x_{rs} = x_{sr} \text{ for all } s, t \in R, \tag{14.6}$$
- Transitivity: (If r and s are in the same cluster and s and t are in the same cluster, then r and t are in the same cluster.)
$$x_{rs} + x_{st} - x_{rt} \leq 1 \text{ for all } r, s, t. \tag{14.7}$$

Any (0-1)-matrix $X = (x_{rs})$ satisfying (14.5), (14.6), and (14.7) defines the classes of an equivalence relation $\mathcal{R}$ defined on the records where $r\mathcal{R}s$ if and only if $x_{rs} = 1$. The clusters (peer groups) are the equivalence classes of $\mathcal{R}$.

Recall that we are also given a target value L. Our overall objective is for any pair $\{r, s\}$ of records to be in the same cluster if $d(r, s) < L$ and in different clusters if $d(r, s) \geq L$. To this end, for each $\{r, s\}$, we define a penalty p_{rs} to be incurred by any pair of records which violate this condition as follows:

$$p_{rs} = \begin{cases} d(r,s) - L, & \text{if } x_{rs} = 1 \text{ and } d(r,s) > L, \\ & [r \text{ and } s \text{ are in the same cluster}], \\ L - d(r,s), & \text{if } x_{rs} = 0 \text{ and } d(r,s) \leq L, \\ & [r \text{ and } s \text{ are in different clusters}]. \end{cases} \tag{14.8}$$

Our optimization problem then becomes:

$$\begin{aligned} \text{minimize} \quad & \textstyle\sum(p_{rs} : r, s \in R) \\ \text{subject to} \quad & (14.5),\ (14.6) \text{ and } (14.7) \\ & p_{rs} \geq (d(r,s) - L) - M(1 - x_{rs}), \quad \text{for all } r, s \in R \\ & p_{rs} \geq (L - d(r,s)) - M(x_{rs}), \quad \text{for all } r, s \in R \\ & x_{rs} \in \{0, 1\} \quad \text{for all } r, s \in R \\ & p_{rs} \geq 0 \quad \text{for all } r, s \in R, \end{aligned} \tag{14.9}$$

where M is a value at least as large as the maximum value of $d(r, s)$ over all pairs r, s of records.

As mentioned earlier, this approach could be used if the number of records is small, but will become computationally intractable if the number is large.

14.5 Detecting Suspicious Behavior

Assume that peer groups (clusters) have been created based on some combination of selected attributes. Now each cluster is analyzed to determine "normal" behavior and, more importantly, outlier behavior. For example, we might decide to investigate the total annual billings for all providers belonging to a selected peer group. We compute the mean μ and the standard deviation σ of these total billings. If the set of total billings for all providers belonging to the group is normally distributed, then about 99.7% of the values would lie within three standard deviations of the mean. Suppose that $\mu = \$180{,}000$ and $\sigma = \$20{,}000$. If we wanted to investigate those providers whose billings are in the top 0.15% of the population, we would investigate those providers billing more than $240,000.

This might produce too few or too many targets for investigation. In this case we could increase or decrease the limit of $240,000 as necessary to get a suitable number. By determining how many standard deviations from the mean the new target lies, we can estimate the fraction of the population that is targeted.

Determination of outlier behavior for a peer group begins by defining a target value which is computed from an attribute or a combination of attributes. This is usually done by a domain expert who is familiar with the problem being solved and can apply judgment as to what could indicate fraudulent behavior. For example, a target value could be the ratio of the annual tax paid by providers to the total amount of their annual billings. In this case, a small value might warrant investigation. The actual selection of target value is often as much an art as a science and depends on the skill and experience of the domain expert.

There still remains an important question: What is an appropriate model for the distribution of the target value? For example, a certain target value could be modeled by a bell curve, a skewed distribution or a fat tail distribution. There are statistical measures for evaluating how well a model of a certain type matches the data but often the most useful method is a dashboard. This provides a way for an analyst to view a number of different visualizations of the data on a screen at the same time. These visualizations can include a display of different distributions applied to sets of different possible target values. The analyst(s) can then select suitable models and target values. Then, based on these, outliers can be selected for investigation. Sometimes certain candidates for investigation show up with several different data models and target values. This helps give more confidence in the selection of providers.

This approach for selection of investigation targets has several important features. First, it can be repeated as often as desired, which means that if characteristics of records change, for example, claimants change some characteristics of their claims, then the peer groups can be re-created and possibly different outliers will be selected. Second, it becomes difficult for fraudsters to attempt to game the system because they do not know the basis for formation of the peer groups or of the selection of outliers belonging to the peer groups.

14.6 A Commercial Software Offering

Many fraud detection systems originated in the private sector and were subsequently adapted to the public sector. One such system is IBM's Fraud and Abuse Management System (FAMS). It was created in the early 1990s in partnership with CIGNA, a major health insurance provider, and has been refined continually since then. After it was deployed by several health insurance companies it was recognized that the analytic engine that had been created, called the Entity Profile Management System (EPMS), could be used for other applications in the area of fraud detection. These applications include detection of under reporting of tax (tax fraud) and detection of insider fraud within a company. This last application deals with a particularly problematic situation: trusted employees committing crimes misusing customer information. These are outlined in Section 14.8.

The basis of EPMS is peer group profiling. This is the process of describing sets of individuals, providers, insurers and transactions by sets of features and scoring these features individually based on their distributions.

The system supports a variety of distribution curves. These include bell curves, inverted bell distributions and a variety of distributions exhibiting left and right skews. For certain features, high values may represent an outlier. An example is the number of insurance claims by a provider. For other features, ultra low values may be suspicious. For example, an unusually small number of prescribed lab tests for patients having large amounts of claims for a certain medical diagnosis could be unusual. In the case of bell curves, either high or low values would be considered suspicious.

EPMS is designed to be used by domain experts who are familiar with the area of medical fraud, or more generally, with whatever type of fraud is being prevented. It provides a dashboard style interface which enables the expert to explore different combinations of attributes, score them based on the selected distribution curves, and thereby identify peer groups that are highly likely to exhibit fraudulent behavior.

The features are placed into business groups, for example, based on demographics, insurance claims, or historical records. These groups are not used in the evaluation of a combination of attributes, but are more amenable for human consumption. Each group is scored based on the associated distribution curves and the group score may be weighted based on the expert's experience and domain knowledge. These groups are then summarized into a composite score for a set of individuals, providers, insurers or transactions.

Rank based scoring provides a new algorithm used to generate feature, group and composite scores. The score is associated with the rank, the ordinal position, of a value in a sorted list. Curves such as Growth, Decline, Bell and U-Bell are still applied to each feature. In the case of a growth curve applied to a feature, as values reach the most extreme value they will receive higher scores. EPMS uses two algorithms. One calculates the score of a feature. The other algorithm combines these scores and weights into a group or composite score.

A high score could be triggered by a single extreme attribute and would result in a high score. However, a combination of non-extreme attributes could also produce a high score. This is important. Criminals who commit a small number of big crimes are easy to detect. What is more difficult to detect are people whose records contain a small number of slightly abnormal features over a long period of time. An example of this is robbing a bank! Skimming a fraction of a cent off every transaction is not easily detected, but can result in significant gain over time. Persons committing a single large robbery usually end up in jail, but criminals who skim a small amount of money over a long period of time are much harder to detect.

The scores are then scaled to integers in the range 0 to 1,000, where 1,000 denotes the most extreme outlier. They are presented from high to low because the developers found that users seemed to respond better to that range than the range of continuous values between 0 and 1 normally used by statisticians.

The purpose of the score is not to make a judgment but to provide a prioritized list to the investigating officer (auditor) who is the final decider in the overall process. This investigating officer is the most expensive and difficult to obtain resource. The business value of EPMS is to make optimal use of this limited resource.

Companies view reduction of waste due to fraud and abuse as a common goal and, for that reason, they are willing to share their experiences and findings with other companies. For this reason, a FAMS users group was created which permitted the exchange of usage tips as well as the effective peer groups that were discovered and what was deemed normal behavior. This was important because often claimants who were abusing the system would apply the same approaches to a variety of insurance carriers. Sharing the details of detected fraud and abuse could significantly reduce the time required to detect and combat new types of fraudulent claims.

14.7 Verify New York

In 2005, the State of New York wanted to find ways to reduce the $44.5 billion of annual medicaid expenditures without sacrificing the quality of the program.

Reducing fraud and waste was an attractive target. However, there were certain issues that needed to be addressed if the system was going to work in that environment.

A challenge was that in New York State, the medicaid program is handled independently by each of the sixty-two counties, with some coordination at the state level. The level of sophistication of the counties with advanced analytics solutions was highly variable. As a result, the decision was made to pilot a new version of FAMS which would have three features: First, it would be tuned to handle Medicaid claims. Second, it would access data from the state medical repository when requested and authorized by a county. Third, the results of the analysis which would be applied on a per county basis would be performed by a secure hosted service provided by IBM. The results of the analysis would be delivered to the counties in the form of written reports. This system was called "Verify NY."

On September 15th, 2005 State Senator Thomas Morahan posted an announcement that Rockland County was piloting IBM's fraud detection software to detect Medicaid fraud and abuse. The month after this announcement, the value of medicaid claims in Rockland County decreased by approximately 15%, even though no fraud investigations had been completed. A news story announcing the introduction of an anti-fraud system can itself have a significant deterrent effect.

The delivery of the system as a hosted service made it much more cost effective than it would have been to install and maintain separate systems in each of the sixty-two counties. However, it also gave the developers the new challenge of how to present the results in a form that could be used by human investigators. Not only did this system need to identify outliers but it also had to explain, in human understandable terms, what made that provider an outlier.

14.8 Detecting Tax Fraud and Insider Fraud

Following the creation of EPMS/FAMS and its successful use in combating health care fraud and abuse, other applications were developed which used EPMS to detect unusual behavior in other areas. It was used to identify income tax filers who seemed to be underreporting income and tax paid. The approach was similar to what had been done for detecting health care fraud. Tax filers were clustered into peer groups based on a variety of attributes. Standard behavior was determined for each group and outliers were identified.

A different application was to combat insider fraud within a company. For example, a bank teller may look up Social Security Numbers for several clients in the course of a day. However, if a teller looked up several hundred such numbers in the last half hour of a shift, this could be a cause for concern. In this case the application would signal an immediate alarm to a supervisor which would enable intervention. The underlying principles are the same: define clusters characterizing normal behavior and then look for outliers.

14.9 Notes and Sources

14.2. A good introduction to the broad field of fraud detection in health care is the paper [83].

14.4. The method of Condorcet Clustering described here is presented in the text book by Stéphane Tufféry [142]. See also the original paper by Michaud and Marcotorchino [89].

14.6. Often companies producing packages to combat fraud keep the details of their methods proprietary. For information on the specific approach described in this chapter, see Anderson et al. [4]. IBM's FAMS package has been installed at over forty healthcare insurance companies.

Chapter 15

Predictive Policing

I love catching people – it's what I live for – but what I'd rather do is live in a place and work in a place where crime didn't happen.

– Charlie Beck

Contents

On a weekday afternoon in July 2011, several Santa Cruz, California police officers were camped out in a downtown parking garage looking for car burglars. The officers spotted two women peering into car windows, and when they approached the women, the officers discovered that one had outstanding warrants, and the other was carrying illegal drugs. The presence of the police officers in the garage was unusual; they were given the tip by a computer program that predicted car burglaries would occur with high probability on that day, at that time, and in that garage. Two arrests were made that afternoon that most likely would not have happened without the help of predictive policing.

Predictive policing refers to the use of crime data together with computers and analytics to predict the locations where crime is more likely to happen, and therefore where more officers should be deployed. Prediction in policing is not a new practice; a search warrant is the response to a prediction that evidence will be found at a certain location, and police officers and detectives are often tasked with the job of predicting where the suspect fled or how the crime occurred. However, since many police departments have fewer police officers than they need, the use of analytics to predict crime may allow police departments to use their resources more efficiently. This chapter discusses several different ways that these methods are currently being used for predictive policing in major cities across the country, including Boston, Los Angeles and New York City.

Similar to the use of analytics in other fields, the key challenge in predictive policing is learning how to best use the different data sources available to build intelligent models. Some of the techniques that have been used include hot spots and crime mapping, data mining, optimization of police deployment, geospatial prediction, and social network analysis. We will discuss three different approaches to predictive policing in this chapter.

15.1 A Dynamic Crime Index

The Boston Regional Intelligence Center (BRIC), a subsection of the Boston Police Department, is tasked with the job of analyzing all of the crime in Boston, Massachusetts. To assist in the analysis of crime, the BRIC, together with a team of researchers from MIT, developed a Dynamic Crime Index that predicts the expected amount of crime for each neighborhood in the city of Boston. The tool is primarily used to synthesize all of the available historical data to determine how actual crime levels compare with expected crime levels. Before this tool was developed, crime levels were compared to the levels at the same time the previous year. The Dynamic Crime Index instead takes all of the historical data and yearly trends into account. When the crime in a certain neighborhood exceeds the expected amount of crime, an alert is given to the BRIC analysts to investigate what has been happening in that neighborhood, and police officers are warned to monitor that area better. The crime index also helps the analysts to determine which neighborhoods are expected to have a high level of crime. This is important to ensure that a red flag is only raised if the crime is outside the normal range for that neighborhood.

Data-driven crime prevention started with CompStat (Computer Statistics), a software program introduced by the New York Police Department (NYPD) in 1993. CompStat uses geographic information systems to generate crime maps that can be used by officers in meetings to employ new strategies to cut crime. The program is credited with decreasing crime, and is used in many cities across the United States. However, CompStat is not set up to use the data in real time or to provide a holistic view of crime, which are goals of the predictive policing methods discussed here.

Data

The main source of data used to calculate the Dynamic Crime Index is the Boston Police Department's incident database, which contains entries for all of the incident reports. These are reports given by officers after they have responded to dispatch calls. Each entry in this database has numerous fields, including the type, location, and time of the incident.

The type of incident is encoded using codes in the Uniform Crime Reporting (UCR) manual provided by the FBI. Additionally, the BRIC has created a crime code classification system that aggregates these crime types into groups. This analysis focuses on the following crime groups: homicide, assault, robbery, burglary (residential and commercial), larceny, and auto theft.

The location of each incident is categorized into a police district, and a reporting area. The reporting areas are smaller areas defined by the police department. The smaller reporting areas are used to match each crime incident to a neighborhood in Boston. The reason for a neighborhood analysis was the fact that other organizations (like the Census Bureau, the Boston Redevelopment Authority, and the Boston Public Health Commission) all report statistics based on neighborhoods. The following neighborhoods are used in the analysis: Allston/Brighton, Back Bay, Central, Charlestown, Dorchester, East Boston, Fenway, Hyde Park, Jamaica Plain, Mattapan, North End, Roslindale, Roxbury, South Boston, and West Roxbury. A map of the neighborhoods and police districts is shown in Figure 15.1. Note that the methods described here can also be applied to the police districts instead of neighborhoods.

The incident database used includes all incidents in Boston from January 2006 until May 2011. A monthly time scale is used, due to the known seasonality of crime (increased crime levels during warmer weather and decreased crime levels during colder weather). Additionally, each time interval must contain enough crime incidents to provide a sufficiently large sample size.

Methodology

The crime index uses all known data in the incident database to make predictions about future crime levels. Data from January 2006 through December 2010 was used to build the model, and data from January through May of 2011 was used to validate the model.

The first step of the method is to compute the historical average crime for each neighborhood, month, and crime type. Table 15.1 shows this computation for larceny in the month of January. The first column lists the fifteen different neighborhoods. The next five columns give the known number of larcenies in each of these neighborhoods in the month of January for the years 2006 though 2010. The last column averages the numbers in each row to give a historical average number of larcenies for each neighborhood in January. A

Figure 15.1: A map of the neighborhoods and police districts in Boston.

Table 15.1: Average Crime Computation for Larceny in January, for each neighborhood of Boston.

	2006	2007	2008	2009	2010	Average
Allston/Brighton	107	101	120	79	80	97.4
Back Bay	165	184	164	174	168	171
Central	220	265	206	188	224	220.6
Charlestown	38	31	14	22	19	24.8
Dorchester	162	177	165	159	162	165
East Boston	38	43	51	48	52	46.4
Fenway	47	71	56	66	73	62.6
Hyde Park	32	31	22	33	23	28.2
Jamaica Plain	67	61	76	49	66	63.8
Mattapan	49	55	58	53	48	52.6
North End	12	19	21	10	8	14
Roslindale	19	26	20	24	21	22
Roxbury	173	197	170	160	128	165.6
South Boston	55	69	83	53	76	67.2
West Roxbury	34	31	31	18	39	30.6

similar computation is done for all other months and all other crime types.

While the historical average crime takes all of the known data into account, it does not necessarily provide accurate crime forecasts for 2011. There may have been an increasing or a decreasing trend in the amount of crime for any number of reasons. Therefore, scaling factors are computed to account for these possible trends. Since each neighborhood and each crime type may have behaved in a different way, a different scaling factor is computed for each neighborhood and crime type. For example, if the number of larcenies in Roxbury has been increasing in the past five years but the number of larcenies in East Boston has been decreasing in the past five years, both of these trends are captured. All months are taken into account when computing the trends so that any abnormalities in the data are cancelled out and the true trend is seen. Figure 15.2 gives an example of one yearly trend. Each point is the number of larcenies in Allston/Brighton during the given year, divided by the historical average number of larcenies in Allston/Brighton. The line shown in the plot is found through a simple linear regression, which gives the best fitting linear trend in the data. If this line is extended one year further, it gives the estimated scaling factor for 2011. Since Allston/Brighton has a decreasing larceny trend, the average number of larcenies is scaled down. This trend gives a scaling factor of 0.80 for 2011, and so we will multiply all monthly historical averages for Allston/Brighton and larceny by 0.80 when forecasting crime. As an example, the historical average of the number of larcenies in January in Allston/Brighton is 97.4 (see Table 15.1). Thus the prediction for 2011 is $97.4 \times 0.80 = 77.92$. Note that this is a standard approach to forecasting, and can be used in many other application areas.

Figure 15.2: Allston/Brighton larceny trend. The points give the average number of larcenies in Allston/Brighton for the particular year, divided by the historical average number of larcenies in Allston/Brighton. The line is the best fitting linear regression line through the points.

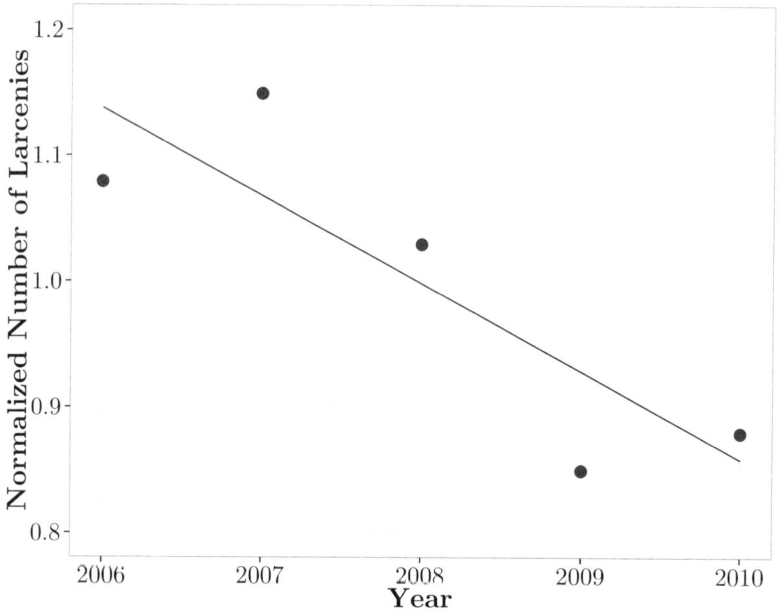

After finding the linear trends and scaling factors for each crime type and neighborhood, predictions for 2011 can be made. Note that while predictions for 2011 are made here, this method can easily make predictions for any year by using previous yearly data to compute the historical averages and yearly trends.

In addition to making precise predictions, we define a range in which we expect the actual number of incidents to fall (for each crime type, neighborhood, and month). For example, if a prediction of 80 is made for a particular neighborhood, but it has an expected range of 10, we would expect the number of incidents to fall within 10 of the prediction most of the time, or between 70 and 90. This is due to the fact that we do not expect to be able to predict the number of crimes exactly, and there will typically be some error between the prediction and what actually happens. If the actual amount of crime is within the expected range, then nothing unexpected has occurred. On the other hand, if the actual amount of crime is outside of the expected range, then we would say that something unexpected has occurred, and should be investigated.

To compute the expected range, the errors between the predictions and what has actually happened are analyzed. For the years 2006 through 2010, we look at the predictions we would have made using the historical average and the scaling factor from the yearly trend line. Since we know what actually happened for these five years, we can compute the absolute value of the difference between the prediction and the actual value:

$$\text{Error} = |\text{Prediction} - \text{Actual}|.$$

Thus if the prediction is 80 larcenies, but there are actually 85 larcenies, the error would be 5. We then find the ninetieth percentile value of all of the errors for a particular neighborhood and crime type, meaning the error value for which ninety percent of the error values are less than or equal to it. We chose the ninetieth percentile value as a cautious estimate for what the error will actually be. Note that we did this computation for each individual neighborhood and crime type, since we might expect a higher or lower amount of error depending on which neighborhood and which crime type we are referring to. For the rest of this section, we will refer to the expected range as the "90% range."

Results

We computed the index based on data from 2006 to 2010. We then tested it by analyzing how the model's predictions compare to actual data for the first five months of 2011. This is an out of sample experiment, meaning that the method was not developed using this data. It shows how well the crime index does on data it has never seen before.

Figure 15.3 shows the prediction, the 90% range, and the actual crime levels for the South Boston neighborhood and the crime type auto theft. The horizontal axis is the first five months of 2011, and the vertical axis is the number of auto thefts in South Boston for each of these months. The dark blue line gives the prediction, the shaded blue area gives the 90% range, and the black squares give what actually happened. This figure shows that the crime index predictions were very accurate for South Boston auto theft.

As another example, Figure 15.4 shows the prediction, the 90% range, and the actual crime levels for the Roxbury neighborhood and the crime type robbery. The predictions for January, February, March, and May were very accurate, but the actual crime level in April was much higher than predicted, even significantly above the 90% range. This is a sign that something unusual could have happened in Roxbury in April, and indicates that this is a neighborhood and crime type that deserves further investigation.

In this application and many others, being able to communicate the results of analytics with the end-user is critical. A set of equations or a huge table of predictions would not be very useful to the Boston Police Department. A visualization allows the analysts and officers to quickly understand what is happening. For more about data visualizations, see Chapter 21.

To assess the accuracy of the crime index, the method was compared to the method of using last year's crime levels to predict this year's crime levels.

Figure 15.3: Predictions for South Boston auto theft. The line gives the predictions, the shaded area gives the 90% range, and the black squares show what actually happened.

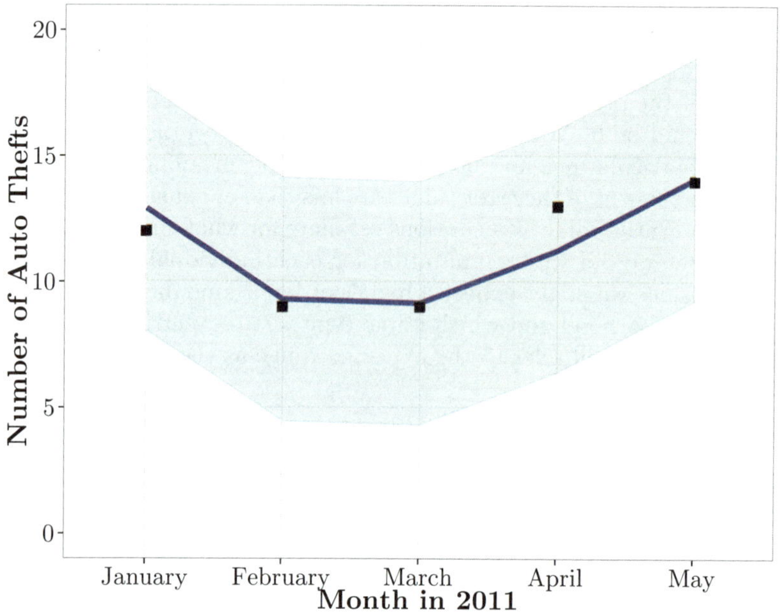

In the method where only last year's data is used, the prediction for each month, neighborhood, and crime type in 2011 is the actual crime levels for that same month, neighborhood, and crime type in 2010. Table 15.2 compares the average errors (for each crime type for the first five months of 2011) of using the crime index with the method of using last year's numbers. The first column lists the crime type, the second column gives the average error using the crime index, the third column gives the average error using last year's crime data, and the fourth column gives the percentage improvement in the average error by using the crime index instead of just last year's data. In terms of percentage improvement, the crime index is significantly better than using last year's data for larceny, robbery, assault, and homocide. It does slightly better than using last year's data for auto theft, and slightly worse than using last year's data for burglary.

A Simple Method with a Significant Edge

The crime index described in this section does not use sophisticated analytics, but it is able to give an edge over the methodology that was previously used to predict and assess crime in Boston. Within months, the BRIC in the Boston

Figure 15.4: Predictions for Roxbury robbery. The line gives the predictions, the shaded area gives the 90% range, and the black squares show what actually happened.

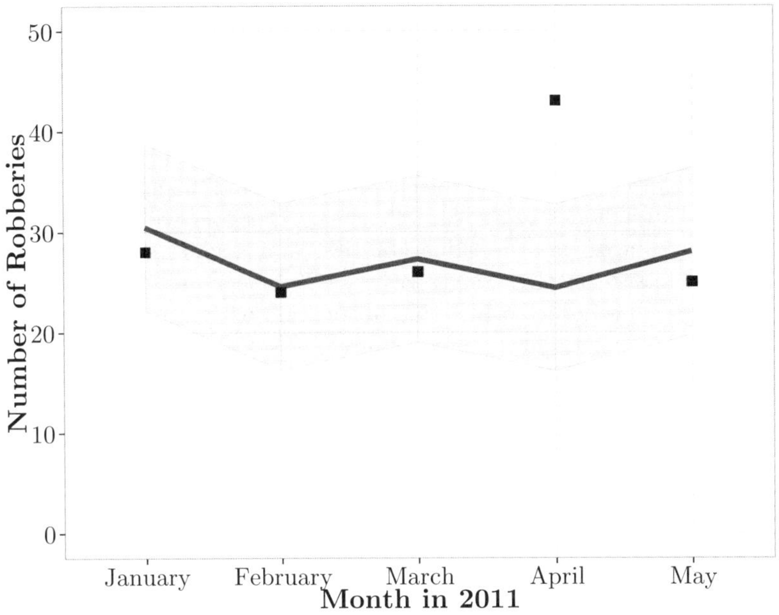

Table 15.2: Comparison of the Dynamic Crime Index with the approach of just using last year's crime, for each crime type.

	Average Error Using Crime Index	Average Error Using Last Year	Percentage Improvement
Larceny	11.42	14.64	22%
Robbery	3.07	3.83	20%
Burglary	6.24	6.09	−2%
Assault	3.83	6.20	38%
Auto Theft	3.84	3.91	2%
Homocide	0.31	0.37	16%

Police Department was able to use the Dynamic Crime Index as a new program to report abnormalities in crime patterns. When it comes to predicting crime, the analysts, police officers, and detectives do not care about how sophisticated the method is; they want something that works. This crime index shows the significant amount of potential for analytics to improve the current techniques being used in police departments across the country.

15.2 What Burglaries and Earthquakes Have in Common

The police departments in several California cities, including Santa Cruz and Los Angeles, have seen remarkable results from using a very new type of predictive policing. Like other methods, the ultimate goal is to predict where crime will happen, and put officers on the scene before the crime occurs. However, the analytics behind this work is very novel. Previous criminological research has shown that certain types of crime, like burglaries and gang violence, often behave like earthquakes. There is typically one hard to predict initial event (like the initial earthquake or initial burglary), and then several subsequent events (like aftershocks or repeat offenses). Burglars will repeatedly attack certain areas due to known vulnerabilities, and a gang shooting may cause retaliatory violence in the same territory. This leads to "crime clusters," or crimes that were committed in a similar location within a short time span.

Similarly, the event of an earthquake is well known to increase the likelihood of additional earthquakes in the same area (called *aftershocks*). Between 2004 and 2005 in Southern California, there were over 700 pairs of earthquakes of magnitude 3.0 or greater than occurred within 110 kilometers of each other and within less than 10 days of each other. After 10 days, the likelihood of repeat earthquakes significantly diminished; there were only about 200 pairs of earthquakes in Southern California of magnitude 3.0 or greater than occurred within 110 kilometers of each other and between 10 and 20 days of each other.

Models have been developed to capture this effect, known as Epidemic Type Aftershock-Sequences (ETAS) models. These models use a technique called "self-exciting point processes," which rely on probabilistic models to capture the repeat behavior. These models work by dividing earthquakes into two categories: background events and aftershock events. Background events occur independently from other earthquakes, which then elevate the risk of an aftershock event according to the magnitude of the background event, the distance from the background event, and the amount of time since the background event has occurred. A diverse group of researchers from several different California universities, including mathematicians, an anthropologist, and a criminologist, have developed a similar program to predict residential burglaries.

The Mathematics of the Method*

A self-exciting point process model is defined by the "conditional intensity" of the model, denoted by $\lambda(t, x, y)$. This represents the rate at which burglaries (or other types of events for other applications) occur at a specific location (x, y), and at a specific time t. All locations are defined by their coordinates (x, y) on a map of the area, where x is the horizontal coordinate, and y is the vertical coordinate.

Suppose there have been N previous burglaries. We denote each previous burglary by four numbers: the identifying number of the burglary k, where k ranges from 1 to N; the time of the burglary t_k, which is often taken to be the midpoint of the time window for which the burglary could have occured; the x-coordinate of the burglary x_k; and the y-coordinate of the burglary y_k. For simplicity, we will denote a previous event k by (t_k, x_k, y_k). These previous burglaries provide data for the model. In this research, 5,376 reported residential burglaries were used to build the model, thus $N = 5{,}376$. These burglaries all occurred in an 18km by 18km region of the San Fernando Valley in Los Angeles in 2004 and 2005.

Given this data, a general mathematical form of $\lambda(t, x, y)$ is given by

$$\lambda(t, x, y) = \nu(t)\mu(x, y) + \sum_{\{k:t_k<t\}} g(t - t_k, x - x_k, y - y_k).$$

The first term is the product of two functions, $\nu(t)$ and $\mu(x, y)$, and represents the rate at which burglaries occur at time t and in location (x, y) independently of previous burglaries (this captures the events that are not considered aftershocks, like the first big earthquake that occurs in an area without many previous earthquakes). The first function, $\nu(t)$, estimates the rate at which burglaries occur at time t, which typically accounts for things such as the weather, seasonality, and the time of day. It is assumed that there are factors correlated with the time that may increase the rate at which burglaries happen, independently of anything else. For example, it is known that crime typically increases in the summer and also increases on Friday and Saturday. Thus, the function $\nu(t)$ should give larger numbers when the time t is during these times. The second function, $\mu(x, y)$, estimates the rate at which burglaries occur in the location (x, y) without another burglary causing the event. It is known that some areas have higher burglary rates, just based on the location. This could be due to economic conditions in the area, the presence of gangs, or other factors.

The second term in the equation for $\lambda(t, x, y)$, given by

$$\sum_{\{k:t_k<t\}} g(t - t_k, x - x_k, y - y_k),$$

represents the estimated rate at which burglaries occur at time t and location (x, y) as a consequence of the occurrence of previous burglaries. It takes the sum over all previous burglaries k that occurred before time t, or for which $t_k < t$. The sum is of the function $g(t - t_k, x - x_k, y - y_k)$, which takes into account the time between the previous burglary and the current time t, and the distance between the previous burglary and the location (x, y). The function g can also take many forms, but it typically increases as the time and distance of the previous event approach the time t and location (x, y). The functions ν, μ, and g can be estimated using an iterative procedure, like that described in the Google PageRank computation in Chapter 11.

If $\lambda(t, x, y)$ is high, then the model predicts that there will be a high rate of burglaries at time t and in location (x, y). This can also be seen as a high probability that a burglary will occur at time t and location (x, y).

The Model in Action

Given this model, police officers are equipped with "hot-spot maps," which show the areas for which $\lambda(t, x, y)$ is predicted to have the highest values. By using the idea that burglaries often occur at similar times and in similar spaces together with the idea that some burglaries occur independently of other burglaries (just like earthquakes), this work is able to make the hot-spot maps much more accurate than just using the past data alone.

The Santa Cruz Police Department started using this technology in July 2011. Within the first month, it helped officers pre-empt several crimes and led to five arrests. The model was calibrated with eight years of crime data, and new data is added each day. Officers are given a list of the ten highest-probability "hot-spots" at the beginning of each day. They then check these areas during the times that they are not out on service calls. Before they started to use this program, officers would make these checks based on hunches or experience alone. With the addition of this technology, the officers feel that either their intuition about the high crime locations was validated or that they were given new focus areas that were previously unknown.

Following the success of the program in Santa Cruz, it was implemented in the Foothill Division, north of downtown Los Angeles, in November 2011. Los Angeles Police Chief Charlie Beck believes that predictive policing is the best way for him to use the limited resources that he has more efficiently. As of April 2012, burglaries were down 33% and violent crime was down 21%. This success has encouraged Beck to expand the technology to other areas of Los Angeles.

15.3 Real Time Crime Centers

One of the most important ingredients in any predictive policing model is data. Without data, it would be impossible to build models to predict and assess crime. Due to the Real Time Crime Center (RTCC) at the New York City Police Department, analysts in New York never have to worry about not having enough data. The RTCC was opened in 2005, and is a technical information hub designed to aid criminal investigations by giving detectives more information than the standard descriptions of the suspect, such as height and weight. The RTCC has access to many databases, which hold over 120 million criminal complaints, arrests, and 911 call records dating back ten years. They also include criminal records, parole files, and more than 31 million records of crime committed nationwide. Detectives in the RTCC look for information in these databases that they then send to officers on the street. There are databases for tattoos, body marks, teeth, and even a database for the way people walk, noting any limps and how severe they are.

One of the key components of the RTCC is data analysis. The RTCC staff employs data analytics to use the massive amount of information available to them. They can visualize patterns and trends on maps and search through the free text of multiple sources simultaneously to find patterns. Before this software existed, police officers would spend days or weeks sifting through paper records and field reports. Now, officers have instant access to the information electronically. This gives officers and detectives more time to solve the crimes, rather than many hours spent digging through police reports and databases.

The Importance of Visualizations

With over 120 million records, it is critical to display information in the RTCC in a clear and comprehensive way. For this, the RTCC analysts rely heavily on visualizations, not only for internal use, but also for officers in the field. Whenever an incident occurs, they can visualize the location on a map, and better understand the type of area and how this incident relates to other incidents in the past.

In addition to geographic maps, they use a technique called "link analysis." This displays all of the information known for an incident in a network of items and links between them. The items can include weapons, people, locations, and other components of the crime. An example of this type of visualization is shown in Figure 15.5. This particular visualization is from the Times Square bombing attempt in May of 2010. The suspect was captured two days after the incident, in part because of the advanced technology used in the RTCC. The graph links the suspect with information about the car, location, and items found. This type of visualization is also helpful in making other arrests in connection with a crime.

Throughout the United States

There are now real time crime centers in many cities throughout the United States. The Memphis Police Department's RTCC has started using IBM's predictive analytics software together with this data, to predict crime trends, deploy officers, and identify "hot spots," places for which crime is predicted to occur with high probability. The Memphis Police Department is calling this initiative Blue CRUSH, or Criminal Reduction Utilizing Statistical History, and it has been built in partnership with the University of Memphis' Department of Criminology and Criminal Justice. Blue CRUSH works together with the data in the RTCC.

The Houston Police Department, responsible for the largest city in the state of Texas, receives about one million calls for service annually. With this amount of activity, their RTCC, which opened in 2008, is able to not only help quickly solve crimes, but also to increase officer safety. The police department

Figure 15.5: An example of a link analysis visualization shown to President Barack Obama when he visited the New York Police Department's Real Time Crime Center in 2010, after the May 1, 2010 Times Square bombing suspect was captured.

can use an officer's location to let them know if new crimes have been reported in the area.

The city of Alburquerque, New Mexico also set up an RTCC in 2013, with the mission of getting police officers all of the information they need before heading to the scene of a crime, and to provide them with real time information while they are there. They call the RTCC "the bridge," because it is able to bridge the wealth of data available with officers in the field.

15.4 Notes and Sources

The information in this chapter about predictive policing in general comes from a U.S. Department of Justice strategy article [144].

15.1. The material in this section is from Bertsimas, Frankovich, and O'Hair [21].

15.2. The information about the work done in California comes from several newspaper articles [110, 116, 54] and an academic research paper [98].

15.3. The information about Real Time Crime Centers comes from several online videos [134, 119] and news articles [123, 138, 66, 59]. Figure 15.5 comes from Reuters News Agency.

Chapter 16

Network Science and Policing

Society does not consist of individuals but expresses the sum of interrelations, the relations within which these individuals stand.

– Karl Marx

Contents

Violent street gangs are major perpetrators of criminal activity in the United States, especially in larger cities. Police forces are introducing so-called "smart policing" tactics with the goal of reducing the activity and impact of gangs. Traditionally, these approaches have been focused on the allocation of law enforcement resources to increase arrests with the hope of deterring criminal behavior.

In this chapter, we describe a different type of smart policing, which has the goal of intelligently targeting individual gang members and offering them incentives to leave their gang. This process of encouraging disenrollment from a gang, referred to as *pulling levers*, is already employed in cities such as Boston and Chicago. However, selecting which specific gang members to target is still largely unanswered and often performed using ad-hoc methods.

We describe here an analytics-based approach to selecting targets for disenrollment programs. The underlying principle is that if the members targeted for disenrollment are well chosen, then other gang members may also defect. The goal is to find a set of gang members to target whose defection would maximally degrade the gang's operations. This takes into account the cost of inducing the targeted members to defect as well as the potential degradation to the gang caused by defection of the targeted members plus those other members induced to defect by the departure of the targeted gang members. This is called the "social incentive influence" (SII) problem. We describe an approach to solving SII and the results of experimental results, including tests on applying SII to real-world police data.

This application belongs to the growing field of *social networks*. This is a rapidly growing area of data analytics which not only considers the characteristics of individuals but also the types and strengths of the interactions between different individuals. We introduce this topic and give some examples after providing more detail on gang disincentive programs.

This chapter provides an example of how analytics based methods can be created for new problems which do not fit into standard models. This requires an accurate understanding of the characteristics of the problem as well as recognizing hard and soft constraints. A *hard constraint* is one which must be satisfied by a solution. A *soft constraint* is one that we would like to have satisfied, but for which we are willing to accept "small" violations. In addition, often applying analytics to solve real problems requires creation of effective heuristics – methods which cannot be shown to always provide optimal solutions, but which generally work well in practice.

16.1 Gangs and Policing in Chicago

Law enforcement partners work with social service providers and victims advocacy groups to attempt to abate gang violence by pulling whatever levers need to be applied to induce selected members of street gangs to leave the gang. The overall goal is to target key gang members who can be induced to leave a gang and who, by leaving the gang, may influence other members to leave as well.

Recent successes with this approach to deterring violence include the Boston Gun Project's *Operation CeaseFire*, *Project Safe Neighborhoods* in Chicago, and continue with the on-going *Group Violence Reduction Strategy* in Chicago. The types of levers applied, and the degree to which they are employed, depends upon the particular situation.

One approach commonly used to facilitate these interactions between law enforcement and street gang members begins with law enforcement engaging known gang members on the street as part of regular patrol activities. Although performed with the goal of focused deterrence, this type of interaction seems to have the least impact. Time spent with the gang member is often limited and the remaining levers (social service providers and victims groups) are generally absent. As a result, the message conveyed to the street gang member is incomplete or biased towards the criminal enforcement aspect. Moreover, the selection of targeted gang members is often random, the result of an opportunistic sighting of a gang member on the street.

A second approach, which we describe here, starts by inducing gang members to attend a call-in. This is a prearranged meeting organized by law enforcement, social service providers, and victims groups during which messages of non-violence are conveyed. It is a full-spectrum effort: law enforcement makes clear to attendees that further violence will be met with relentless police operations and enforcement efforts, social service providers offer information on how members can exit the street gang and obtain educational and vocational training, and victims groups tell stories of losses caused by gang activity as part of a plea for violence cessation.

Attendees at call-in sessions are typically of two types. Gang members currently on probation or parole are compelled to attend. Other gang members are invited to attend. This is where the selection process plays an important role. Invitees may be selected via some form of social network analysis. Often, a large amount of discretion is afforded local law enforcement in selecting invitees. This allows local gang experts and command staff members to identify key members of the gang or gang members whom they know or suspect to be influential and invite them to the call-in.

This process can be very successful if the agency has access to these experts or knowledge of the gang's organizational structure. However, there is often no guarantee that the people invited are, in fact, genuinely influential in the gang as opposed to being just the "most well known to law enforcement" members of the gang. In law enforcement, where financial, personnel, and time resources are increasingly constrained, turning a more objective and analytical eye toward invitee selection grows increasingly important.

A main objective of gang disenrollment programs is to invite to call-ins those gang members who, should the efforts to disenroll them be successful, are most likely to influence additional gang members to defect with them. There is, however, a key question: how easy is it to convince influential members to leave the gang? A recent empirical study exploring non-criminal online social networks suggests that highly influential individuals are typically not susceptible. Experience indicates that taking both influence and susceptibility into account are necessary for the behavior to spread and so become cost effective.

In some cases, gang members thought to be influential successfully convinced others to defect from the gang. In Chicago, in the summer of 2013, the district personnel (local plainclothes gang officers) knew a person whom they deemed to be influential and targeted him for intervention. When he was contacted he indicated that he had already gotten a job outside of the gang, but knew several other gang members who could use the offered social services and disenrollment opportunities. He personally contacted twenty fellow gang members, seven of whom walked into the local social services facility to join the disenrollment program.

16.2 Social Networks

The approach we describe for deciding whom to target is developed in the context of *social networks*. The concept of a *network* is both old and broad. A network consists of *nodes* representing *entities* and *links* which join pairs of nodes thereby defining relationships between pairs of entities. Here are some examples:

- A network in public transit could represent the bus and subway lines in a city. Here the nodes could be the subway stations and bus stops. The links could be the pairs of stations and stops which are adjacent on a subway line or bus line.

- The entities of a communication network may represent the devices served by the network and the links could represent pairs of devices joined by a direct link.

- A GPS system stores a detailed network representing all intersections and streets, together with relevant data, like speed limits and average travel times, for the area covered.

All these networks have the characteristics that they are usually carefully constructed so that they can support their desired function and they are relatively static. It is often a big job to add new nodes or links.

Social networks were introduced in the social sciences to enable the study of relationships between individuals, groups, organizations, or even entire societies. Nodes usually represent one or more types of entities. Links represent the various interactions that can occur between pairs of entities of the same type or pairs of entities of different types. There will often be different types of nodes as well as different types of links.

Links may be directed or undirected, depending on what is being represented. For example, the nodes of a multi-generational population network could represent the people being studied. Two nodes could be joined by a directed link if one of the people represented by a node is a parent of the other and the direction could be from parent to child. In this case, the direction of a link has a logical meaning. Two nodes could be joined by an undirected link if the two people represented by the nodes knew each other. In this case, for an undirected link, the relationship is symmetric.

This example of a social network differs in several ways from a transportation network or a communication network. First, it tends to grow in a somewhat haphazard fashion. Second, it is quite dynamic. New persons can be created (births) and other people may disappear (deaths). New relationships can be formed and other relationships may be allowed to fade away. These networks may have structural properties which may enable inferring properties of the communities they represent. However, this will not be part of the application we discuss here.

The basic social network approach to understanding entities and their interactions is through properties of relations between and within units, rather than properties of the entities themselves. Many different types of relations, singular or in combination, can form these network configurations. For this reason network analytics can be applied to a broad range of situations. In social science, these fields of study include communication studies, economics, information science, organizational studies, social psychology, and sociology.

A well known example of a social network is the *co-stardom* network. This represents the collaboration graph of film actors. Nodes correspond to the movie actors and two nodes are joined by a link if they performed (received a credit) in the same movie. These links are undirected.

Kevin Bacon is a well known film actor who has appeared in many films and who is believed to be quite central in the co-stardom network. The Bacon number of any actor in this network is the number of links in a shortest path in the network joining the node representing the actor to the node representing Kevin Bacon. If there is no such path, then the Bacon number is defined as infinity. The only actor having Bacon number equal to zero is, naturally, Kevin Bacon himself. Every actor who appeared in a film with Kevin Bacon has Bacon number equal to 1.

A party game popular with film buffs is called *Six degrees of Kevin Bacon.* An actor (living or dead) is named and the challenge is to determine the Bacon number of the actor. Surprisingly, most actors not only have finite Bacon numbers, but these numbers are usually small. Charlie Chaplin has a Bacon number of two. Lindsay Lohan also has a Bacon number of two - she and Kevin Bacon both appeared in different films with Robert de Niro. Al Jolson and Rudolph Valentino both have Bacon numbers of three.

"The Oracle of Bacon" is a remarkable web site, conceived of and created in 1996 by Brett Tjaden and rebuilt and maintained since 1999 by Patrick Reynolds. It is based on the 3.2 million people in The Internet Movie Database.

Not only does it provide (an upper bound on) the Bacon number for any actor, but it also provides a variety of interesting statistics. For example, the average Bacon number of all actors in the database (excluding the 12% who have an infinite Bacon number) is 3.009.

The idea of computing the Bacon number was based on the *Erdös number*, which first appeared in a 1969 article by Casper Goffman in *The American Mathematical Monthly*. In this case the nodes represented published mathematicians and links joined pairs of nodes corresponding to pairs of mathematicians who appear as co-authors of a publication reviewed in *Math Reviews*.

A related idea of "Six Degrees of Separation" is much older, originally set out by the Hungarian author Frigyes Karinthy in his 1929 short story, "Chains." In this case every living person was represented by a node and a link was created joining every pair of people who knew each other. The proposition was that every pair of people was joined by a chain of at most six links. This is very difficult to verify or refute, as no database of all living persons and their acquaintances exists.

The *diameter* of a network is the maximum distance between any pair of nodes in the network. Here distance is measured as the minimum number of links in any path joining the two nodes. Thus the Six Degrees of Separation claim is that the Living Person/Acquaintance network has diameter six. According to The Oracle of Bacon, there is one actor with Bacon number ten and there are nine actors with Bacon number nine. Therefore, the diameter of the network is at most 19, because every two nodes are joined to the node representing Kevin Bacon by paths having length at most nine or ten. However, the diameter is probably much lower than 19.

16.3 Centrality

A basic concept of social networks is *centrality* - to what degree is a node central to a network. There are various types of centrality; the appropriate choice for an application depends on the type of network and the properties being analyzed. Here are some of the most often used measures:

Degree Centrality. The *degree* of a node in a network is the number of links adjacent to the node. If a network has the possibility of multiple links between pairs of nodes, such as a variant of the co-stardom network in which we create a link for every film in which a given pair of actors appear, then the number of nodes at distance one from a given node may be less than the degree of the node. According to "The Oracle of Bacon," Kevin Bacon is connected by a single link to 3,042 other nodes. So the degree centrality of the corresponding node is 3,042.

Closeness Centrality. The *distance* $d(u, v)$ between nodes u and v in a network is defined to be infinity if there is no path joining them and the length of a shortest path joining the nodes otherwise. The *farness* $F(v)$ of a node v is defined as the average of these distances over all nodes in the network for which the distance from v is finite. The *closeness centrality* $Cl(v)$ of a node is the reciprocal of the farness $F(v)$. That is, $Cl(v) = 1/F(v)$. The reason for taking the reciprocal is to yield a measure between 0 and 1 such that the higher the value of $Cl(v)$, or, equivalently, the lower the value of $F(v)$, the more central is the node.

Again, according to "The Oracle of Bacon," the farness of the node corresponding to Kevin Bacon is 3.009. Therefore, its closeness is 0.3323. It is not the node with the highest closeness in the database. This honor goes to the node w representing Eric Roberts for which $F(w) = 2.832$ and so $Cl(w) = 0.3531$. This is only slightly higher than that of the better known Samuel L. Jackson, ranked number 5, for which $F(w) = 2.864$ and $Cl(w) = 0.3491$.

Betweenness Centrality. A *geodesic* in a network is a shortest path between any two nodes. Every link itself is a geodesic. A two edge path in the network joining nodes u and v is a geodesic provided that there is no link joining u and v directly. The *betweenness centrality* of a node w is based on the fraction of all geodesics on which it lies. It identifies those nodes which lie on shortest paths between other pairs of nodes. More precisely, for each pair st of nodes, let σ_{st} denote the number of different geodesics joining nodes s and t.

For any node v different from s and t, let $\sigma_{st}(v)$ be the number of these geodesics that contain v. Then, the fraction of geodesics joining s and t that contain node v is $\sigma_{st}(v)/\sigma_{st}$ The betweenness centrality of node v is obtained by summing these fractions over all pairs of nodes not containing v. That is, the betweenness centrality of node v is defined as

$$\sum \left(\frac{\sigma_{st}(v)}{\sigma_{st}} : s, t \in N, s, t \neq v \right).$$

This can be normalized by dividing by the number of pairs of distinct nodes s, t not containing v, which is $\binom{n-1}{2} = \frac{(n-1)(n-2)}{2}$.

If nodes s and t are adjacent then the distance between them is 1, and no node different from s and t lies on a geodesic joining them. So adjacent pairs (s, t) contribute nothing to the calculation.

Betweenness centrality in social network analysis identifies nodes that lie on a large number of geodesics joining pairs of nodes. An application to the *co-stardom* network is not obvious. However, if we are interested in disrupting gang activity, it could be relevant. Assuming members communicate using shortest paths of connections between members, then a node with high betweenness centrality would lie on a large number of these paths. Inducing the member associated with the node to defect could have a disruptive effect on gang communications.

Eigenvector Centrality. Google's page rank, which we discuss in Chapter 11, is closely related to the notion of *eigenvector centrality*. It computes "influence" scores for every node in the network based on the principle that connections to nodes which themselves have high scores should count more than connections to nodes with low scores.

Figure 16.1 provides an example of a social network in which the most central node according to each of these four criteria is different. However, these notions of centrality do not capture the following features of our application:

- gang members selected as targets for defection may influence others to defect,
- we are not limited to selecting a single target.

A method that does provide an effective way of identifying the most influential set of gang members to target is described in the next section.

16.4 The Social Incentive Influence Problem*

In some situations, a person's condition or choices are heavily influenced by others who are "close," in some sense. Marketers know that if a person decides to buy a product, likes it, and then recommends it to friends, this will often induce friends to buy the product. This motivates the question that often appears in user satisfaction surveys: Would you recommend this product to friends? A similar effect also affects the spread of communicable diseases – the likelihood of a person catching a cold normally increases as the number of people contacted who have colds increases.

The general term for this phenomenon is a *diffusion process*. In this section, we describe a form of this phenomenon designed to maximize the number of members who will defect from a gang – the "pulling levers" strategy. This is called the *Social Incentive Influence (SII)* problem. Here are some key features:

1. **Slow diffusion process.** Leaving a gang can be a major life decision for an individual, so the spread of this idea will likely take time. Further complicating the matter is that there may be changes to the gang structure while the diffusion process is occurring, based on events such as arrests, homicides, and gang conflict and cooperation.

Figure 16.1: Social Network and Centrality Measures.

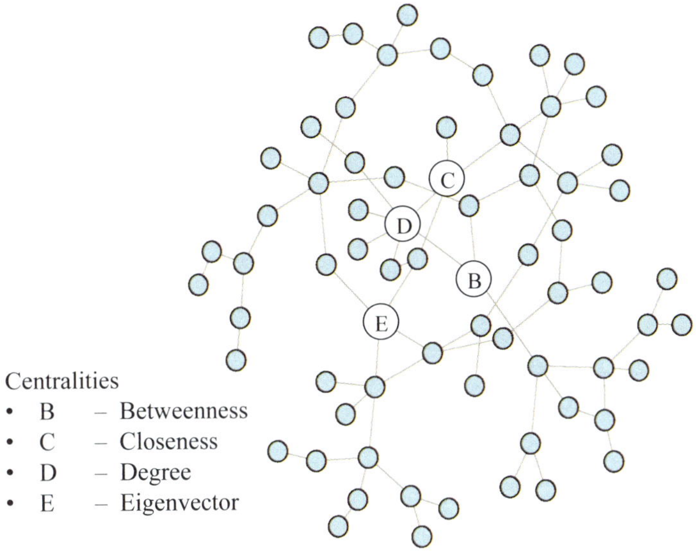

2. **Interaction with the population during the diffusion process.** Not only does the diffusion process take time to occur in this domain, but also law enforcement personnel will often make multiple attempts to "pull levers" as the diffusion occurs.

3. **Geographic locations and strength of connections.** Often, law enforcement data has an inherent geospatial component. Street gangs are usually inherently territorial so, in the SII model, geospatial information is used to infer the strength of connections in a social network.

4. **Notion of cost.** Cost becomes an important factor in gang disenrollment programs. Law enforcement personnel are attempting to encourage a major change in the life of the targeted gang members. Conducting a call-in session costs time, money, and other resources. In general not all gang members will be equally susceptible to this type of intervention - some may require more or less effort to be convinced to defect. Further, there are real costs associated with encouraging disenrollment. For example, in North Carolina personalized letters are created for the gang members that show the individual how his association with others involved in violence puts him or her at risk. A similar tactic is used in Chicago, where the letters are often delivered

to the homes of the gang members. This utilizes police manpower and resources hence further increasing the cost.

5. **Profit maximization.** The *benefit* is the value each expected invitee provides to the diffusion process. This enables a profit-maximizing model with the goal of maximizing the difference between the expected benefit and the cost.

Now we can describe the Social Incentive Influence model.

The social network. We define a social network $G = (V, E)$ where V is a set of nodes and E is a set of directed edges. The nodes in V represent the gang members and an arc directed from node u to node v indicates that defection by the member corresponding to u has some influence on a defection decision by the person corresponding to node v. The actual amount of influence will depend on the geographic distance between u and v as outlined below. If it is believed that u has no influence on v defecting, then there is no arc uv in the network.

This network will typically be constructed by a combination of police records, intelligence provided by former gang members, participation in social programs and ad hoc observations.

Cost of incenting a member to leave a gang. For the gang member corresponding to node v, the cost c_v of pulling lever actions sufficient to induce that member to leave the gang is estimated.

Benefit of getting a gang member to quit. The *benefit value* $b \geq 0$ estimates the value of getting a person to leave the gang. This could be the result of "pulling levers" on the person directly or of the person being influenced by others whom were directly induced to leave the gang. (Different values b_v could be defined for different nodes v, but for our present discussion, we assume that every member's decision to leave produces the same benefit.)

Amount of influence of one gang member on another. We assume that each gang member has a geolocation. This enables computation of the distance $d(u, v)$ between the gang members represented by nodes u and v. If defection of gang member u is believed to influence member v to defect (the arc uv exists in the social network), the amount of influence of u on v depends on the distance $d(u, v)$.

This is defined by a *degree of influence* p_{uv} of u on v between 0 and 1. This estimates the probability that v will defect if u defects.

The properties we would like p_{uv} to satisfy are

- gang members located close to each other have high influence on each other;

- gang members located far from each other have low influence on each other;
- the influence of one gang member on another increases as the distance between their locations decreases.

Figure 16.2 illustrates a geolocation based influence function. The x-axis represents the geodistance $d(u, v)$ between pairs of nodes in the network, scaled to a range of 1 to 20. The y-axis represents p_{uv}, ranging from 0 (no influence) to 1 (maximum influence) based on the distance between the pairs of nodes.

Note that p_{uv} is almost 1 if $d(u, v)$ is small and it drops to almost zero as $d(u, v)$ increases. This type of influence function is called an *exponential distance decay function.* We can view p_{uv} as the probability that v will leave the gang if u leaves the gang. Then, $1 - p_{uv}$ can be viewed as the probability that u leaving the gang will *not* induce v to leave the gang.

This influence function is defined by

$$p_{uv} = e^{-(d(u,v)/\gamma)^r} \tag{16.1}$$

where γ, r are finite positive parameters, and e is the base of the natural logarithm. The parameter γ is used as a scaling parameter - we set it to be the average distance between two nodes connected by an edge. The parameter r controls the shape of the distance decay curve. In this example, $\gamma = 8$ and $r = 2$. What is important is that this enables us to compute p_{uv} from $d(u, v)$.

Figure 16.2: Influence Function.

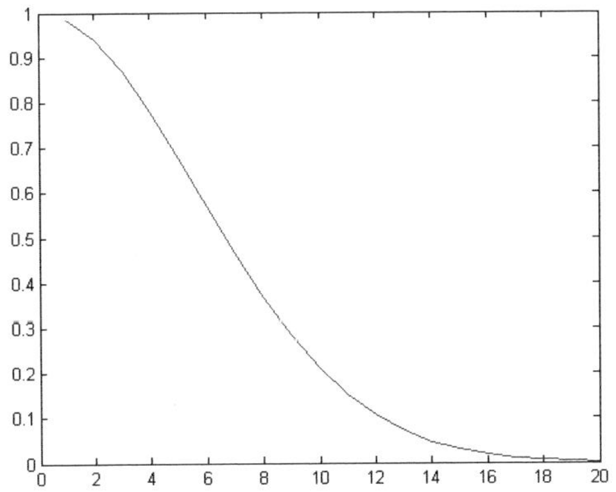

The Diffusion Process. Suppose a set X of gang members decides to leave the gang as the result of pulling levers programs. How will this influence other gang members to defect? The social network described above identifies those gang members who may be affected. These are the gang members for which the corresponding nodes in the network are the heads of an arc from one or more nodes in X. See Figure 16.3. In this figure, nodes u, v and w are influenced by one, four and two members of X respectively. Node z is not influenced by anyone in X.

Let v be a gang member not in X and let X_v be the set of members of X adjacent to v in the network. Then, X_v is the set of gang members whose defection could influence v to defect. For any s in X_v, the probability of v defecting because s defected is p_{sv}, and the probability of v staying in the gang in spite of s defecting is $1 - p_{sv}$. We assume that these probabilities are independent. Then, the probability of v staying in the gang in spite of all members of X_v defecting is the product of $(1 - p_{sv})$ for all $s \in X_v$, denoted by

$$\prod_{s \in X_v} (1 - p_{sv}).$$

Therefore, the probability that v defects because at least one member of X_v defects is

$$\Big(1 - \prod_{s \in X_v} (1 - p_{sv})\Big).$$

Therefore, the expected number of members who will defect if the members in X defect is

$$f(X) = |X| + \sum_{v \in V \setminus X} \Big(1 - \prod_{s \in X_v} (1 - p_{sv})\Big). \qquad (16.2)$$

This $f(X)$ is an example of a a *diffusion process function.*

Figure 16.3: Diffusion.

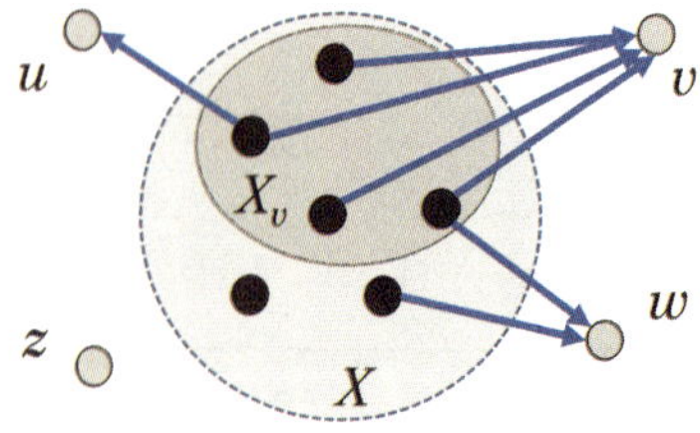

For some applications, a diffusion process will be iterated over several time periods to capture a possible cascading effect of an action. However, the disenrollment process here is modeled as a "one-step" influence model which only considers the immediate effect of the process over a single time step. This is because law-enforcement analysts typically use the most current data available to make decisions about which gang members to target for each iteration of this model. Attempts will be made to influence targeted individuals, after which changes to the social network (both resulting from the outreach and other external factors) will be incorporated before repeating the cycle. Because we expect the time for each iteration to be significant, the social network will generally change after each iteration.

The Profit of a Disenrollment Program. The net profit $\mathrm{p}(X)$ obtained by successfully convincing a set X of gang members to disenroll is defined as

$$\mathrm{p}(X) = b \cdot f(X) - \sum_{v \in X} c_v. \tag{16.3}$$

That is, $\mathrm{p}(X)$ is the difference between the benefit created by having $f(X)$ gang members defect and the cost of convincing those gang members in X to defect.

The SII Problem. We now have all components necessary to formally define the social incentive influence (SII) problem:

Given

- a social network $G = (V, E)$,
- a diffusion process function $f(X)$,
- a cost c_v of each node $v \in V$ and
- a benefit value b,

find $X^* \subseteq V$ which maximizes $\mathrm{p}(X)$ for all $X \subseteq V$.

A solution X^* to this problem will identify an optimal set of gang members to target.

However, there is one more obstacle remaining: SII belongs to the class of $\mathcal{NP}$-hard problems. These are problems for which no algorithm is known which can both guarantee an optimum solution and for which the running time grows at a rate which is bounded by a polynomial function of the size of the problem. If such an algorithm were known, then there would be an efficient algorithm for a huge class of problems, including well-known difficult problems such as the Traveling Salesman Problem and solving integer optimization problems. So most people believe that no such efficient algorithm exists.

This means that some instances of SII may be very hard to solve. When faced with such problems, we are unlikely to be able to develop efficient algorithms that will find optimal solutions for all possible instances. Instead, we need to develop heuristics which will, hopefully, produce good solutions to the particular instances of the problem which we would like to solve. We address this in the next section.

16.5 A Heuristic for SII

In this section, we describe an algorithm for SII, called SII-Approx. It cannot be guaranteed to find an optimal solution, but in practice it usually finds a good solution. In the section following, we describe some experimental results with this heuristic which show that, for many instances of SII, the solution it produces is equal to or quite close to the optimal solution.

The idea of the algorithm is simple, and is outlined in Figure 16.4. As the algorithm runs, it computes two sets: X is the set of nodes which it commits to including in the final solution; and $\bar{X}$ is the set of nodes which are either in the final solution or still candidates to be included in the final solution. The algorithm considers each node in turn and estimates whether the profit is better if we include it in X or remove it from $\bar{X}$. It does whichever is more profitable.

The distance function $d(u, v)$ is used indirectly. It enables the algorithm to compute the degree of influence p_{uv} for each edge $(u, v) \in E$, see equation (16.1). These, in turn, enable the computation of $f(X)$, the expected total number of gang members who will defect if the members corresponding to nodes in X defect because of lever pulling programs, see equation (16.2). This together with b and $(c_v : v \in V)$ enables us to compute $\mathrm{p}(X)$, see equation (16.3).

16.6 How Good is the Heuristic?

Two factors determine the effectiveness of a heuristic. The first is the quality of the solution it produces. The second is the time it takes to obtain the solution. It is generally difficult to obtain a good bound on a heuristic's solution quality. This is because it is usually not known in advance when the heuristic will be run, and even if the heuristic finds a solution that looks good, it is hard to figure out how close it is to being optimal when we do not know the value of an optimal solution.

For the problem SII, it is possible to determine the optimal solution X^* to a small problem by computing $\mathrm{p}(X)$ for every subset of the nodes and then letting X^* be a set for which this is maximized. This approach, called *complete enumeration*, can be computed in reasonable time for networks having twenty of fewer nodes. Then, SII-Approx can be applied to the problem and the solution X it obtains can be compared with X^*.

Figure 16.4: The SII-Approx algorithm.

SII-Approx

Input:

- Social network $G = (V, E)$,
- disenrollment cost c_v for each node $v \in V$,
- benefit of disenrollment b,
- distance function $d(u, v)$ defined for each pair uv of nodes.

Output: Heuristic solution X to SII.

Algorithm:

1. $X = \emptyset, \bar{X} = V$
2. **for all** $v \in V$
   $a = \mathrm{p}(X \cup \{v\}) - \mathrm{p}(X)$
   $b = \mathrm{p}(\bar{X} \setminus \{v\}) - \mathrm{p}(\bar{X})$
   if $a \geq b$ **then** $X = X \cup \{v\}$ **else** $\bar{X} = \bar{X} \setminus \{v\}$
   end for
3. **return** X.

A first test dataset consisted of arrest records of individuals from March 2010 - March 2013 in a single police district in Chicago. This data set included both arrest locations and relationships among the individuals. From this data a social network, called the *arrest network*, consisting of 1,836 nodes and 2,531 edges, was created. The nodes corresponded to the individuals and two nodes were joined by an edge if the two individuals were arrested together.

The solution X found by SII-Approx was compared to an optimal solution X^* found by complete enumeration of all possible sets X. This was done by constructing 20 connected test networks from the overall police network ranging in size from 11 to 20 nodes. The cost c_v was set to 1 for all $v \in V$ and the benefit b was also set to 1. In many cases SII-Approx found the optimal solution. The worst ratio of $p(X)$ to $p(X^*)$ obtained in these tests was 0.70. The average-case found was much better at 0.92.

This arrest network could be enriched by adding other edges to the network incorporating other relationships between the individuals which can be obtained from sources such as observations by police patrolmen and information from correctional facilities.

Similar tests were also run on other randomly generated data sets. In all cases the results obtained were better than the results obtained when running on the samples we generated from the arrest network. (This is a common phenomenon - often heuristics do better on random problems than they do on problems based on data from real problems.)

In order to analyze the runtime, the times of SII-Approx were compared with those of complete enumeration. See Figure 16.5.

Note that the vertical scale is a log scale, so the apparent straight line behavior corresponds to the fact that the run time of complete enumeration grows exponentially with the number of nodes, whereas the run time of SII-Approx grows roughly as the number of edges in the network grow, which is much smaller. This clearly shows that SII-Approx is a much faster way to get a good, although not necessarily optimal, solution to the problem.

A second analysis was performed to see how the run time of SII-Approx grew as the size of the network increased. See Figure 16.6. Times were computed on a moderately powerful workstation. For the size of the datasets used by the Chicago police department (less than 5,000 nodes), the run time was less than ten hours which showed that this is a viable approach even with a prototype implementation.

Figure 16.5: Speedup of SII-Approx Compared to Complete Enumeration.

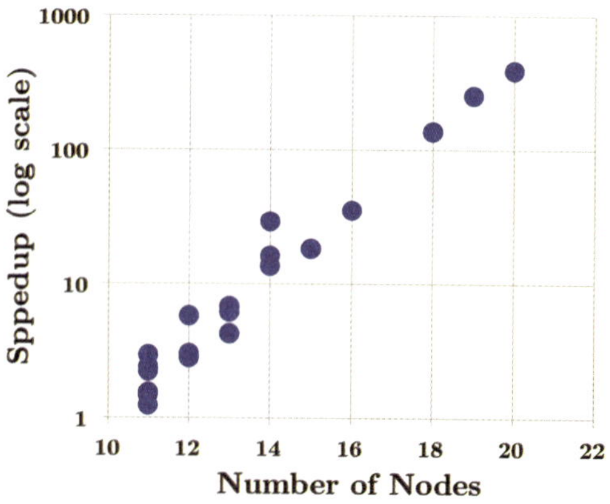

Figure 16.6: Network Size vs. Runtime.

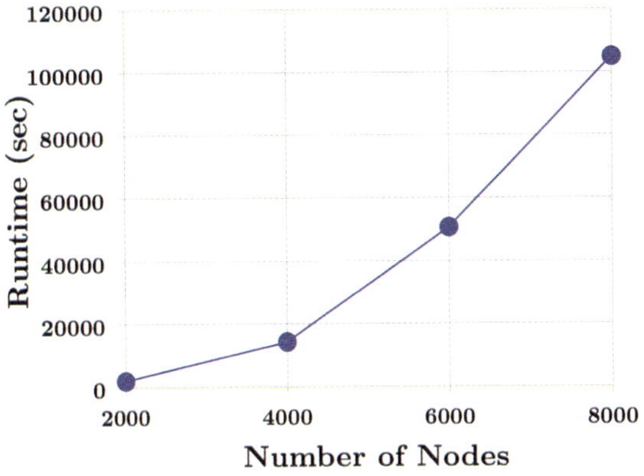

16.7 Notes and Sources

This chapter is based on the paper by Shakarian et al. [126] where the SII problem and its relation to smart policing is introduced. The SII problem itself is a variant of a very general problem called an "influence maximization problem" [75].

16.1. The use of social network analysis to select invitees to gang disenrollment meetings is introduced in Braga et al. [30]. An empirical study exploring non-criminal online social networks that suggests that highly influential individuals are typically not susceptible is Aral and Walker [6].

16.2. Good general references to social networks and their applications are McCulloh et al [92], Barabási [11], Easley and Kleinberg [43, 44] and Newman [104].

The link to the website "The Oracle of Bacon" is [141]. It is based on the Internet Movie Database [70].

The *Erdös number* was intoduced in a 1969 article by Casper Goffman in *The American Mathematical Monthly* [53].

16.4. The model on which the Social Incentive Influence Problem is based is a general social network maximum influence problem introduced in Kempe et al. [75]. Figure 16.1 was constructed by Luke Gerdes.

16.5. The SII-Approx algorithm described here processes the nodes in random order. The paper by Shakarian et al. [126] reports an improvement to solution quality obtained by processing the nodes in the order of their *Cluster Rank*.

Part VI

Management of Operations

Chapter 17

Increasing Revenue with Analytics

We haven't got the money, so we've got to think.

– Ernest Rutherford

Contents

In 1976, the Senior Vice President of Marketing for American Airlines, Bob Crandall, called for a brainstorming session that ran until late in the night. The airfare regulations were changing, and charter airlines had started selling seats for fares far less than those offered by more traditional airlines, like American. Bob Crandall knew that American Airlines needed to lower their fares to compete. Initially, the general belief was that airlines needed to lower costs. However, they finally realized revenue, not costs, was the problem. American's planes were only flying half full, which meant that they were carrying millions of empty seats each year. This started a focus in the airline industry on discovering new ways to increase revenue, with American Airlines as a front-runner. By 1992, Bob Crandall had become the Chairman and CEO of American Airlines, and revenue management techniques had generated billions of dollars in increased revenue for the company.

With 183 of its 576 rooms still available, a returning customer at Harrah's Cherokee Casino & Hotel (the Cherokee) can still be denied a room. This happens even when the customer is known to bet an average of \$2000 a night, meaning that the Cherokee will gain about \$140 in profit from his gambling alone. The revenue management system at the Cherokee has recommended that this customer be offered a complimentary room at a neighboring hotel. Even to those who are familiar with revenue management, this seems unusual. Why pay for a room at another hotel when there are so many rooms at the Cherokee still available? This decision was made by the revenue management system used by the Harrah's casinos and hotels, which has increased the revenue per room across the hotel chain by 15%. The system recommends not giving a room at the Cherokee to this particular customer, because historical data has shown that it is more profitable overall to leave rooms at the casino available for higher paying customers, even if the rooms might occasionally end up empty!

This chapter discusses two major successes of revenue management techniques. We first discuss the case of American Airlines, the company that created a revolutionary way to increase revenue using analytics. While revenue management was first used in the airline industry, today the field has influenced almost every industry. One notable example is the use of revenue management in the casino industry, illustrated here with the example of Harrah's Cherokee Casino & Hotel. Companies using revenue management techniques have been able to increase profits when other companies could not survive. Today, revenue management systems are crucial to the marketing and operations of many companies.

17.1 The Right Strategy

Revenue management (RM) increases company profitability by using analytics to control reservations for airline seats, hotel rooms, or other products. The primary aim of revenue management is selling the "right product to the right customer at the right time and for the right price." By using revenue management, many important questions of a business are answered: what to

Figure 17.1: Traditional pricing without revenue management. The market clearing price P^* occurs where the supply and demand curves meet. For customers who are willing to pay more than P^*, the shaded region represents the difference between the price that a consumer would pay and the price that a consumer actually pays. Therefore, the area of the shaded region represents the amount of lost revenue in this setting.

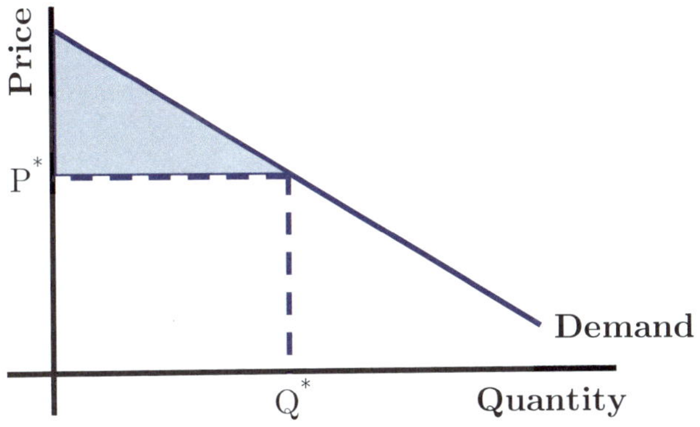

sell, when to sell, to whom to sell, and for how much. In order to achieve this, the company must understand customers' perception of product value and align the right prices and availability to each customer segment.

One of the key aspects of revenue management is pricing. Traditionally, given a fixed quantity of an item for sale, the recommended price is the maximum value that allows the seller to sell all inventory, according to the forecasted demand curve. Figure 17.1 shows this traditional setting. The quantity of the product is shown on the x-axis, and Q^* is the amount in inventory. The price of the product is shown on the y-axis. The demand for the product increases with a lower price, as shown by the demand curve. The recommended price, P^*, is marked as the maximum price that would allow all inventory to be sold. If the price was set higher than P^*, the demand would be less than the amount in inventory. If the price was set lower than P^*, the demand would exceed the amount in inventory. However, when the price is set to P^*, there are many customers who are willing to pay more, but still only pay the set price P^*. The shaded region in Figure 17.1 represents these customers and the difference between what they are willing to pay and what they actually pay. Therefore, the area of the shaded region represents the total amount of lost revenue by only setting one price for all customers.

With a revenue management approach, different prices are set for the same product. The product looks the same to all of the customers (coach class

Figure 17.2: Pricing with revenue management. Three prices are set, and more customers pay the price they are willing to pay. The shaded regions represent the amount of lost revenue due to customers paying a lower price than they are willing to pay.

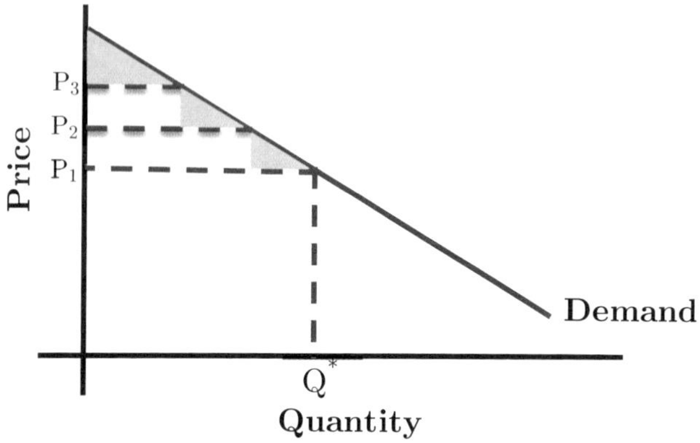

airline seats, standard hotel rooms, etc.), but the goal is to get the customers who are willing to pay more to do so. This scenario is depicted in Figure 17.2. Three different prices are set: P_1, P_2, and P_3. Customers willing to pay more than P_1 but less than P_2 pay P_1, customers willing to pay more than P_2 but less than P_3 pay P_2, and customers wiling to pay more than P_3 pay P_3. There is still some lost revenue due to customers paying less than the maximum amount they would be willing to pay (shown by the shaded regions), but much less than without RM. It can also be observed that by creating more price levels, more customers will pay the price that they are willing to pay, and less revenue will be lost.

Revenue management is often very useful and it may seem that every industry should want such a system. However, there are a few characteristics that an industry must have for a revenue management system to apply. One is that they must have a fixed capacity, such as a fixed number of seats on an airplane, or a fixed number of rooms in a hotel. Another requirement is an analytics-based reservations system. Revenue management is an intricate process, and without an electronic reservation system that is sufficiently advanced, it would be very difficult to use RM. Also, setting different prices for different customers has to be feasible, meaning that it cannot be obvious to customers that they are paying a higher price than their neighbor. This would not work very well in a store setting, where a product is sitting on a shelf with a price tag. (Although, prices in stores are often changed fairly regularly, with the help of a technique called *dynamic pricing*.) Many industries that use revenue management also have frequent cancellations and no-shows, a high fixed cost but low variable cost, and highly perishable inventories. Both of the examples that we present in this chapter have these characteristics, and are viewed as more traditional applications of RM. However, RM is starting to be used in more and more application areas, including energy, healthcare, manufacturing, apparel, and restaurants.

17.2 Revenue Management at American Airlines

Revenue management was first used in the airline industry. Several major changes in airline policy made revenue management ideal for this industry: the introduction of computer reservation systems in the late 1960s, and the deregulation of airline schedules and prices in 1978, which permitted the introduction of discount fares. Prior to deregulation, airlines were only allowed to fly certain routes, and each route was controlled by a certain airline like Northwest, Eastern, and Southwest. Additionally, the fares were determined by the federal Civil Aeronautics Board (CAB), based on mileage and other costs. After the Airline Deregulation Act of 1978, any airline was allowed to fly anywhere, and the fares were determined by the airlines and the market. This suddenly opened up many new possibilities for airlines.

Additionally, the airline industry has many characteristics that make it ideal for revenue management techniques, including a relatively fixed seat capacity, high fixed costs but low variable costs, a variety of customer types, and the ability to sell tickets to customers without the customers seeing what other customers paid. The decision-making process for airlines is so large and complex that controlling the inventory of seats can only be accomplished with automated models.

American Airlines is considered to be the first airline that successfully implemented a revenue management system. The company had been using analytical models as early as the 1960s, and after deregulation they developed a system to automatically update availability and prices, called SABRE (semi-automated business research environment). In the 1980s, American Airlines starting using the first RM software available, and by 1992 almost all of their profit was coming from the implementation of RM practices. By this time, almost every airline had implemented an RM system. American Airlines estimated a benefit from using RM of $1.4 billion from 1989-1992, and over $500 million during each year after 1992.

Without an RM system, it was impossible for an airline to manage inventory allocation. If a mid-size airline has 1,000 daily departures, with 200 seats on each flight, there are 200,000 seats available each day. Additionally, many passengers make reservations months in advance. If there are 200 days maintained in the reservation system, this means that at any one time, forty million seats are available to be reserved and must be maintained in inventory. This means that volume alone is a challenge for reservation systems. When discount fares, connecting flights, and overbooking are taken into account, the challenge becomes even greater. To solve a system-wide problem, an optimization problem with hundreds of millions of variables would be necessary, which is very challenging to solve. To reduce the size of the problem, American Airlines reduced the large revenue management problem into three more manageable subproblems: traffic management, discount allocation, and overbooking. While we will briefly discuss each of these techniques in the remainder of this section, keep in mind that airlines typically view the details of their revenue management systems as highly confidential, and optimizing revenue is a complex problem.

Traffic Management

After deregulation, airlines were allowed more flexibility in scheduling. While this opened up opportunities for increased revenue, it also added extra complications. Passengers could take connecting flights, and so one flight leg could serve people going to many different destinations. In 1980, shortly after deregulation, about 10% of flights were connecting flights. Five years later, in 1985, about 66% of flights were connecting flights. To handle this new situation, airlines developed the hub-and-spoke system. Figure 17.3 shows a small example of how the hub-and-spoke system works. Dallas/Fort Worth (DFW) serves as the hub, and passengers travel through DFW to get to farther destinations. In this network, passengers can take four different one-leg flights: PDX to DFW, LAX to DFW, DFW to JFK, and DFW to MIA. Additionally, they can take four different connecting flights: PDX to JFK, PDX to MIA, LAX to JFK, and LAX to MIA. Using connecting flights, the airline can use four flight routes to serve customers traveling between eight different origin and destination pairs. (Note that passengers cannot fly between PDX and LAX, or JFK and MIA using these flight routes.)

Discount Allocation

There are two basic types of customers for airlines: vacation or leisure travelers, and business travelers. Often, leisure travelers have more flexibility to book their trip far in advance and want to pay less for airfare. Business travelers often book flights days before wanting to travel and are willing to pay a much higher fare. This inspired airlines to offer two different products: (a) a more expensive ticket that could be purchased at any time, had no restrictions and was fully refundable, and (b) a cheaper ticket that required a three week advanced purchase, a Saturday night stay and enforced penalties for any changes after purchasing the ticket. As more advanced systems became available, even more fare classes could be defined. For example, "super saver" tickets could be offered to customers who booked their flights even further in advance at a deep discount. However, there are several decisions that still need to be made: at what price should the tickets be offered, how many tickets of each type should

Figure 17.3: A simple airline network with one hub (DFW) and four spoke cities (PDX, LAX, JFK, MIA).

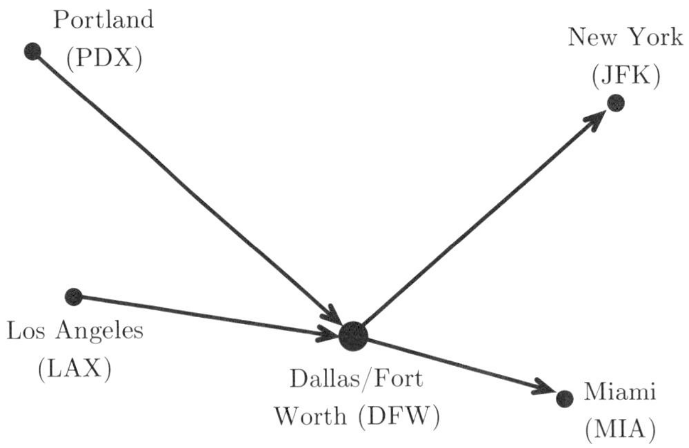

be offered, and when should the tickets be offered. Ideally, an airline would like to fill their flights with business customers, since they are willing to pay more for their tickets. However, if an airline rejects leisure customers looking for tickets and does not fill their seats with business customers, they have lost revenue. Thus, airlines need a way to determine how many tickets they will set aside for more expensive customers who may want to buy tickets later.

These decisions can be modeled with an optimization problem. For more about the method of optimization, see Chapter 21. In this section, we will present a simplified version of the optimization problem that is solved today by ignoring the timing of the flights. This includes both the scheduling of the flight itself (day of the week and time of the day), and the amount of time left before the flight when a ticket is purchased (often referred to as *lead time*). Both of these timing issues are important for revenue management and should be incorporated in the optimization problem, but for simplicity we will assume here that timing is not an issue. We direct the reader to the notes and sources in Section 17.5 for more information.

Suppose that the price of each type of ticket has already been decided (by the marketing department) and we are trying to decide how many seats to reserve for each fare class and each itinerary in the airline's schedule. We will assume that there are three different fare classes: regular, discount, and super saver. Additionally, suppose that there are only three flights offered: LAX to DFW, LAX to JFK, and DFW to JFK. Note that while there are three different flights, there are only two flight legs being used: LAX to DFW and DFW to

Table 17.1: Decision variables for the number of seats to be offered on each route and for each fare class.

Flight Route	Fare Class	Variable	Revenue ($)	Demand
LAX to DFW	Regular	x_1	100	20
	Discount	x_2	90	40
	Super Saver	x_3	80	60
LAX to JFK	Regular	y_1	215	80
	Discount	y_2	185	60
	Super Saver	y_3	145	70
DFW to JFK	Regular	z_1	140	20
	Discount	z_2	120	20
	Super Saver	z_3	100	30

JFK (as in Figure 17.3). This means that all customers flying from LAX to JFK have a layover in DFW. The expected demand for each of these flights has been estimated based on historical data and demand forecasting models.

To solve this optimization model, we need a decision variable for the number of seats that should be reserved for every flight and fare class combination. For example, we need one decision variable for regular seats from LAX to DFW, one decision variable for discount seats from LAX to DFW, and one decision variable for super saver seats from LAX to DFW. Table 17.1 lists all of the decision variables for the different routes and fare classes, as well as the revenue expected from a ticket (more revenue for longer flights and more expensive fare classes) and the expected demand for each type of ticket. With three flight routes and three fare classes, we have nine decision variables. This is a very small fraction of the number of variables that have to be used in a realistic airline network. American Airlines has over 160,000 different flight and fare combinations in a given day, resulting in over 50 million decision variables when solving the problem over a time horizon of one year. To handle this, they use sophisticated optimization techniques and computing resources.

To maximize revenue, we would like to sell as many regularly priced tickets as possible. Additionally, some routes are more expensive than others, and we would like to give priority to customers wishing to fly on the more expensive routes. However, the optimization problem can get complicated, for several reasons. In this example, the revenue may be higher if we sell the seats on a connecting flight to two different customers rather than a single customer, but if a ticket is sold for only one leg of the connecting flight, we lose revenue. In some cases, passengers might be willing to pay a premium for a direct (one leg) flight, potentially making it more profitable to sell a seat on a connecting flight to a single customer.

We have to consider both capacity constraints and demand constraints. We have two different capacity constraints, one for each flight leg. Since LAX to DFW is a popular flight leg, the airline has decided to have a capacity of

300. The flight leg from DFW to JFK only has a capacity of 200. Therefore, the capacity constraints are as follows:

$$x_1 + x_2 + x_3 + y_1 + y_2 + y_3 \leq 300,$$

$$y_1 + y_2 + y_3 + z_1 + z_2 + z_3 \leq 200.$$

The demand constraints limit the number of seats to be reserved for each flight class to be greater than zero, but less than the expected demand for that flight and fare class. For example, the demand constraints for the flight LAX to DFW and the fare class Regular are:

$$0 \leq x_1 \leq 20,$$

since the expected demand for this type of ticket is 20 (Table 17.1). Putting all of these constraints together, we have the following optimization problem:

maximize:

$$100x_1 + 90x_2 + 80x_3 + 215y_1 + 185y_2 + 145y_3 + 140z_1 + 120z_2 + 100z_3$$

subject to:

$$\begin{aligned}
&x_1 + x_2 + x_3 + y_1 + y_2 + y_3 \leq 300\\
&y_1 + y_2 + y_3 + z_1 + z_2 + z_3 \leq 200\\
&0 \leq x_1 \leq 20\\
&0 \leq x_2 \leq 40\\
&0 \leq x_3 \leq 60\\
&0 \leq y_1 \leq 80\\
&0 \leq y_2 \leq 60\\
&0 \leq y_3 \leq 70\\
&0 \leq z_1 \leq 20\\
&0 \leq z_2 \leq 20\\
&0 \leq z_3 \leq 30.
\end{aligned}$$

The objective is to maximize total revenue, subject to the capacity and demand constraints. Using an optimization solver, the optimal solution to this problem is $x_1 = 20$, $x_2 = 40$, $x_3 = 60$, $y_1 = 80$, $y_2 = 60$, $y_3 = 40$, $z_1 = 20$, $z_2 = 0$, $z_3 = 0$. The total revenue for this solution, or the optimal objective function value, is $47,300.

Even for this simple problem, the optimal solution gives some interesting results. If we were to use a "greedy" method, meaning that we would iteratively fill up the seats with the customers paying the most, we would satisfy the demand for all types of customers on the LAX to JFK flight, since even the super saver tickets on this flight are more expensive than the regularly priced tickets on either of the other flights. Therefore, the greedy solution would set $y_1 = 80$, $y_2 = 60$, and $y_3 = 60$, which fills up the plane flying from DFW to JFK. These customers also take up capacity on the first leg of the trip, LAX to DFW, but there are 100 seats left to fill. These would be filled by setting $x_1 = 20$, $x_2 = 40$, and $x_3 = 40$. This solution gives $46,000 in total revenue, which is about 3% less than the optimal revenue from solving the optimization problem. This may seem like a small amount of lost revenue, but when we consider all of the flights and fare classes for which an airline needs to make decisions, the optimal solution can provide a significant edge.

The solution to this optimization problem tells the airline how many seats they should reserve for each type of customer, given the expected demand and the capacity. However, in addition to being able to directly solve for each decision variable, a major benefit of an optimization approach is that the solution provides a *shadow price* for each constraint. This shadow price tells us how much the objective (total revenue) would change by increasing the right hand side of the constraint by one additional unit. These shadow prices, sometimes referred to as *bid prices*, are used in practice to decide whether or not an additional seat should be offered for a particular flight and fare class. See Chapter 21 for more about shadow prices.

There are a few potential problems with this simple optimization model. One is that as soon as the reserved number of regular priced tickets have been sold, only discount tickets are available, even though some customers may still be willing to buy tickets at the regular price. Airlines address this issue by making seats reserved for discount classes available to more expensive classes, which is called "nesting." Thus, in our example with three classes, all of the tickets would be available to regular customers, the discount and super saver tickets would be available to the discount customers, and only the super saver tickets would be available to the super saver customers.

Another potential source of lost revenue comes from customers who are willing to pay a higher price but manage to get a discount ticket. The airlines handle this situation in many ways. One method is by offering the tickets for different prices at different times, trying to target the different types of customers. The super saver tickets are offered months in advance, when the business customers are not looking to buy tickets. However, the leisure travelers, who are looking for discount prices, are able to buy these tickets.

Overbooking

For a flight that is sold out at departure, about 15% of the seats still end up being unused. This is due to passenger cancelations and no-shows. To decrease this percentage, airlines often overbook flights, meaning that they intentionally sell more reservations for a flight than the number of seats on the flight. By doing this, the airline takes the risk that more passengers may show up for a flight than there are seats on the aircraft. When this happens, the airline will often ask for passengers who are willing to take a different flight in exchange for vouchers that can be redeemed on a future flight with the airline, hotel and meal accommodations if necessary, and accommodation on a later flight. Even if the over-demand is handled by volunteers delaying their flights, the airline does incur a cost which cuts into revenue. If too few passengers are willing to take this offer, then what are called "involuntary oversales" occur, which cause some passengers to be "bumped" to a later flight. This causes an additional cost of lost customer goodwill.

To select the best overbooking level for a flight, American Airlines has developed an optimization model that balances the additional revenue that can be gained from overbooking against the cost of overselling the flight. This model tries to maximize the net revenue when oversale costs are taken into account. Figure 17.4 shows how the system works. The "Passenger Revenue" line shows that as the number of seats sold increases, the total revenue from selling tickets to passengers increases. (For simplicity, we assume in the figure that the total revenue from ticket sales increases linearly, meaning that all tickets are sold for the same price. However, as we have already seen in this chapter, the revenue can increase by different amounts depending on the types of tickets that are sold.) The "Oversale Cost" line shows that as seats are sold beyond the capacity of the plane, the cost to the airline increases nonlinearly. This captures costs such as having to give passengers complimentary tickets, and lost goodwill. When these two lines are combined (the "Passenger Revenue" and the "Oversale Cost"), we get the "Net Revenue" line shown in the figure. This line tells us that there is some benefit to selling seats beyond the capacity of the plane, but at a certain point the revenue starts decreasing because the costs are just too high. The number of seats sold that yields the maximum Net Revenue gives the number of seats that should be sold by the airline.

Finding the maximum value of Net Revenue is a nonlinear optimization problem with a constraint on the expected number of oversales per flight (too many oversales would reduce passenger satisfaction). Overbooking levels are recalculated many times before a flight departs. The parameters of the model, including the probability a passenger will cancel or be a no-show and the oversale cost, are forecast using several other models.

17.3 Casino Revenue Management at Harrah's Cherokee

While most revenue management systems yield revenue improvements between 3% and 5%, hotels and casinos in the Harrah's chain have seen improvements up to 15%. The most significant increases have occurred at Harrah's Cherokee Casino Resort (the Cherokee), located in North Carolina. The casino is owned by the Eastern Band of Cherokee Indians and operated by Caesars Entertainment Corporation (formerly known as Harrah's Entertainment from 1995 to 2010). The Cherokee was opened in 1997 with the mission of using casino profits for the benefit of the Cherokee Indian community. Due to the unique mission of the management and a deal that was made with the state of North Carolina, the casino does not offer many table games such as roulette and craps. It does offer blackjack, poker, and slot machines. Alcohol was not served

Figure 17.4: The optimal overbooking level is the unique maximum of the Net Revenue curve. The Net Revenue is calculated as the Passenger Revenue minus the Oversale Cost.

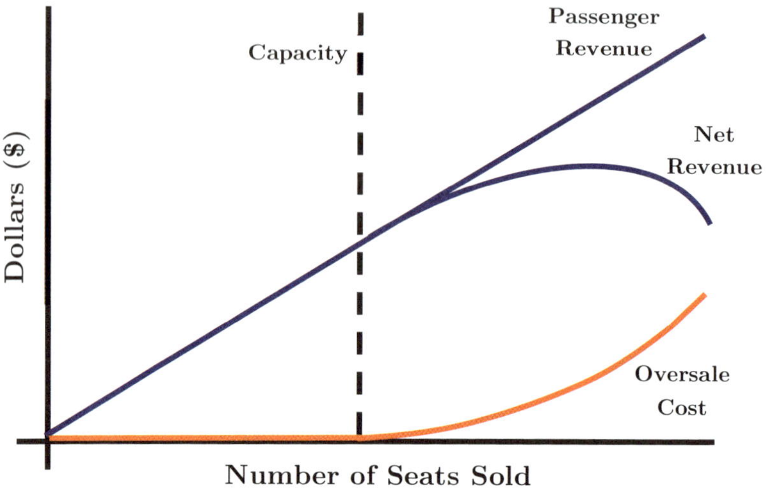

until the end of 2009. Even without serving alcohol, the Cherokee returned a 60% profit margin on gross revenue, which is double the industry norm. The hotel currently has 1,108 rooms, having recently expanded from 576 rooms as part of a $633 million expansion project. Most hotel rooms are offered free of charge, and yet Cherokee guests generate $565 per night of revenue on average, mostly due to gambling and food.

Caesars Entertainment Corporation is one of the largest gambling companies in the world. The corporation has a history of using analytics to make decisions. The CEO, Gary Loveman, is a former Harvard Business School professor who has published articles about using analytics at Harrah's hotels and casinos.

Revenue management in casinos differs from other revenue management applications for several reasons. One major reason is that the highest paying customers are willing to pay twenty to fifty times more than that of the lowest paying customers, while in other industries the highest paying customers are typically only willing to pay up to five times that of other customers. This means that the cost of filling a room with a low paying customer when it could have gone to a higher paying customer is much higher for casinos. Additionally, customers self-segment themselves (each customer controls his or her own revenue generation by deciding how much they want to gamble) so there is no need for the industry to set restrictions to get more customers to pay the price they are willing to pay. Instead of setting a fixed number of different prices as in Figure 17.2, each customer selects how much they spend and thus there is no consumer surplus at all.

In 2008, when the hotel had 576 rooms, the Cherokee was averaging a 98.6% occupancy rate January through November. Consequently, they only extended hotel stays to their best customers, and purchased blocks of rooms at neighboring hotels for second-tier customers. The challenge was determining which customers should be offered hotel stays. The Cherokee has implemented a customer-tracking program to help with this problem. Each customer is given a "Total Rewards" card, which customers enter into each gambling device they use. Information about how much the customer bets is tracked by the system. Customers are incentivized to use their rewards cards with offers for complimentary rooms, meals, casino chips, and other perks. Approximately 83% of bets made at the Cherokee are tracked with this system. With this program, the Cherokee can assign a value to each known customer, which is equal to the average amount of money that they wager times the house percentage. It is this value that allows the Cherokee to implement an advanced RM system.

Applying RM to the Cherokee

Given the value that is assigned to each customer, the Cherokee can split their customers into segments. A customer's value, equal to the average amount of money that the customer wagers times the house percentage, is called the "expected wagering profit" (EWP). Table 17.2 divides the customers into ten segments based on EWP. Customer segment 0 (CS0) is the highest gambling segment, and contains all customers with an EWP of more than $1,000 per night. The last segment, CS9, is for customers who are not in the database.

The total *unconstrained* demand per day is calculated for each customer segment, meaning the "true" demand if there were unlimited rooms in the hotel and every potential customer could be accommodated. Since a customer is asked to provide their rewards number before requesting a reservation, the system not only tracks accepted requests, but also rejected requests. The only complication is accounting for denied requests through third-party channels, such as Travelocity, Expedia, and Orbitz. The Cherokee system estimates this demand by assuming that the same percentage of requests that are denied through the Cherokee system are also denied through third-party systems.

Using historical data about similar days, demand trends, seasonality, and special events, the system is able to make forecasts about the expected demand for a day in the future. Since the demand is expected to increase as the day approaches, different forecasts are made for each day in a 90 day period leading up to the specific day. Forecasts are also made for each individual customer segment.

With these forecasts, the revenue management system is able to allocate available rooms to the ten customer segments. The system controls all of the regular rooms, and the casino staff directly books the VIP customers and schedules all suite bookings. Before the current expansion, the RM system was used to book 547 of the 576 rooms (the standard rooms).

The RM system for the Cherokee solves an optimization problem that is very similar to the one used for airline revenue management. For simplicity, we will assume that customers can only book rooms for one night, and we are solving the room allocation problem for a particular night. The model can be extended to accommodate multiple-night stays.

The decision variables are how many rooms to reserve for customers in each customer segment. The objective is to maximize the total revenue of these customers, where the revenue for customers in each segment is represented by the historical average amount that a customer in that segment spends in the casino. The constraints consist of a capacity constraint, insuring that the total number of rooms allocated (the sum of all of the decision variables) does not exceed the capacity of the hotel (547 rooms), and demand constraints for each customer segment. The total number of rooms allocated to a customer segment should not exceed the forecasted demand for that segment and for the day we are solving the optimization problem for.

Table 17.3 lists the decision variables for the optimization problem with ten segments and the expected revenue per customer from each segment. For the unknown customer segment, CS9, the Cherokee has estimated a $100 revenue from gaming on average.

With these decision variables and expected revenue, the optimization problem is as follows:

maximize:

Table 17.2: The ten customer segments (CS0 - CS9), and the expected wagering profit (EWP) for each segment.

Segment	**EWP ($)**
CS0	$\geq$ 1,000
CS1	800-999
CS2	600-799
CS3	400-599
CS4	300-399
CS5	200-299
CS6	100-199
CS7	50-99
CS8	0-50
CS9	Unknown

$$1{,}500x_0 + 900x_1 + 700x_2 + 500x_3 + 350x_4 + 250x_5 + 150x_6 + 75x_7 + 25x_8 + 100x_9$$

subject to:

$$x_0 + x_1 + x_2 + x_3 + x_4 + x_5 + x_6 + x_7 + x_8 + x_9 \leq 547$$
$$0 \leq x_0 \leq d_0$$
$$0 \leq x_1 \leq d_1$$
$$0 \leq x_2 \leq d_2$$
$$0 \leq x_3 \leq d_3$$
$$0 \leq x_4 \leq d_4$$
$$0 \leq x_5 \leq d_5$$
$$0 \leq x_6 \leq d_6$$
$$0 \leq x_7 \leq d_7$$
$$0 \leq x_8 \leq d_8$$
$$0 \leq x_9 \leq d_9,$$

where d_i represents the forecasted demand for segment i on the night for which we are solving the optimization problem.

The model is re-optimized every 24 hours and after five additional rooms have been booked. This is to update the forecasted demand and change the number of allocated rooms if necessary. Additionally, shadow prices are used in practice to decide whether or not a room request should be accepted, and these also need to be updated multiple times each day (similarly to the airline revenue management example). Often, the Cherokee does not offer any rooms to customers in lower customer segments. On many weekend summer nights, only customers in segment CS0 are offered rooms, due to the high demand.

Table 17.3: The ten customer segments, decision variables, and expected profits.

Segment	Decision Variable	Expected Revenue ($)
CS0	x_0	1,500
CS1	x_1	900
CS2	x_2	700
CS3	x_3	500
CS4	x_4	350
CS5	x_5	250
CS6	x_6	150
CS7	x_7	75
CS8	x_8	25
CS9	x_9	100

While the same revenue management principles from airlines can be applied to casinos, there are several aspects that make this problem different. One is that the revenues in the objective of the optimization problem are determined by the customer's behavior on the day they are at the casino, not by the marketing department. Another is that casinos have a lot of last minute reservations, which makes it even more necessary to have a dynamically updated RM system. Additionally, the no-show rate is very small at the Cherokee, and so an overbooking system is not necessary. Even when customers do not show up, there are always other customers in the casino looking for rooms. The total rewards tracking system and the demand forecasting are crucial to the RM system. Without this important data, the system would not be as profitable and would not return as high of a margin on revenue.

17.4 A Technique for All Industries

While revenue management started as a solution for airlines to deal with deregulation, it is now being used in almost every industry imaginable. Revenue management systems can be applied in healthcare, restaurants, manufacturing, apparel, energy, and many more areas. Almost every company is looking to increase revenue, and RM systems are now considered by many companies to be an indispensable part of their marketing and operating strategies.

There are several attributes of revenue management systems that make them so widely used:

1. The gains in revenue often come from existing products and customers. Revenue management systems are designed to find ways to increase revenue without changing the company.

2. Product prices are more accurately aligned with what customers are willing to pay. Advanced demand forecasting systems help the company to target the right customers with the right prices at the right time.

3. Rapidly evolving computer technology has made it possible for companies to implement revenue management systems and to solve more advanced and complex optimization problems. This enables companies to re-optimize daily to change their strategies based on realized demand, and to implement the optimization solutions in real-time.

Without revenue management and the analytics used, airlines, hotels, and other industries that traditionally use revenue management can no longer compete. For industries in which revenue management systems are not traditionally used, the analytics methods can provide them with an edge over the competition.

17.5 Notes and Sources

For more information about revenue management in general, we direct you to Talluri and van Ryzin [137].

17.2. The information about airline revenue management is from two important papers in the field: Smith et al. [131], and Glover et al. [51].

17.3. The information about the Cherokee Casino comes from Metters et al. [94].

Chapter 18

A Life-Saving Analytics Operation

An approximate answer to the right problem is worth a good deal more than an exact answer to an approximate problem.

– John Tukey

Contents

In July of 2006, a woman arrived at an emergency department in Illinois complaining of nausea, shortness of breath, and chest pain. After waiting two hours for treatment, her name was called. Unfortunately, the staff was too late; she had died of a heart attack while waiting. She had the classic symptoms of a heart attack and should have been put on cardiac monitoring immediately.

While emergency department staff members are trained to take care of the most ill people first, long emergency room waits have become commonplace. Between 1997 and 2008, the number of annual emergency department visits in the United States increased by 33%, from 94.9 million to 124 million. At the same time, many emergency departments across the country were closed due to financial difficulty, causing a huge increase in wait times, with an average wait of nearly four hours.

Many emergency departments are taking action to improve operations in an effort to decrease waiting times. The Emergency Department (ED) at Beth Israel Deaconess Medical Center (BIDMC) in Boston, Massachusetts, has invested in creating a "Dashboard" software system. The data underlying the Dashboard is an accurate, thorough and real-time representation of the status of the ED, including information about patients in the ED and ED resources such as staff and beds. Such complete and reliable data has enabled in-depth analysis of ED operations and exploration of ways to seek improvement.

In this chapter, we discuss a simulation model of the ED that was developed to allow the staff to analyze performance and evaluate the impact of different operational decisions, such as increasing the number of beds, reducing the bed cleaning time, and introducing a point of care lab testing device. This model was developed by a team of MIT researchers using the expertise of ED staff and one year of detailed data. The MIT team spent several days and nights in the ED at the BIDMC shadowing doctors and nurses. This resulted in a much greater understanding of the ED operations and of the behavior of the doctors and nurses, leading to an improved simulation model. Frequent meetings and close collaboration between the MIT team and the leadership of the ED resulted in several of the recommendations being implemented. Using this simulation model, the MIT team proposed and analyzed policies for reducing the waiting times in the ED by 35%. We show in this chapter how an accurate simulation model can provide an organization with a useful and easy-to-use tool to discover ways to improve operations.

18.1 The Emergency Department at BIDMC

Beth Israel Deaconess Medical Center (BIDMC) is a Harvard teaching hospital and a leading medical institution. The Emergency Department (ED) is always open and is staffed by specialty trained, board-certified emergency medicine physicians and trauma trained nurses. The ED treats nearly 55,000 patients each year from the Boston metropolitan area.

Each patient in the ED at BIDMC goes through a series of processes: registration, triage, waiting, bed assignment, assignment to medical staff, lab tests, radiology exams, diagnosis, and admission to the hospital or discharge. Relevant information and timestamps about each of these processes are recorded in the Dashboard data collection system.

The first timestamp occurs immediately when a patient checks in at the ED. Additionally, when a patient is registered, important information about the patient is recorded, including a visit number, a permanent patient number, date of birth, and chief complaint. After the patient undergoes triage, more information is recorded, including severity or acuity level on a scale of 1-5, also known as the Emergency Severity Index (ESI).

Generally, several timestamps occur simultaneously when a patient leaves the waiting room. First, a timestamp simply documents the fact that the patient has left the waiting room. It is also at this time that the patient is assigned to a bed as well as a nurse, a medical resident, and an attending physician. Information is recorded about the time the bed is assigned as well as the bed number. The Dashboard system also records which nurses, residents, and attending physicians are assigned to a particular patient at a particular time, and who replaces them when a shift change occurs.

As the patient undergoes treatment, the Dashboard records information about which labs and radiology exams are ordered, when they are ordered, when they are processed, what the results are, and when the results are available. The system also records the final disposition of the patient (usually admitted to the hospital or discharged but occasionally something else) and the final numerical diagnosis/diagnoses, which are based on the International Classification of Diseases (ICD). If the patient is admitted to the hospital, the Dashboard records when an inpatient bed is requested, when that bed is assigned, and when that patient is finally admitted. It also records when each patient leaves the emergency department (whether to be discharged, admitted to the hospital, transferred, etc.).

BIDMC provided the MIT team with patient visit data for all visits to the ED from February 1, 2005 through January 31, 2006. This dataset included over 47,000 patients. Also included in the data was the status/utilization of overall ED resources in 10 minute intervals.

18.2 The Simulation Model

Based on analysis of the available data and discussion with ED staff, the team of researchers decided to model ED operations with beds as the critical resource and ESI level as the primary classification of the urgency of the patient's condition. The team had also considered a model of the ED with nurses as the critical resource. However, beds seemed more critical based on the frequent overcrowding in the ED and the use of temporary hallway beds to try to accommodate patient demand. In addition, the team considered separating the patients based on final disposition (admit to the hospital, discharge or observation) or final diagnosis (clusters of ICD codes), but ESI level proved to be the most relevant way to classify patients, especially considering the fact that beds are assigned to patients based on ESI level.

The simulation model (Figure 18.1) used to analyze ED operations consists of five processes that are discussed in more detail in the rest of this section: arrivals, triage, waiting room, bed and room occupation, and exit.

Arrival Process

One of the main challenges faced by emergency departments is the fluctuating nature of arrivals. While average patient demand is often predictable, there are occasional surges that stretch resources beyond capacity, leaving hospital staff feeling overworked and hospital patients feeling neglected. Examples include the surge during the Boston Marathon bombing and the severe Boston winter of 2015. Emergency department crowding has been identified as a major barrier to receiving timely emergency care in the United States. It is also on the busiest days that patient waiting times reach their highest levels. In order to perform a reliable analysis of ED operations, it became necessary to incorporate

Figure 18.1: BIDMC emergency department simulation model. Upon arrival to the ED, patients go through the triage process and then wait in the waiting room area. When a bed becomes available, they are assigned a bed in the ED. After diagnosis and treatment, about 70% of the patients are discharged, and about 30% of the patients are admitted to the hospital for further treatment.

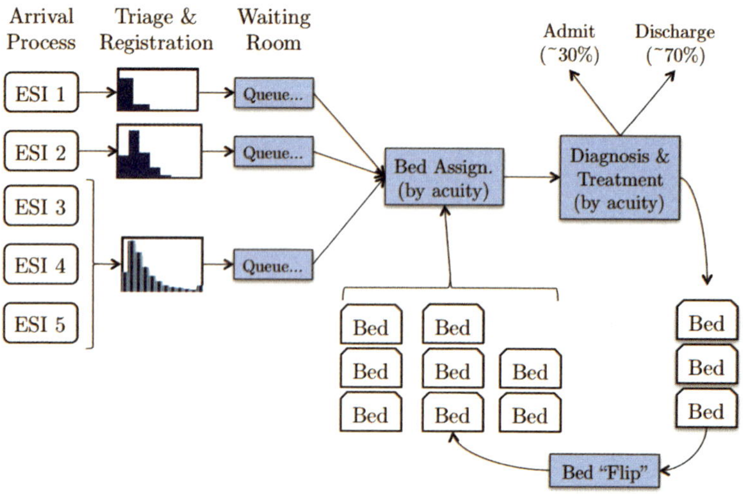

an accurate estimate of patient arrival rates, which took into account these fluctuations, into the simulation model.

The arrival rate of patients to the ED was estimated using linear regression analysis based on time of day, day of the week, and previous arrivals. For more about linear regression, see Chapter 21.

Table 18.1 shows the results of this linear regression analysis to predict the number of arrivals in 8 hour blocks. Using a random 70% of the data points to generate the model, the resulting value of R^2 is 0.84. Results of the regression indicate that time of day has the greatest impact on the arrival rate. The period from 8 am to 4 pm is the busiest time of the day in terms of arrivals while the period from midnight to 8 am is the slowest period of the day. Results also indicate that arrivals occur more frequently on weekdays than on weekends, and that there is a positive correlation between the arrival rate at a given point in time and the number of arrivals that occurred exactly two to four days prior to that moment.
The validation of the model also yielded strong results; using the remaining 30% of the data to test the model, the R^2 value was also 0.84.

The model above was considered the best model because of its simplicity and high correlation to historical data. Several other models were considered with various combinations of the variables used above, as well as the following variables:

- Time of Day in 1 hour blocks
- Time of Day in 6 hour blocks
- Time of Day in 12 hour blocks
- Day of Week (Mon, Tues, Wed, Thurs, Fri, Sat, Sun)
- Day of Week (Monday, Midweek, Friday, Saturday, Sunday)
- Number of Arrivals 0-4 days earlier in 8 hour blocks

Table 18.1: Output from the linear regression model used to estimate the number of arrivals in eight hour blocks.

Variable	Estimate	t-Stat
(Intercept)	28.99	8.49
Time of Day (12am to 8 am)	-24.66	-61.61
Time of Day (8 am to 4 pm)	17.55	44.06
Time of Day (4 pm to 12am)	7.11	17.4
Day of Week (Weekend)	-1.93	-6.14
Day of Week (Weekday)	1.93	6.14
# Arrivals 48-96 hrs earlier	0.05	4.14

- Number of Arrivals 0-4 days earlier in 12 hour blocks
- Number of Arrivals 0-4 days earlier in 24 hour blocks
- Holiday
- Temperature/Precipitation

The arrival rates used in the simulation were the arrival rates generated from the linear regression analysis in Table 18.1. Within each 8 hour block, there is a fixed arrival rate based on the time of day, day of week, and previous arrivals. Patient inter-arrival times within this 8 hour block are generated from an exponential probability distribution with density function $\lambda e^{-\lambda x}$ at the prescribed arrival rate λ.

Triage Times

It is in triage where the Emergency Severity Index (ESI) or acuity level is determined for each patient. This index helps give ED staff an estimate of the resources a patient will require as well as the priority in which the patient should be seen. Patients with ESI-1 are the most serious patients and require immediate attention. Patients with ESI-5 are the least severe and can wait several hours to be seen by a doctor. Table 18.2 shows the number and percentage of arrivals for each ESI level from February 1, 2005 to January 31, 2006. The majority of patients who enter the ED are ESI-3 patients.

Although triage times were not explicitly captured in the Dashboard, there was one timestamp when each patient arrived at the ED and another timestamp when each patient left the waiting room. Triage occurred at some point between these two timestamps. Although not all of this time was necessarily spent in triage (much of the time is often spent waiting for an available room or nurse), it was assumed that the time patients spent waiting when no one else was in the waiting room must have been time in triage. It was also possible to recreate from the data the number of patients already waiting in the waiting room when each patient arrived. Triage times were therefore estimated to be the time patients spent waiting to leave the waiting

Table 18.2: Patient severity (ESI-1 = most severe).

	Arrivals	% of Patients
ESI-1	1,165	2.45%
ESI-2	10,910	22.95%
ESI-3	28,372	59.69%
ESI-4	6,756	14.21%
ESI-5	332	0.70%
Total	47,535	100.00%

room (i.e., time from presentation until leaving waiting room) when the waiting room was empty upon arrival. Table 18.3 contains triage time statistics. The average triage time per patient is 15.4 minutes. This time is lower for more severe patients who are often rushed into a bed to begin receiving treatment immediately upon arrival.

Waiting Room

Patients of ESI-1 are given first priority to leave the waiting room when rooms become available. ESI-2 patients are given the next priority. ED Policy states that ESI-3 patients would have next highest priority, followed by ESI-4 and ESI-5. However, the data shows that often the less severe patients (ESI-3, 4, and 5) are not necessarily served in order of priority but are often served on a first-come first-serve basis regardless of priority. The simulation model incorporated this strategy by giving highest priority to ESI-1 patients, second highest priority to ESI-2 patients, and treating the remaining patients on a first-come first-serve basis.

Room Occupation

At the time of the study, there were 46 rooms in the ED at BIDMC, each containing a single bed. One room was reserved for ESI-1 patients, and the remaining 45 rooms could be used by patients of any ESI level. Technically, the rooms of the ED were divided into zones with special purposes such as observation, fast track, or acute zones. However, each room had the capability of serving any type of patient. For this simulation, all rooms were considered equal, with the exception of one room reserved for the acute ambulance arrivals. Although in reality patients can be and often are reassigned from room to room,

Table 18.3: Triage time distribution (minutes).

	All	ESI-1	ESI-2	ESI-3	ESI-4	ESI-5
Mean	15.4	2.1	8.0	17.0	22.4	20.0
Std Dev	19.9	8.6	9.8	21.1	23.3	16.2
99th Percentile	96.0	41.9	44.0	102.1	116.8	68.7
95th Percentile	51.0	11.9	26.0	53.0	66.8	50.4
90th Percentile	36.0	1.0	19.0	39.0	50.0	41.1
75th Percentile	20.0	0.0	11.0	22.0	29.0	25.8
50th Percentile	9.0	0.0	5.0	11.0	15.0	16.5
25th Percentile	4.0	0.0	1.0	5.0	8.0	8.0
10th Percentile	0.0	0.0	0.0	1.0	4.0	5.0
5th Percentile	0.0	0.0	0.0	0.0	2.0	3.7
1st Percentile	0.0	0.0	0.0	0.0	0.0	2.1

for the simulation a patient was assigned to one room only and eventually departed from the originally assigned room.

Bed times (the amount of time a patient spends in an ED bed) were explicitly recorded in the Dashboard system, and these times were used in the simulation model (Table 18.4). Although ESI-1 patients are the most severe, they have shorter bed times than ESI-2 and ESI-3 patients because they are almost always given inpatient beds immediately when admitted to the hospital. Other less severe patients generally have to wait much longer to be admitted to the ED. ESI-4 and ESI-5 patients have the shortest average bed times simply because generally their conditions are so minor that they can be treated relatively quickly and released.

Patient Exit and Bed "Flip" Times

Historically at BIDMC, approximately 65% of ED patients are discharged while approximately 30% are admitted to the hospital. The rest are transferred to other hospitals or leave before receiving full treatment. Because the simulation model is restricted to the ED and not the entire hospital, when a patient exits, he or she simply vacates the assigned bed and leaves the system. After the bed and room are cleaned, they become available for the next patient.

Bed cleaning times are not explicitly recorded by the Dashboard system. There is, however, data available for when beds are occupied versus how long beds sit empty. The bed cleaning or "flip" time must therefore be some portion of the time the bed sits empty. In order to estimate the bed "flip" times the model assumes that when the ED is very busy (i.e., many people in the waiting room) the bed "flip" process will begin as soon as the bed is vacated and, as soon as the bed "flip" is complete, the highest priority patient will be assigned to the now available bed. Figure 18.2 plots the mean, median, and standard

Table 18.4: Bed time distribution (hours). Note that all patients are assigned to beds in the ED.

	All	**ESI-1**	**ESI-2**	**ESI-3**	**ESI-4**	**ESI-5**
Mean	6.46	5.69	8.41	6.63	2.95	1.85
Std Dev	5.77	4.47	6.27	5.70	3.24	1.92
99th Percentile	27.75	22.43	30.00	27.51	18.52	11.46
95th Percentile	18.80	14.98	22.32	18.90	7.89	4.71
90th Percentile	13.12	11.80	16.70	13.37	5.37	3.45
75th Percentile	8.08	6.99	9.82	8.23	3.35	2.28
50th Percentile	4.90	4.47	6.69	5.06	2.17	1.42
25th Percentile	2.73	2.78	4.62	2.98	1.35	0.77
10th Percentile	1.48	1.71	3.12	1.73	0.75	0.33
5th Percentile	0.93	1.07	2.27	1.07	0.40	0.13
1st Percentile	0.05	0.21	0.73	0.03	0.00	0.00

Figure 18.2: Empty bed times versus number of patients in waiting room.

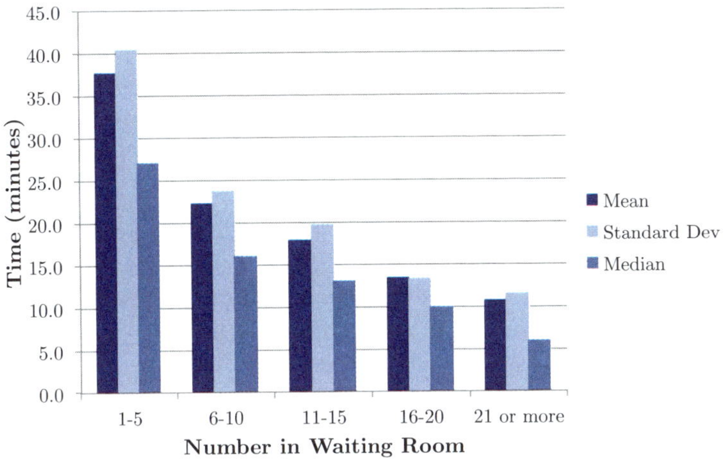

deviation for the empty bed times versus the number of patients in the waiting room.

Interestingly, as pressure mounts on the system, the time that beds sit empty decreases. This may indicate that the work rate increases and beds are cleaned faster as the number of people in the waiting room grows large or simply that as more people arrive they are placed in beds faster. The MIT team discussed this finding with the nurses and, after observing the data, they admitted that they were feeling the pressure to clean the beds faster.

For the simulation model, the bed "flip" times correspond to the mean time a bed sits empty as found in Figure 18.2. For example, when there are 5 or fewer people in the waiting room, the bed "flip" takes 37.6 minutes, and when there are between 6 and 10 people in the waiting room, the bed "flip" lasts for 22.2 minutes, etc.

The complete simulation model was coded in the Python programming language. Each run of the model simulated 10 years of ED operations and over 450,000 patient arrivals.

Reality Check

The developers of this model went to great lengths to ensure that the arrival rates, triage times, waiting room priority, bed times, and bed cleaning times accurately reflect the actual times/processes that occur at BIDMC. Several other criteria were used to ensure that the simulation model accurately reflects reality. These criteria include a comparison of daily arrivals, waiting times, and patient length of stay.

Daily Arrivals

The arrival process drove the simulation, and in order to accurately model ED operations correctly, it became very important to ensure that the number of patient arrivals in the simulation model each day matched the historical number of patient ED arrivals each day at BIDMC. This is especially important considering the increased strain that is placed on ED resources when the arrival rate increases. Although staffing levels can be raised somewhat to meet increased demand, there is a fixed amount of space available to observe, diagnose, and treat patients. Thus, as the number of arrivals increases, the bottleneck effect of beds becomes more and more pronounced.

Figure 18.3 is a histogram of both the historical average number of daily ED arrivals at BIDMC from 2/01/05 to 1/31/06 and the average number of daily arrivals predicted by the simulation model. In both cases, the number of daily arrivals is between 115 and 140 patients a majority of the time. Having fewer than 95 patient arrivals or greater than 165 patient arrivals per day is very rare. The figure confirms that the arrival process of the simulation model appears to be a reasonable representation of reality.

Waiting Times

The time patients spend waiting is perhaps the most important measure of how closely the simulation model matches reality. Unlike other indicators in the simulation such as the arrival process, triage times, and time patients spend in a bed, which are explicitly controlled, the waiting times are dependent on everything else happening in the simulation, including the arrival process, triage

Figure 18.3: Histogram of number of actual and simulated daily arrivals.

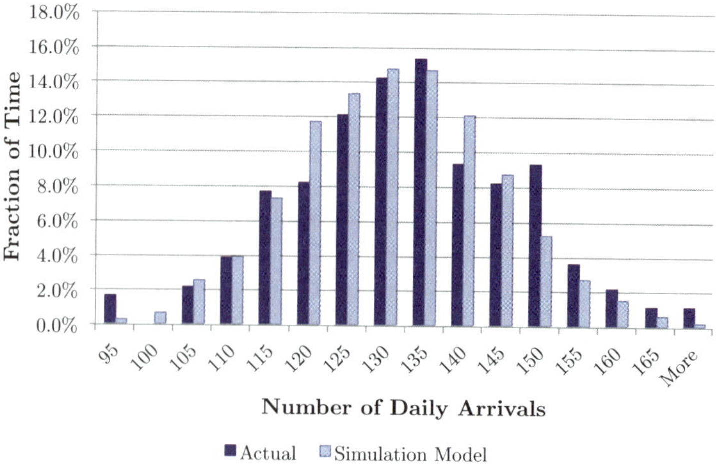

times, waiting room priority, bed times, and bed cleaning times. Ensuring that the waiting times of patients in the simulation model match the historical waiting times of ED patients from 2/1/05 to 1/31/06 provides a reasonably high level of confidence that the simulation model accurately reflects reality.

One important consideration to note is that because the Dashboard system does not include timestamps for the triage process, the waiting times considered here represent the time from when a patient first presents at the ED until that patient leaves the waiting room and is assigned a bed. Therefore, triage times are included in the waiting times for both the historical data and the simulation model.

Tables 18.5 and 18.6 show the waiting times for patients both historically at BIDMC and in the simulation model. The average waiting time for all patients in the simulation model is only 2.2% higher than the actual average waiting time. Other average waiting times and percentiles for the simulation model generally match reality very closely.

Length of Stay

As a final confirmation of the validity of the simulation model, the historical length of stay for patients from 2/1/05 to 1/31/06 is compared with the simulated length of stay (Tables 18.7 and 18.8). This represents the time from

Table 18.5: Actual waiting times (minutes).

	All	ESI-1	ESI-2	ESI-3	ESI-4	ESI-5
Mean	40.7	3.0	12.0	49.6	55.3	51.3
Std Dev	62.0	8.7	12.8	68.4	69.1	65.1
99th Percentile	286.6	57.6	57.8	305.3	306.4	317.7
95th Percentile	176.1	18.5	37.4	197.9	206.5	176.1
90th Percentile	119.7	9.2	28.8 1	41.7	148.8	134.5
80th Percentile	58.8	1.2	19.2	81.0	89.8	82.0
50th Percentile	15.0	0.0	7.3	21.2 2	9.4	24.6

Table 18.6: Simulated waiting times (minutes).

	All	ESI-1	ESI-2	ESI-3	ESI-4	ESI-5
Mean	41.6	3.9	12.3	50.6	56.6	54.8
Std Dev	63.9	1.6	3.0	77.0	80.1	78.1
99th Percentile	289.8	57.6	59.2	306.2	314.2	323.4
95th Percentile	178.7	23.4	39.1	199.6	206.1	206.9
90th Percentile	124.5	11.8	29.2	144.1	152.8	151.8
80th Percentile	63.6	3.6	19.5	85.8	95.5	88.2
50th Percentile	15.0	0.0	7.5	22.6	29.4	24.6

when a patient first arrives until departure from the ED, either by discharge or admittance to the hospital. The overall average length of stay from the simulation model exactly matches the actual overall average length of stay. Other indicators from the simulation model also closely match those from the actual data.

18.3 "What-if" Analyses

By effectively modeling the patient throughput process in the emergency department at BIDMC, it is possible to analyze several "what-if" scenarios that are important to ED staff and may increase patient throughput. These "what-if" scenarios include adding additional beds, reducing the bed "flip" times, adopting a policy of reserving extra beds for more serious patients (a "nested" bed policy), and investing in a point of care (POC) troponin test to rapidly diagnose patients with chest pain. We will first discuss the effects of each policy individually and then discuss how they can be combined for even bigger improvements.

Additional Beds

The ED at BIDMC has identified beds as a critical resource. At the time of the study, there were 46 permanent beds available in the ED. Results for the additional bed analysis are shown in Table 18.9. According to our simulation model, the addition of one bed would lead to a 13.2% overall decrease in average waiting time, from 41.6 minutes to 36.1 minutes. Also, reducing the number of available beds from 46 to 45 would lead to a 16.6% overall increase in average waiting time. Finally, adding four additional beds would lead to a 39.3% overall decrease in average waiting time. For each of the scenarios, one bed is held in

Table 18.7: Actual patient length of stay (hours).

	All	ESI-1	ESI-2	ESI-3	ESI-4	ESI-5
Mean	7.14	5.70	8.60	7.46	3.90	2.69
Std Dev	5.73	4.47	6.28	5.71	3.36	2.09
99th Percentile	28.23	22.43	30.17	28.17	19.41	12.73
95th Percentile	19.55	14.98	22.55	19.84	8.97	6.12
90th Percentile	13.77	11.77	16.92	14.22	6.63	4.56
80th Percentile	9.72	7.82	11.23	10.12	4.97	3.70
50th Percentile	5.60	4.47	6.87	5.92	3.13	2.17
20th Percentile	3.10	2.46	4.38	3.42	1.90	1.25
10th Percentile	2.20	1.73	3.30	2.48	1.40	0.82
5th Percentile	1.60	1.17	2.45	1.88	1.07	0.60
1st Percentile	0.77	0.22	1.02	0.95	0.55	0.37

Table 18.8: Simulated patient length of stay (hours).

	All	ESI-1	ESI-2	ESI-3	ESI-4	ESI-5
Mean	7.14	5.76	8.60	7.45	3.89	2.77
Std Dev	5.68	4.45	6.12	5.70	3.34	2.26
99th Percentile	29.44	23.83	30.06	30.49	20.06	14.10
95th Percentile	19.48	14.55	22.60	19.92	9.26	6.69
90th Percentile	13.52	12.30	16.58	14.99	6.85	5.09
80th Percentile	9.88	7.74	10.60	9.93	5.07	3.87
50th Percentile	5.22	4.34	7.39	6.18	2.90	2.10
20th Percentile	2.90	3.38	4.70	4.05	1.63	1.01
10th Percentile	1.98	1.46	4.62	1.98	1.25	0.76
5th Percentile	1.81	1.46	2.17	1.82	1.25	0.67
1st Percentile	1.25	1.46	1.99	1.73	1.14	0.67

Table 18.9: Percentage change in average waiting time from baseline scenario (current number of beds is 46).

Number of Beds	All (%)	ESI-1 (%)	ESI-2 (%)	ESI-3 (%)	ESI-4 (%)	ESI-5 (%)
45	16.58	6.60	6.37	17.71	16.00	17.15
46	0.00	0.00	0.00	0.00	0.00	0.00
47	-13.23	-5.94	-5.31	-14.13	-12.76	-12.65
48	-23.89	-11.32	-10.24	-25.43	-23.05	-23.39
49	-32.47	-15.95	-14.53	-34.50	-31.33	-32.18
50	-39.33	-20.80	-18.40	-41.72	-37.89	-39.20

reserve for ESI-1 patients, and bed reassignment times are consistent with the baseline model as presented in Figure 18.2.

Bed "Flip" Times

The time required for cleaning and reassigning beds was not readily available from the data. However, there is evidence to suggest that several minutes were required from when a patient leaves a bed until that bed is ready for the next patient to enter. This analysis investigated the effect that reducing bed "flip" times would have on patient waiting times. Complete results for the analysis are presented in Table 18.10. A reduction of 5 minutes in the bed "flip" times would lead to a 7.18% overall decrease in average patient waiting time and a bed "flip" reduction of 10 minutes would lead to a 13.71% decrease in average patient waiting time. After some discussions, the nurses accepted the recommendation and felt it was realistic to implement.

"Nested" Beds

The "Nested Bed" Policy is the idea of reserving certain beds for patients of certain acuity levels. This idea was motivated by the use of nested fare classes in airlines as a way to maximize revenue. The current policy at BIDMC was to reserve one bed for ESI-1 patients who arrive via ambulance. These patients can occupy any available bed in the ED, but patients not in this category cannot occupy the bed reserved for ESI-1 patients. The "nested" bed analysis extended that idea for ESI-1 and ESI-2 patients and multiple beds. For the following scenarios denoted A-B, A refers to the number of beds out of 46 that are available exclusively for ESI-1 patients, and B refers to the number of beds that are available for either ESI-1 or ESI-2 patients. To further clarify this policy, ESI-1 patients can occupy any of the 46 beds in the ED, ESI-2 patients can occupy any of the 46 beds in the ED except for the A beds, and ESI-3, ESI-4, and ESI-5 patients can occupy any of the 46 beds in the ED except for the A and B beds.

Results of the analysis are summarized in Table 18.11. Note that changing from the current 1-0 policy to a 1-1 policy would increase overall average waiting time by 0.8%, ESI-3 average waiting time by 0.99%, ESI-4 average waiting time by 0.91%, and ESI-5 average waiting time by 1.14%, and yet reduce ESI-2 average waiting time by 1.51% and reduce ESI-1 average waiting time by 1.25%. The leadership of the ED accepted the recommendation to changing from the current 1-0 policy to a 1-1 policy.

Point of Care Troponin Test

The physicians at BIDMC Emergency Department have recommended a point of care (POC) troponin test as a possible way to increase throughput at BIDMC. This point of care device would substantially reduce the amount of time required to identify the troponin levels in patients with chest pain. When troponin levels are high, this can be a strong indication of heart damage. Of the 47,537 patients who arrived at the BIDMC ED from 2/1/05 to 1/31/06, 3,185 patients had chest

Table 18.10: Percentage change in average waiting time from baseline scenario.

Cleaning Time Reduction (min)	All (%)	ESI-1 (%)	ESI-2 (%)	ESI-3 (%)	ESI-4 (%)	ESI-5 (%)
0	0.00	0.00	0.00	0.00	0.00	0.00
5	-7.18	-3.33	-2.75	-7.68	-6.91	-7.00
10	-13.71	-5.25	-5.76	-14.63	-13.15	-13.47
15	-19.42	-8.79	-8.32	-20.71	-18.60	-18.98
20	-24.40	-11.87	-10.90	-25.96	-23.40	-23.96
25	-28.54	-14.33	-13.22	-30.33	-27.39	-27.86

pain as a chief complaint. However, only 2,632 of these patients with chest pain as a chief complaint had a troponin lab test.

Although there are several factors that affect the final disposition (i.e., discharge vs. admit to the hospital) of patients in the ED, for the purposes of this analysis it is assumed that once the results are available using a POC troponin test, the disposition of that patient can be immediately determined. Thus, a patient can either immediately be discharged or will have an inpatient bed requested. These assumptions may be optimistic but they represented a first-cut approximation to analyzing the benefits of the POC troponin device.

Table 18.12 depicts the percentage of patients presenting with chest pain. In order to simulate the arrival of patients with chest pain to the ED, 0.6% of ESI-1 patients, 18.4% of ESI-2 patients, etc. were randomly assigned to be a chest pain patient.
Furthermore, only a certain fraction (Table 18.13) of those patients with chest pain will eventually be admitted to the hospital as an in-patient. The rest are discharged, transferred, or leave before treatment is complete.

Generally, it can take several hours after an inpatient bed is requested before a patient is actually admitted to the hospital. There are two factors responsible for this. First, it takes a great deal of coordination between the ED and hospital staff to accomplish the transfer, and second, sometimes there are very few available inpatient beds to which the patients can be admitted. In the case of chest pain patients, it takes on average 5.12 hours to actually be admitted to the hospital after an inpatient bed is requested by the ED. For the

Table 18.11: Percentage change in average waiting time from baseline 1-0 policy.

New Policy (A-B)	All (%)	ESI-1 (%)	ESI-2 (%)	ESI-3 (%)	ESI-4 (%)	ESI-5 (%)
0-0	-6.59	35.07	-2.33	-7.18	-6.35	-5.94
0-1	-5.93	31.70	-3.64	-6.35	-5.63	-5.22
0-2	-5.14	29.18	-4.98	-5.38	-4.74	-4.04
0-3	-4.28	26.41	-6.43	-4.33	-3.74	-2.89
0-4	-3.29	22.26	-7.76	-3.14	-2.66	-1.86
1-0	0.00	0.00	0.00	0.00	0.00	0.00
1-1	0.80	-1.25	-1.51	0.99	0.91	1.14
1-2	1.71	-2.99	-2.90	-2.09	1.93	2.35
1-3	2.80	-5.26	-4.51	3.40	3.14	4.03
1-4	4.03	-7.36	-6.10	4.89	4.45	5.45
2-0	10.96	-24.61	4.21	11.79	10.58	11.26
2-1	11.93	-25.75	2.41	13.00	11.66	12.64
2-2	13.08	-25.96	0.65	14.40	12.90	14.36
2-3	14.44	-26.44	-1.11	16.01	14.39	15.98
2-4	15.99	-27.21	-2.99	17.84	16.09	18.05

simulation analysis, once the disposition of a chest pain patient is determined, he or she will either be immediately discharged or transferred to the hospital after 5.12 hours if admittance is necessary.

Table 18.14 shows the effects of reducing the time required to determine the disposition of chest pain patients. If ED physicians were able to reduce the time necessary to determine the disposition of troponin patients from four or five hours to one hour using the troponin test, average patient waiting time would decrease by over 21%. It is important to note that the critical factor here is not how long it takes to determine the troponin levels but how long it takes to determine the disposition of the patient. Reducing the time to determine the troponin levels will certainly help reduce the time to determine disposition, but other factors may affect this time as well. Note that even though ESI-4 and ESI-5 do not have a significant number of chest pain patients, they have a significant reduction in waiting time, because the people with chest pain clear out of the system faster.

Combined Effects

Four separate policies have been evaluated individually to estimate the respective isolated effect of implementing each policy. Another interesting idea is to consider changing policies simultaneously and determine the net effect. For example, the ED staff could invest in a POC troponin device and create an extra bed for patients to occupy. Table 18.15 shows the net effect that changing several policies could have. If the ED staff invests in the POC troponin device, adds an extra bed, reduces the bed cleaning time by 5 minutes, and reserves an additional bed for ESI 1-2 patients (a 1-1 nested bed policy), the predicted average waiting time of each patient would be reduced by over 34%.

Future "What-ifs"

Besides the policies already considered here, several other "what-if" scenarios have been proposed and may be considered for future evaluation using the simulation model. One such scenario involves determining the effectiveness of adding a "Fast-Track" zone to the ED which exclusively serves less severe

Table 18.12: Percentage of patients presenting with chest pain.

ESI Level	Total	Chest Pain	% of ESI Level
All	47,537	3,185	6.7
ESI-1	1,165	7	0.6
ESI-2	10,910	2,003	18.4
ESI-3	28,372	1,148	4.1
ESI-4	6,756	25	0.4
ESI-5	332	2	0.6

Table 18.13: Percentage of chest pain patients admitted to the hospital.

ESI Level	Chest Pain	Admitted	% of ESI Level
All	3,185	1,484	46.6
ESI-1	7	7	100.0
ESI-2	2,003	1.159	57.9
ESI-3	1,148	318	27.7
ESI-4	25	0	0.0
ESI-5	2	0	0.0

patients. Several hospitals have adopted this policy in order to reduce waiting time for patients who generally have shorter lengths of stay. This policy presumes to create space and reduce the number of people in the waiting room when the demand for the ED becomes high.

Another proposal for future evaluation includes seeking to identify key groups of patients who cause significant delays to the system as a whole. Such groups might include MRI patients or psychiatric patients. Identifying such groups and quantifying the negative impact on wait times caused by them may provide motivation to discover solutions and make improvements in the way ED personnel administer treatment to these groups.

18.4 The Strength of Simulation

The Dashboard data provided by BIDMC has allowed for extensive and accurate modeling of emergency department operations. The simulation model described

Table 18.14: Percentage change in average waiting time from baseline scenario.

Time to Determine Disposition of Chest Pain Patients	All (%)	ESI-1 (%)	ESI-2 (%)	ESI-3 (%)	ESI-4 (%)	ESI-5 (%)
15 min	-25.03	-12.23	-10.64	-26.64	-24.18	-24.99
30 min	-23.97	-11.55	-10.11	-25.53	-23.14	-23.70
1 hr	-21.75	-10.42	-9.20	-23.15	-21.04	-21.04
2 hr	-16.87	-6.67	-6.92	-18.00	-16.24	-16.33
3 hr	-11.69	-5.15	-4.66	-12.47	-11.30	-11.62
4 hr	-6.40	-2.84	-2.23	-6.86	-6.19	-6.54
5 hr	-0.54	-0.76	0.00	-0.60	-0.47	-0.60
6 hr	5.58	1.81	2.28	5.95	5.38	5.79

Table 18.15: Percentage change in average waiting time from baseline scenario by successively applying the proposed changes.

	All (%)	ESI-1 (%)	ESI-2 (%)	ESI-3 (%)	ESI-4 (%)	ESI-5 (%)
1 hr troponin	-21.75	-10.42	-9.20	-23.15	-21.04	-21.04
+Extra Bed	-30.73	-16.18	-13.55	-32.65	-29.70	-30.65
+5 min Faster Flip	-34.83	-18.31	-15.74	-37.01	-33.52	-34.77
+1-1 Nested Policy	-34.48	-19.26	-16.64	-36.56	-33.11	-34.41

in this chapter is an example of how simulations can be used to model reality and evaluate decisions. The model was able to provide insight to the staff at BIDMC regarding several possible improvements to their congestion problems. Especially because of the excellent communication between the research team and the leadership of the ED, the simulation model had a lot of credibility among the members of the leadership team of the ED. Correspondingly, several of the recommendations were adopted: bed flip minutes, nested beds, and additional beds.

Additionally, the research team was able to give the staff in the ED at BIDMC a tool that they could use in the future to evaluate decisions. The design of the product was such that they were able to use it in practice and easily understand the output. While the accuracy of the model was important, it was equally important to build a tool that could be used in practice.

18.5 Notes and Sources

Simulation analysis of emergency department operations has been used to evaluate policy changes. Saunders et al. [120] and Connelly and Bair [37] quantify the effect that the number of physicians, nurses, and beds had on patient throughput time in emergency room operations. The story in the introduction was reported in the American Medical News [133]. Gannon et al. [49] analyzed one year of ED data from BIDMC in order to identify process inefficiencies and recommend solutions with the goal of reducing patient throughput time. The material in this chapter is based on the work of Bertsimas, Carr and Noyes [17], which further analyzes the proposals in [49] and quantifies the impact that these and other proposals will have on ED operations at BIDMC.

18.1. The information about BIDMC is from their website [26].

18.3. The idea of using nested fare classes in airlines as a way to maximize profit is from [31].

Part VII

Finance

Chapter 19

An Analytical Valuation of Stock Options

There's no such thing as a free lunch.

– Robert A. Heinlein

Contents

In 1997, the Nobel prize in Economic-Sciences was awarded to Robert Merton and Myron Scholes. These economists, in collaboration with the late Fisher Black, developed a pioneering methodology and the so called "Black–Scholes formula" for the analytical valuation of stock options (also known as financial derivatives). Their work has paved the way for economic valuations in many other areas, has generated new types of financial instruments, and has facilitated more efficient risk management methods.

In this chapter, we introduce the key idea of pricing options: the no-arbitrage principle. This principle says that it should not be possible to make arbitrary profits without any risk, which implies that two financial instruments that have exactly the same payoff in all states of the market should have exactly the same price. By utilizing the no-arbitrage principle, we show how analytics can be applied to price financial derivatives.

19.1 What are Options and Why are They Important?

Options are derivative contracts that give the holder the right, but not the obligation, to buy or sell the underlying instrument at a specified price, called the *strike price*, on or before a specified future date called the *expiration date*. In this section, we will discuss the two main types of options: call options and put options. A call (put) option gives the holder the right to buy (sell) a stock at a specified price. Throughout this chapter, we will focus on European options. A *European call option* provides the holder the right to buy the underlying stock at a specified strike price K on a specified future date T. If S_T denotes the price of the stock at time T, then the payoff of the option is $S_T - K$, if $S_T \geq K$, and it is 0, if $S_T < K$. This implies that the payoff of a European call option is given as the maximum of $S_T - K$ and 0:

$$\max(S_T - K, 0).$$

A popular way for companies to compensate highly valued employees is to award them "employee stock options," which give employees the right, but not the obligation, to buy the stock of the company at a pre-specified price, typically the price of the stock at the time of the award. For example, if an employee receives 1,000 call options with a strike price of \$53, and the price of the stock after four years becomes \$93, then the employee can exercise the options, buying them at \$53 and selling them in the market for \$93, making a profit of \$40,000. It is common that options vest over time and can not be transferred to another person. These restrictions attempt to align the employee's interest with that of the company's. Another substantial reason that companies issue employee stock options as compensation is to preserve cash flow and to receive tax deductions.

On the other hand, the *European put option* provides the holder the right to sell the underlying stock at a specified strike price K on a specified future date T. In this case, the payoff of the option is $K - S_T$, if $S_T \leq K$, and it is 0, if $S_T > K$. This implies that the payoff of a European put option is given as the maximum of $K - S_T$ and 0:

$$\max(K - S_T, 0).$$

Let us consider a concrete example of the use of put options. Consider a major United States manufacturing firm, with the majority of its employees in the United States, but most of its revenue comes from Europe. In other words, the majority of the costs of the company are in US dollars, while the majority of its revenue is in Euros. Currency exchange rates fluctuate significantly, so if the Euro weakens relative to the US dollar, then the amount of dollars the company receives decreases. To be protected against this happening, companies buy insurance, often called "a put option" that gives them the right to sell Euros at a pre-specified price, thus ensuring that the financial impact to the company will not be too severe because of currency rate fluctuations. For example, suppose the company buys 100 million put options on the Euro with a strike price of 1.33 (1 Euro=1.33 Dollars). If the exchange rate becomes 1.27 and the company exercises the put option, it will gain 6 million dollars, thus ensuring that the loss of revenue due to the weakening of the Euro will be offset by the gain in the put options.

There is another popular style of option, called the *American option*. An American option gives the holder of the option the ability to exercise the option on or before its expiration. In the United States, all issued options are of the American style.

In addition to protection from adverse outcomes, options lead to leveraging that can substantially increase returns from investments. Leveraging is the act of controlling more assets with less money. When a call option is bought, the hope is that the stock will increase in value. The cost of the option is far less than the cost of buying 100 shares of stock. For example, it would cost \$6,000 to buy 100 shares of a stock currently worth \$60 a share. If the price for a call option with strike price \$60 is \$4, one could buy the option for only \$400. If one bought the stock and the price of the stock becomes \$66, then the 100 shares would be worth \$6,600, a 10% return relative to the cost of \$6,000. However, if one bought the option, the position would be worth \$600, which represents a 50% return relative to the cost of \$400.

19.2 The Pricing of a One-Period Option

In this section, we introduce the key idea of options pricing by focusing on European call options and considering an option that matures in $T = 1$ period, say one month. We consider a stock with current price S_0 that has the very simple dynamics depicted in Figure 19.1(a). After one period, the stock price either increases to $S_1 = S_0 \cdot u$ (where $u > 1$), with probability q, or decreases to $S_1 = S_0 \cdot d$ (where $d < 1$), with probability $1 - q$. The quantities q, u and d are estimated from data. For more information, see Section 19.4.

For example, if the period is one month, $S_0 = \$100$, $u = 1.05$, $d = 0.97$ and $q = 0.6$, then the stock price after one month will be \$105 with probability 0.6 or \$97 with probability 0.4. In addition to the stock, a risk free asset can be used, for example, cash. A dollar invested in the risk free asset always becomes r dollars after one period. For example, if $r = 1.002$, then cash delivers a 0.2% return after one month. This translates to an annual return of $1.002^{12} = 1.02426$, which is approximately a 2.4% return per year. Note that the stock can potentially have much higher returns than the risk-free asset, but it comes with a higher risk.

Now consider a call option with strike price K that matures after one period. The payoff of one option is

$$\max(S_1 - K, 0).$$

For example, if $K = \$100$ in the example we considered above, after one period the option will be worth \$5 with probability 0.6 or it will be worth \$0 with probability 0.4. Recall that in the case that the stock price goes down, we will not exercise the option, and therefore our payoff is zero. More generally, we denote the payoff of the option by C_u, if the price of the stock goes up, and by C_d, if the price of the stock goes down. As another example, if $K = \$96$, then $C_u = \$9$ and $C_d = \$1$. The dynamics of the option are depicted in Figure 19.1(b).

The key question in this section is to determine the fair price C of the option. Note that in our case, the payoff of this option is given by

$$C_u = \max(S_0 \cdot u, 0), \quad C_d = \max(S_0 \cdot d, 0).$$

Let us now introduce the key idea of options pricing. Instead of buying an option, we could instead invest \$$x$ in the stock and \$$B$ in the risk-free asset.

Figure 19.1: The one period dynamics of (a) the stock price and (b) the option.

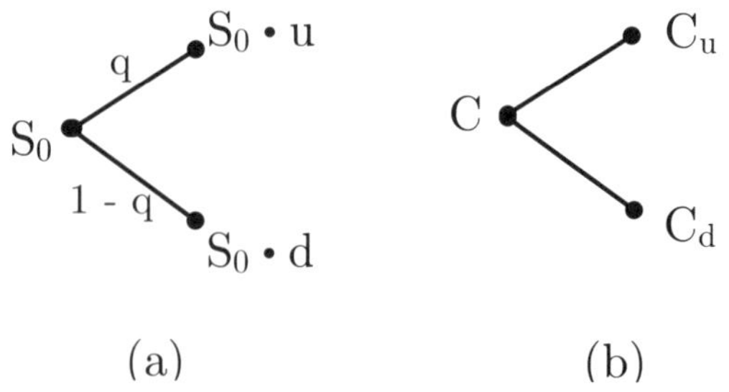

What would the value of our portfolio be after one period? If the stock goes up, then our portfolio will be worth

$$\$(x \cdot u + B \cdot r).$$

If the stock goes down, then our portfolio will be worth

$$\$(x \cdot d + B \cdot r).$$

We can select x and B so that the payoffs of the option and of this portfolio are the same:

$$\begin{aligned} x{\cdot}u \ + \ B{\cdot}r &= C_u, \\ x{\cdot}d \ + \ B{\cdot}r &= C_d. \end{aligned}$$

Solving this linear system of two equations in two unknowns (x and B) we obtain

$$x = \frac{C_u - C_d}{u{-}d}, \qquad B = \frac{u{\cdot}C_d - d{\cdot}C_u}{(u{-}d) \cdot r}. \tag{19.1}$$

Note that the amounts x and B can be negative, which means that we short sell[1] the stock if $x < 0$ or we short sell the risk free asset if $B < 0$.

The option and the portfolio we created have exactly the same payoffs independent of whether the stock goes up or down. By the no-arbitrage principle, they should have the same price. Why is this so? If these two financial instruments did not have the same price, then an investor can buy one (the least expensive) and short sell the other (the most expensive). After one period, the investor would make a guaranteed profit independent of whether the stock goes up or down. By investing higher and higher amounts in this scheme, higher and higher profits can be made, which is of course implausible. The **no-arbitrage principle** states exactly this: it is not possible to make arbitrary profits without any risk, which implies that two financial instruments that have exactly the same payoff in all states of the market should have exactly the same price.

The cost of the portfolio we have created is $\$(x + B)$. By the no-arbitrage principle, the cost of the option should also be $C = x + B$. Substituting the values for x and B from Eq. (19.1), we find that the price of the option should be

$$\begin{aligned} C &= \frac{C_u - C_d}{u{-}d} + \frac{u{\cdot}C_d - d{\cdot}C_u}{(u{-}d) \cdot r} \\ &= \frac{1}{r}\left[p{\cdot}C_u \ + \ (1{-}p) \cdot C_d\right], \qquad p = \frac{r{-}d}{u{-}d}. \end{aligned} \tag{19.2}$$

[1] Short selling an asset worth \$100 today means that we obtain \$100 right now and we owe the asset. If the asset decreases in value to say \$93, then we buy the asset for \$93 and make \$7 profit. If the asset appreciates in value to say \$103, then we have a loss of \$3.

Suppose that the stock goes up with probability p (instead of q), and down with probability $1 - p$. Under this assumption the expected payoff of the option is $p{\cdot}C_u + (1{-}p) \cdot C_d$ and the present value of this expected payoff is $(p{\cdot}C_u + (1{-}p) \cdot C_d)/r$. Thus, a nice interpretation of formula (19.2) is that the price of the option is the present value of the expected payoff of the option, not using the original probability q, but with probability p, which is called the risk neutral probability. Note that the price of the option is independent of the probability q!

Let us calculate the price of the option in the example we are considering. With $K = \$100$, $C_u = \$5$, $C_d = \$0$, $r = 1.002$, $u = 1.05$ and $d = 0.97$, we have that

$$x = \frac{C_u - C_d}{u{-}d} = \$62.50, \quad B = \frac{u{\cdot}C_d - d{\cdot}C_u}{(u{-}d) \cdot r} = -\$60.50,$$

meaning that the price C of the option should be $x + B = \$2.0$.

19.3 The Pricing of a Multi-Period Option

In this section, we determine the price of an option that matures in T periods. The dynamics of the underlying stock are as in the previous section: in each period the stock price S_0 either increases to $S_0{\cdot}u$ (where $u > 1$), with probability q, or decreases to $S_0 \cdot d$ (where $d < 1$), with probability $1 - q$. For $T = 2$ these dynamics are depicted in Figure 19.2.

This figure shows us that the price of the stock after two periods, S_2, is:

$$S_2 = \begin{cases} S_0 \cdot u^2, & \text{with probability } q^2, \\ S_0 \cdot u \cdot d, & \text{with probability } 2(1-q)q, \\ S_0 \cdot d^2, & \text{with probability } (1-q)^2. \end{cases}$$

Figure 19.2: The two period dynamics of the stock price.

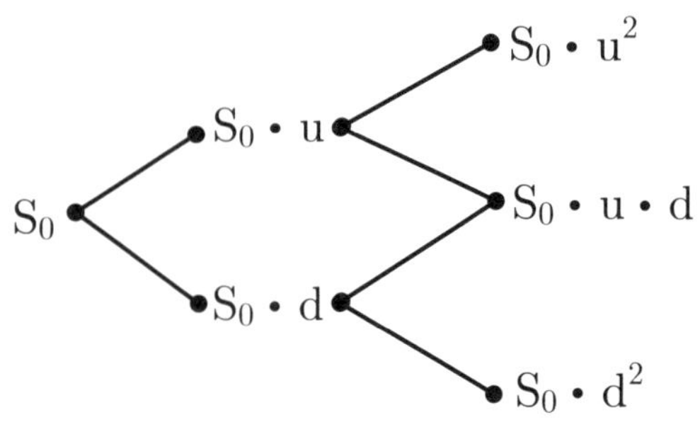

Now, let us consider the option payoff. After one period, the payoff of the option is C_u, if the stock goes up by u, and C_d, if the stock goes down by d. After two periods, we denote the final payoff of the option by C_{uu}, if the stock goes up in both periods, by C_{ud}, if the stock goes up in one period and down in the other, and by C_{dd}, if the stock goes down in both periods. The dynamics of the option are depicted in Figure 19.3.
By definition, the final payoff of the option is $\max(S_2 - K, 0)$. Therefore, we have that

$$C_{uu} = \max(S \cdot u^2 - K, 0), \quad C_{ud} = \max(S \cdot u \cdot d - K, 0), \quad C_{dd} = \max(S \cdot d^2 - K, 0).$$

According to formula (19.2), we can link the payoff C_{uu} and C_{ud} to the price of the option C_u after one period. By doing so, we obtain the following formula:

$$C_u = \frac{1}{r}\big[p\, C_{uu} \;+\; (1-p)\, C_{ud}\big], \quad p = \frac{r-d}{u-d}.$$

Similarly, we can link the payoffs C_{ud} and C_{dd} to the price of the option C_d after one period to obtain:

$$C_d = \frac{1}{r}\big[p\, C_{ud} \;+\; (1-p)\, C_{dd}\big], \quad p = \frac{r-d}{u-d}.$$

Additionally, we can directly use formula (19.2), which tells us that

$$C = \frac{1}{r}\big[p\, C_u \;+\; (1-p)\, C_d\big].$$

Substituting the first two equations into the third, we get:

$$C = \frac{1}{r^2}\big[p^2\, C_{uu} \;+\; 2\,p(1-p)\, C_{ud} \;+\; (1-p)^2\, C_{dd}\big].$$

Figure 19.3: The two period dynamics of the option payoff.

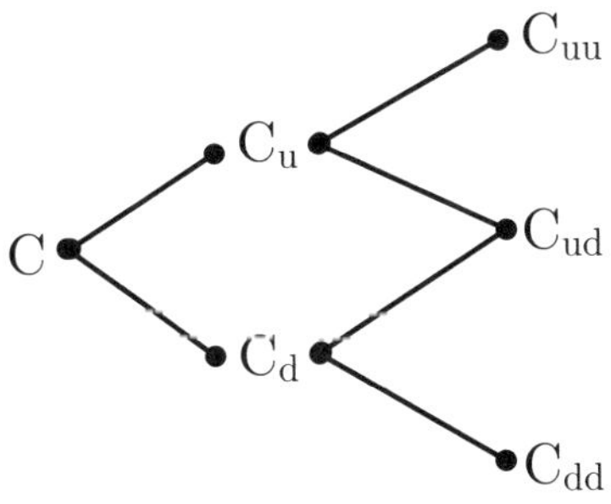

Let us see a concrete example, using the data from the end of the previous section. We have $u = 1.05$, $d = 0.97$, $r = 1.002$ and $S_0 = K = 100$. This implies that

$$p = \frac{r-d}{u-d} = 0.4,$$

$$\begin{aligned}
C_{uu} &= \max(100 \times (1.05)^2 - 100, 0) &&= \$10.25,\\
C_{ud} &= \max(100 \times 1.05 \times 0.97 - 100, 0) &&= \$1.85,\\
C_{dd} &= \max(100 \times (0.97)^2 - 100, 0) &&= \$0,\\
C_u &= \frac{1}{r}\left[p\, C_{uu} \;+\; (1-p)\, C_{ud}\right] &&= \$5.20,\\
C_d &= \frac{1}{r}\left[p\, C_{ud} \;+\; (1-p)\, C_{dd}\right] &&= \$0.74,\\
C &= \frac{1}{r}\left[p\, C_u \;+\; (1-p)\, C_d\right] &&= \$2.52.
\end{aligned}$$

Lastly, we can generalize this derivation to multiple periods T, to obtain that the price C of a European call option with strike price K, on a stock with current price S_0 that goes up by u (with probability q) and down by d (with probability $1-q$) is given by

$$C = \frac{1}{r^T} \sum_{n=0}^{T} \binom{T}{n} p^n\, (1-p)^{T-n} \max(S_0 \cdot u^n \cdot d^{T-n} - K, 0),$$

where $p = \frac{r-d}{u-d}$, r is the risk free rate, and $\binom{T}{n} = \frac{T!}{n!(T-n)!}$ (with $n! = 1 \times 2 \times \ldots \times (n-1) \times n$).

Extensions

The methodology based on the no-arbitrage principle we outlined in this section extends to put options, American options and options with dividends. Unfortunately, when there are transaction costs, taxes or other real world effects, the methodology does not extend well in that we can not find a portfolio that matches the payoff of the option. Instead, the idea of ϵ-arbitrage has been proposed as a way to replicate the payoff of the option as closely as possible. See the notes and sources in Section 19.6 for more information.

19.4 Calibration of Parameters and a Real World Example*

In this section, we describe a general methodology to select parameters u, d and q to calibrate the binary tree dynamics for the stock returns we presented in the previous section. We then apply this methodology in a real world example.

Calibration of Parameters

The return of a stock after t units of time, denoted by R_t, is typically modeled as a log-normal distribution with mean $\mu \cdot t$ and variance $\sigma^2 \cdot t$. This means that the logarithm of the return R_t obeys a normal distribution with mean $\mu \cdot t$ and variance $\sigma^2 \cdot t$. See [22] for a review of the normal distribution.

Under the binomial tree dynamics, we assume that every Δt time steps the stock goes up by u (with probability q) and down by d (with probability 1-q). Over t units of time, there will be $n = t/\Delta t$ such up or down movements. Consider the stock price S_n after n up or down movements. During these n up or down movements, let J be the number of times the stock went up (with probability q each time). Thus, J obeys the binomial distribution with parameters n and q. See [22] for a review of the binomial distribution. In particular, the expected value of J is $E[J] = n \cdot q$ and the variance of J is $Var[J] = n \cdot q \cdot (1-q)$. Then, the return of the stock after $t = n \cdot \Delta t$ time units is:

$$R_t = \frac{S_n}{S_0} = u^J \cdot d^{n-J},$$

which leads to

$$\log(R_t) = \log\left(\frac{S_n}{S_0}\right) = J \cdot \log\left(\frac{u}{d}\right) + n \cdot \log d.$$

Thus,

$$E[\log R_t] = E[J] \cdot \log\left(\frac{u}{d}\right) + n \cdot \log d,$$

$$Var[\log R_t] = Var[J] \cdot \log^2\left(\frac{u}{d}\right).$$

Substituting $E[J] = n \cdot q$ and $Var[J] = n \cdot q \cdot (1-q)$, we obtain that

$$E[\log R_t] = \left(q \cdot \log\left(\frac{u}{d}\right) + \log d\right) \cdot t/\Delta t,$$

$$Var[\log R_t] = q \cdot (1-q) \cdot \log^2\left(\frac{u}{d}\right) \cdot t/\Delta t.$$

We want to select the parameters u, d and q so that as $\Delta t \to 0$ the expected value $E[\log R_t]$ and variance $Var[\log R_t]$ approach $\mu \cdot t$ and $\sigma^2 \cdot t$, respectively. The meaning of $\Delta t \to 0$ is that the model approaches continuous time. If we select

$$\begin{aligned} u &= e^{\sigma\sqrt{\Delta t}} \\ d &= e^{-\sigma\sqrt{\Delta t}} \\ q &= \frac{1}{2} + \frac{1}{2}\frac{\mu}{\sigma}\sqrt{\Delta t} \end{aligned}$$

we can verify that

$$E[\log R_t] = \mu \cdot t,$$

$$Var[\log R_t] \to \sigma^2 \cdot t, \quad \text{as } \Delta t \to 0.$$

A Real World Example

Consider a stock with annual price volatility, denoted by σ, of 20%. The current price is $S_0 = \$62$ and the stock does not pay dividends. Also consider a call option that has an expiration of 5 months with a strike price of $K = \$60$. The annual risk-free rate is 10% compounded monthly. We want to use the methodology developed in the previous section to determine the price of this option.

We consider a period length of one month, $\Delta t = 1/12$, and a volatility of $\sigma = 0.2$. To calibrate the parameters u and d in terms of Δt and σ we have

$$\begin{aligned} u &= e^{\sigma\sqrt{\Delta t}} &&= 1.05943 \\ d &= e^{-\sigma\sqrt{\Delta t}} &&= 0.94390 \\ r &= 1 + 0.1/12 &&= 1.00833 \\ p &= \frac{r-d}{u-d} &&= 0.55770. \end{aligned}$$

Note that the probability q is not needed for determining the price of the option.

The price of the stock after five consecutive up movements is $S_0 \cdot u^5 \approx \$82.75$ and the corresponding payoff of the option in this case is

$$\max(S_0 \cdot u^5 - K, 0) = \max(62 \cdot 1.05943^5 - 60, 0) = \$22.75.$$

As another example, the price of the stock after 4 up and 1 down movements is $S_0 \cdot u^4 \cdot d \approx \$73.72$ and the corresponding payoff of the option in this case is

$$\max(S_0 \cdot u^4 \cdot d - K, 0) = \$13.72.$$

Figure 19.4 depicts the binomial tree representing the stock dynamics and the final payoff of the option.

Now, starting with the final payoffs, we can calculate the price of the option backwards. For example,

$$\begin{aligned} C_{uuuu} &= \frac{1}{r}(p\,C_{uuuuu} + (1-p)\,C_{uuuud}) \\ &= \tfrac{1}{1.00833}(0.557 \times 22.75 + (1 - 0.557) \times 13.72) = \$18.60. \end{aligned}$$

Figure 19.4 depicts the binomial tree representing the stock dynamics and the final payoff of the option. The value of the option is calculated backwards as we indicated above. The price of the option is therefore as indicated above, which turns out to be \$5.85.

19.5 Impact

The options pricing formula led to a boom in options trading and legitimised scientifically the activities of the Chicago Board Options Exchange and other options markets around the world. It is widely used, although often with adjustments and corrections, by options market participants. Many empirical tests have shown that the Black–Scholes price is "fairly close" to the observed prices, although there are well-known discrepancies due to transaction costs, taxes and exogenous market effects. In addition, the method has been used to price many financial instruments such as preferred shares, loans and other debt instruments.

There is a vast variety of options that exist in the real world. Examples include Bermudan options that may be exercised only on specified dates on or before expiration; Asian options whose payoff is determined by the average underlying price over some preset time period; Barrier options that have the characteristic that the underlying security's price must pass a certain level or "barrier" before it can be exercised; Binary options that pay the full amount if the underlying security meets the defined condition on expiration, otherwise it expires worthless; and Exotic options whose payoffs include complex financial structures. Valuing options accurately is critically important as significant

Figure 19.4: The five period dynamics of the stock and the option price. The numbers on top represent the price of the stock and the numbers on the bottom represent the price of the option. For example, $82.75 in the upper right is the price of the stock and $22.75 is the price of the option, if the stock increases in value every period.

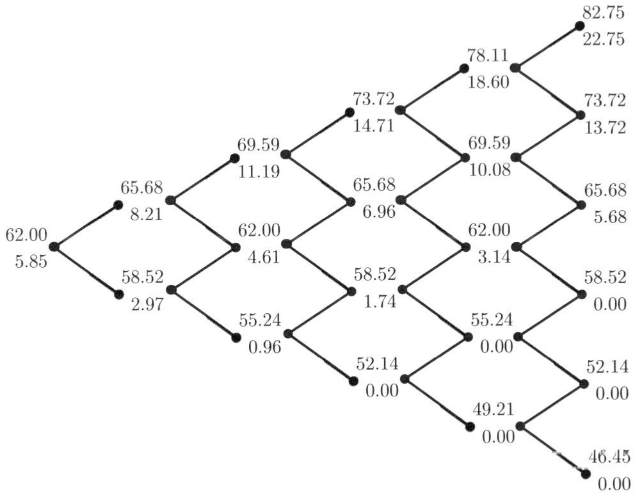

arbitrage opportunities are created if the valuation is incorrect.

In many ways, the analytics of options pricing has revolutionized the financial industry by creating a new discipline called financial engineering that has contributed to the tremendous growth of markets for financial derivatives. Major investment banks have large departments that employ scientists trained in this discipline, who are responsible for pricing financial derivatives with ever-increasing complexity. Thousands of traders and investors now use the analytics of options pricing every day to value stock options in markets throughout the world.

19.6 Notes and Sources

The presentation in this chapter follows Cox, Ross and Rubistein [38] who presented the binomial tree model that simplifies the original approach of Black and Scholes. Black and Scholes [28] derived the Black–Scholes formula, which estimates the price of the option over time. Merton [93] was the first to publish a paper expanding the mathematical understanding of the options pricing model, and coined the term "Black–Scholes options pricing model." Merton and Scholes received the 1997 Nobel Prize in Economics for their work. Though ineligible for the prize because of his death in 1995, Black was mentioned as a contributor by the Swedish Academy. For a personal account of how Black and Scholes discovered the Black–Scholes formula see [27].

19.3. For extensions of options pricing to put options, American options and options with dividends see the book *Options, Futures, and Other Derivatives* by John C. Hull [62]. The ϵ-arbitrage idea is described in Bertsimas, Kogan, and Lo [23].

Chapter 20

The Analytics Edge in Asset Management

Far more money is made buying high and selling at even higher prices.

– Richard Driehaus

Contents

The asset management industry is one of the largest industries in the world. There are thousands of asset management firms which can be broadly characterized as *fundamental* or *quantitative*. A fundamental asset management firm has a team of analysts and portfolio managers who use experience, human intuition and some quantitative tools to decide which assets to buy and sell and at what times. The basis for decisions is an estimate of the future prospects of a stock based on factors such as the executive team, the product mix, competition, and the sector of activity. The majority of asset management firms belong to this category. They do not employ rigorous analytical methods to construct and trade portfolios. On the other hand, a quantitative asset management firm uses computer systems and historical data to design, implement, and trade stock and bond portfolios.

In general, as the assets under management increase, a fundamental investment process needs to employ larger and larger teams to invest the increased assets. On the other hand, a quantitative investment process, with its ability to electronically analyze thousands of securities and to rigorously control trading costs, can have a much larger investment capacity. Asset management firms like AQR, Barclays and INTECH rely almost exclusively on quantitative strategies, while others, such as Pimco, Blackrock, Citadel or GMO use a mixture of quantitative and fundamental methods.

In 2010, the quantitative division of Riversource Investments, the asset management arm of Ameriprise Financial, a large financial services firm, was responsible for managing $10 billion of assets in a variety of equity and asset allocation funds. The group had grown from managing $1 billion in assets in 2002. The quantitative division consisted of eight professionals and used a variety of analytics-based methods to manage the assets.

In this chapter, we discuss the key analytics concepts that are important to the successful quantitative asset management process based on the experience of Riversource Investments. We focus on the management of a stock fund consisting of United States large capitalization securities. The approach could easily be adapted to United States stock funds consisting of medium and small capitalizations, international developed funds, emerging market funds, funds from specific sectors and fixed income and asset allocation funds. Rather than giving a encyclopedic perspective of the quantitative asset management arena, the goal of the chapter is to familiarize the reader with the key concepts in asset management: alpha models and portfolio construction.

20.1 Mutual Funds

A mutual fund is a type of professionally managed investment fund that pools money from many investors to purchase securities. In the United States, mutual funds must be registered with the U.S. Securities and Exchange Commission (SEC), overseen by a board of directors, and managed by a Registered Investment Advisor. Mutual funds are also subject to an extensive and detailed regulatory regime set forth in the Investment Company Act of 1940. There are three types of U.S. mutual funds: open-end funds, unit investment trusts, and closed-end funds. The most common type, open-end funds, must be willing to buy back shares from investors every business day. Unit investment trusts (UITs) can only issue to the public once, when they are created. UITs generally have a limited life span, established at creation. Investors can redeem shares directly with the fund at any time (similar to an open-end fund) or wait to redeem them upon the trust's termination. Closed-end funds generally issue shares to the public only once, when they are created through an initial public offering. Their shares are then listed for trading on a stock exchange. Investors who no longer wish to invest in the fund cannot sell their shares back to the fund (as they can with an open-end fund). Instead, they must sell their shares to another investor in the market.

Mutual funds are further classified based on their principal investments. The four main categories of funds are money market funds, bond or fixed income funds, stock or equity funds, and hybrid funds. Funds may also be categorized as index (or passively managed) or actively managed.

The first mutual funds were established in Europe in the 1770s. Mutual funds were introduced to the United States in the 1890s, and they became popular in the 1920s. These early funds were generally closed-end funds. The first open-end mutual fund, called the Massachusetts Investors Trust (now part of the MFS family of funds), with redeemable shares was established in 1924. However, closed-end funds remained more popular than open-end funds throughout the 1920s. In 1929, open-end funds accounted for only 5% of the industry's $27 billion in total assets. After the stock market crash of 1929, Congress passed a series of acts regulating the securities markets in general and mutual funds in particular. The Securities Act of 1933 requires that all investments sold to the public, including mutual funds, be registered with the SEC and that they provide prospective investors with a prospectus that discloses essential facts about the investment. The Securities and Exchange Act of 1934 requires that issuers of securities, including mutual funds, report regularly to their investors; this act also created the Securities and Exchange Commission, which is the principal regulator of mutual funds in the United States. The Revenue Act of 1936 established guidelines for the taxation of mutual funds, while the Investment Company Act of 1940 governs their structure.

When confidence in the stock market returned in the 1950s, the mutual fund industry began to grow again. By 1970, there were approximately 360 funds with $48 billion in assets. The introduction of money market funds in the high interest rate environment of the late 1970s dramatically boosted industry growth. The first retail index fund, First Index Investment Trust, was formed in 1976 by The Vanguard Group, headed by John Bogle; it is now called the "Vanguard 500 Index Fund" and is one of the world's largest mutual funds, with more than $195 billion in assets as of January, 2015.

Fund industry growth continued into the 1980s and 1990s, as a result of three factors: a bull-market for both stocks and bonds, new product introductions (including tax-exempt bond, sector, international and target date funds) and wider distribution of fund shares. Among the new distribution channels were retirement plans. Mutual funds are now the preferred investment option in certain types of fast-growing retirement plans, specifically in 401(k) and other defined contribution plans and in individual retirement accounts (IRAs), all of which surged in popularity in the 1980s. At the end of 2013, there were over 15,000 mutual funds in the United States with combined assets of $17 trillion and $30 trillion worldwide. Mutual funds play an important role in U.S. household finances; by the end of 2013, funds accounted for 22% of household financial assets. Their role in retirement planning is particularly significant. Roughly 60% of assets in 401(k) plans and individual retirement accounts were invested in mutual funds.

Active versus Passive Funds

Among equity funds, a large capitalization U.S. fund consists of securities that are publicly traded in the U.S. stock exchanges (NYSE and NASDAQ) and that typically have market capitalization of above $5 billion. There are two major indices that serve as a benchmark for United States large capitalization funds: the S&P 500 and the Russell 1000. The members of the S&P 500 index are selected by a committee, while the weights of the companies in the S&P 500 index are proportional to their market capitalization. This index covers about 75% of the total capitalization of the American equity market. The members and the weights of the Russell 1000 Index are chosen by quantitative rules. The index has a total weighted average market capitalization of $81 billion, the median market capitalization is approximately $4.6 billion and the smallest company in the index has a market capitalization of $1.8 billion. There are many companies that offer funds whose value is based on these indices at low cost. There are many large cap index funds, like the Schwab S&P 500 Index SWPPX and the Vanguard VFINX that aim to offer the performance of the S&P 500 index at low cost. Table 20.1 compares the performance of the index funds SWPPX and VFINX relative to the S&P 500 index. Over long horizons, these funds underperform the S&P 500 Index as they incur management costs.

Table 20.1: The performance of the index funds SWPPX and VFINX relative to S&P 500 index in the fourth quarter of 2014.

Total Return	**1-Year**	**3-Year**	**5-Year**	**10-Year**	**15-Year**
SWPPX	16.66	22.62	15.94	7.94	4.59
VFINX	16.58	22.56	15.88	7.86	4.42
S&P500	16.86	20.93	15.96	8.06	4.66

An index fund is an example of a *passive fund.* Vanguard, a company founded in 1975, has been a pioneer of passive funds at low cost. Today, Vanguard manages \$2.5 trillion. On the other hand, the typical objective of a U.S. large cap *active fund* is to outperform the S&P 500 index after management fees. For this reason, the management fees are higher; they can be anywhere from three to fifteen times the fees of a passive fund.

There are two major categories of active funds: traditional and quantitative. A traditional active fund employs analysts that follow companies in various industries and uses human intuition to build a portfolio of companies. A quantitative fund employs analytics to build a portfolio. The idea of using mathematical principles in investments appears in the work of Edward Thorp, who applied a systematic, analytics driven process to discover and exploit a number of pricing anomalies in the securities markets. The key ingredients of a quantitative asset management process for stocks are:

1. Alpha Models, which are algorithmic ways to rank stocks. They rely on predictive analytic methods.

2. Portfolio construction models, which are optimization-based methods that decide the portfolio weight for each stock, i.e., the fraction of the overall portfolio value invested in this stock, in order for the portfolio to have desirable characteristics.

3. Simulation models that offer insights on how investment ideas will behave in various market conditions.

In the rest of this chapter, we discuss these ingredients using a U.S. large capitalization portfolio as an example.

20.2 Alpha Models

Quantitative asset management starts with historical data, including historical financial information on the prices, dividends, corporate actions (mergers, acquisitions), and earnings. An example of a database containing this information about global companies throughout the world is Compustat, which started in 1962. Understanding and maintaining this data is a critical part of the quantitative asset management process. In this section, we review the two principal quantitative alpha models that are constructed using the data from such databases: value investing and momentum investing. There is pervasive evidence of the effectiveness of both styles of investing.

Value Investing

The idea of value investing is attributed to Benjamin Graham (1894-1976), a professional investor, who began teaching it at Columbia Business School in 1928 and subsequently refined it with David Dodd through various editions of their famous book Security Analysis. Graham had many disciples in his lifetime including Warren Buffett, who credits Graham as grounding him with a sound intellectual investment framework. Buffett described Graham as the second most influential person in his life after Buffett's own father.

We will start by giving an example of a simple model of value investing. Our buyable universe of stocks is the largest 500 companies in the United States based on market capitalization. We will develop a value investing alpha model on a monthly basis. Let $EARN_{j,t}$ be the earnings from operations of company j during month t. These values are used as a simple measure of past earnings capacity which should have prediction power in the future. Earnings are typically reported quarterly, so in order to obtain an annual number, we include the sum of the four most recent past quarters. We let $MCAP_{j,t}$ be the market capitalization of company j at month t. Then

$$\alpha^v_{j,t} = \frac{EARN_{j,t}}{MCAP_{j,t}},$$

is the *value alpha* of company j at month t. It represents a measure of the profitability of company j at month t.

Table 20.2 depicts the value alphas in November 2014 of the 10 largest companies in the U.S. by market capitalization. Among these companies, Exxon Mobil has the highest value alpha. According to value investing, we should invest more heavily in companies that have a high value alpha. Intuitively, such companies are *relatively* inexpensive; they have high earning capability relative to their market price. By holding these companies, after some period of time, we expect the market price to increase, leading to superior returns. In the words of Warren Buffet, one of the most successful value investors of the 20th century, an investor should "buy companies with strong histories of profitability and with a dominant business franchise."

There are multiple ways to obtain a particular portfolio weight based on the value alpha and the market capitalization of the company. Let $R^v_{j,t}$ represent the rank of company j at month t according to the value alphas (higher numbers indicate better ranks). These ranks are depicted in the last column of Table 20.2. An advantage of ranks as opposed to the alphas is that they are more robust as earnings change because of restatements. While, the value alphas might change significantly due to restatements, the ranks change much less. As an example of creating portfolio weights from ranks, we might choose a weight for company j at month t proportional to

$$MCAP_{j,t} \times R^v_{j,t}.$$

if we do this for the ten largest U.S. securities, Apple will have a weight of 27.6% and Exxon Mobil will have a weight of 18.4%.

Momentum Investing

Richard Driehaus (born in 1942) is sometimes considered the father of momentum investing but the strategy can be traced back earlier to Richard

Donchian (1905-1993). In the words of Driehaus, "far more money is made buying high and selling at even higher prices." Evidence of the efficacy of momentum style of investing is pervasive.

We now develop the idea of momentum investing. Let $RET_{j,t}$ be the return in the last three months of company j at month t. The return includes both price appreciation as well as dividends. For example, if the price three months ago was \$60, the current price is \$62 and there was a \$1 dividend paid per share, the return is \$3/60=5%.

We define the momentum alphas to be

$$\alpha_{j,t}^{m} = RET_{j,t}$$

and we let $R_{j,t}^{m}$ be the rank based on the momentum alphas. Under the momentum style of investing, companies that have high returns are expected to continue to have high returns. The philosophical underpinning of the momentum style of investing is that investors tend to go with winners.

Table 20.3 depicts the momentum alphas of the 10 largest companies in the United States by market capitalization. According to momentum investing, we invest more in companies that have a high momentum alpha with the intuition that such companies will continue to produce high returns.

Typically, momentum and value alphas offer "style diversification" in portfolios. In the bull-market of the late 1990s, momentum style investing was particularly strong, whereas value investing was out of favor. However, in the bear-market of the early 2000s, value investing was particularly strong, whereas momentum investing did not do well. By having both momentum and value alphas to influence the portfolio, we achieve diversification in the portfolio.

A concrete way to construct portfolio weights from the alpha models is to average the ranks of the value alpha and the momentum alpha. For example,

Table 20.2: The value alphas for the ten largest U.S. companies by market capitalization in November 2014.

Company	**Ticker**	**EARN \$ bil.**	**MCAP \$ bil.**	α^{v}	**Rank $R_{j,t}^{v}$**
Apple	AAPL	39.51	697.51	5.66	8
Exxon Mobil	XOM	34.30	383.39	8.94	10
Microsoft	MSFT	21.37	394.09	5.42	4
Google	GOOG	12.88	367.56	3.50	1
Berkshire Hathaway	BRK.A	20.71	365.83	5.66	7
Johnson and Johnson	JNJ	17.32	303.00	5.16	3
Wells Fargo	WFC	21.81	282.62	7.71	9
Wal-Mart	WMT	15.44	282.10	5.47	5
General Electric	GE	15.05	266.02	5.65	6
Procter & Gamble	PG	10.26	244.35	4.19	2

the weight of the target portfolio of company j at month t could be proportional to

$$MCAP_{j,t} \times \frac{R^v_{j,t} + R^m_{j,t}}{2}.$$

We use the term *target portfolio* to signify that this portfolio only reflects the value and momentum alphas. It does not take into account other real world issues, like risk, liquidity and transaction costs. In the next section, we discuss how we can construct portfolios based on ideas from optimization.

20.3 Portfolio Construction

The alpha models of the previous section lead to a target portfolio that does not account for several real world issues, such as risk, sectors exposure, liquidity and transaction costs. In this section, we present a mixed integer optimization approach to show how to construct a portfolio that accounts for such issues.

We define a portfolio by specifying a weight $w_0(i)$, where $w_0(i)$ is the fraction of the portfolio invested in stock $i = 1, \ldots, N$. The weights are nonnegative numbers that sum to one. We will denote the weights of the current portfolio by

$$\mathbf{w}_0 = \big(w_0(1), w_0(2), \ldots, w_0(N)\big).$$

From the alpha models, we can derive a target portfolio, whose weights are proportional to the quantities $MCAP_{j,t} \times \frac{R^v_{j,t}+R^m_{j,t}}{2}$. We call

$$\mathbf{w}_t = \big(w_t(1), w_t(2), \ldots, w_t(N)\big)$$

the target portfolio weights, where $w_t(i)$ is the fraction of the target portfolio invested in stock $i = 1, \ldots, N$. Our objective is to create a set of final portfolio

Table 20.3: The momentum alphas for the ten largest United States companies by market capitalization for November 2014.

Company	Ticker	α^{m}	Rank
Apple	AAPL	16.49	10
Exxon Mobil	XOM	-8.27	1
Microsoft	MSFT	5.92	5
Google	GOOG	-5.21	2
Berkshire Hathaway	BRK.A	8.35	7
Johnson and Johnson	JNJ	5.03	4
Wells Fargo	WFC	6.59	6
Wal-Mart	WMT	15.95	9
General Electric	GE	2.81	3
Procter & Gamble	PG	9.58	8

weights

$$\mathbf{w}_f = \big(w_f(1), w_f(2), \ldots, w_f(N)\big)$$

that has the following characteristics:

(a) **The overall portfolio should be close to the target portfolio.** Since the target portfolio $\mathbf{w}_t$ was created taking into account the key drivers of the investment process (the alpha models), the portfolio $\mathbf{w}_f$ should be as close as possible to $\mathbf{w}_t$. This requirement is captured by the objective function

$$\min \sum_{i=1}^{N} \big|w_f(i) - w_t(i)\big|.$$

In order to model the absolute value in a linear way, we introduce the auxiliary variables $y(i)$ for every stock i and instead have as the objective function

$$\min \sum_{i=1}^{N} y(i),$$

and add the constraints:

$$w_f(i) - w_t(i) \leq y(i), \quad -\big(w_f(i) - w_t(i)\big) \leq y(i), \text{ for all } i.$$

Note that because we are minimizing, at least one of the two constraints is binding, forcing $y(i)$ to equal $|w_f(i) - w_t(i)|$ at optimality.

(b) **The combined weight of stocks in different economic sectors should be close to that of the target portfolio.** Within different sectors of the economy, the target and final portfolios should also be as close as possible. Examples of sectors include energy, utility and financial services firms. This requirement is captured by adding a constraint

$$\sum_{s=1}^{K} \left| \sum_{i=1}^{N} M_s(i)\big(w_f(i) - w_t(i)\big) \right| \leq \delta_{\text{sec}},$$

where $M_s(i)$ is a 0/1 index denoting membership of stock i in sector s, and δ_{sec} is a user-specified total allowed difference in sector exposure between the final and the target portfolios.

In order to model the absolute value in a linear way, we introduce the auxiliary variables $x(s)$ for every sector s and rewrite the constraint as

$$\sum_{s=1}^{K} x(s) \leq \delta_{\text{sec}},$$

and add the additional constraints:

$$\sum_{i=1}^{N} M_s(i)(w_f(i) - w_t(i) \leq x(s), \quad -\sum_{i=1}^{N} M_s(i)(w_f(i) - w_t(i) \leq x(s).$$

(c) **Our final portfolio should have a small number of stocks.** It is desirable to have a portfolio with a small number of stocks. Consequently, we define

$$y_{\mathrm{s}}(i) = \begin{cases} 1, & \text{if } w_f(i) > 0, \\ 0, & \text{if } w_f(i) = 0. \end{cases}$$

The requirement that our portfolio only have a small number of stocks is captured by the constraint

$$\sum_{i=1}^{N} y_{\mathrm{s}}(i) \leq \delta_{\mathrm{s}},$$

where δ_{s} is the largest allowable number of stocks in the portfolio. In order to link the variables $y_{\mathrm{s}}(i)$ and $w_f(i)$, we also add the constraint

$$w_f(i) \leq y_{\mathrm{s}}(i), \text{ for all } i.$$

(d) **Our final portfolio should have a high return.** It is desirable to have a final portfolio with high return. This is captured by the constraint

$$\sum_{i=1}^{N} \alpha(i) w_f(i) \geq \overline{\alpha},$$

where $\alpha(i) = (\alpha_i^v + \alpha_i^m)/2$ is the average alpha of stock i, and $\overline{\alpha}$ is the desired return for the portfolio.

(e) **Our portfolio should have low illiquidity.** It is desirable to have a portfolio that avoids stocks that are hard to sell quickly. In particular, as the position in a stock increases beyond the average daily trading volume, it is increasingly difficult, and thus increasingly more expensive, to liquidate the stock. Moreover, the cost of liquidating a position in a stock increases in a nonlinear way as the portfolio weight increases. To capture this effect, we consider the piecewise linear cost function $f_{\mathrm{lq}}(i, w_f(i))$ depicted in Figure 20.3 that penalizes, in a nonlinear way the final stock position in the portfolio. The illiquidity function $f_{\mathrm{lq}}(i, x)$ is modeled as

$$\begin{cases} \mathrm{ls}(1,i)x, & 0 \leq x \leq \mathrm{lq}(i), \\ \mathrm{ls}(2,i)(x - \mathrm{lq}(i)) + \mathrm{ls}(1,i)\mathrm{lq}(i), & \mathrm{lq}(i) \leq x \leq 2 \cdot \mathrm{lq}(i), \\ \mathrm{ls}(3,i)(x - 2 \cdot \mathrm{lq}(i)) + \mathrm{ls}(2,i)2 \cdot \mathrm{lq}(i), & 2 \cdot \mathrm{lq}(i) \leq x \leq 4 \cdot \mathrm{lq}(i). \end{cases}$$

The parameter lq(i) is proportional to the average daily trading volume of stock i, while regression is used to estimate the slopes ls($1,i$), ls($2,i$), ls($3,i$). Note that the nonlinearity is captured by assuming that the slopes satisfy:

$$\text{ls}(1,i) \leq \text{ls}(2,i) \leq \text{ls}(3,i).$$

To bound the illiquidity of the portfolio we add the constraint

$$\sum_{i=1}^{N} f_{\text{lq}}\big(i, w_f(i)\big) \leq \delta_{\text{lq}},$$

where δ_{lq} is a bound on the the illiquidity of the portfolio. This constraint models the desire to accumulate positions in stocks that are too illiquid, i.e., too expensive to liquidate.

In order to model this constraint in a linear way we introduce the auxiliary variables $x_1(i), x_2(i), x_3(i)$ for every stock i and write the constraint as

$$\sum_{i=1}^{N} ls(1,i)x_1(i) + ls(2,i)x_2(i) + ls(3,i)x_3(i) \leq \delta_{\text{lq}},$$

while introducing additional constraints

$$w_f(i) = x_1(i) + x_2(i) + x_3(i), \text{ for all } i,$$

$$0 \leq x_1(i) \leq lq(i), \quad 0 \leq x_2(i) \leq lq(i), \quad 0 \leq x_3(i) \leq 2lq(i), \text{ for all } i.$$

The idea is that if $w_f(i) = 2.5lq(i)$, then

$$x_1(i) = lq(i), \; x_2(i) = lq(i), \; x_3(i) = 0.5lq(i),$$

and the illiquidity will be

$$ls(1,i) \times lq(i) + ls(2,i) \times lq(i) + 0.5 \times ls(3,i) \times lq(i).$$

(f) Our portfolio should have low transaction costs.
It is critical to portfolio performance to keep the total transaction costs as small as possible. These costs directly reduce the performance of the fund. In particular, as the trading position increases relative to the average daily trading volume of a stock, transaction costs become higher because portfolio trades have an impact in the market. The transaction cost from trading stock i is captured by a piecewise linear convex function $f_{\text{tc}}\big(i, |w_f(i) - w_0(i)|\big)$ depicted in Figure 20.3. The parameter vol(i) represents the average daily trading volume of stock i, while regression is used to estimate the corresponding slopes.

To bound the transaction cost we add the constraint

$$\sum_{i=1}^{N} f_{\text{tc}}\big(i, |w_f(i) - w_0(i)|\big) \leq \delta_{\text{tc}},$$

where δ_{tc} is a bound on the the transaction costs.

In order to model this constraint in a linear way we introduce the auxiliary variables $f(i)$ and $z_1(i)$, $z_2(i)$ and $z_3(i)$ and write the constraint as

$$\sum_{i=1}^{N} cs(1,i)z_1(i) + cs(2,i)z_2(i) + cs(3,i)z_3(i) \leq \delta_{\text{tc}},$$

while introducing additional constraints

$$f(i) = z_1(i) + z_2(i) + z_3(i), \text{ for all } i,$$

$$w_f(i) - w_0(i) \leq f(i), \quad -\big(w_f(i) - w_0(i)\big) \leq f(i), \text{ for all } i,$$

$$0 \leq z_1(i) \leq 0.1vol(i), \text{ for all } i.$$

$$0 \leq z_2(i) \leq 0.2vol(i), \text{ for all } i.$$

$$0 \leq z_3(i) \leq 0.2vol(i), \text{ for all } i.$$

Figure 20.1: The illiquidity function. This function captures the fact that the cost of liquidating a position in a stock increases in a nonlinear way as the portfolio weight increases.

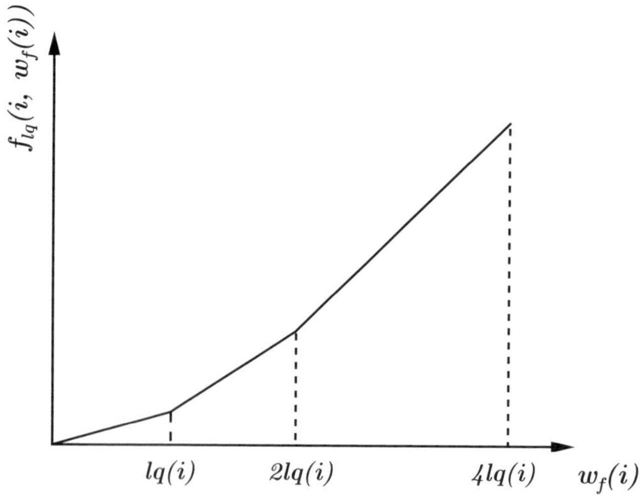

Figure 20.2: The transaction cost function.

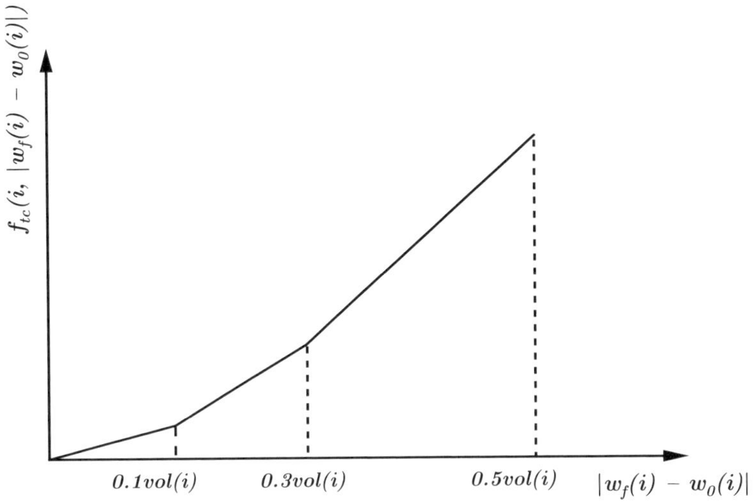

(g) **A small number of transactions.**
Typically each trade costs a fixed amount independent of the number of shares traded and a variable amount that depends on the number of shares traded. In part (f) we modeled the variable part of the transaction costs. Here we model the fixed part of the transaction costs. A transaction is made if there is a difference between the current and the final portfolio. For this reason we define

$$y_t(i) = \begin{cases} 1, & \text{if } \left|w_f(i) - w_0(i)\right| > 0, \\ 0, & \text{if } \left|w_f(i) - w_0(i)\right| = 0. \end{cases}$$

Then, to constrain the number of transactions we add the constraint

$$\sum_{i=1}^{N} y_t(i) \leq \delta_t,$$

where δ_t is the largest number of transactions we are allowed to make in each trading period. We note that from part (f) the auxiliary variable $f(i)$ is equal to $\left|w_f(i) - w_0(i)\right|$. In order to link the variables $y_t(i)$ and $f(i)$, we also add the constraint

$$f(i) \leq y_t(i), \text{ for all } i.$$

(h) **Low benchmark risk.**
A key idea in asset management is the idea of benchmark risk, which is typically measured with respect to the weight of a benchmark like the S&P 500 index. Let $b(i)$ be the weight of stock i in the benchmark (for example, the S&P 500 index) and $\sigma_{i,j}$ be the historical covariance[1] of companies i and j. The quantities $\sigma_{i,j}$ are typically calculated from the historical covariances during the last six months and are updated monthly. To bound the benchmark risk we add the constraint

$$\sum_{i,j=1}^{N} \sigma_{i,j}(w_f(i) - b(i))(w_f(j) - b(j)) \leq \delta_{\text{BR}},$$

where δ_{BR} is a bound on the allowed benchmark risk of the portfolio. If δ_{BR} is set to zero, the optimal solution will have $w_f(i) = b(i)$ for all stocks i, and therefore, the portfolio becomes a passive fund.

As we use both binary and continuous variables and the benchmark risk constraint involves a quadratic function, the overall model belongs to the class of *mixed-integer quadratic optimization problems*, which can be solved by commercial solvers. For example, we can optimize the model with 1,000 different stocks (N=1,000) in under a minute using state of the art software such as Gurobi or CPLEX.

20.4 Simulation and Performance

Once the alpha models and the portfolio construction process were implemented, the quantitative division of Riversource Investments simulated the overall process to find the best possible parameters used both in the alpha models as well as in the portfolio construction process. These parameters included, how much value versus momentum to include in the portfolio and the various user defined parameters δ_{sec}, δ_{s}, $\overline{\alpha}$, δ_{lq}, δ_{tc}, δ_{t} and δ_{BR} presented in the previous section. Data from the 1970s until 2003 was used to launch the Riversource Large Core Quantitative fund (AQEAX, now called Columbia Large Core Quantitative Fund), utilizing a combination of the methods outlined in this chapter.

In simulations for the period 1970-2003, this fund had an annual outperformance of more than 4%, or 400 basis points (bps), relative to the S&P 500 before management fees, while having the capacity to manage several

---

[1] Given historical returns $r_{i,t}$ and $r_{j,t}$ for companies i and j at times $t = 1, \ldots, T$, let $\overline{r}_i = \sum_{t=1}^{T} r_{i,t}/T$ be the average return of company i and $\overline{r}_j = \sum_{t=1}^{T} r_{j,t}/T$ be the average return of company j. Then, the empirical covariance between stocks i and j is estimated by

$$\sigma_{i,j} = \frac{\sum_{t=1}^{T}(r_{i,t} - \overline{r}_i)(r_{j,t} - \overline{r}_j)}{T}.$$

billion dollars. The fund was managed by the team that created it until May 2010. The assets of the fund in 2010 were over $4 billion. The annualized return from 2002 to 2010 was 4.48%, while the return of the S&P 500 for the same period was 2.24%, leading to an outperformance of 224bps before management fees. The management fees depended on the assets an investor invested, but they were in the neighborhood of 100bps. While the simulation results were more optimistic, the overall process worked successfully.

In addition to strong performance, the quantitative approach has had a major impact on the ability of the quantitative division to more effectively manage a large number of assets and a large number of funds, given a group of only eight investment professionals. The quantitative division was able to launch many new funds and grew from managing $1 billion in 2002 to $12 billion in 2010. In addition to managing the large cap core U.S. portfolio, the quantitative division was able to manage asset allocation funds, large value, large growth, mid cap, small cap, international and emerging stock funds.

20.5 Concluding Remarks

The analytics approach outlined in this chapter underscores several principles:

1. Every idea the investment team used in the portfolio was thoroughly and rigorously simulated. Only when the idea proved itself in simulations, was it used in managing the portfolio.

2. The simulation process revealed certain periods during which performance had not been as strong, which necessitated more research on the overall process.

3. While the alpha models have proven their value over a long period of time, continuous research on new models is necessary.

4. Even though during the 1970-2007 period a variety of market conditions had been observed, the global credit crisis of 2008 had not been observed previously and it presented a challenge to the quantitative division, as well as many other quantitative funds. However, in the period 2010-2104, quantitative funds did very well.

20.6 Notes and Sources

Dimitris Bertsimas was consulting portfolio manager and head of the quantitative division during the period 2002-2010 of Riversource Investments. His group, consisting of eight professionals, was responsible to manage over $10 billion of assets in a variety of equity and asset allocation funds.

20.2. The idea of using mathematical principles in investments appears in the work of [140]. The idea of value investing is attributed to Benjamin Graham (1894-1976), who subsequently refined it with David Dodd through various editions of their famous book [58]. One of the most famous books on investing is [57]. The first academic study on the efficacy of the momentum style of investing is due to [72]. For an explanation of the over-performance of momentum strategies see [73].

20.3. Markowitz [90] introduced a quadratic optimization model for constructing portfolios and won the Nobel prize in 1990. Bertsimas, Darnell and Soucy [19] introduced mixed integer optimization methods to manage portfolios in the asset management company GMO. This chapter is based on their work.

Part VIII

Methods and Exercises to Put the Analytics Edge into Action

Chapter 21

Analytics Methods

The value of an idea lies in the using of it.

– Thomas A. Edison

Contents

In this chapter, we give a brief overview of several analytics methods that were referenced throughout the book. We do not cover all of the analytics methods discussed, but we try to cover many different methods that can be used for descriptive, predictive, and prescriptive analytics. Tutorials and resources for recommended software options can be found in the Online Companion for this book (www.dynamic-ideas.com/analytics-edge). For a more technical and comprehensive understanding of the methods presented here, we give several references in Section 21.7.

21.1 Linear Regression

Linear regression is one of the most common methods for making predictions. It is used to determine how an outcome variable, called the *dependent variable*, can best be expressed as a linear combination of a set of known input variables, called the *independent variables.* The dependent variable is typically denoted by y and the independent variables are denoted by $x_1, x_2, \ldots, x_k$, where k is the number of different independent variables. We are interested in finding the best possible coefficients $\beta_0, \beta_1, \beta_2, \ldots, \beta_k$ such that our predicted values:

$$\hat{y} = \beta_0 + \beta_1 x_1 + \beta_2 x_2 + \ldots + \beta_k x_k$$

are as close as possible to the actual y values. There are many different ways to define the "best" coefficients. For basic linear regression, this is achieved by minimizing the sum of the squared differences between the actual values, y, and the predictions $\hat{y}$. These differences, $(y - \hat{y})$, are often called *error terms* or *residuals.*

As an example, we saw in Chapter 1 that Orley Ashenfelter developed the following multiple linear regression equation to predict wine quality:

> Wine Quality = -12.145 + (0.001173 × Winter Rainfall) + (0.616 × Average Growing Season Temperature) - (0.00386 × Harvest Rainfall) + (0.0238 × Age of Vintage).

Here, the dependent variable is "Wine Quality" and the four independent variables are "Winter Rainfall," "Average Growing Season Temperature," "Harvest Rainfall" and "Age of Vintage." By using a data set and minimizing the sum of the squared differences between the actual values and the predicted values, Ashenfelter discovered that the best coefficients were $\beta_0 = -12.145$, $\beta_1 = 0.001173$, $\beta_2 = 0.616$, $\beta_3 = -0.00386$ and $\beta_4 = 0.0238$.

Evaluating a Model

Once a linear regression model is constructed, it is important to evaluate the quality of the model. When a linear regression model is created with a statistical package, a lot of additional information is typically generated about the model in addition to the coefficient estimates, or the β values.

Significance

One important piece of information to consider when evaluating the model is the significance of the independent variables. In a linear regression model, a coefficient is considered *significant* if the coefficient estimate is significantly different from zero according to the data used to build the model. A coefficient of zero means that the value of the independent variable does not change the prediction for the dependent variable. If a coefficient is not significantly different than zero, then we should probably remove the variable from the model, since it is not helping predict the dependent variable.

More specifically, a *standard error* value can be computed for each coefficient. This value gives a measure of how much the "true" coefficient is likely to vary from the estimate value, given the data used to build the model. Keep in mind that the standard error only holds for the data used to build the model. If the dataset is not representative of future data, the model might not perform as well.

A *t-value* for a coefficient is also often computed, which is the coefficient estimate divided by the standard error (it will be negative if the coefficient is negative, and positive if the coefficient is positive). A larger absolute t-value means that the coefficient is more significant (we want independent variables with a small standard error relative to the coefficient estimate). So we ultimately want independent variables with large absolute t-values. A probability that a coefficient is actually zero given the data can also be computed (called a p-value), and the linear regression model output in any software package will often make it easy to tell which variables are significant. For a more mathematically rigorous treatment of these topics, see the references in Section 21.7.

Removing Independent Variables

If there are insignificant independent variables in the model, we should consider removing these variables, for several reasons. One is that having too many independent variables compared to the number of data observations can cause the model to *overfit* to the data used to build the model. This leads to a model that does really well at predicting the outcome for data it has seen before, but really poorly at predicting the outcome for new observations.

If there is significantly more data than independent variables, then overfitting is not really a concern, and leaving in independent variables that are insignificant will not hurt the predictive ability of the model. But it might still be better to remove the insignificant variables for another important reason: simplicity and interpretability of the model. A model with unnecessary independent variables requires more data, and makes the model more complex than it needs to be. Simpler models that are just as accurate should be preferred to more complex models that do not improve the accuracy of prediction. However, a modeler should be careful when removing independent variables because there are interactions going on between the independent variables that can change when a variable is removed. We discuss this more below.

The Metric R^2

Another important evaluation of a linear regression model is to compute the R-squared, or R^2, value. The R^2 of a linear regression model can be computed with the following equation:

$$R^2 = 1 - \frac{\sum_{i=1}^{n}(y_i - \hat{y}_i)^2}{\sum_{i=1}^{n}(y_i - \bar{y})^2},$$

where n is the number of data observations, y_i is the actual value of the dependent variable for observation i, $\hat{y}_i$ is the predicted value of the dependent variable for observation i, and $\bar{y}$ is the mean value of the dependent variable, for all observations. The numerator of the fraction is called the *sum of squared errors (SSE)* and the denominator of the fraction is called the *total sum of squares (SST)*.

The R^2 value can be interpreted as the proportion of the total variation of the dependent variable that is accounted for by the independent variables used in the regression equation. A different interpretation of R^2 is that it measures the value added of the model over a "baseline" model of predicting the average of the dependent variable for all observations. It is unit-less and takes values between 0 and 1. The worst case is an R^2 of 0, because it means that using the independent variables to make predictions is no better than just predicting the mean of the dependent variable for all observations. The best case is an R^2 of 1, because it means that the model perfectly predicts the variation of the dependent variable, and we do not make any errors.

Generally, a higher R^2 value implies a better regression model, but this can be very dependent on the application area. A valuable model for a hard problem (like predicting stock prices) can have a low R^2 because the problem is so challenging, and a less valuable model for an easy problem can have a high R^2 because the problem is so easy (like predicting revenue of a product using the number of items sold). Therefore, it is important to evaluate the use of a model in practice in addition to computing the R^2 value.

Refining the Model

If it has been determined that one or more insignificant independent variables should be removed from the model, it is typically easy to rebuild the model without a few independent variables. However, the independent variables should be removed one at a time. This is due to interactions between the independent variables, specifically something called *multicollinearity*. Multicollinearity means that two independent variables are highly correlated. If there is multicollinearity in the model, two independent variables are basically representing the same thing. This can make the variables seem insignificant when they actually should be significant. By removing just one of them, it can be discovered that the other variable is significant in the model.

If there are multiple insignificant independent variables in the model, a general rule for which variable to remove first is to remove the one that is the least significant. However, expert human judgment can also be a good strategy for deciding which of two insignificant variables to remove first, based on intuition about the model.

Making Predictions

An important final step to validate a linear regression model is to make predictions on new data, which is often called *out-of-sample* data or a *test set*. If a linear regression model is not good at predicting unseen data, it might be overfit to the training data.

To make predictions, the new data should be plugged into the linear regression equation. For example, recall Ashenfelter's linear regression equation to predict the quality of wine:

> Wine Quality = -12.145 + (0.001173 × Winter Rainfall) + (0.616 × Average Growing Season Temperature) - (0.00386 × Harvest Rainfall) + (0.0238 × Age of Vintage).

Suppose we have two new data points about wine prices, which Ashenfelter did not use to build his model, described in Table 21.1.

Using the linear regression equation, we can predict that for Test Point 1,

> Wine Quality = -12.145 + (0.001173 × 717) + (0.616 × 16.17) - (0.00386 × 122) + (0.0238 × 4) = -1.719,

and for Test Point 2,

Table 21.1: Out-of-sample data for Ashenfelter's wine equation.

Variable	Test Point 1	Test Point 2
Winter Rainfall	717	578
Average Growing Season Temperature	16.17	16.00
Harvest Rainfall	122	74
Age of Vintage	4	3

Wine Quality = -12.145 + (0.001173 × 578) + (0.616 × 16.00) - (0.00386 × 74) + (0.0238 × 3) = -1.825.

Note that we do not need the values of the dependent variables to make predictions. This is important, because often it is necessary to make future predictions before the results are realized (for example, think about predicting the winner of the Academy Awards the week before the results are revealed). But suppose that we know that the actual Wine Quality of the first data point is -1.540, and the actual Wine Quality of the second data point is -1.996. Then we can compute our accuracy on this out-of-sample data by computing the test set R^2.

First, we can compute the sum of squared errors:

$$SSE = (-1.719 - (-1.540))^2 + (-1.825 - (-1.996))^2 = 0.061.$$

Then we can compute the total sum of squares:

$$SST = (-1.426 - (-1.540))^2 + (-1.426 - (-1.996))^2 = 0.338,$$

where -1.426 is the average wine quality of the data used to build the model. Note that we use the mean of Wine Quality in the *training set* to calculate SST. This is because we are trying to compare ourselves against how well we could do by just guessing the mean. In reality, we often have to make out-of-sample predictions before we know the outcome, and so we can not use the test set mean. To make this calculation match what will occur in practice, we should use the training set mean. (Note that this convention makes it so that the R^2 of a model on the test set can sometimes be negative!)

So the R^2 on our test set is

$$R^2 = 1 - \frac{0.061}{0.338} = 0.82$$

This is promising, but we would want to get a larger test set to be more confident of this result. Computing how good a model is at making out-of-sample predictions is crucial for evaluating the predictive power of the model.

21.2 Logistic Regression

Logistic regression is a predictive method that handles cases where the dependent variable, y, only has two possible outcomes, called *classes*. Examples of dependent variables that could be used with logistic regression are predicting whether a new business will succeed or fail, whether or not a loan will be approved, and whether a team will win or lose a game. These are all called *classification* problems, since the goal is to figure out which class each observation belongs to.

Similar to linear regression, logistic regression uses a set of independent variables to make predictions, but instead of predicting a continuous value for the dependent variable, it predicts the probability of membership in each of the possible outcomes, or classes.

The two possible outcomes are often denoted as 1 and 0. For example, if our possible outcomes were "success" or "failure," then we could denote success by 1 and failure by 0. If our possible outcomes were "yes" or "no," then we could denote yes by 1 and no by 0. We will refer to the two possible classes as 1 and 0 for the rest of this section.

Logistic regression consists of two steps. The first step is to compute the probabilities of the two different outcomes. Thus, for each observation i, we are computing $P(y_i = 1)$, or the probability the observation belongs to class 1, and $P(y_i = 0)$, or the probability the observation belongs to class 0. Since we only have two possible outcomes, we know that $P(y_i = 0) = 1 - P(y_i = 1)$ according to the basic properties of probability (the sum of the probabilities for all possible outcomes must equal 1). So logistic regression with two classes only needs to predict $P(y_i = 1)$ for each observation i, since we can easily compute $P(y_i = 0)$.

In the second step of logistic regression, we use a *cutoff*, or *threshold*, value to classify each observation into one of the classes. A common cutoff value is 0.5, meaning that if $P(y_i = 1) \geq 0.5$ we will classify observation i into class 1 and if $P(y = 1) < 0.5$ we will classify observation i into class 0. Simply, we will classify each observation into the class with the highest probability. However, other cutoff values can be chosen, and in some cases are more appropriate. For example, if the probability of belonging to class 1 is a low probability event, a lower cutoff value might be sufficient. We discuss this more later in this section.

The Logistic Regression Model

The probabilities in logistic regression are computed using an equation that is similar to the equation used for linear regression. In linear regression, our equation to predict y was $y = b_0 + b_1x_1 + b_2x_2 + \ldots + b_kx_k$. Since in logistic regression we want our prediction to be a probability, we use a nonlinear function that will only produce values between 0 and 1:

$$P(y = 1) = \frac{1}{1 + e^{-(b_0 + b_1x_1 + b_2x_2 + \ldots + b_kx_k)}}$$

This is called the *logistic response function* and it predicts the probability of an observation belonging to class 1. For more technical details about the logistic response function, see the references in Section 21.7.

To make this equation easier to understand, we define what is known as the *odds* of belonging to class 1:

$$Odds = \frac{P(y = 1)}{P(y = 0)} = \frac{P(y - 1)}{1 - P(y = 1)}.$$

This metric is very popular in gambling games and many other areas. Instead of talking about the probability of an outcome, we can refer to the odds of an outcome. When the probability of class 1 is equal to the probability of class 0, the odds equal one. When the probability of class 1 is larger than the probability of class 0, the odds are larger than one, and when the probability of class 1 is smaller than the probability of class 0, the odds are smaller than one. So the odds capture how likely outcome 1 is to "win" over outcome 0. If we substitute the logistic response function into this equation for $P(y = 1)$, we have (after some algebraic manipulation):

$$Odds = e^{b_0+b_1x_1+b_2x_2+...+b_kx_k}.$$

By taking the logarithm of both sides we get that:

$$log(Odds) = b_0 + b_1x_1 + b_2x_2 + \ldots + b_kx_k,$$

where the right hand side looks like our linear regression equation. The $log(Odds)$ is called the *Logit*, and it is modeled like the dependent variable in a linear regression equation. Sometimes this equation is easier to understand, because it is more clear how the coefficients affect the Logit. The interpretation of the coefficients for the Logit is the same as that for linear regression. If the coefficient of an independent variable is positive, then it leads to a larger logit value (assuming the independent variable takes positive values), which in turn leads to higher Odds, or a higher probability of class 1. On the other hand, if the coefficient of an independent variable is negative (assuming the independent variable takes positive values), then it leads to a smaller logit value, or a lower probability of class 1.

Selecting a Cutoff Value

The logistic response function predicts the probability of outcome 1. Sometimes this probability is useful, since it gives a measure of confidence in the prediction. For example, if we predicted the probability of belonging to class 1 for one observation to be 0.99, and for another observation to be 0.6, we are more confident for the first observation that class 1 is the correct class.

However, logistic regression is most often used to classify each of the data points into one of the classes. To do this, a cutoff or threshold value needs to be selected. Once a threshold value is selected, all observations with probabilities above this value are classified into class 1, and all observations with probabilities below this value are classified into class 0.

Different threshold values can yield different amounts of error in the predictions. In a classification problem, an error occurs when we classify an observation into one class, but it actually belongs to a different class. The accuracy of the model is the number of observations that the model classifies correctly. Most of the time, a model will make some errors, and for this reason there are several approaches to determining the appropriate threshold value. A popular default value is 0.5, with the rationale that an observation should be classified into the class for which its probability is the highest. However, a different threshold value can be selected, because one type of error is seen as worse than the other. Whenever the probabilities are converted to class predictions, there are two types of errors that can be made: *false positives* and *false negatives.* A false positive error is when the model predicts class 1, but in reality the observation belongs to class 0. A false negative error is when the model predicts class 0, but in reality the observation belongs to class 1. If a higher threshold is selected, more false negative errors will be made, because class 1 will only be predicted if the probability is really high. If a lower threshold is selected, more false positive errors will be made, because class 1 will be predicted more often.

Let us think about this in terms of some applications. One application where decision-makers often have an error preference is in disease prediction. Suppose a model is built to predict whether or not someone will develop heart disease in the next 10 years (like the model we saw in Chapter 7 about the Framingham Heart Study). We will consider class 1 to be the outcome in which the person does develop heart disease, and class 0 the outcome in which the person does not develop heart disease. If a high threshold is selected, false negative errors are more likely, which means that the model predicts that the person would not develop heart disease, but they actually did. If a lower threshold is selected, false positive errors are more likely, which means that the model predicts the person will develop heart disease, but they actually did not. In this example, a false positive error is often preferred by the decision-maker. Unnecessary resources might be spent treating a patient who did not need to worry, but fewer patients go untreated (which is what a false negative error does).

Now, consider spam filters. Almost every email provider has a built in spam filter that tries to detect whether or not an email message is spam. We can classify spam messages as class 1 and non-spam messages as class 0. Then, if we build a logistic regression model to predict spam, we might want to select a high threshold. Why? In this case, a false positive error means that we predicted a message was spam, and sent it to the spam folder, when it actually was not spam. We might have just sent an important email to the junk folder! On the other hand, a false negative error means that we predicted a message was not spam, when it actually was. This creates a slight annoyance for the user (since they have to delete the message from the inbox themselves) but at least an important message was not missed. Additionally, each time a user deletes a spam message, many email providers allow them to mark it as spam, so the system can learn from its mistakes.

We can formalize this error trade-off with a Receiver Operator Characteristic curve, or ROC curve. An ROC curve plots the false positive rate of a model on the x-axis, and the true positive rate (the percentage of class 1 observations that the model classified correctly) of the model on the y-axis for different threshold possibilities. An example ROC curve is shown in Figure 21.1.

The line shows how the false positive rate and true positive rate vary with different threshold values for a particular model. A lower threshold corresponds to values in the top right of the plot, since by selecting a lower threshold we predict an outcome of 1 more often. This allows us to maximize our true positive rate, but it also increases the false positive rate. A higher threshold corresponds to values in the bottom left of the plot.

Ideally, we want the ROC curve to be as close to the top left corner of the plot as possible, since it gives a high true positive rate and a low false positive rate. This motivates an important metric for classification problems: the AUC, or area under the curve. The AUC of a model gives the area under the ROC curve, and is a number between 0 and 1. The higher the AUC, the more area under the ROC curve, and the better a model is at distinguishing between the two different classes. The AUC of a model can be interpreted as follows: if a model were handed two random observations from the dataset used to build the ROC curve, one belonging to one class and one belonging to the other class, the AUC gives the percentage of the time that we expect the model to predict the two observations correctly. If we were to just guess which observation was which, this would be an AUC of 0.5. (The ROC curve in this case would be a straight line from the bottom left corner of the plot to the top right corner of the plot.) So a model with an AUC greater than 0.5 is doing something

Figure 21.1: An example ROC curve for a logistic regression model.

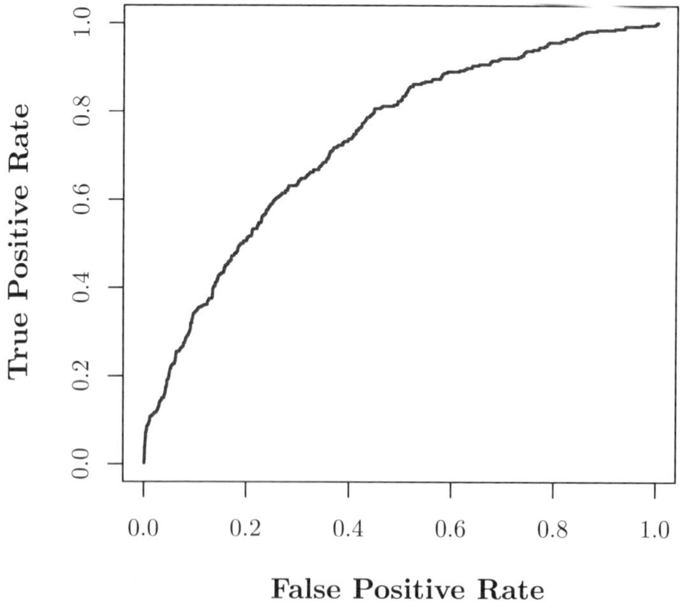

smarter than just guessing, but we want the AUC of a model to be as close to 1 as possible.

Once a logistic regression model is constructed and a threshold value is selected, the model should be tested on out-of-sample data. Similarly to linear regression, this can be done by plugging the new data into the logistic response function to get probability predictions, and then using the threshold value to get class predictions. To evaluate the model's predictive ability, the accuracy of the model, error rates, and AUC can be computed on the test set.

In the next section, we discuss two additional methods that can be used for both classification and regression.

21.3 CART and Random Forests

Classification and regression trees (CART) and random forests are both tree-based methods. These are flexible data-driven methods for determining an outcome using splits, or logical rules, on the independent variables. Unlike linear and logistic regression, we do not need to assume that the outcome variable depends linearly on the independent variables. CART and Random Forests can be used for both a continuous outcome (like in linear regression) and a categorical outcome (like in logistic regression).

CART

The simpler of the two methods is CART. In a CART model, a single tree is constructed, and for this reason, CART models are very easy to interpret, and are popular for applications where the method needs to be easy to explain. This interpretability and the ability to capture nonlinearities in the data are two major benefits of CART.

As a small example, suppose we want to classify whether applicants to a job position will be given an interview. To construct the tree, we start with the training data provided in Table 21.2.

There are currently 5 applicants who have already been informed of whether or not they will receive an interview, and two independent variables that we will use to build our model: highest level of education and previous experience in the field. Based on this data, we can use CART to build the tree shown in Figure 21.2.

This tree correctly labels all of the given data, and can be used to predict whether or not a new applicant will be given an interview by following the splits down the tree, from top to bottom. For example, if an application is received from Fred who does not have previous experience, we predict that he will not receive an interview. If another application is received from Gloria who has previous experience and a Master's degree, we predict that she will receive an interview. Note that it could also be the case that the split on the highest level of education should exclude people with too much education; it could be

Figure 21.2: CART tree for the job application example.

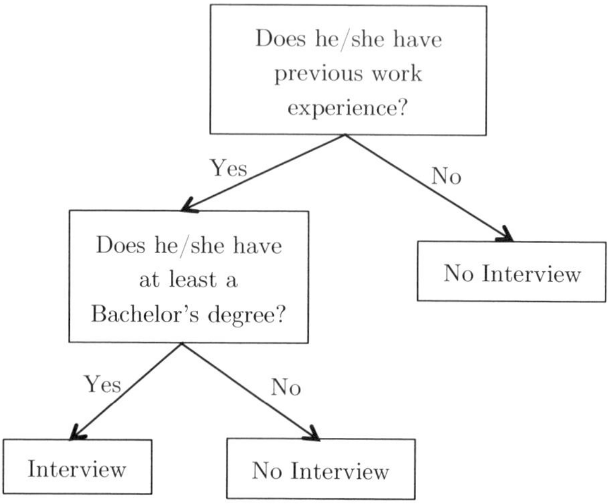

that for this particular position, anything above a Master's degree would make the candidate over-qualified. By using a CART tree, this type of nonlinear relationship could easily be detected.

Each split in a CART tree is always based on a single independent variable, and a CART tree can be given all available independent variables. If a particular independent variable is decided to not be significant, the CART tree will not use that variable at all to make a split. For this reason, a CART tree is often useful to find the significant variables when tens, or even hundreds, of independent variables are available.

The splits used in a CART model divide the observations into smaller

Table 21.2: Data for a small set of job applicants.

Name	Highest Level of Education	Experience	Interview
Andrew	MBA degree	Yes	Yes
Betty	Some College	Yes	No
Charlie	Bachelor's degree	No	No
Diane	Bachelor's degree	Yes	Yes
Edward	PhD	No	No

groups, called *leaves* or *buckets*. In this example, all of the applicants without previous experience were placed into one bucket, all of the applicants with previous experience but without a bachelor's degree or higher were placed into a second bucket, and all of the applicants with previous experience and at least a bachelor's degree were placed into a third bucket. These splits are selected to make the buckets as homogenous or "pure" as possible, meaning that we want each of the buckets to contain observations belonging to just one class. This is not always possible, since we might have two observations with exactly the same values of the independent variables, but different dependent variable values. For example, we could have two applicants with previous experience and MBA degrees, but one received an interview and the other did not. There is no possible split on our two independent variables that would put these observations into different buckets.

There are a number of ways to measure how pure a split is, including what are known as the *Gini index* and an *entropy measure*. We will not describe the specifics of these methods here, but the main idea is that they give a higher "purity" measure to a bucket with a higher proportion of observations belonging to the same class.

Even if it is possible to divide the observations into pure buckets, it may not be a good idea. It could lead to overfitting of the training data, meaning that the model will not extend well to data that it has never seen before. One popular method to prevent overfitting from happening is called "pruning" the tree. In this approach, a complete tree is constructed to make the buckets as pure as possible, and then certain branches are deleted if they do not reduce the impurity of the buckets by a high enough value. Other approaches are to set parameter values to limit the number of splits in the tree, to set a minimum number of observations that must be in a group before a split is attempted, or to set a minimum number of observations that must be in each final group of the tree.

The choice of these parameters can often influence the accuracy of the model, and several different parameter choices should be tested. One way of doing this is with a technique called *cross-validation*. Another is by creating a *validation* set of data. Then, for several different parameter values, a model is built using the training set, and its accuracy is assessed on the validation set. Whichever parameter choice performs the best on the validation set should be selected for the final model. Then, the performance of the final model is assessed on the test set. The validation set is needed so that the test set remains a true out-of-sample test. If the test set is used to select the parameter value, the test set was used to build the model and no longer represents how the model will perform on new data.

For each bucket or leaf of a CART tree, the typical prediction is to predict the majority outcome of all of the observations in the training set that belong in that bucket (assuming we have a classification problem). We can instead assign a probability to each observation of belonging to each class by computing the percentage of observations in the corresponding bucket that belong to each class. Then these probabilities can be thresholded to capture different error preferences, similarly to logistic regression (note that predicting the majority outcome is like using a threshold of 0.5).

CART can easily be used to predict an outcome with more than two classes, or a continuous outcome. With a continuous outcome, the prediction for each group is the average value of the dependent variable over all training points that were classified into that group. In a CART model, regardless of the outcome type, keep in mind that all observations that are classified into the same group, or bucket, will have the same prediction.

After building a CART model, a couple of steps should be taken to assess the validity and evaluate the performance of the tree:

1. Plot the tree and look at each of the decision rules. Check to see if they make sense intuitively. Rules that seem strange could still be accurate, or it could be a sign that the data needs to be examined. This is also a good way to see which independent variables are the most important for the model, by seeing which ones were used in the tree.

2. Assess the accuracy of the tree on a test set. The predictions should be compared to the actual values by using a classification matrix (for a categorical outcome) or by computing the R^2 value (for a continuous outcome).

CART often performs well across a wide range of situations, requires little effort from the analyst, and is easily understandable by the user of the model. It can also be used to detect which variables out of a large number of possible choices are the most important, since the most significant independent variables will appear at the top of the tree. CART models work best when there are large amounts of data, but a variation of this method, called random forests, was designed to improve the performance of trees on smaller datasets.

Random Forests

The method of random forests, developed by Leo Breiman and Adele Cutler, was designed to improve the prediction accuracy of CART. It works by building a large number of CART trees which each "vote" on the outcome to make a final prediction. Unfortunately, this makes the method less interpretable than CART, so often the modeler needs to decide which is more important: the interpretability of the model, or attaining the maximum possible accuracy.

A random forest builds many trees by randomly selecting a subset of observations and a subset of independent variables to use for each tree. We could not just run CART many times, because we would get the same tree every time. Instead, each tree is given a random subset of the independent variables from which it can select the splits, and a training set that is a *bagged* or *bootstrapped* sample of the full dataset. This means that the data used as the training data for each tree is selected randomly with replacement from the full dataset. As an example, if we have five data points in our training set, labeled $\{1, 2, 3, 4, 5\}$, we might use the five observations $\{3, 2, 4, 3, 1\}$ to build the first tree, the five observations $\{5, 1, 2, 3, 2\}$ to build the second tree, etc. Notice that some observations are repeated, and some are not included in certain training sets. This gives each tree a slightly different training set, and helps make each tree see different things in the data.

Just like in CART, there are some parameters that need to be selected for a random forest model. The first is the number of trees to build, which is typically set to a few hundred. The more trees that are built, the longer the model will take to build, but if not enough trees are built, the full potential of the model might not be realized. Another parameter is needed to control the size of the trees. A popular choice is to set a minimum number of observations that can be in a bucket, or subset, of a tree. This is the same as one of the parameters that can be used in a CART model. Random forest models have been shown to be less sensitive to the parameters of the model, so it is typically sufficient to set the parameters to reasonable values. To test different parameter settings, the same validation approach described for building a CART model can be used here.

Unfortunately, it can be hard to interpret a random forest model because it consists of a large number of trees. For this reason, it is typically viewed as more of a "black box" method, meaning that it is not easily interpretable. If interpretability and understanding the model are key objectives for a particular application, then a random forest model is probably not the best model to use.

21.4 Clustering

Clustering is different from the other analytics methods we have discussed so far in this chapter, in that it is an *unsupervised* learning method. This means that the goal of clustering is not to predict an outcome, or dependent variable. It is instead to segment a set of observations into similar groups, based on the available data. Figure 21.3 gives an example of how a set of points can be clustered into three groups, just using the distance between the points. The points are assigned to a group based on how close together they are.

Although clustering is not designed to predict an outcome variable, clustering can still be useful to improve the accuracy of predictive models. The data can be clustered into similar groups, and then used to build a predictive model for each group. We saw an example of this in Chapter 8, "Medical Monitoring and Predictive Diagnosis." A word of caution: this tends to work best for large datasets, since it is easy to overfit a model to the training set using this technique.

There are many different algorithms for clustering, which differ in how the clusters are built and the properties of the clusters produced from the method.

In this chapter, we will cover Hierarchical clustering and k-means clustering, two of the most popular clustering methods. In Chapter 14, a third clustering method is presented, called Condorcet Clustering.

Distance

Before a clustering algorithm can be applied, the distance metric that will be used to define the distance between two points and the distance between two clusters needs to be selected.

The most popular and standard way to compute the distance between two points is Euclidean distance, which is defined as follows for data points $\mathbf{x}$ and $\mathbf{y}$:

$$d(\mathbf{x}, \mathbf{y}) = \sqrt{(x_1 - y_1)^2 + (x_2 - y_2)^2 + (x_3 - y_3)^2 + \ldots + (x_k - y_k)^2}.$$

For each attribute of the data points (here we are assuming there are k attributes), Euclidean distance computes the difference between the two data points and squares it. Then these values are added across all attributes and the square root is taken.

In addition to Euclidean distance, there are many other distance metrics that could be used. One is called *Manhattan distance*, which computes the distance between two points as the sum of the absolute values of the differences between the attributes, instead of the sum of squares. Another is called *maximum coordinate distance*, which defines the distance as the largest difference between the two data points in any attribute. In the rest of this chapter, we will use Euclidean distance. For an example of a non-Euclidean distance metric, see Chapter 14.

Another important distance that we have to define for clustering is the distance between two clusters, or groups of points. One way of doing this is called *minimum distance*, which defines the distance between two clusters as the distance between the data points in the clusters that are the closest together. Figure 21.4 shows how we would define the distances between each cluster in our example. Each black line gives the distance between a pair of clusters.

Figure 21.3: Example of how points can be clustered into groups.

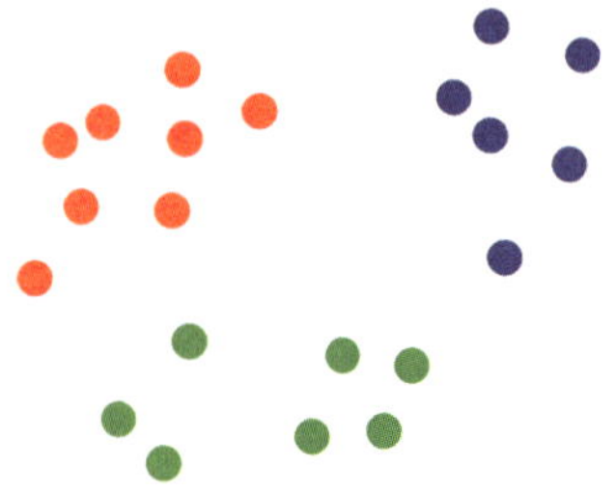

Figure 21.4: Example of minimum distance between clusters.

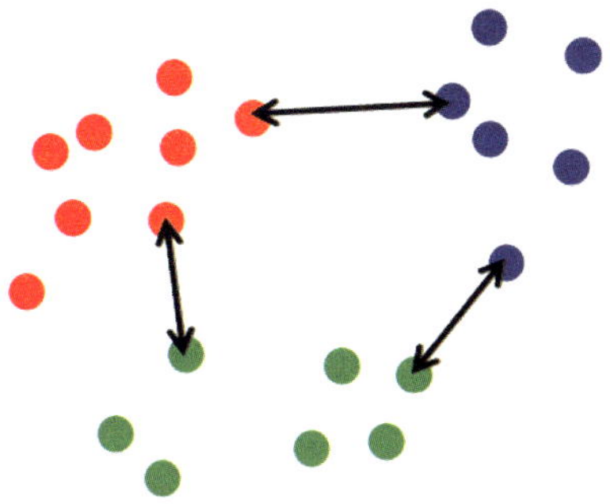

As we saw with the distance between two points, there are also several ways of defining the distance between two clusters. We could instead use *maximum distance*, which defines the distance between two clusters as the distance between the points that are the farthest apart. Another option is *centroid* distance, which defines the distance between two clusters as the distance between the cluster centroids. The centroid of a cluster is the point that is the average (in each attribute) of all of the data points in the cluster. Figure 21.5 shows the centroid of each cluster as a black square. The distance between two clusters would then be the distance between the two squares, or centroids. Note that each of these distances ultimately requires that we compute the distance between two points, for which we can use Euclidean distance.

Distance can be highly influenced by the scale of the different attributes, so it is important to consider normalizing the data before computing distances. For example, suppose that the observations are companies. One of the

Figure 21.5: Example of centroid distance between clusters.

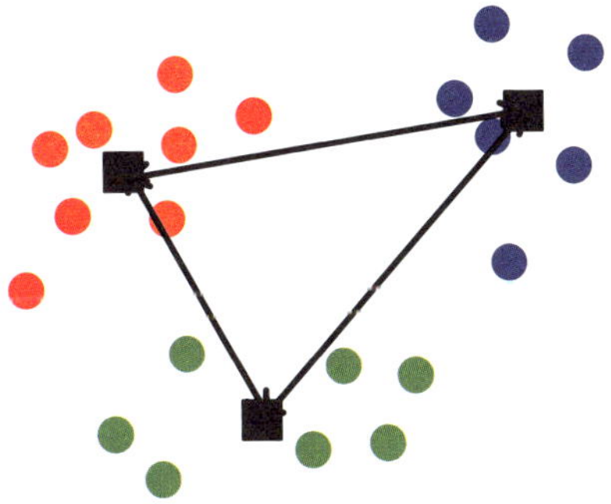

attributes could be annual revenue, in dollars, and another attribute could be age of the company, in years. The revenue variable would dominate in the distance calculation because it is much larger than the years variable. The variables can be normalized to be on the same scale by subtracting the mean and dividing by the standard deviation (for each variable).

Hierarchical Clustering

In this section, we will discuss *agglomerative hierarchical clustering*, which starts with each observation in its own cluster. So if there are n data points, or observations, it starts with n clusters. Then, the distance between each pair of clusters (or points) is computed, and the two closest clusters are combined (resulting in $n - 1$ clusters). This is repeated until all of the data points are in a single cluster. (A different form of hierarchical clustering, called divisive hierarchical clustering, starts with all of the points in a single cluster and iteratively splits the cluster into two pieces. We will be referring to the agglomerative form of hierarchical clustering throughout this section.)

This clustering process is called *hierarchical* because the clusters are nested. When two clusters are combined, the new cluster can be thought of as "above" the other clusters. This can be visualized with a *dendrogram*. A small example of the hierarchical clustering process and the resulting dendrogram is shown in Figure 21.6. In this example, there are four data points shown on the left of the figure (colored red, green, blue, and black) and therefore the clustering process starts with four clusters. The two closest are the red and green points, so they are combined first. The next closest are the red/green cluster and the blue point, so they are combined next, and then lastly, the black data point is combined with the others. This process is shown in the dendrogram to the right of the points. Each of the points is shown on the bottom, and the process by which they are combined is shown with the gray lines. The height of the lines approximately shows how far apart the two clusters were when they were combined.

Hierarchical clustering is done without first selecting the number of clusters desired. This is nice because the algorithm can be run without having to know the appropriate number of clusters for the problem. However, in many applications, a specific number of clusters is ultimately needed. This can be done after the hierarchical process is complete by looking at the dendrogram. Imagine a horizontal line cutting across the dendrogram. The number of vertical lines of the dendrogram that the horizontal line crosses shows how many clusters would be selected. That number of clusters tends to be a good choice if the horizontal line has a lot of "wiggle room," meaning that the horizontal line can move up and down without running into a horizontal line of the dendrogram. Figures 21.7 and 21.8 show the horizontal line and wiggle room for three clusters or two clusters. For this particular dataset, the dendrogram tells us that two clusters is a better choice, because the clusters were farther apart when they were combined (more wiggle room). However, when selecting the number of clusters for a particular problem, the decision-maker should also consider how many clusters make sense for the particular application.

Figure 21.6: Small example of hierarchical clustering and the resulting dendrogram.

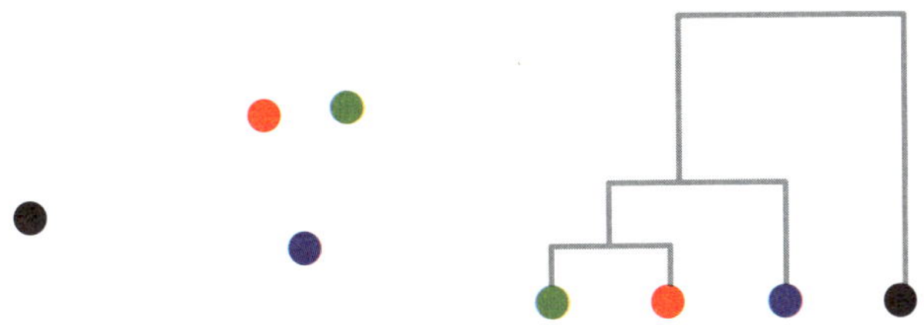

Figure 21.7: Selecting the number of clusters using a dendrogram.

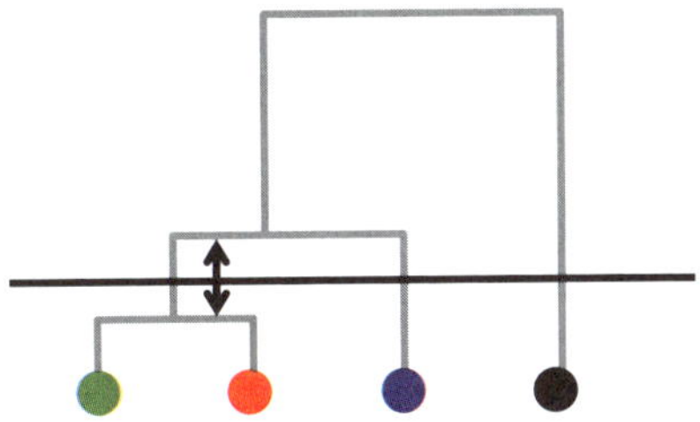

Figure 21.8: Selecting the number of clusters using a dendrogram.

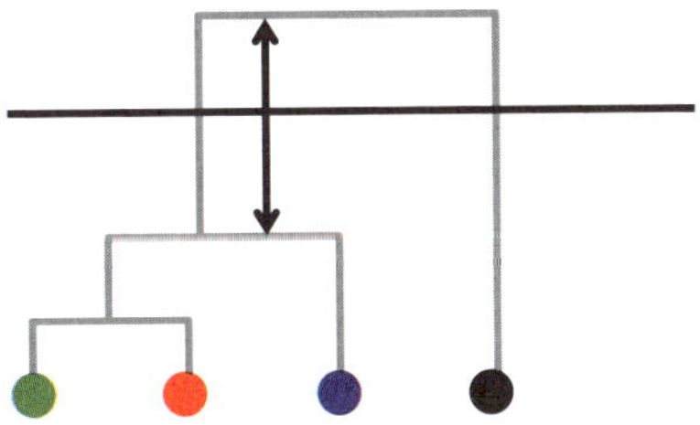

K-Means Clustering

Instead of forming the clusters in a hierarchical way, k-means clustering iteratively re-assigns data points to clusters. First, the number of clusters desired has to be selected. It is often useful to run hierarchical clustering first to better understand which number of clusters would be good, or to think about the number of clusters that would be appropriate for the given problem. Alternatively, the clustering algorithm can be run several times with different choices for the number of clusters.

Once the number of clusters has been selected, each data point is randomly assigned to one of the clusters and each cluster centroid is computed. Then, each data point is re-assigned to the closest cluster centroid, and the cluster centroids are re-computed. This process repeats until no data point needs to be reassigned. It can also be stopped by defining a maximum number of iterations.

The largest benefit of the k-means clustering algorithm is that it is very fast, and works with small and large datasets. This is not true for hierarchical clustering, because of the distance computations required. Hierarchical clustering will not work if the dataset is too large, so in some situations, hierarchical clustering might not be an option. However, a dendrogram can not be used with the k-means clustering algorithm to assist in selecting the number of clusters. A different type of visualization, called a *scree plot*, can help in selecting the appropriate number of clusters for any clustering algorithm. For more information, see the references in Section 21.7.

Regardless of the clustering algorithm used, the resulting clusters should be analyzed and explored to see if they are meaningful. This can be done by looking at basic statistics in each cluster, like the mean, minimum, and maximum values in each cluster and each variable. If the clusters have a feature in common that was not used in the clustering, like an outcome variable, then this often indicates that the clusters might help improve a predictive model.

21.5 Data Visualization

In this section, we will discuss the meaning of data visualization, why it is often useful to visualize data to discover hidden trends and properties, and a few different types of visualizations.

Data visualization is defined as a mapping of *data properties* to *visual properties*. Data properties are usually numerical or categorical, like the mean of a variable, the maximum value of a variable, or the number of observations with a certain property. Visual properties are attributes like (x, y) coordinates, colors, sizes, or shapes. Both types of properties can be useful for understanding a dataset.

To motivate the need for data visualization, let us consider a famous example called "Anscombe's Quartet." This example consists of four small datasets, each with two attributes. The data is given in Table 21.3. Just looking at the data, it is hard to notice anything special about the different

Table 21.3: Data for Anscombe's Quartet.

$\mathbf{X}_1$	$\mathbf{Y}_1$	$\mathbf{X}_2$	$\mathbf{Y}_2$	$\mathbf{X}_3$	$\mathbf{Y}_3$	$\mathbf{X}_4$	$\mathbf{Y}_4$
10.00	8.04	10.00	9.14	10.00	7.46	8.00	6.58
8.00	6.95	8.00	8.14	8.00	6.77	8.00	5.76
13.00	7.58	13.00	8.74	13.00	12.74	8.00	7.71
9.00	8.81	9.00	8.77	9.00	7.11	8.00	8.84
11.00	8.33	11.00	9.26	11.00	7.81	8.00	8.47
14.00	9.96	14.00	8.10	14.00	8.84	8.00	7.04
6.00	7.24	6.00	6.13	6.00	6.08	8.00	5.25
4.00	4.26	4.00	3.10	4.00	5.39	19.00	12.50
12.00	10.84	12.00	9.13	12.00	8.15	8.00	5.56
7.00	4.82	7.00	7.26	7.00	6.42	8.00	7.91
5.00	5.68	5.00	4.74	5.00	5.73	8.00	6.89

datasets. It turns out that the mean and standard deviation of the **X** variable is the same for all four datasets, and the mean and standard deviation of the **Y** variable is the same for all four datasets. Additionally, the correlation between **X** and **Y** is the same for all four datasets, and the regression equation to predict **Y** from **X** is even the same for all four datasets! So are these datasets very similar?

Figure 21.9 shows a scatterplot of each of the four datasets. By visualizing the data, we can see that they are actually very different. The first dataset (in the top left of the plot) looks like an appropriate dataset for linear regression, with a clear linear relationship between $\mathbf{X}_1$ and $\mathbf{Y}_1$. The second dataset (in the top right of the plot) looks quadratic, and the third dataset (in the bottom left of the plot) looks perfectly linear with an outlier. The fourth dataset is perhaps the most unusual, with all of the points lying on a vertical line except for one. Without visualizing the data, we might not have noticed these differences, and we would have ignored valuable information that we could use when building a model.

Beyond detecting patterns that are hard to notice by looking at the numerical data, visualization is also useful for interpreting a model and communicating results. Often, the person who built the model is not the person who will be implementing or using the model. With the correct visualizations, the task of describing a model or a dataset to the end user can be much easier.

Throughout the rest of this section, we will describe a few different visualizations. All of the images shown here were created in R using the `ggplot2` package. For more about this package and how to create these visualizations yourself, see the R Manual in the Online Companion.

Figure 21.9: Visualization of Anscombe's Quartet.

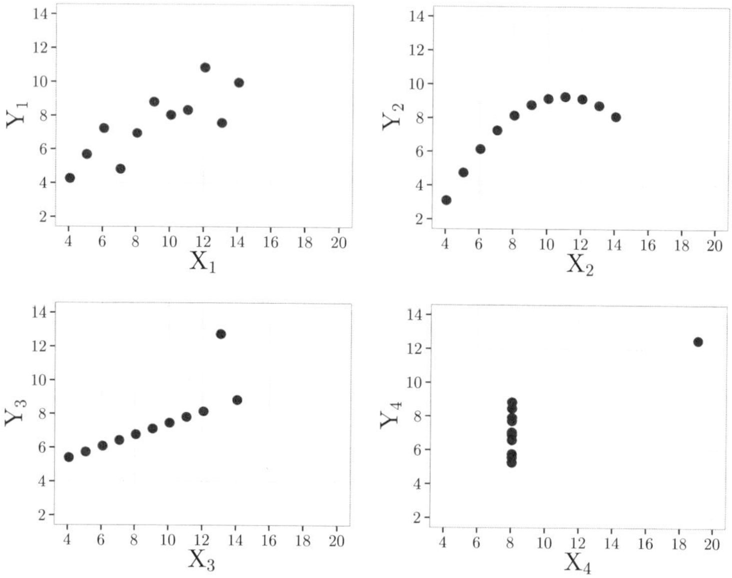

Scatterplots and Line Graphs

Two basic visualizations are scatterplots and line graphs. While they are very simple ways of visualizing data, they can also be the cleanest and most understandable visualizations in some situations.

Scatterplots

Scatterplots can be useful for quickly visualizing data trends in two dimensions. As an example, Figure 21.10 shows a basic scatterplot of per capita gross national income compared to fertility rate for all countries, according to the World Health Organization (WHO). Each point is a country, per capita gross national income is on the x-axis, and fertility rate is on the y-axis.

By coloring the points or changing the shapes, scatterplots can also be used to visualize data in more than two dimensions. Figure 21.11 shows the same scatterplot, but now the points are colored by the region the points belong to. This plot easily allows us to see something we might not have observed before: The points from different regions are located in different areas of the plot.

Figure 21.10: Scatterplot of gross national income per capita versus fertility rate (number of children per woman) for all countries.

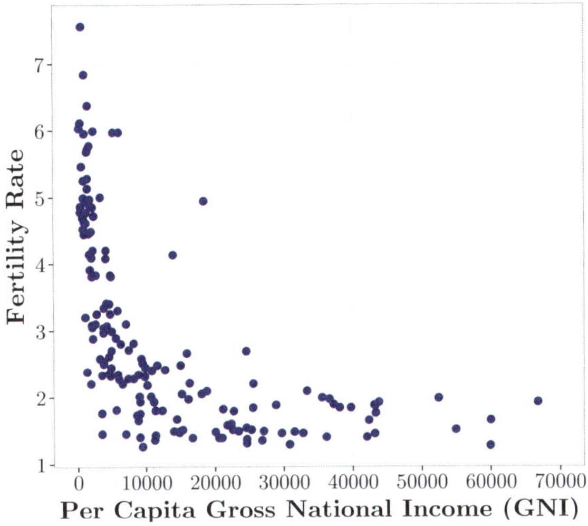

Line Graphs

Line graphs are often very useful for visualizing data with a time component. For example, Figure 21.12 gives the number of motor vehicle thefts in the city of Chicago by day of the week.

This plot helps us easily observe that the number of motor vehicle thefts in Chicago (on average) is higher on Friday and lower on Sunday. If we want to also visualize how crime changes with the hour of the day, a heat map is a useful visualization.

Heat Maps

A great way to visualize frequency data on two attributes (like the frequency of crime according to the day of the week and the hour of the day) is by using a heat map. A heat map creates a grid in two dimensions, with one attribute on the x-axis and the other on the y-axis. There is a square in the grid for every possible pair of the two attributes. For example, in our crime plot, we will have $7 \times 24 = 168$ squares in our grid, one for each hour of each day.

To see this more concretely, Figure 21.13 shows a heat map for motor vehicle thefts in the city of Chicago. The legend on the right helps us understand the plot. The darker the color is, the more motor vehicle thefts in that hour and day.

Figure 21.11: Scatterplot of gross national income per capita versus fertility rate in the WHO dataset, with each point colored by the region it belongs to.

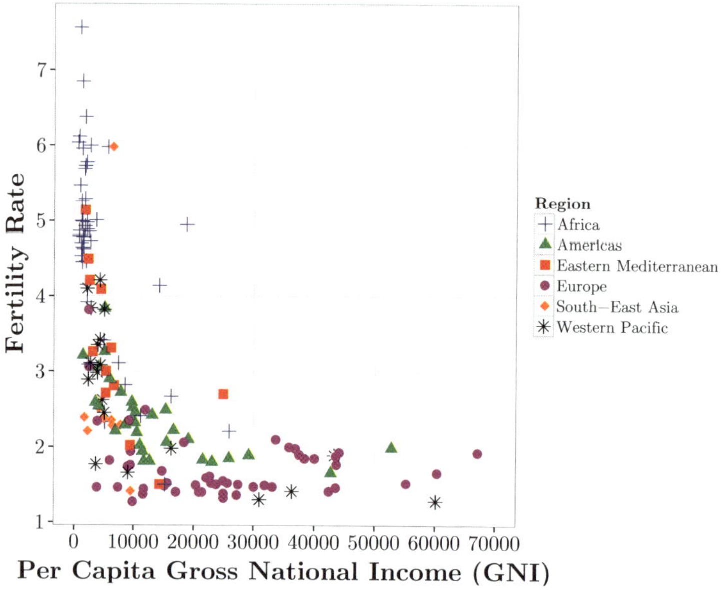

It is common to change the color scheme of a heat map depending on the application. For example, crime maps are often shown with a red color scheme (like the ones shown here), to give the crime "hot spots."

Geographical Maps

Heat maps are often shown on a geographical map to visualize an attribute based on location. For example, Figure 21.14 shows the number of motor vehicle thefts across the city of Chicago. This is a great visualization for crime "hot spots," and is frequently used in policing to visualize crime trends.

United States Map

A common visualization used by organizations like the Centers for Disease Control (CDC) and the World Health Organization (WHO) is a country or world map, with the different states or countries colored according to some attribute, like obesity, high school graduation, or unemployment.

As an example, Figure 21.15 gives an unemployment map of the United States from 2009, during the peak of the Great Recession. By looking at this map, we can easily see that some states had significantly higher unemployment rates than others in 2009.

Figure 21.12: Line graph of the number of motor vehicle thefts in the city of Chicago by day of the week.

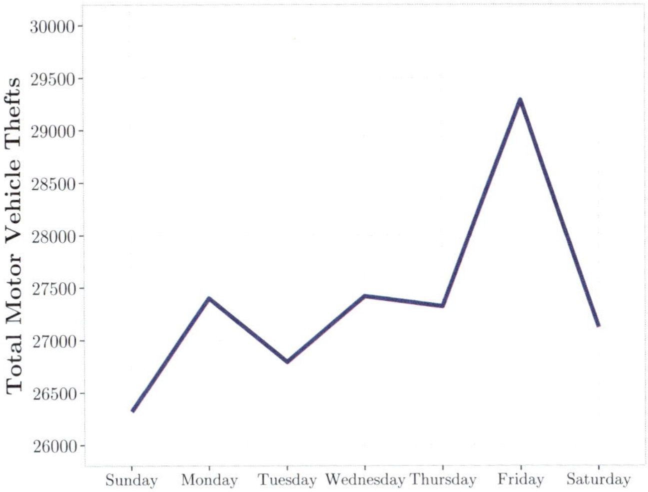

Figure 21.13: A heat map of the number of motor vehicle thefts in the city of Chicago by day of the week and hour of the day. The regions that are the most blue have had the highest number of motor vehicle thefts historically.

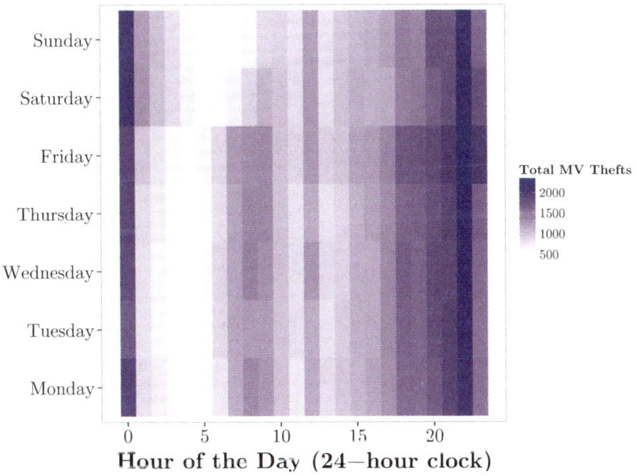

Visualizations can be used to better understand data, but they can also lead to misconceptions about the data if used incorrectly. We do not

Figure 21.14: Heat map of the number of motor vehicle thefts in the city of Chicago by geographic location.

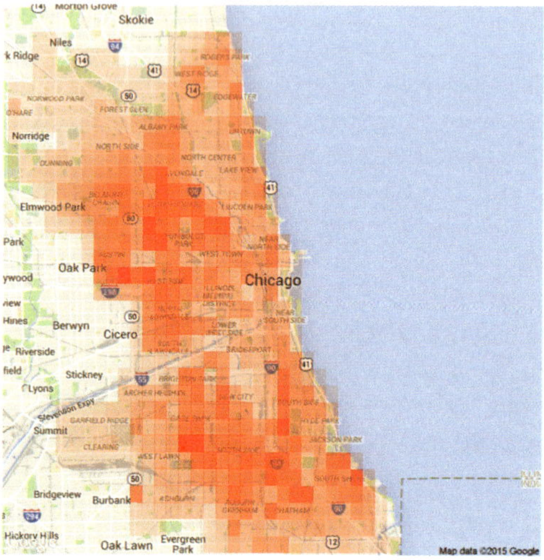

Figure 21.15: A heat map on a map of the United States, showing the unemployment rate in 2009.

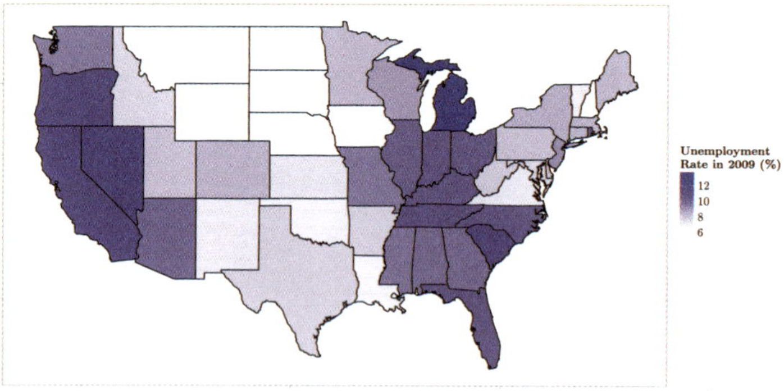

want to conclude from this map that Michigan was hit the hardest by the Great Recession without comparing the unemployment rates to those in 2005. When used appropriately, visualizations can be an incredibly powerful way to understand and describe data.

21.6 Linear and Integer Optimization

Linear and integer optimization are methods used to select optimal decisions. The key components of an optimization model are the decision variables, the objective, and the constraints.

The decision variables in an optimization model represent the choices faced by the decision maker. In a linear optimization model, they can take continuous values in a range. Examples are the number of gallons of crude oil to use to produce gasoline, the number of bushels of vegetables to produce in a given season, and the intensity of beams in radiation therapy. In an integer optimization model, the decision variables are constrained to take integer values (..., -3, -2, -1, 0, 1, 2, 3, ...) or binary values (0 or 1). Examples of integer or binary decision variables are whether or not to invest in a stock, assigning nurses to shifts, the number of new machines to purchase in a factory, and the number of items to stock in a store. Ultimately, an optimization model is used to find the optimal values of these decision variables.

The objective in a linear or integer optimization model is to maximize or minimize a linear function of the decision variables. Examples are to maximize total revenue, to minimize total cost, or to maximize social welfare. This is the ultimate goal of the optimization model.

The constraints in a linear or integer optimization model are linear equations of the decision variables that must be satisfied by the solution of the model. They often represent feasibility problems in the model; if the constraints are not met, the solution will not work. Examples of possible constraints are to not sell more of a product than the amount that was produced and to not exceed the estimated demand.

If the constraints and/or the objective are not linear, then the optimization model is called *nonlinear*. There are many different types of optimization models, but linear and integer optimization models are some of the most practical and widely used types of optimization models. For more technical details, see the references in Section 21.7.

The Formulation

Optimization models are typically written as a set of equations. As an example, here is a simple optimization model:

$$\begin{aligned} \text{maximize} \quad & 617x_1 + 238x_2 \\ \text{subject to} \quad & x_1 + x_2 \leq 166 \\ & x_1 \leq 100 \\ & x_2 \leq 150 \\ & x_1 \geq 0 \\ & x_2 \geq 0. \end{aligned}$$

This is a small example of an airline optimization problem. The airline is trying to decide how many seats to offer at the regular price of \$617 (x_1) and how many seats to offer at the discount price of \$238 (x_2) to maximize total revenue. The capacity of the airplane is 166 seats, so they do not want to offer more seats than 166 ($x_1 + x_2 \leq 166$). Additionally, they have estimated the demand of regular seats to be 100, and the demand of discount seats to be 150. They do not want to offer more seats than the demand, since additional seats are unlikely to be purchased ($x_1 \leq 100$ and $x_2 \leq 150$). Lastly, the airline can not sell a negative number of seats, so both decision variables are constrained to be non-negative ($x_1 \geq 0$ and $x_2 \geq 0$).

The optimal solution for this problem is $x_1 = 100$ and $x_2 = 66$, with an objective value of $\$617 \times 100 + \$238 \times 66 = \$77{,}408$. Why? The airline would like to sell as many regular seats as possible, since the revenue from a regular seat is higher than that of a discount seat. So, they sell the maximum number of regular seats that they can, according to the constraints. The remaining seats are offered as discount seats.

While this problem can be solved by inspection, real-world optimization problems are typically much larger. Imagine this problem with hundreds of different flights and tens of different types of tickets. Additionally, the problem gets even more complex when connecting flights are taken into account.

To solve optimization models in practice, there are many different commercial and open-source solvers. Small optimization models can be solved with spreadsheet software, which is a very intuitive way of setting up and solving a model. Larger problems require more advanced software, and there are many options available. For more information, see the software manuals in the Online Companion.

Sensitivity Analysis

An important step in solving an optimization model is to perform *sensitivity analysis.* The solution to the optimization model is often sensitive to some of the parameter values. For example, if we increase the capacity of the airplane in our simple example, will the optimal solution change? How about if the demand for regular seats increases? Or the demand for discount seats increases?

First, let us think about what would happen if the demand for discount seats increases. Since the current optimal solution does not even meet the current demand for discount seats, this will not change the optimal solution at all! The discount demand could even decrease all the way down to 66 without affecting the optimal solution. This is not true for the regular demand. If the regular demand increases, we will want to sell an additional regular seat instead of a discount seat. For each additional unit of regular demand, this will increase our optimal objective function value by $\$617 - \$238 = \$379$, since we are selling a regular ticket instead of a discount ticket.

This motivates the definition of the *shadow price* of a constraint for a linear optimization model, which is the marginal revenue of increasing the right hand side of the constraint by one. So the shadow price of the discount demand constraint is \$0, while the shadow price of the regular demand constraint is \$379. However, these values only hold if the constraint is increased to a certain level. Think about what would happen if the regular demand increased by 67. For the first 66 units of increase, the shadow price is \$379. But then the capacity of the airplane is full, and any additional increase in regular demand does not matter since there are no more seats left to sell. So the shadow price for the regular demand constraint is \$379, with an *allowable increase* of 66.

While exploratory sensitivity analysis (changing parameter values and resolving the model) can be done for any type of optimization model, shadow prices are particularly useful for linear optimization models. For more technical details, see the references in Section 21.7.

21.7 Notes and Sources

For a more mathematically rigorous treatment of the statistical methods described here, we refer you to "An Introduction to Statistical Learning" by James et al. [71]. For a more mathematically rigorous treatment of the optimization methods described here, we refer you to "Introduction to Linear Optimization" by Bertsimas and Tsitsiklis [25].

For additional resources describing data mining methods for business, we refer you to "Data Mining for Business Intelligence" by Shmueli et al. [129], and for additional resources describing regression, simulation, and optimization methods for business, we refer you to "Data, Models, and Decisions" by Bertsimas and Freund [22].

21.1. The wine quality data referenced here comes from the Liquid Assets website (http://www.liquidasset.com/winedata.html).

21.5. The World Health Organization (WHO) data used for the scatterplots comes from the Global Health Observatory Data Repository (http://apps.who.int/gho/data/?theme=main), the Chicago crime data used for the line graph and heat maps comes from the City of Chicago website (http://www.cityofchicago.org), and the unemployment data comes from the United States Bureau of Labor Statistics (http://www.bls.gov/).

Chapter 22

Analytics Explorations and Dives

He who would search for pearls must dive below.

– John Dryden

Contents

This chapter contains several exercises to explore and dive into the analytics topics presented in Chapter 21. We assume knowledge of the corresponding section in Chapter 21, and may use topics presented in previous sections. These are in-depth exercises; each problem uses a dataset from a particular application area (some of which have been slightly modified for anonymity) and explores that dataset in detail. You will need to use an analytics software to complete the exercises. Manuals for software recommended by the authors are provided in the Online Companion for this book (www.dynamic-ideas.com/analytics-edge). All datasets can also be found in the Online Companion, and the sources for the data are described in Section 22.8.

22.1 Linear Regression Exercises

The exercises in this section are designed to help the reader better understand the method of linear regression, and to practice building linear regression models.

Predicting Life Expectancy in the United States

In this problem, we will be examining the dataset *StateData.csv*, which has data from the 1970s on all fifty US states. If you are using R, this dataset is actually built in. Try typing `?state` in your R console for more information. A description of the variables in the dataset is given in Table 22.1.

a) Let us start by exploring the data.

i) First, create a scatterplot of all of the states by putting `Longitude` on the x-axis and `Latitude` on the y-axis. The shape of the plot should be the familiar outline of the United States. Turn in the plot, and explain how you generated it.

ii) Which region of the United States (West, North Central, South, or Northeast) has the highest average high school graduation rate? Note that this problem requires that you split the states into regions, and then compute the mean high school graduation rate for each region. (We are not asking you to calculate a weighted average by population, just a simple average across states.)

iii) Create a box plot of the variable `Murder` for each `Region` (so you should have four box plots in total). Describe the statistical distribution of the murder rate for each region. For example, which region has the highest median murder rate? The largest range of values?

b) Now build a linear regression model to predict life expectancy (`LifeExp`), using the following variables as independent variables:

Table 22.1: Variables in the dataset *StateData.csv*.

Variable	Description
`Population`	Population estimate of the state in 1975.
`Income`	Per capita income in the state in 1974.
`Illiteracy`	Illiteracy rates in 1970, as a percentage of the state's population.
`LifeExp`	The life expectancy in years of residents of the state in 1970.
`Murder`	The murder and non-negligent manslaughter rate per 100,000 population in 1976.
`HighSchoolGrad`	The high-school graduation rate in the state in 1970.
`Frost`	The mean number of days with minimum temperature below freezing from 1931 to 1960 in the capital or a large city of the state.
`Area`	The land area (in square miles) of the state.
`Longitude`	The longitude of the center of the state.
`Latitude`	The latitude of the center of the state.
`Region`	The region (Northeast, South, North Central, or West) that the state belongs to.

`Population`, **`Income`**, **`Illiteracy`**, **`Murder`**, **`HighSchoolGrad`**, **`Frost`**, and **`Area`**. Use the entire dataset **`StateData`** to build the model.

i) What is the regression equation produced by your model? Include all of the coefficients and the independent variables they correspond to.

ii) What is the interpretation of the coefficient for **`Income`**?

iii) Create a scatterplot with **`Income`** on the x-axis, and **`LifeExp`** on the y-axis. Does this relationship agree with the coefficient for **`Income`** in your linear regression model? Why or why not?

c) Now re-build your linear regression model, finding the set of independent variables that you think is the best for predicting **`LifeExp`**. You can use any subset of the seven independent variables used in the previous question. Use the significance of the coefficients, the R^2 of the model, and the interpretability of the model when selecting the final set of independent variables.

i) What is your new linear regression equation?

ii) Compare and contrast this model to the one you built with all seven independent variables, paying special attention to the R^2 of the model and the significance of the coefficients.

iii) Using your simplified model, create a vector of predictions for the dataset **StateData** (this is just the data used to build the model). Which state does your model predict to have the lowest life expectancy? Which state actually has the lowest life expectancy? Which state does your model predict to have the highest life expectancy? Which state actually has the highest life expectancy?

Climate Change

There have been many studies documenting that the average global temperature has been increasing over the last century. The consequences of a continued rise in global temperature will be dire. Rising sea levels and an increased frequency of extreme weather events will affect billions of people. In this problem, we will study the relationship between average global temperature and several other factors. The file *ClimateChange.csv*, which is available in the Online Companion, contains climate data from May 1983 to December 2008. The variables are described in Table 22.2.

a) Start by splitting the dataset into a *training* set, consisting of observations up to and including 2006, and a *testing* set, consisting of observations after 2006. You will use the training set to build your model, and the testing set to evaluate the predictive ability of your model.

Then, build a linear regression model to predict **Temp**, using all of the other variables as independent variables (except **Year** and **Month**). You should use the training set that you just created to build the model.

i) What is the linear regression equation produced by your model?

ii) Evaluate the quality of the model. What is the R^2 value? (Note that this is called "Multiple R-squared" in some software output.) Which independent variables are significant?

iii) Current scientific opinion is that N2O and CFC-11 are greenhouse gases: gases that are able to trap heat from the sun and contribute to the heating of the Earth. However, you should see that the regression coefficients of both the N2O and CFC-11 variables in this model are negative, indicating that increasing atmospheric concentrations of either of these two compounds is

Table 22.2: Variables in the dataset *ClimateChange.csv*.

Variable	Description
`Year`	The observation year.
`Month`	The observation month.
`Temp`	The difference in degrees Celsius between the average global temperature in the observation month and a reference value.
`CFC.11`	The atmospheric concentration of trichlorofluoromethane (commonly referred to as CFC-11), expressed in ppbv (parts per billion by volume – i.e., 397 ppbv of CFC-11 means that CFC-11 constitutes 397 billionths of the total volume of the atmosphere).
`CFC.12`	The atmospheric concentration of dichlorodifluoromethane (commonly referred to as CFC-12), expressed in ppbv.
`CO2`	The atmospheric concentration of carbon dioxide (CO2), expressed in ppmv (parts per million by volume).
`N2O`	The atmospheric concentration of nitrous oxide (N2O), expressed in ppmv.
`CH4`	The atmospheric concentration of methane (CH4), expressed in ppmv.
`Aerosols`	The mean stratospheric aerosol optical depth at 550 nm.
`TSI`	The total solar irradiance (TSI) in W/m^2, which is the rate at which the sun's energy is deposited per unit area.
`MEI`	Multivariate El Nino Southern Oscillation index (MEI), a measure of the strength of a weather effect in the Pacific Ocean.

associated with lower global temperatures. What is the simplest explanation for this contradiction?

iv) Compute the correlations between all independent variables in the training set. Which independent variables is `N2O` highly correlated with (absolute correlation greater than 0.7)? Which independent variables is **CFC.11** highly correlated with (absolute correlation greater than 0.7)?

b) Now build a new linear regression model, this time only using **MEI**, **TSI**, **Aerosols**, and **N2O** as the independent variables. Remember to use the training set to build the model.

i) How does the coefficient for **N2O** in this model compare to the coefficient in the previous model?

ii) How does the quality of this model compare to the previous one? Consider the R^2 value and the significance of the independent variables when answering this question.

c) We have developed an understanding of how well we can fit a linear regression model to the training data, but now we want to see if the model quality holds when applied to unseen data. Using the simplified model you created in part (b), calculate predictions for the testing dataset. What is the R^2 on the test set? What does this tell you about the model?

Forecasting Hyundai Elantra Sales

An important application of predictive models is understanding sales. For a company that produces and sells a product, having excess inventory can lead to additional warehouse storage costs, or outdated products. Having too little inventory can lead to lost sales and unmet demand. If the company can predict sales before producing the product, they can better match production with customer demand.

In this problem, we will predict the monthly sales in the United States of the Hyundai Elantra car. The Hyundai Motor Company is a major automobile manufacturer based in South Korea. The Elantra is a car model that has been produced by Hyundai since 1990 and is sold all over the world, including the United States. We will build a linear regression model to predict monthly sales using economic indicators of the United States as well as Google search queries. The data for this problem is contained in the file *Elantra.csv*, and can be found in the Online Companion. Each observation in the file is a month, from January 2010 to February 2014. The variables are described in Table 22.3.

a) Start by splitting the dataset into a training set and testing set. The training set should have all observations for 2010, 2011, and 2012. The testing set should have all observations for 2013 and 2014.

Then, build a linear regression model to predict monthly Elantra sales (**ElantraSales**) using **Unemployment**, **Queries**, **CPI.Energy**, and **CPI.All** as the independent variables. Use the training set to build the model.

Table 22.3: Variables in the dataset *Elantra.csv*.

Variable	Description
`Month`	The observation month (1 = January, 2 = February, 3 = March, etc.).
`Year`	The observation year.
`ElantraSales`	The number of units of the Hyundai Elantra sold in the United States in the given month and year.
`Unemployment`	The estimated unemployment rate as a percentage in the United States in the given month and year.
`Queries`	A (normalized) approximation of the number of Google searches for "hyundai elantra" in the given month and year.
`CPI.All`	The consumer price index (CPI) for all products for the given month and year. This is a measure of the magnitude of the prices paid by consumer households for goods and services.
`CPI.Energy`	The monthly consumer price index (CPI) for energy for the given month and year.

i) What is the linear regression equation produced by your model? Make sure to give the coefficients for each of the independent variables.

ii) What is the R^2 of the model?

iii) Which variables are significant? What does this tell you about the model?

b) We would like to improve our linear regression model by modeling seasonality. In predicting demand and sales, seasonality is often very important since demand tends to be periodic in time. For example, demand for jackets and coats tends to be higher in winter versus summer, while demand for sunscreen tends to be higher in the summer. We will incorporate seasonality into our model by using the `Month` variable.

Build a new linear regression model, this time using the `Month` variable as an additional independent variable. Again, use the training data to build your model.

i) Describe your new model. What is the regression equation? What is the R^2? Which variables are significant?

ii) We are currently modeling **Month** as a numeric variable (1 = January, 2 = February, 3 = March, etc.). This causes our model to see February as "larger" than January, March as "larger" than February, etc. Is this the right way to model this variable? What would happen if we made **Month** a categorical variable instead?

c) Create a new linear regression model, this time with **Month** modeled as a categorical variable. You can do this by changing the values of **Month** to "January," "February," etc. or, if you are using R, by converting **Month** to a factor variable.

i) Describe your new model. What is the regression equation? What is the R^2? Which variables are significant?

ii) Using this model, make predictions on the test set. Remember to convert the **Month** variable to a categorical variable in the test set before making predictions. What is the R^2 of the model on the test set?

d) From what you saw in this problem, what can you conclude about predicting Hyundai Elantra sales? Do you think these conclusions generalize to predicting sales for other products?

e) If you could collect additional independent variables for this problem, which variables do you think would be useful for predicting sales?

22.2 Logistic Regression Exercises

The exercises in this section are designed to help you better understand the method of logistic regression, and to practice building logistic regression models.

Predicting the Baseball World Series Champion

While analytical methods have been shown to be very useful in predicting the *regular season* performance of players and teams in baseball, predicting the *World Series* champion is a different story. For a small series of games, luck can win out over skill, and it is generally believed that anything can happen. In this exercise, we will use data on baseball teams in Major League Baseball (MLB) to try to predict the World Series winner at the beginning of the playoffs.

The data for this exercise is in the file *Baseball.csv* (available in the Online Companion). Each observation corresponds to a team that made it to the playoffs in a given year. This dataset has 13 variables, which are described in Table 22.4.

Table 22.4: Variables in the dataset *Baseball.csv*.

Variable	Description
`Team`	A code for the name of the team.
`League`	The Major League Baseball league the team belongs to, either AL (American League) or NL (National League).
`Year`	The year of the corresponding record.
`RS`	The number of runs scored by the team in that year.
`RA`	The number of runs allowed by the team in that year.
`W`	The number of regular season wins by the team in that year.
`OBP`	The on-base percentage of the team in that year.
`SLG`	The slugging percentage of the team in that year.
`BA`	The batting average of the team in that year.
`RankSeason`	The ranking of the regular season record for the teams (1 is best) in that year.
`RankPlayoffs`	The ranking of the team in the playoffs in that year (the team winning the World Series gets a RankPlayoffs value of 1).
`NumCompetitors`	The number of teams in the playoffs in that year (ranges from 2 to 10).
`WonWorldSeries`	Whether or not the team won the World Series (1 if they won, and 0 otherwise).

a) Let us start by exploring our dataset.

i) Each row of *Baseball.csv* represents a playoff team's performance in a particular year. Through the years, different numbers of teams have been invited to the playoffs. How has the number of teams making it to the playoffs each year changed, according to this dataset?

ii) Given that a team has made it to the playoffs, it is much harder to win the World Series if there are 10 teams competing for the championship versus just two. Therefore, we have the variable **`NumCompetitors`** in our dataset. **`NumCompetitors`** contains the number of total teams making the playoffs in the year of the observation. For instance, **NumCompetitors** is 2 for the 1962 New York Yankees, but it is 8 for the 1998 Boston Red Sox. Without knowing anything else about the teams in the playoffs, can you think of a simple model that uses **NumCompetitors** to predict the probability of a team winning?

b) Let us now build logistic regression models to predict the World Series winner.

i) When we are not sure which of our variables are useful in predicting a particular outcome, it is often helpful to build bivariate models, which are models that predict the outcome using a single independent variable. Build a bivariate logistic regression model using each of the following variables as the independent variable to predict **WonWorldSeries**, and the entire dataset as the training set each time: **Year**, **RS**, **RA**, **W**, **OBP**, **SLG**, **BA**, **RankSeason**, **NumCompetitors**, and **League**. You should have created 10 logistic regression models. Describe each of the models by giving the regression equation and the accuracy of the model. For which models is the independent variable significant? In your opinion, which are the best models and why?

ii) Now, build a logistic regression model using all of the variables that you found to be significant in the bivariate models as the independent variables, and the entire dataset to train the model. Are all of the independent variables significant in this model? Why would some independent variables be significant in the bivariate model using that variable, but then not significant in a model that uses more than one independent variable? Be sure to provide numerical evidence for your claim.

iii) Using any number of the independent variables that you found to be significant in the bivariate models, find what you think is the best model, and justify why you think it is the best. How many independent variables are used in your final model?

iv) Do your findings in this problem confirm or reject the claim that the playoffs is more about luck than skill? Why?

Predicting Parole Violators

In many criminal justice systems around the world, inmates deemed not to be a threat to society are released from prison under the parole system prior to completing their sentences. They are still considered to be serving their sentences while on parole, and they can be returned to prison if they violate the terms of their parole.

Parole boards are charged with identifying which inmates are good candidates for release on parole. They seek to release inmates who will not commit additional crimes after release. In this problem, we will build and validate a model that predicts if an inmate will violate the terms of his or her parole. Such a model could be useful to a parole board when deciding to approve or deny an application for parole.

The file *Parole.csv* contains data from 2004 on parolees who served no more than 6 months in prison and whose maximum sentence for all charges did not exceed 18 months. All parolees in the dataset either successfully completed the term of their parole during 2004 or violated the terms of their parole in 2004. The variables in this dataset are described in Table 22.5.

Table 22.5: Variables in the dataset *Parole.csv*.

Variable	Description
`Male`	1 if the parolee is male, and 0 if female.
`RaceWhite`	1 if the parolee is white, and 0 otherwise.
`Age`	The parolee's age in years when he or she was released from prison.
`State`	The parolee's state, either Kentucky, Louisiana, Virginia, or Other. These three states were selected due to having a high representation in the dataset.
`TimeServed`	The number of months the parolee served in prison (limited by the inclusion criteria to not exceed 6 months).
`MaxSentence`	The maximum sentence length for all charges, in months (limited by the inclusion criteria to not exceed 18 months).
`MultipleOffenses`	1 if the parolee was incarcerated for multiple offenses, and 0 otherwise.
`Crime`	The parolee's main crime leading to incarceration, either Larceny, Drugs (representing a drug-related crime), Driving (representing a driving-related crime), or Other.
`Violator`	1 if the parolee violated their parole, and 0 if the parolee completed their parole without violation.

Using this dataset, answer the following questions.

a) How many parolees do we have data for? Of the parolees that we have data for, what percentage violated the terms of their parole?

b) Randomly split the data into a training set and a testing set, putting 70% of the data in the training set. Then, build a logistic regression model to predict the variable **`Violator`** using all of the other variables as independent variables. You should use the training dataset to build the model.

i) Describe your resulting model. Which variables are significant in your model?

ii) Consider a parolee who is male, of white race, aged 50 years at prison release, from the state of Maryland, served 3 months, had a maximum sentence of 12 months, did not commit multiple offenses, and committed a larceny. According to your model, what is the probability that this individual is a violator? (HINT: You should use the coefficients of your model and the Logistic Response Function to solve this problem.)

iii) Now compute the model's predicted probabilities for parolees in the testing set. Then create a confusion matrix for the test set using a threshold of 0.5. What is the model's false positive rate on the test set? False negative rate? Overall accuracy?

iv) Compare your accuracy on the test set to a *baseline* model that predicts every parolee in the test set is a non-violator, regardless of the values of the independent variables. Does your model improve over this simple model?

v) Consider a parole board that might use your model to predict whether parolees will be violators or not. The job of a parole board is to make sure that a prisoner is ready to be released into free society, and therefore parole boards tend to be particularly concerned about releasing prisoners who will violate their parole. Would the parole board be more concerned by false positive errors or false negative errors? How should they adjust their threshold to reflect their error preferences?

vi) Compute the AUC of the model on the test set, and interpret what the number means in this context. Considering the AUC, the accuracy compared to the baseline model, and what happens when the threshold is adjusted, do you think this model is of value to a parole board? Why or why not?

c) Our goal in this problem has been to predict the outcome of a parole decision, and we used a publicly available dataset of parole releases for predictions. It is always important to evaluate a dataset for possible sources of bias, especially when the dataset only contains a subset of the observations of interest.

The *Parole.csv* dataset contains all individuals released from parole in 2004, either due to completing their parole term or violating the terms of their parole. However, it does not contain parolees who neither violated their parole nor completed their term in 2004, causing non-violators to be underrepresented. This is called *selection bias* or *selecting on the dependent variable*, because we used our dependent variable (parole violation) to select only a subset of all relevant parolees to include in our analysis. How could we improve our dataset to best address selection bias?

Loan Repayment

In the lending industry, investors provide loans to borrowers in exchange for the promise of repayment with interest. If the borrower repays the loan, then the lender profits from the interest. However, if the borrower is unable to repay the loan, then the lender loses money. Therefore, lenders would like to minimize the risk of a borrower being unable to repay a loan.

In this exercise, we will use publicly available data from LendingClub, a website that connects borrowers and investors over the internet. The dataset is in the file *Loans.csv* (available in the Online Companion). There are 9,578 observations, each representing a 3-year loan that was funded through the LendingClub.com platform between May 2007 and February 2010. There are 14 variables in the dataset, described in Table 22.6. We will be trying to predict **`NotFullyPaid`**, using all of the other variables as independent variables.

a) Let us start by building a logistic regression model.

i) First, randomly split the dataset *Loans.csv* into a training set and a testing set. Put 70% of the data in the training set. What is the accuracy on the test set of a simple baseline model that predicts that all loans will be paid back in full (**`NotFullyPaid`** = 0) ? Our goal will be to build a model that adds value over this simple baseline method.

ii) Now, build a logistic regression model that predicts the dependent variable **`NotFullyPaid`** using all of the other variables as independent variables. Use the training set as the data for the model. Describe your resulting model. Which of the independent variables are significant in your model?

iii) Consider two loan applications, which are identical other than the fact that the borrower in Application A has a FICO credit score of 700 while the borrower in Application B has a FICO credit score of 710. Let Logit(A) be the value of the linear logit

Table 22.6: Variables in the dataset *Loans.csv*.

Variable	Description
`CreditPolicy`	1 if the customer meets the credit underwriting criteria of LendingClub.com, and 0 otherwise.
`Purpose`	The purpose of the loan (one of "Credit Card," "Debt Consolidation," "Educational," "Major Purchase," "Small Business," or "Other").
`IntRate`	The interest rate of the loan, as a proportion (a rate of 11% would be stored as 0.11). Note that borrowers judged by LendingClub to be more risky are assigned higher interest rates.
`Installment`	The monthly installments ($) owed by the borrower if the loan is funded.
`LogAnnualInc`	The natural log of the self-reported annual income of the borrower.
`Dti`	The debt-to-income ratio of the borrower (amount of debt divided by annual income).
`Fico`	The FICO credit score of the borrower.
`DaysWithCrLine`	The number of days the borrower has had a credit line.
`RevolBal`	The borrower's revolving balance (amount unpaid at the end of the credit card billing cycle).
`RevolUtil`	The borrower's revolving line utilization rate (the amount of the credit line used relative to total credit available).
`InqLast6mths`	The borrower's number of inquiries by creditors in the last 6 months.
`Delinq2yrs`	The number of times the borrower had been 30+ days past due on a payment in the past 2 years.
`PubRec`	The borrower's number of derogatory public records (bankruptcy fillings, tax liens, or judgments).
`NotFullyPaid`	1 if the loan was not paid back in full, and 0 otherwise.

function of loan A not being paid back in full, according to our logistic regression model, and define Logit(B) similarly for loan B. What is the value of Logit(A) - Logit(B)?

iv) Now predict the probability of the test set loans not being paid back in full. Store these predicted probabilities in a variable named **PredictedRisk** and add it to your test set (we will use this variable in later parts of the problem). What is the accuracy of the logistic regression model on the test set using a threshold of 0.5? How does this compare to the baseline model?

v) What is the test set AUC of the model? Given the accuracy and the AUC of the model on the test set, do you think this model could be useful to an investor to make profitable investments?

b) LendingClub assigns the interest rate to a loan based on their estimate of that loan's risk. This variable, **IntRate**, is an independent variable in our dataset. In this part, we will investigate just using the loan's interest rate as a "smart baseline" to order the loans according to risk.

i) Using the training set, build a logistic regression model that predicts the dependent variable **NotFullyPaid** using **IntRate** as the only independent variable. Is **IntRate** significant in this model? Was it significant in the first logistic regression model you built? How would you explain this difference?

ii) Use the model you just built (with only one independent variable) to make predictions for the observations in the test set. What is the highest predicted probability of a loan not being paid back in full on the test set? How many loans would we predict would not be paid back in full if we used a threshold of 0.5 to make predictions?

iii) Compute the test set AUC of the model. How does this compare to the model using all of the independent variables? In your opinion, which model is stronger? Why?

c) Let us now see how our logistic regression model can be used to identify loans that are expected to be profitable.

i) If the loan is paid back in full, then the investor makes interest on the loan. However, if the loan is not paid back, the investor loses the money invested. Therefore, the investor should seek loans that best balance this risk and reward.

To compute interest revenue, consider a \$$c$ investment in a loan that has an annual interest rate r over a period of t years. Using continuous compounding of interest, this investment pays back $c \times e^{rt}$ dollars by the end of the t years. How much does a \$10 investment with an annual interest rate of 6% pay back after 3 years, using continuous compounding of interest? (HINT: Remember to convert the percentage to a proportion before doing the math.)

ii) While the investment has this value after collecting interest, the investor had to pay c dollars for the investment. What is the profit to the investor if the investment is paid back in full? What is the profit to the investor if the investment is *not* paid back in full?

iii) Compute the profit of a \$1 investment in each loan, and save your result to a variable named **Profit**. Keep in mind that the profit computation should depend on the value of the variable **NotFullyPaid**. What is the maximum profit of a \$1 investment in any loan in the testing set?

iv) A simple investment strategy of equally investing in all the loans would yield a profit \$20.94 for a \$100 investment. But this simple investment strategy does not leverage the prediction model we built earlier in this problem. Instead, let us analyze an investment strategy in which the investor only purchases loans with a high interest rate (a rate of at least 15%) to maximize return, but amongst these loans selects the ones with the lowest predicted risk of not being paid back in full. We will model an investor who invests \$1 in each of the most promising 100 loans.

First, create a new dataset called **HighInterest** consisting of the test set loans with an interest rate of at least 15%. What is the average profit of a \$1 investment in one of these high-interest loans? What proportion of the high-interest loans were not paid back in full?

v) Next, sort the loans in the **HighInterest** dataset by the variable **PredictedRisk** that we computed earlier in the problem. Create a new dataset called **SelectedLoans** that consists of the 100 loans with the smallest values of **PredictedRisk**.

What is the profit of an investor who invested \$1 in each of these 100 loans? How many of the 100 selected loans were not paid back in full? How does this compare to the simple strategy of investing in all loans, which yielded a profit of \$20.94 for a \$100 investment?

d) One of the most important assumptions of predictive modeling often does not hold in financial situations, causing predictive models to fail. What do you think this is? As an analyst, what could you do to improve the situation?

22.3 CART and Random Forests Exercises

The exercises in this section are designed to help you better understand the methods of Classification and Regression Trees (CART) and Random Forests, and to practice building these models.

Letter Recognition

One of the earliest applications of predictive analytics was automatic recognition of letters, which is used in applications like sorting mail at post offices. In this problem, we will build a model that uses attributes of images of four letters in the Roman alphabet – A, B, P, and R – to predict which letter a particular image corresponds to.

In this problem, we have more than two classifications that are possible for each observation, like the situation in Chapter 8, when D2Hawkeye built a model to classify expected healthcare cost. Such problems are called *multi-class classification problems.*

The file *Letters.csv* (available in the Online Companion) contains 3116 observations, each of which corresponds to a certain image of one of the four letters A, B, P and R. The images came from 20 different fonts, which were then randomly distorted to produce the final images; each such distorted image is represented as a collection of pixels, each of which is "on" or "off." For each such distorted image, we have available certain attributes of the image in terms of these pixels, as well as which of the four letters the image is. These variables are described in Table 22.7.

a) To warm up, start by predicting whether or not the letter is "B." First, create a new variable called `IsB` in your dataset, which takes value "Yes" if the letter is B, and "No" if the letter is not B. Then randomly split your dataset into a training set and a testing set, putting 50% of the data in each set.

   i) Before building models, let us consider a baseline method that always predicts the most frequent outcome, which is "not B." What is the accuracy of this baseline method on the test set?

   ii) Build a CART tree to predict whether or not a letter is a B, using the training set to build your model. Remember to not use the variable `Letter` as one of the independent variables in the model, as this is related to what we are trying to predict! Select reasonable parameter values for the model, and justify your parameter choices. What is the accuracy of this CART model on the test set?

   iii) Now, build a random forest model to predict whether or not the letter is a B. Again, select reasonable parameter values for the model, and justify your parameter choices. What is the accuracy of the model on the test set?

Table 22.7: Variables in the dataset *Letters.csv*.

Variable	Description
`Letter`	The letter that the image corresponds to (A, B, P or R).
`Xbox`	The horizontal position of where the smallest box covering the letter shape begins.
`Ybox`	The vertical position of where the smallest box covering the letter shape begins.
`Width`	The width of this smallest box.
`Height`	The height of this smallest box.
`Onpix`	The total number of "on" pixels in the character image.
`Xbar`	The mean horizontal position of all of the "on" pixels.
`Ybar`	The mean vertical position of all of the "on" pixels.
`X2bar`	The mean squared horizontal position of all of the "on" pixels in the image.
`Y2bar`	The mean squared vertical position of all of the "on" pixels in the image.
`XYbar`	The mean of the product of the horizontal and vertical position of all of the "on" pixels in the image.
`X2Ybar`	The mean of the product of the squared horizontal position and the vertical position of all of the "on" pixels.
`XY2bar`	The mean of the product of the horizontal position and the squared vertical position of all of the "on" pixels.
`Xedge`	The mean number of edges (the number of times an "off" pixel is followed by an "on" pixel, or the image boundary is hit) as the image is scanned from left to right, along the whole vertical length of the image.
`XedgeYcor`	The mean of the product of the number of horizontal edges at each vertical position and the vertical position.
`Yedge`	The mean number of edges as the images is scanned from top to bottom, along the whole horizontal length of the image.
`YedgeXcor`	The mean of the product of the number of vertical edges at each horizontal position and the horizontal position.

iv) Compare the accuracy of your CART and Random Forest models. Which one performs better? For this application, do you think interpretability or accuracy is more important?

b) Let us now move on to the problem that we were originally interested in, which is to predict whether or not a letter is one of the four letters A, B, P or R. The variable in our dataset which we will be trying to predict is `Letter`.

i) In a multi-class classification problem, a simple baseline model is to predict the most frequent class of all of the options for every observation. For this problem, what does the baseline method predict, and what is the baseline accuracy on the testing set? Do you think this simple baseline method is a useful benchmark for this problem? Why or why not?

ii) Now build a classification tree to predict `Letter`, using the training set to build your model. (Remember not to use the variable `IsB` in the model, as this is related to what we are trying to predict!) Select reasonable parameter values and justify your parameter choices. What is the test set accuracy of your CART model?
(HINT: When you are computing the test set accuracy using a classification matrix, you want to add everything on the main diagonal and divide by the total number of observations in the test set.)

iii) Now, build a random forest model to predict `Letter`, using the training data – again, do not forget to remove the `IsB` variable. What is the test set accuracy of your random forest model?

iv) Compare the accuracy of your CART and Random Forest models for this problem. Which one would you recommend for this problem? Is your choice different from the model you recommended in part (a)?

State Data Revisited

In this problem, we will be revisiting the United States dataset that was used in Section 22.1 to practice building tree models with a continuous outcome. Start by downloading the data file *StateData.csv* from the Online Companion. A description of the variables in the dataset is given in Table 22.1 of Section 22.1.

a) Let us start by building a linear regression model.

i) First, build a linear regression model to predict `LifeExp` using the following seven variables as the independent variables:

Population, **Murder**, **Frost**, **Income**, **Illiteracy**, **Area**, and **HighSchoolGrad**. Use the entire dataset to build the model. What is the R^2 of the model?

ii) Now, build a linear regression model to predict **LifeExp** using the following four variables as the independent variables: **Population**, **Murder**, **Frost**, and **HighSchoolGrad**. Again, use the entire dataset to build the model. What is the R^2 of the model?

iii) Compare these two models. What are we achieving by removing independent variables? What is the equivalent procedure in a CART model?

b) Now, build a CART model to predict **LifeExp** using the following seven variables as the independent variables: **Population**, **Murder**, **Frost**, **Income**, **Illiteracy**, **Area**, and **HighSchoolGrad**. Use the validation set approach discussed in Section 21.3 to select between three reasonable parameter values. Use all of the data to build the model. Make sure that you are building a regression tree, and not a classification tree (the nodes at the end of the leaves should have values around 70).

i) Plot the tree. Which of the independent variables appear in the tree? Do you find the linear regression model or the CART model easier to interpret?

ii) Compute the predicted life expectancies for the dataset using the CART model, and calculate the R^2 of the predictions. How does this compare to the R^2 of the linear regression model?

iii) Now change the parameter value you used to prevent the tree from overfitting. Plot this tree, and compute the R^2. How does this tree compare to the linear regression model, and to the first CART model you built?

c) Now, build a random forest model to predict **LifeExp** using the following seven variables as the independent variables: **Population**, **Murder**, **Frost**, **Income**, **Illiteracy**, **Area**, and **HighSchoolGrad**. Select reasonable values for the number of trees and other parameter settings, and justify your choices. Use all of the data to build the model.

Then, compute the predicted life expectancies for the dataset using the random forest model, and calculate the R^2 of the predictions. How does this model compare to the linear regression model, and the CART models?

d) Which of the four models you built do you expect to be the better model, if out-of-sample accuracy is very important? How about if understanding the given dataset is the most important? Or if interpretability is the most important? Justify your answers.

Vandalism on Wikipedia

Wikipedia is a free online encyclopedia that anyone can edit and contribute to. It is available in many languages and is growing all the time. On the English language version of Wikipedia, there are currently 4.3 million pages and approximately 130,000 edits per day.

One of the consequences of being editable by anyone is that some people vandalize pages. This can take the form of removing content, adding promotional or inappropriate content, or changing the meaning of an article. With this many articles and edits per day, it is difficult for humans to detect all instances of vandalism and revert (undo) them. As a result, Wikipedia uses bots - computer programs that automatically revert edits that look like vandalism. In this assignment, we will attempt to develop a vandalism detector that uses analytics to distinguish between a valid edit and vandalism.

The data for this problem is based on the revision history of the page "Language," and can be found in the file *Wikipedia.csv*. Wikipedia provides a history for each page that consists of the state of the page at each revision. Rather than manually considering each revision, a script was run that checked whether edits stayed or were reverted. If a change was eventually reverted then that revision was marked as vandalism. This may have resulted in some misclassifications, but the script performs well enough for our needs.

The variables in the dataset are described in Table 22.8.

a) Start by exploring the dataset.

Table 22.8: Variables in the dataset *Wikipedia.csv*.

Variable	Description
`Vandal`	1 if this edit was vandalism, and 0 if not.
`Minor`	1 if the user marked this edit as a "minor edit," and 0 if not.
`LoggedIn`	1 if the user made this edit while using a Wikipedia account, and 0 if they did not.
`HTTP`	1 if the edit contained a web address, and 0 otherwise.
`NumWordsAdded`	The number of unique words added.
`NumWordsRemoved`	The number of unique words removed.

i) How many cases of vandalism were detected in the history of this page?

ii) What is the average number of words that were added? What is the average number of words that were removed?

iii) Which variable is the most correlated (positively or negatively) with the variable `Vandal`?

b) Now, randomly split the data into a training set and a testing set. You should put 70% of the data in the training set. What is the accuracy on the testing set of a simple baseline method that always predicts "not vandalism" for every edit?

c) Build a CART model to predict `Vandal`, using all of the other variables as independent variables. You should use the training set to build the model, and use the validation set approach discussed in Section 21.3 to select between a few different reasonable parameter values.

i) Plot the CART tree. Which variables were used in the tree? Which variables appear to be the most significant?

ii) What is the accuracy of the model on the test set?

d) Now build a random forest model to predict `Vandal`, using all of the other variables as independent variables. Again, use the training set to build the model. Select reasonable parameter values (you do not need to use validation for the random forest model). Then compute the accuracy of the model on the test set. How does it compare to the CART model?

e) It is often important to think about the business implications for a model. With this in mind, answer the following questions:

i) Do you think the model you built could be useful to Wikipedia to detect vandalism? Why or why not?

ii) If you could collect more data about the edits, what variables would you want? Why?

iii) The data used in this problem was collected from the page about Language. Do you think this model would easily extend to other pages? Why or why not?

22.4 Clustering Exercises

The exercises in this section are designed to help you better understand the methods of Hierarchical Clustering and K-Means Clustering, and to practice using these algorithms.

Document Clustering

Document clustering, or text clustering, is a very popular application of clustering algorithms. A web search engine, like Google, often returns thousands of results for a simple query. For example, if you type the search term "jaguar" into Google, over 400 million results are returned. This makes it very difficult to browse or find relevant information, especially if the search term has multiple meanings, like this one. If we search for "jaguar," we might be looking for information about the animal, the car, or the Jacksonville Jaguars football team.

Clustering methods can be used to automatically group search results into categories, making it easier to find relevant results. This method is used in the search engines PolyMeta and Helioid, as well as on FirstGov.gov, the official Web portal for the U.S. government. The two most common clustering algorithms used for document clustering are Hierarchical and K-means.

In this exercise, we will be clustering articles published on Daily Kos, an American political blog that publishes news and opinion articles written from a progressive point of view. The file *DailyKos.csv* can be found in the Online Companion for this book, and contains data on 3,430 news articles or blogs that have been posted on Daily Kos. These articles were posted in 2004, leading up to the United States Presidential Election. The leading candidates were incumbent President George W. Bush (Republican candidate) and Senator John Kerry (Democratic candidate). Foreign policy was a dominant topic of the election, specifically, the 2003 invasion of Iraq.

There are 1,545 variables in this dataset – each of the variables in the dataset is a word that has appeared in at least 50 different articles (1,545 words in total). For each document, or observation, the variable values are the number of times that word appeared in the document. (If you are familiar with text analytics, this approach is called *bag of words*.)

a) Start by building a Hierarchical Clustering model to cluster documents using all of the variables in the dataset. Indicate which distance metrics you used for distances between the observations and distances between the clusters.

i) Building a hierarchical clustering model will probably take a significant amount of time on this dataset. Why?

ii) Plot the dendrogram of your hierarchical clustering model. Using the dendrogram and thinking about this particular application, which number of clusters would you recommend? Keep in mind that document clustering would most likely be used by Daily Kos to show readers categories to choose from when trying to decide which articles to read.

iii) Assign each observation to a cluster, using the number of clusters you recommended in the previous subproblem. How many observations are in each cluster?

iv) In the previous chapter, we analyzed the centroids of the clusters by looking at the average values of all of the variables in each cluster. We do not want to do that here though, since we have over 1,000 variables! Instead, split your dataset into a dataset for each cluster, using your cluster assignments.

Then, find the six most frequent words in each cluster. If you are using R, and your dataset for the first cluster is called `HierCluster1`, this can be done with the command: `tail(sort(colMeans(HierCluster1)))`.

Describe each cluster. Is there a cluster that is mostly about the Iraq war? Is there a cluster that is mostly about the democratic party? It might be helpful to know that in 2004, Howard Dean was one of the candidates for the Democratic nomination for the President of the United States, John Kerry was the candidate who won the democratic nomination, and John Edwards was the running mate of John Kerry (the Democratic Vice President nominee).

b) Now cluster the documents using K-means clustering. Choose the same number of clusters that you recommended for Hierarchical clustering.

i) How many observations are in each cluster? Is your answer the same as it was with Hierarchical clustering? Why or why not?

ii) Just like you did for Hierarchical clustering, split your dataset into a dataset for each K-means cluster, and analyze the most frequent words in each cluster. Are the clusters similar to the Hierarchical clusters? Can you find a similar Hierarchical cluster for each K-means cluster? Keep in mind that the order of the clusters (which cluster is labeled as 1, which cluster is labeled as 2, etc.) is meaningless – for example, Hierarchical cluster 3 might be very similar to K-means cluster 1.

c) **Extra Credit:** Try repeating this problem with a different number of clusters than you originally selected. How do your results compare between the two selections? Do you prefer one number of clusters over the other? Are you able to make different observations about the data when the number of clusters changes?

Market Segmentation for Hubway

Market segmentation is a strategy that divides a broad target market of customers into smaller, more similar groups, and then designs a marketing strategy specifically for each group. Clustering is a common technique for market segmentation since it automatically finds similar groups within a given dataset.

In this problem, we will see how clustering can be used to find similar groups of registered users of the Boston, Massachusetts bike-sharing program Hubway. Users of Hubway can check out a bicycle from one of 140 stations located throughout the Boston area, and return the bike to a different station. Users pay a membership fee, which includes unlimited trips up to 30 minutes in duration at no additional cost. Trips longer than 30 minutes cost additional "overtime" fees.

The dataset *HubwayTrips.csv* contains data from trips taken by registered users of Hubway from June 2012 through September 2012. The dataset contains nine variables, described in Table 22.9. Our goal in this problem will be to cluster trips to ultimately find interesting insights about the types of trips customers of Hubway tend to take.

Table 22.9: Variables in the dataset *HubwayTrips.csv*.

Variable	Description
`Duration`	The time of the trip in seconds.
`Morning`	Whether or not the trip started in the morning, between the hours of 6am and 12pm (1 if yes, and 0 if no).
`Afternoon`	Whether or not the trip started in the afternoon, between the hours of 12pm and 6pm (1 if yes, and 0 if no).
`Evening`	Whether or not the trip started in the evening, between the hours of 6pm and 12am (1 if yes, and 0 if no).
`Night`	Whether or not the trip started during the night, between the hours of 12am and 6am (1 if yes, and 0 if no).
`Weekday`	Whether or not the trip started on Monday, Tuesday, Wednesday, Thursday, or Friday (1 if yes, and 0 if no).
`Weekend`	Whether or not the trip started on Saturday or Sunday (1 if yes, and 0 if no).
`Male`	Whether or not the user was male (1 if yes, and 0 if no).
`Age`	The age of the user, in years.

a) When clustering data, it is often important to normalize the variables so that they are all on the same scale.

i) Why is it important to normalize the data? What would you expect to happen when clustering the Hubway dataset if we did not normalize the variables?

ii) Normalize all of the variables in the *HubwayTrips.csv* dataset (for each variable, you should subtract the mean and divide by the standard deviation). Each of the variables in the normalized dataset should have mean 0 and standard deviation 1. Turn in output from the software you are using that shows the mean and standard deviation of each of the variables in your normalized dataset.

b) Run the K-Means clustering algorithm on your normalized dataset with 10 clusters.

i) How many trips are in each of the clusters?

ii) Compare the clusters by looking at the mean values of the variables (the cluster centroids). Note that you may want to look at the unnormalized data, but you could also look at the normalized data (whichever is more interpretable to you). How would you describe each cluster to the marketing department at Hubway?

iii) Do you think some clusters are more interesting than others? Which ones?

iv) Looking at these results, do you think it would be helpful to have *more* clusters or *fewer* clusters than 10? Why?

c) Run the K-Means clustering algorithm on your normalized dataset again with a different number of clusters. You should change the number of clusters to correspond to your recommendation in the last subproblem.

i) How many trips are in each of the clusters?

ii) Like you did in the previous problem, compare the clusters by looking at the mean values of the variables (the cluster centroids). How would you describe each cluster to the marketing department at Hubway?

iii) How do these results compare to the 10 cluster results? Do you think you got better insights by changing the number of clusters?

Clustering Stock Returns

When building portfolios of stocks, investors seek to obtain good returns while limiting the variability in those returns over time. This can be achieved by selecting stocks that show different patterns of returns. In this problem, we will use clustering to identify clusters of stocks that have similar returns over time; an investor might select a diverse portfolio by selecting stocks from different clusters.

For this problem, we will use the dataset *NasdaqReturns.csv*, which contains monthly stock returns from the NASDAQ stock exchange during 2000-2009. The companies selected in this dataset are limited to those that were listed on the stock exchange for this entire time period and whose stock price never fell below $1. The NASDAQ is the second-largest stock exchange in the world, and it lists many technology companies. The variables in the dataset are described in Table 22.10.

a) Let us start by exploring the dataset.

i) How many companies are in this dataset? How many companies are there in each of the industries?

ii) In the aftermath of the dot-com bubble bursting in the early 2000s, the NASDAQ was quite tumultuous. In December 2000,

Table 22.10: Variables in the dataset *NasdaqReturns.csv*.

Variable	Description
`StockSymbol`	The symbol identifying the company of the stock.
`Industry`	The industry the stock is classified under.
`SubIndustry`	The sub-industry the stock is classified under.
`Ret2000.01 - Ret2009.12`	The return for the stock during the variable's indicated month. The variable names have the format "RetYYYY.MM," where YYYY is the year and MM is the month. For instance, variable Ret2005.02 refers to February 2005. The value stored is a proportional change in stock value during that month. For instance, a value of 0.05 means the stock increased in value 5% during the month, while a value of -0.02 means the stock decreased in value 2% during the month. There are 120 of these variables, for the 120 months in our dataset.

how many stocks in this dataset saw their value *increase* by 10% or more? *Decrease* by 10% or more?

iii) Entering the Great Recession, most stocks lost significant value, but some sectors were hit harder than others. In October 2008, which industries had the worst average return across all stocks in that industry?

b) Let us now cluster the stocks according to the monthly returns. For the remainder of this problem, make sure that you are just clustering the observations based on the variables `Ret2000.01 - Ret2009.12` (`StockSymbol`, `Industry`, and `SubIndustry` should not be used to cluster the observations). You can do this by creating a new dataset only containing the variables `Ret2000.01 - Ret2009.12`, or you can just give these variables to the clustering algorithm.

i) In this analysis, we will not normalize our data prior to clustering. Why is this a valid approach for this problem and dataset?

ii) Cluster the data using Hierarchical clustering. Clearly indicate which distance metrics you used for point distances and cluster distances. Plot the resulting dendrogram. What do you think are reasonable choices for the number of clusters to select, based on the dendrogram? How about for the application? Select a specific number of clusters to use for the rest of the problem, and justify your choice.

iii) Extract cluster assignments from your hierarchical clustering model, using the number of clusters you selected in the previous problem. Describe each cluster, using the number of observations in the cluster, the industry of the companies in the cluster, and the subindustry of the companies in the cluster. (Since we never changed the order of the observations, you can use the cluster assignments together with the original dataset to extract information about the industry and subindustry.)

iv) For some months, we expect there to be significant differences between the returns of stocks in different clusters. For February 2000, do some clusters have negative average returns while other clusters have positive average returns? How about for March 2000?

v) Now run the K-means clustering algorithm on this data (when clustering, only use the variables `Ret2000.01 - Ret2009.12`). You should select the same number of clusters that you used for Hierarchical clustering. Extract cluster assignments from your K-means clustering model, and compare them to the Hierarchical cluster assignments. Are the clusters similar or different?

c) In the introduction to this problem, we discussed the value of a diverse portfolio and how we might achieve this objective by selecting stocks from different clusters. Propose a diverse portfolio of stocks using the results of your clusters. When selecting your stocks, how do you think you could best use the results of the Hierarchical clustering algorithm *and* the K-means clustering algorithm?

22.5 Visualization Exercises

The exercises in this section are designed to help you better understand the power of data visualization, and to practice creating clear and useful visualizations. Unlike the other exercise sections, this one depends on use of the software R, in order to teach new visualizations and how to implement them. Before starting these exercises, please make sure you have reviewed Section 21.5 and the Visualization section of the Analytics Edge R Manual, available in the Online Companion. You will also need to install and load the R package `ggplot2` for all of the exercises in this section.

Visualizing Attributes of Parole Violators

In this problem, we will use the dataset *Parole.csv* that we used in Section 22.2 to visualize attributes of parole violators (the file can be found in the Online Companion, and a description of the variables is given in the "Predicting Parole Violators" problem of Section 22.2). We will create visualizations using histograms, which can be used as an alternative to heat maps to visualize information in three dimensions.

Read the dataset *Parole.csv* into R, and call the resulting data frame `Parole`.

a) We need to specify a dataset, aesthetic, and geometry when creating visualizations in `ggplot`. To create a histogram, the geometry will be `geom_histogram`.

Create a histogram to learn about the distribution of the age of parolees, by typing the following command in your R console:

```
> ggplot(data = Parole, aes(x = Age)) + geom_histogram()
```

By default, `geom_histogram` divides the data into 30 bins. Change the width of the bins to 5 years by adding the argument `binwidth = 5` to `geom_histogram` and running the above command again. Note that by default, histograms create bins where the left endpoint is included in the bin, but the right endpoint is not. So the first bin in this histogram represents parolees who are between 15 and 19 years old.

The last bin in this histogram represents parolees who are between 65 and 69 years old.

Please turn in all visualizations you create for this problem, as well as answering the questions.

i) Looking at the histogram you just generated, what is the age bracket with the most parolees? The least?

ii) Now redo the histogram, adding the argument `color="blue"` to `geom_histogram`. What does this argument do?

b) Now let us see how the age distribution of male parolees compares to the age distribution of female parolees. To create separate histograms for male and female parolees, type the following command in your R console:

```
> ggplot(data = Parole, aes(x = Age)) +
geom_histogram(binwidth = 5) + facet_grid(Male ~ .)
```

The histogram for female parolees is shown on the top of the resulting plot, and the histogram for male parolees is shown on the bottom.

i) Discuss how these two histograms differ, and any insights you gained about the data by creating this plot.

ii) Now change the `facet_grid` argument to be `facet_grid(. ~ Male)` instead of `facet_grid(Male ~ .)`. What does this do?

iii) An alternative choice to creating separate histograms is to simply color the different groups differently. To color the data points by group, we need to tell `ggplot` that a property of the data (male or not male) should be translated to an aesthetic property of the histogram. We can do this by setting the `fill` parameter within the aesthetic to `Male`. Run the following command in your R console to produce a histogram where data points are colored according to the variable `Male`:

```
> ggplot(data = Parole, aes(x = Age, fill = Male)) +
geom_histogram(binwidth = 5, position="identity",
alpha=0.5)
```

The new arguments to `geom_histogram` prevent the bars from being stacked, and make the bars semi-transparent. Which of the histograms (faceting or overlaying) do you think better visualizes this data? Why?

c) Now let us explore another aspect of the data: the amount of time served by parolees. Create a basic histogram like the one we created in part (a), but this time with **TimeServed** on the x-axis. Set the **binwidth** to one month.

i) What is the most common length of time served, according to this histogram?

ii) Change the **binwidth** to 0.1 months. Now what is the most common length of time served, according to the histogram? What does this tell you about interpreting visualizations?

iii) Now, suppose we suspect that it is unlikely that each type of crime has the same distribution of time served. To visualize this, change the **binwidth** back to 1 month, and use **facet_grid** to create a separate histogram of **TimeServed** for each value of the variable **Crime**. What does this histogram show you in terms of the amount of time served for different crime types?

iv) Now, instead of faceting the histograms, overlay them. Remember to set the **position** and **alpha** parameters so that the histograms are not stacked. Also, make sure to indicate that the **fill** aesthetic should be **Crime**. Which of the histograms (faceting or overlaying) do you think better visualizes this data? Why?

Visualizing Network Data

With the popularity of social networking sites like Facebook, Twitter, and LinkedIn, many companies and researchers are now very interested in understanding how information can be determined by looking at a social network. The connections between different entities are often best represented with a graph, which is a visualization comprised of vertices (also often called "nodes") and edges connecting those nodes. In this exercise, we will see how to visualize networks using the **igraph** package in R.

We will use anonymized data from Facebook; this data comes from the SNAP library, a website that collects datasets on large social and information networks. In our visualizations, the vertices in our network will represent Facebook users and the edges will represent these users being Facebook friends with each other. This information is contained in the files *Users.csv* and *Edges.csv*, available in the Online Companion. Read both of these files into R, and call the resulting data frames **Users** and **Edges**.

Edges contains variables **V1** and **V2**, which label the endpoints of edges in our network. Each row represents a pair of users in our graph who are Facebook friends. From this row, we will know that these two users are friends with each other.

`Users` contains information about the Facebook users, or the vertices in our network. The dataset contains the four variables described in Table 22.11.

Please turn in all visualizations you create for this problem, as well as answering the following questions.

a) Let us start by understanding the data we have.

i) How many Facebook users are there in our dataset?

ii) What is the average number of friends per user in our dataset? (HINT: Use the number of edges to answer this question.)

iii) Out of the students who listed a school, what is the most common locale?

iv) Is it possible that either school A or B is an all-girls or all-boys school?

b) Install and load the **`igraph`** package in R by using the **`install.packages`** and **`library`** functions.

Now create and plot a graph representing the users and edges with the following commands:

```
> g = graph.data.frame(Edges, FALSE, Users)
> plot(g, vertex.size = 5, vertex.label = NA)
```

Table 22.11: Variables in the dataset *Users.csv*.

Variable	**Description**
`ID`	A unique identifier for this user; this is the value that appears in `V1` or `V2` of `Edges`.
`Gender`	An identifier for the gender of a user (either A or B). Because the data is anonymized, we do not know which value refers to males and which value refers to females.
`School`	An identifier for the school the user attended (either A or AB). Note that users with value "AB" attended school A as well as another school B. Because the data is anonymized, we do not know which schools are represented by A and B.
`Locale`	An identifier for the locale of the user (either A or B). Because the data is anonymized, we do not know what locales are represented by A and B.

The **graph.data.frame** function creates a graph where the first argument gives the edges, the second argument indicates whether or not the graph is directed (in a directed graph the edges only go one way, but in our graph, friendships are undirected, meaning that if A is friends with B, then B is also friends with A), and the third argument is the properties of the vertices. The **plot** command just plots the graph **g**, but makes the vertices a little smaller and removes the vertex labels.

i) In this graph, there are a number of groups of nodes where all the nodes in each group are connected in some way, but the groups are disjoint from one another, forming "islands" in the graph. Such groups are called "connected components." How many connected components with at least 2 nodes are there in the graph?

ii) How many users are there with no friends in the network?

iii) In this graph, the "degree" of a vertex is that user's number of friends. We have already seen that some nodes in our graph have degree 0 (these are the nodes with no friends), while others have a much higher degree. Type **degree(g)** in your R console to compute the degree of all the nodes in your graph g. How many users are friends with 10 or more other Facebook users in this network?

c) Let us now change the color of our vertices according to some of the attributes of the users. By giving the **Users** data frame to the **graph.data.frame** function, the variables **Gender**, **School** and **Locale** from our **Users** data frame are stored as **V(g)$Gender**, **V(g)$School**, and **V(g)$Locale**. We will use these attributes to change the color attribute of our vertices, which is stored as **V(g)$color**. Run the following commands in your R console to change the color to "red" for the vertices with **Gender** equal to "A," and to "gray" for vertices with **Gender** equal to "B":

```
> V(g)$color[V(g)$Gender == "A"] = "red"
> V(g)$color[V(g)$Gender == "B"] = "gray"
```

Then plot the graph again with the **plot** command you used before.

i) Describe the resulting graph. Do the connections between users seem to be related by gender?

ii) Now, color the vertices based on the school that each user in the network attended, and re-plot the graph. Are the two users who attended both schools A and B Facebook friends with each other?

iii) Now, color the vertices based on the locale of the users, and replot the graph. Do the connections between users seem to be related by locale?

Election Forecasting

In this exercise, we will plot the polling predictions and results of the 2012 United States Presidential Election on a map of the United States. The dataset we will use is *Polling.csv* (available in the Online Companion). Read the dataset into R, and call the resulting data frame `Polling`. This dataset has 50 observations (one for each state) and the six variables described in Table 22.12.

Table 22.12: Variables in the dataset *Polling.csv*.

Variable	Description
`State`	The name of the state.
`Rasmussen`	The percentage of voters polled by the polling firm Rasmussen that planned to vote Republican, minus the percentage of voters polled that planned to vote Democratic. If a poll was not conducted in a state, the value is NA.
`SurveyUSA`	The percentage of voters polled by the polling firm SurveyUSA that planned to vote Republican minus the percentage of voters polled that planned to vote Democratic. If a poll was not conducted in a state, the value is NA.
`DiffCount`	The number of polls that predicted a Republican winner in the state minus the number of polls that predicted a Democratic winner in the state. If no polls were conducted in a state, the value is NA.
`PropR`	The number of polls that predicted a Republican winner in the state divided by the total number of polls in the state. If no polls were conducted in a state, the value is NA.
`Republican`	1 if the Republican candidate won in the state, and 0 if the Democratic candidate won in the state.

Note that if you built a model to predict the results of the election, you could also plot your own predictions on the map!

Before starting this problem, make sure you have installed and loaded the **ggplot2**, **maps**, and **ggmap** packages in R.

a) First, go through the following steps to load the states map, merge the data frames, and plot the map (this process is described in more detail in the "Analytics Edge R Manual," available in the Online Companion):

- Load the US map and save it to the variable **statesMap**, using the **map_data** function.
- Merge **statesMap** with **Polling**, matching the observations by the state names, and call the resulting data frame **electionMap**. We need to make sure the observations are in the correct order for plotting, so after creating the data frame **electionMap**, run the following command in your R console:

```
> electionMap = electionMap[order(electionMap$order),]
```

- Plot the map of the United States using the **ggplot** function and the **geom_polygon** geometry, filling each state according to the variable **DiffCount**. If a state has an "NA" value in **DiffCount**, the color of the state will be gray.

Lighter states on this map correspond to ones for which more of the polls predicted a Republican winner, and darker states on this map correspond to ones for which more of the polls predicted a Democratic winner. Which states stick out as ones for which the polls are fairly consistent? Are the polls fairly consistent for most of the states? To answer these questions, it might help to change the colors selected as the two extremes, for example, changing them to blue and red (which happen to be the colors for the Democratic and Republican parties, and will make the states in the middle more pink). You can do so by adding to your plot **scale_fill_gradient(low = "blue", high = "red")**. Play around with the colors to find a scale that helps you better visualize the plot.

b) Now, generate two more plots, the first one filling the color of the states according to the **SurveyUSA** variable, and the second filling the color of the states according to the **Rasmussen** variable. These plots are a bit harder to visualize because there is a lot of missing data, but they have some notable differences.

i) Compare and contrast these plots with each other, and with the **DiffCount** plot from part (a).

ii) In the 2012 election, the state of Florida ended up being a very close race. It was ultimately won by the Democratic party. Do any of the three plots show a confident prediction for this state? If so, was it a correct prediction?

c) Now generate a plot that fills the states according to the actual outcome, given as the variable **Republican**. How do the different polling predictions (**DiffCount**, **Rasmussen**, and **SurveyUSA**) perform in the states you noticed they were confident about? If you were to build a predictive model using this data, is there one polling variable in particular that you would use to predict the outcome?

22.6 Linear Optimization Exercises

The exercises in this section are designed to help you better understand linear optimization, and to practice creating and solving linear optimization problems.

Investment Management Under Taxation

Billions of shares of stock, or fractions of ownership in a business, are traded on the stock market every day. Over half of all adults in the United States own stocks and 1.2 billion people worldwide invest in the stock market. Many people invest in stocks to increase their wealth and to increase their earnings beyond their salary. If the business that you own stock in does well, then your stock value will increase and you will make money.

An individual who owns stock can sell their shares, or a fraction of their shares, to get cash that can be used for a down payment on a home, to buy a new car, or for any other purchase. However, when you sell stock, you have to pay both a transaction fee and tax on the money you gain. If you own many different stocks, you have to decide which stocks and how much to sell to make sure you have enough cash for your purchase. In this problem, we will use linear optimization to decide which shares of stock and how many you need to sell in order to have enough cash to make your purchase, and to maintain a strong portfolio of stocks.

Suppose that, last year, you purchased 150 shares of eight different stocks, for a total of 1,200 shares. Table 22.13 lists the stocks that you purchased, the price you purchased them for last year, the current price, and the price estimate for next year.

If you sell any shares, you have to pay a transaction cost of 1% of the amount transacted. In addition, you must pay a capital-gains tax at the rate of 30% on any capital gains at the time of the sale. For example, suppose that you sell 100 shares of a stock today at \$50 per share, which you originally purchased for \$30 per share. You would receive \$5,000. However, you would have to pay capital-gains taxes of 0.30 × (\$5,000 - \$3,000) = \$600, and you would have to

Table 22.13: Stock information for the "Investment Management Under Taxation" problem.

Stock	**Price Purchased**	**Current Price**	**Price Estimate Next Year**
Yahoo!	\$15.68	\$31.80	\$29.50
General Electric	\$22.10	\$24.28	\$26.31
Microsoft	\$30.39	\$32.50	\$34.55
Bank of America	\$8.93	\$14.16	\$15.23
JPMorgan Chase	\$40.55	\$50.99	\$62.43
Cisco Systems, Inc.	\$18.58	\$24.17	\$26.68
Intel	\$22.54	\$23.67	\$23.85
Pfizer	\$24.84	\$28.77	\$31.66

pay \$50 in transaction costs (1% of \$5,000). Therefore, by selling 100 shares of this stock, you would have a net cash flow of \$5,000 - \$600 - \$50 = \$4,350.

Note that for this problem, none of the stocks decreased in value since the time of purchase, so we do not have to deal with capital losses.

a) You would like to sell enough shares of stock today to generate \$10,000 to use as part of a down payment on a new home. You need to decide how many shares of which stocks to sell in order to generate \$10,000, after taxes and transaction costs, while maximizing the estimated value of your stock portfolio next year. We will formulate this problem as a linear optimization problem.

i) Describe the decision variables for this problem. How many are there?

ii) We will assume for this problem that you can not sell more shares of stock than you own, and you can not buy additional shares. How should you constrain the values of the decision variables to account for this?

iii) Your objective is to maximize the estimated value of your stock portfolio next year. To do this, you should sum the estimated value of each stock next year. Suppose you sell x shares of your stock in Microsoft. What is the estimated value of your Microsoft stock next year?

iv) Write out the objective function of this problem in terms of your decision variables.

v) In addition to the upper and lower bounds on your decision variables, you need to add one constraint to your model to make sure you get $10,000 in cash from selling your stocks, after taxes and transaction costs. Write down this constraint in terms of your decision variables.

b) Set-up and solve this problem in the optimization software you are using. Make sure to maximize your objective, include a constraint for the amount of cash you generate, and upper and lower bounds for the values of your decision variables.

i) What is the optimal solution? Give the values of the decision variables and the objective function value.

ii) As an investor who is seeking to have a diverse portfolio, are you happy with this solution? Why or why not?

c) Suppose you would like to keep at least 75 shares of each of your eight stocks. Adjust the formulation so that you sell no more than 75 shares of each stock, and solve the problem again.

i) What is the new optimal solution? Give the values of the decision variables and the objective function value.

ii) What type of investor might prefer this solution over the previous one? What type of investor might prefer the previous solution over this one?

Gasoline Blending

One of the earliest and most successful applications of linear optimization was in the oil industry in the 1950s. According to Bill Drew, the former manager of research for Exxon Mobil, the company used linear optimization to "schedule our tanker fleets, design port facilities, blend gasoline, create financial models, you name it." In this problem, we will use optimization to blend gasoline. (While the application of this problem is real, the data that we will be using here has been created for this problem.)

Gasoline blending occurs in oil refineries, where crude oil is processed and refined into more useful products, such as gasoline and diesel fuel. We will consider three products: super gasoline, regular gasoline, and diesel fuel. These can be made by mixing three different types of crude oil: crude 1, crude 2, and crude 3. Each product is distinguished by its octane rating, which measures the quality of the fuel, and its iron content, which is a contaminant in the gas. The crude oils each have an octane rating and iron content as well. Table 22.14 shows the required octane ratings and iron contents for each of the products, as well as the known octane ratings and iron contents of each of the crude oils.

The gasoline produced must meet these standards for octane ratings and iron content. The octane rating and iron content of a product is the weighted average of the octane rating and iron content of the crude oils used to produce it. For example, if we produce super gasoline using 20 barrels of Crude 1, 5 barrels of Crude 2, and 10 barrels of Crude 3, the Octane Rating of the super gasoline would be:

$$\frac{(20 \times 12) + (5 \times 6) + (10 \times 8)}{35} = 10.$$

The numerator is the number of barrels of Crude 1 used times the octane rating of Crude 1, plus the number of barrels of Crude 2 used times the octane rating of Crude 2, plus the number of barrels of Crude 3 used times the octane rating of Crude 3. The denominator is the total number of barrels used. Similarly, the iron content of the super gasoline would be:

$$\frac{(20 \times 0.5) + (5 \times 2.0) + (10 \times 3.0)}{35} = 1.43.$$

The objective of the oil company is to *maximize profit*. In this case, profit is the total revenue from selling gasoline and fuel, minus the total cost of the crude oils. The revenue from one barrel of super gasoline is $70, the revenue from one barrel of regular gasoline is $60, and the revenue from one barrel of diesel fuel is $50. The cost of one barrel of Crude 1 is $45, the cost of one barrel of Crude 2 is $35, and the cost of one barrel of Crude 3 is $25.

Lastly, the company can only buy 5,000 barrels of each type of crude oil, and can process no more than 14,000 barrels total of crude oil. Assume that

Table 22.14: Octane Ratings and Iron Content for the Gasoline Blending problem.

Product or Oil	**Octane Rating**	**Iron Content**
Super Gasoline	at least 10	no more than 1
Regular Gasoline	at least 8	no more than 2
Diesel Fuel	at least 6	no more than 1
Crude 1	12	0.5
Crude 2	6	2.0
Crude 3	8	3.0

one barrel of crude oil makes exactly one barrel of gasoline or fuel (nothing is lost in the conversion).

a) Formulate this problem as a linear optimization problem.

  i) What are the decision variables? (HINT: There are 9 of them.)

  ii) What is the objective function?

  iii) What are the constraints?

b) Solve this problem in the optimization software you are using, and describe the optimal solution. What are the values of the decision variables? What is the optimal objective function value? (HINT: When trying to solve this problem, your solver might complain that it is nonlinear. Be careful how you construct the constraints.)

c) Suppose that the company is unhappy with this solution, because they are exceeding the customer demand for regular gasoline. They estimate that the customer demand for super gasoline is 3,000 barrels, the customer demand for regular gasoline is 2,000 barrels, and the customer demand for diesel fuel is 1,000 barrels. They do not want to produce more than the customer demand, since they will lose revenue. Add constraints to your model to make sure that the solution produces no more than the customer demand for each of the products, and re-solve your model.

  i) What is the optimal solution now? How does it compare to the previous optimal solution? Consider the objective value and the decision variable values.

  ii) What other considerations might the company want to include in the model to improve the solution?

d) Suppose that the shadow prices for each of the demand constraints are as follows: 29 for the super gasoline demand constraint, 27 for the regular gasoline demand constraint, and 9 for the diesel fuel demand constraint. The super gasoline shadow price holds to an allowable increase of 1250, the regular gasoline shadow price holds to an allowable increase of 2,500, and the diesel fuel shadow price holds to an allowable increase of 1,250. The "allowable increase" is the amount that you can increase the right-hand side and still use this shadow price. For a larger increase, the shadow price will change, and you have to resolve the model to get the new shadow price.

  Please answer the following questions without re-solving the optimization model.

  i) What does a shadow price of 29 for the super gasoline demand constraint mean?

ii) According to the shadow prices, which type of gasoline should the company advertise to increase demand? Assume that advertising costs \$2 per unit increase in demand regardless of the type of gasoline being advertised.

iii) How much additional profit would the company gain if the super gasoline demand increased by 500?

iv) How much additional profit would the company gain if the super gasoline demand increased by 1,500?

Radiation Therapy

Cancer is the second leading cause of death in the United States, with an estimated 570,000 deaths in 2013. Over 1.6 million new cases of cancer will be diagnosed in the United States alone in 2013. About half of these patients will be treated with radiation therapy, which uses beams of high energy photons to kill cancerous cells.

In this problem, we will optimize treatment decisions for intensity-modulated radiation therapy (IMRT), which was invented in the early 1980s. Since radiation must pass through healthy tissue to reach the tumor, radiation therapy damages both healthy and cancerous tissue. IMRT was invented so that the radiation could "fit" the tumor more closely and reduce the dose to healthy tissue.

This is done by making the intensity profile of each beam non-uniform. Figure 22.1 shows a simple example of how traditional radiation therapy works. There are three beams, which are each aimed at the target, or the cancerous tumor. Unfortunately, the target is surrounded by healthy tissue and some critical structures (these could be a kidney, liver, etc.). So while the positioning of the beams gives a high dose of radiation to the target, it also gives a high dose of radiation to the critical structures.

Figure 22.2 shows how the treatment can be improved with IMRT. Each beam is divided into beamlets, so the intensity of each beamlet can be determined independently. The beams are in the same position, but by altering the intensity of the beamlets, we are able to give a high dose of radiation to the target, while giving a low dose of radiation to the critical structures.

So the fundamental problem is deciding how the beamlet intensities should be selected to deliver a high dose of radiation to the tumor, while minimizing damage to healthy tissue. Oncologists solve this problem by first taking a CT scan of the patient, and dividing the area with the tumor into a grid of *voxels*. In this problem, we will be looking at a patient case with 9 voxels and 6 beamlets. (In practice, there are typically over 100,000 voxels and hundreds of beamlets.) This is shown in Figure 22.3. Beam 1 is divided into three beamlets, which all come in from the right and each give a dose to three voxels. For example, beamlet 1 hits voxel 3, then voxel 2, and then voxel 1. Beam 2 is also divided into three beamlets, which each come in from the top. The voxels are shaded

Figure 22.1: An example treatment plan using traditional radiation therapy.

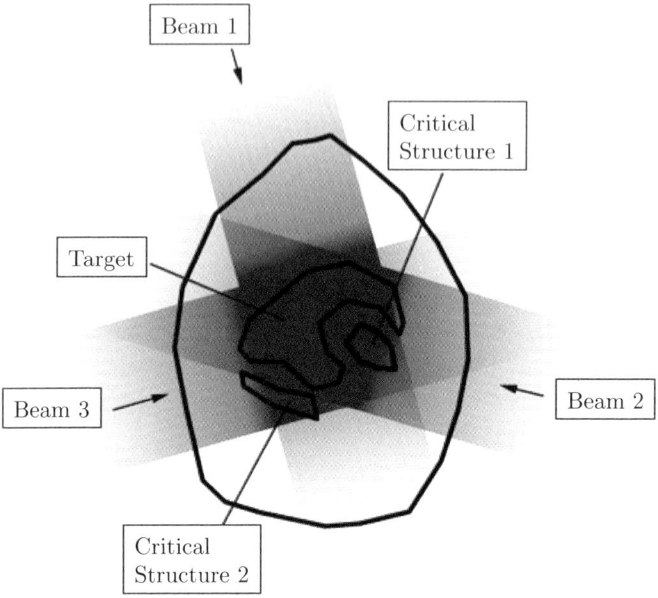

according to what type of tissue they are. The white voxels (voxel 2, voxel 6, voxel 7, and voxel 8) are tumor voxels, the dark blue voxel (voxel 5) is a spinal cord voxel, and the light blue voxels (voxel 1, voxel 3, voxel 4, and voxel 9) are other healthy tissue voxels.

When each beamlet is turned on at unit intensity (beamlet intensity = 1), it gives a different radiation dose to each voxel. This is due to the amount of tissue the beamlet has to go through to reach the voxel, as well as the type of tissue. Figure 22.4 shows the radiation doses to each voxel from the beamlets in Beam 1, and Figure 22.5 shows the radiation doses to each voxel from the beamlets in Beam 2. So if Beamlet 1 is turned on with intensity = 1, it will give a dose of 2 to Voxel 3, 2 to Voxel 2, and 1 to Voxel 1. If it is instead turned on with intensity = 2, it will give a dose of 4 to Voxel 3, 4 to Voxel 2, and 2 to Voxel 1 (the doses are doubled).

The problem we are trying to solve here is to determine what the beamlet intensities should be. Our objective is to minimize the total dose to all healthy tissue (the spinal cord plus other healthy tissue). We also need to make sure that the tumor voxels each get a total dose of at least 7 and the spinal cord voxel gets a total dose of at most 5. Lastly, the intensities should be constrained to be non-negative.

Figure 22.2: An example treatment plan using intensity-modulated radiation therapy (IMRT).

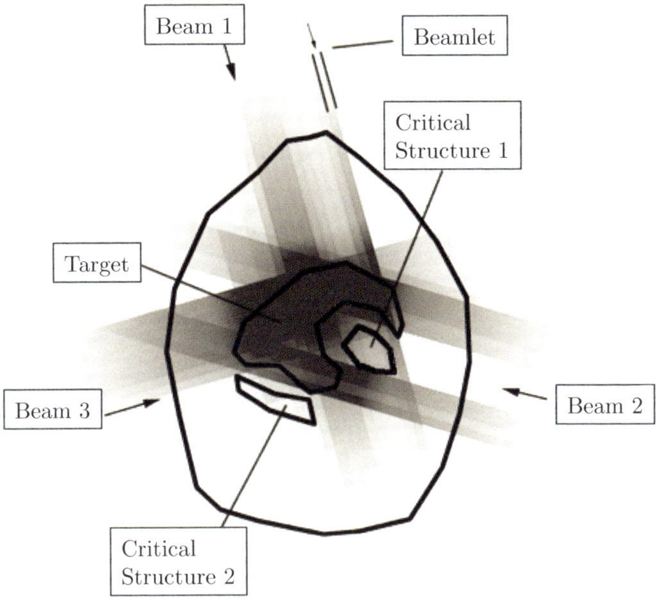

Figure 22.3: An example patient case with nine voxels and two beams. The tumor voxels are shown in white, the spinal cord voxel is shown in dark blue, and other healthy tissue voxels are shown in light blue.

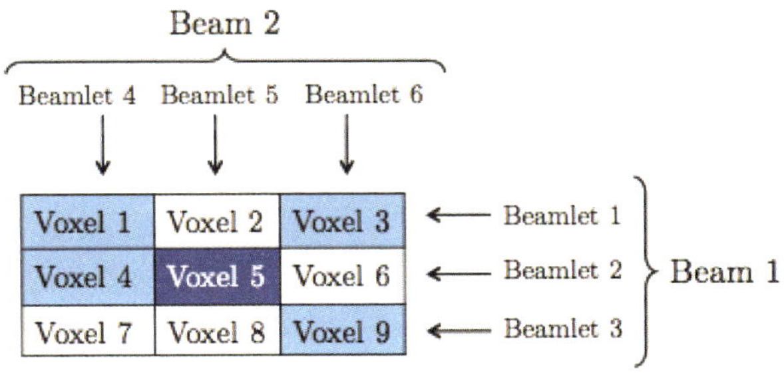

a) Formulate this problem as a linear optimization problem. Be sure to clearly indicate what your decision variables, objective, and constraints are.

Figure 22.4: The dose given to each voxel when Beamlets 1, 2, and 3 are turned on with intensity equal to 1.

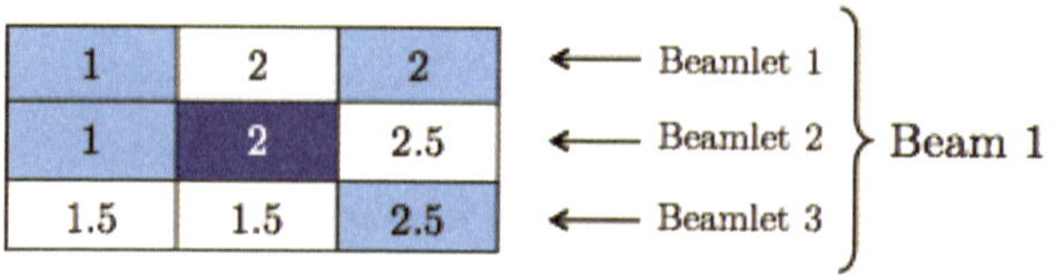

Figure 22.5: The dose given to each voxel when Beamlets 4, 5, and 6 are turned on with intensity equal to 1.

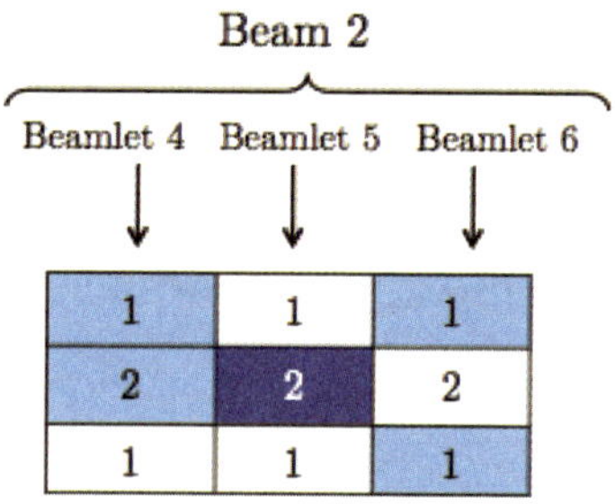

b) Solve this problem in a linear optimization software. What is the optimal solution? Intuitively, does this make sense?

c) Suppose we would like to reduce the dose to the spinal cord as much as possible. We can do this by reducing the maximum dose that the spinal cord can receive. Adjust your spinal cord constraint to make sure that the spinal cord receives a total dose of no more than 4. How does the optimal solution change? Continue reducing the maximum total dose to the spinal cord by trying values of 3, 2, 1, and 0. What happens to the optimal solution? How would you describe this tradeoff to the oncologist?

22.7 Integer Optimization Exercises

The exercises in this section are designed to help you better understand integer optimization, and to practice creating and solving integer optimization problems.

Optimizing Hotel Selection

La Quinta Motor Inns is a mid-sized hotel chain headquartered in San Antonio, Texas. They are looking to expand to more locations, and know that selecting good sites is crucial to a hotel chain's success. Of the four major marketing considerations (price, product, promotion, and location), location has been shown to be one of the most important considerations for multisite firms.

Hotel chain owners who can pick good sites quickly have a distinct competitive advantage, since they are competing against other chains for the same sites. La Quinta used data on 57 existing inn locations to build a linear regression model to predict "Profitability," computed as the operating margin, or earnings before interest and taxes divided by total revenue. They tried many independent variables, such as "Number of hotel rooms in the vicinity" and "Age of the Inn." All independent variables were normalized to have mean zero and standard deviation 1.

The final regression model is given by:

Profitability = 39.05 - (5.41 × State Population per Inn) + (5.86 × Price of the Inn) - (3.09 × Square Root of the Median Income of the Area) + (1.75 × College Students in the Area)

In this problem, we will use this regression model together with integer optimization to select the most profitable sites for La Quinta.

a) Let us start by understanding the regression equation.

  i) According to the regression equation given above, which variables positively affect Profitability? Which variables negatively affect Profitability? Does this intuitively make sense to you?

  ii) Using this regression equation, La Quinta created a spreadsheet model to predict profitability, and routinely uses it to screen potential real estate acquisitions. Suppose that La Quinta is looking to expand their locations in California, and has collected data for 16 different potential sites. This data is given in Table 22.15 and is also available in the Online Companion (*SelectingHotels.xlsx*). For each hotel, we have the location, the price, and the value of each of the independent variables used in the regression equation (normalized to have mean zero and standard deviation one).

  Using the regression equation and the 4 normalized independent variables, what is the predicted profitability of hotel 1?

  iii) Now use the regression equation and the data to compute the predicted profitability for all hotels. Which hotel has the highest predicted profitability? The lowest?

b) La Quinta has a budget of \$10 million to spend on hotels. Suppose we used a "greedy" approach where we selected the most profitable

Table 22.15: Data for the "Optimizing Hotel Selection" problem. Note that the last four variables (Price, Square Root of Median Income, College Students in Area, and State Population Per Inn) are normalized versions of the variables.

	Location	**Price (millions)**	**Price**	**Square Root of Median Income**	**College Students in Area**	**State Population Per Inn**
1	Eureka	$2.925	-0.30	-0.81	-0.54	-1.00
2	Fresno	$10.000	1.70	-0.41	0.31	-0.47
3	Fresno	$3.750	-0.07	-0.41	0.31	-0.47
4	Fresno	$3.500	-0.14	-0.41	0.31	-0.47
5	Fresno	$0.325	-1.04	-0.41	0.31	-0.47
6	Long Beach	$8.950	1.40	0.66	0.48	-0.56
7	Los Angeles	$1.950	-0.58	0.17	3.11	3.11
8	Los Angeles	$1.750	-0.63	0.17	3.11	3.11
9	Los Angeles	$4.900	0.26	0.17	3.11	3.11
10	South Lake Tahoe	$1.650	-0.66	-0.79	-0.59	-0.43
11	South Lake Tahoe	$1.125	-0.81	-0.79	-0.59	-0.43
12	South Lake Tahoe	$2.500	-0.42	-0.79	-0.59	-0.43
13	South Lake Tahoe	$1.975	-0.57	-0.79	-0.59	-0.43
14	South Lake Tahoe	$3.750	-0.07	-0.79	-0.59	-0.43
15	South Lake Tahoe	$1.475	-0.71	-0.79	-0.59	-0.43
16	South Lake Tahoe	$0.750	-0.92	-0.79	-0.59	-0.43

hotels until we ran out of budget. So we would start by buying the hotel we predict to be the most profitable, and then if we had enough budget left, we would buy the hotel we predict to be the second most profitable, and so on.

i) Describe what we would do with this approach. Which hotels would we purchase?

ii) What would our total predicted profitability be? (This is the sum of the predicted profitability of all hotels we purchase.)

iii) If we are trying to maximize our total predicted profitability, is this a good approach? How about if we were trying to maximize the average predicted profitability of the hotels we select? How about if we had a budget of $20 million instead of $10 million?

c) Now, let us build an optimization model to select hotels. We are trying to decide whether or not a hotel should be purchased, while making sure we spend no more than our budget of $10 million. Our objective is to maximize the total predicted profitability.

i) Write out the optimization problem we are trying to solve. Make sure to describe the decision variables, the objective, and the constraints.

ii) Now solve your optimization model. What is the optimal solution? Give the values of the decision variables and the optimal objective function value.

iii) Does the optimal solution make sense intuitively? How does it compare to the greedy solution?

d) La Quinta thinks that buying too many hotels in one city is probably not a good idea, and would prefer to diversify across as many cities as possible. Add constraint(s) to your model to limit the number of hotels purchased in any city to at most 2.

i) What are the constraints that you need to add to the model? Intuitively, do you expect the new optimal objective function value to be larger, smaller, or the same as before?

ii) Solve the new model. What is the optimal solution? Give the values of the decision variables and the optimal objective function value. How does this compare to the previous solution?

e) In no more than one paragraph, describe how you would present your results to La Quinta. Do you have any recommendations for them to improve the regression model? How about to improve the optimization model?

Class Assignments

The Salanter Akiba Riverdale (SAR) Academy is a coeducational, private Modern Orthodox Jewish day school located in New York City. Every summer, the SAR Academy must create class assignments for their elementary school students. Each grade of 80-100 students must be divided into different classes. Requests for assignments are made by parents, teachers, and school therapists. These requests include pairs of students that should be placed together, pairs of students that should not be placed together, and requests for students to be placed in classes that better suit their unique or special academic needs. These requests often conflict with each other, and it falls on the administration to prioritize which requests should be fulfilled over others.

In this exercise, we will solve a simplified version of the problem faced by the SAR Academy with 40 students and two classes. (The full optimization problem is currently being used to assist administrators at the SAR Academy. For more details, see the paper referenced in Section 22.8.) The parents or guardians of each of the 40 students are asked to submit preferences for class 1 or class 2. These preferences often depend on the teaching style of the teachers, the teachers older siblings have had in the past, and characteristics of the class (one class is called an "inclusion class," which is better for students with academic needs). The parents give a ranking of 1 to the class they prefer (their first choice), and a ranking of 2 to their second choice. This data, as well as the gender of each of the students, is given in the spreadsheet *ClassAssignments.xlsx*.

a) The problem faced by the SAR Academy is to decide which students should be assigned to which classes, to satisfy as many of the parent preferences as possible (note that since smaller numbers for the preferences are better, this is a minimization problem). Each student must be assigned to exactly one class, and there should be exactly 20 students in each class.

   i) Formulate this problem as an integer optimization problem. Describe the decision variables, objective function, and constraints.

   ii) Now solve this optimization problem. What is the optimal solution? Give the values of the decision variables as well as the value of the optimal objective function value.

   iii) How many students received their first choice class, according to the parent preferences? (HINT: You should be able to answer this by just looking at the optimal objective function value.)

b) After looking at the optimal solution, the SAR academy decided that they would like to adjust the formulation to better balance the boy/girl ratio in the classes. They would like to limit the number of boys in each class to no more than 12.

   i) What constraint(s) do you need to add to your model to incorporate this adjustment?

   ii) Add the necessary constraints and resolve your model. What is the optimal solution now? How does it compare to the previous solution?

iii) How many students received their first choice class in this new solution, according to the parent preferences?

c) Now, we will add some logical constraints to capture additional preferences of parents, teachers, and school therapists.

i) Students 10 and 11 are twins, and the school has a policy that twins must be placed in different classes. What constraint(s) needs to be added to the model to implement this policy?

ii) Students 4, 9, 15, 25, 30, and 36 are all from the same neighborhood. The school would like to put at least 2 students from this neighborhood in each class. What constraint(s) needs to be added to the model to implement this policy?

iii) The school therapist strongly recommends that students 20 and 21 are placed in the same classroom, that student 1 is placed in classroom 2, and that student 40 is placed in classroom 2. What constraint(s) needs to be added to the model to implement this policy?

iv) Add all of these constraints to your model, and solve it again. What is the optimal solution now? How does the objective value compare to the previous solution, without all of these constraints? What does this tell us?

Gerrymandering New Mexico

In the United States, each state is divided into small regions called districts for the purposes of representation in the House of Representatives, which is one of two chambers of the U.S. Congress. In every even-numbered year, the citizens who reside in each district can vote in an election to determine the U.S. Representative for that district. Representatives hold great power, as they can propose and vote on bills that later can become laws.

Each representative typically is affiliated with one of the two major political parties in the United States: the Democratic Party or the Republican Party. Each party naturally wants to ensure that they have as many representatives in Congress as possible. One way of achieving this is through gerrymandering.

Gerrymandering refers to the process of redrawing district boundaries so as to favor a particular political party. To illustrate this, suppose we have the hypothetical state shown in Figure 22.6, with three districts, indicated by the bold black lines. Each district is further subdivided along a grid into smaller subregions, where each subregion votes unanimously for either party. For simplicity, suppose that in this hypothetical example there is only one voter in each subregion.

Based on the current district boundaries, the blue party has a majority in each district, so each district elects a blue representative. However, suppose we decide to redraw the boundaries as shown in Figure 22.7. The voting didn't change, but now the red party wins two of the three districts.

In this problem, we will be exploring how to systematically manipulate these kinds of boundaries. We will be doing this specifically for the state of New Mexico in the United States, which currently has three districts, as shown in Figure 22.8. It is further subdivided into counties (shown by the faint lines in Figure 22.8). In many states, a district boundary can go through a county, but for this problem we will assume that a county must belong to one and only one district.

We have the voting record from the 2012 election for each county in New Mexico, which we will use as a proxy for how the county will vote in the next election (whether the majority will be Republican or Democratic). In the 2012 House of Representatives election, the Democratic party won in New Mexico's 1st and 3rd districts, while the Republican party won in the 2nd district. This data is provided in the file *Gerrymandering.xlsx*, available in the Online Companion.

Suppose that we have the opportunity to gerrymander New Mexico. We would like to keep three districts, but redesign them so that we expect the Democratic party to take all three districts. Our decisions are which county should be assigned to which district. We need to make sure that each country is assigned to exactly one district, and each district consists of at least one county.

The first scenario we will consider is selecting our objective to maximize the number of votes that the Democratic party wins district 2 by (remember that the Democratic party lost in the 2nd district). If we can get the Democratic party to win district 2 by a margin of at least 100 votes while still winning

Figure 22.6: A hypothetical state, with three districts. With the district boundaries shown here, blue wins every district.

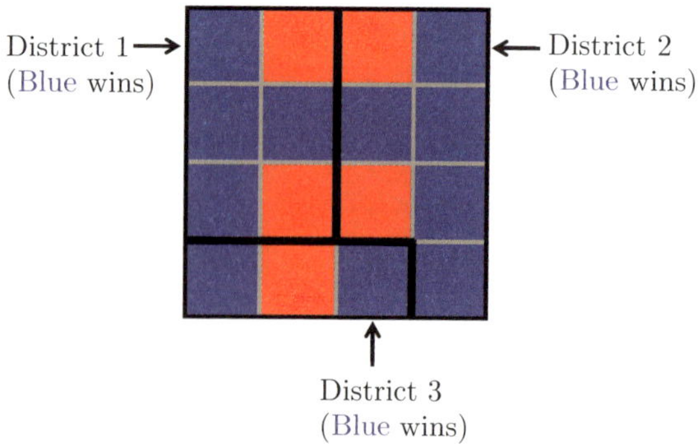

Figure 22.7: A hypothetical state, with three districts. With the district boundaries shown here, blue wins one district and red wins two districts.

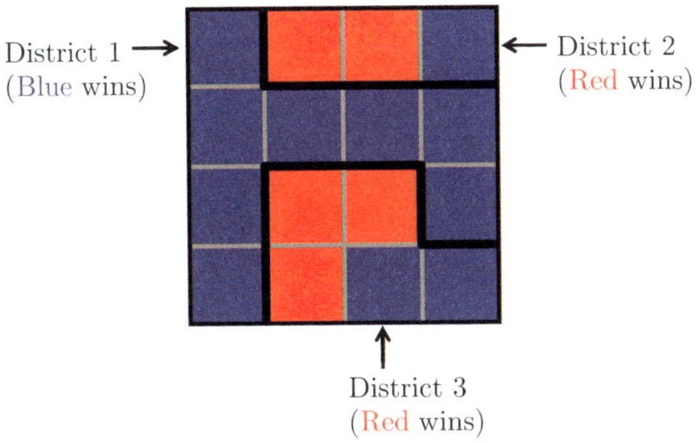

Figure 22.8: The current three district borders in the state of New Mexico.

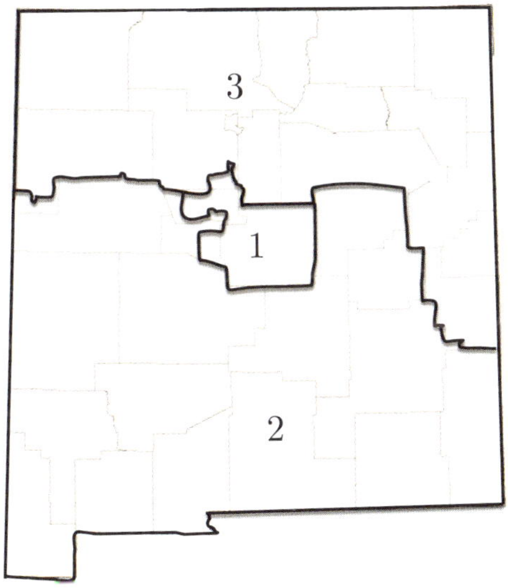

districts 1 and 3 by a margin of at least 100 votes in each district, the Democratic party will win all three districts. So we also need to make sure that the

Democratic party still wins districts 1 and 3 by a margin of at least 100 votes.

a) Formulate this problem as an integer optimization problem. Write out the decision variables, objective function, and constraints. You should use the data provided in the file *Gerrymandering.xlsx*. For the vote difference, you should use the numbers under Scenario 1.

b) Solve this optimization model. What is the optimal solution? By how many votes does the Democratic Party win each of the districts under this redistricting?

c) It would be nice to find a solution for which the Democratic party wins in all three districts, but for which the new assignments are not very different from the existing districts. In the spreadsheet, we have included information about the county assignments in 2012, that is, which counties belong to which districts. (Note that this is an approximate assessment because in New Mexico, districts are not exactly made up of counties.)

  i) Let us change our objective so that it instead maximizes the number of districts that are not reassigned. What should the new objective be?

  ii) Modify your problem to use the new objective. The old objective should become a constraint like the ones we have for districts 1 and 3 - we want to ensure that the Democratic party wins by a margin of at least 100 votes in district 2 as well. Then re-solve the problem. You should still be using the "Scenario 1" column for the vote differences. In the optimal solution, which counties have been re-assigned? How does this compare to the previous solution?

d) In addition to ensuring that the Democratic party wins in each district, we would also like to take into account the following considerations: (1) Exactly one of Santa Fe (county 27) or Dona Ana (county 8) must be in district 2; and (2) Both Socorro (county 29) and Torrance (county 31) must be in the same district.

  i) What constraint(s) do we need to add to our model to make sure that these additional considerations are satisfied?

  ii) Add these constraints to your model and re-solve it. How does the optimal solution compare to the previous optimal solution?

e) So far, we have been using only one voting scenario to design our districts. In this scenario, we have assumed that each county will vote in the representative election of its designated district the same way it voted in the 2012 election (scenario 1 in the spreadsheet). For example, Bernalillo county will vote for the Democratic candidate of its district, with a margin of 42,941 more voters (i.e., the number of Democratic votes from Bernalillo is 42,941 higher than the number of Republican votes).

This is a problematic feature of the model, because voters will not vote in this exact way in future elections. In fact, if they vote sufficiently differently, the democratic party may not be able to win all of its representative elections.

Let us change our formulation to make it more robust to changes in voter behavior. Suppose that in addition to the data we have been using so far (Scenario 1), we also wish to account for two other scenarios: Scenario 2 and Scenario 3. These scenarios are based on forecasts obtained from a separate prediction model. Furthermore, we want to make sure that the Democratic party wins by a large margin, so we will change the constraints to ensure that the Democratic party wins at least 12,000 more votes than the republicans in each district.

To do this, we need to revisit our constraints that ensure that the Democratic party wins each district. In particular, the Democratic Party should win each district with a margin of at least 12,000 votes in every scenario; so instead of three constraints (one for each district), we should have nine constraints (one for each district and scenario pair).

Add these constraints to your model, and re-solve it. What is the optimal solution now? How does it compare to the previous optimal solution?

22.8 Notes and Sources

22.1. The data for "Climate Change" comes from multiple sources: the Climatic Research Unit, University of East Anglia; the Global Monitoring Division of the Earth System Research Laboratory at the U.S. Department of Commerce; the Goddard Institute for Space Studies at NASA; and the SOLARIS-HEPPA project [36, 46, 52, 132].

22.2. The data for "Predicting Parole Violators" comes from the National Corrections Reporting Program at the United States Department of Justice [99].

22.3. The data for "Letter Recognition" comes from the UCI Machine Learning Repository [84].

22.4. The data for "Document Clustering" comes from the UCI Machine Learning Repository [84] with an original source of Daily Kos [40].

22.7. The "Optimizing Hotel Selection" problem is adapted from the paper "Selecting Profitable Hotel Sites at La Quinta Motor Inns" by Kimes and Fitzsimmons [76]. The "Class Assignments" problem is based on the case study "Optimizing the Assignment of Students to Classes in an Elementary School," by Krauss, Lee, and Newman [77].

References

[1] Z. Abrams, O. Mendelevitch, and J. Tomlin, *Optimal Delivery of Sponsored Search Advertisements Subject to Budget Constraints*, Electronic Commerce Conference, (2007), pp. 272–278.

[2] *AdWords*. Wikipedia, The Free Encyclopedia. http://en.wikipedia.org/wiki/AdWords.

[3] *American Diabetes Association*. http://www.diabetes.org/.

[4] G. Anderson, D. Selby, and M. Ramsey, *Insider Attack and Real-Time Data Mining of User Behavior*, IBM Journal of Research and Development, 51 (2007), pp. 465–475.

[5] A. D. Angelical, *How Watson works: a conversation with Eric Brown, IBM Research Manager*. http://www.kurzweilai.net/how-watson-works-a-conversation-with-eric-brown-ibm-research-manager, 2011.

[6] S. Aral and D. Walker, *Identifying Influential and Susceptible Members of Social Networks*, Science, 337 (2012), pp. 337–341.

[7] O. Ashenfelter, D. Ashmore, and R. LaLonde, *Bordeaux Wine Vintage Quality and the Weather*, American Statistical Association, 8 (1995), pp. 7–14.

[8] O. Ashenfelter and R. Quandt, *Liquid Assets*. http://liquidasset.com.

[9] S. Baker, *Final Jeopardy: Man vs. Machine and the Quest to Know Everything*, Houghton Mifflin, New York, 2011.

[10] R. R. Baldwin, W. E. Cantey, H. Maisel, and J. P. McDermott, *The Optimum Strategy in Blackjack*, Journal of the American Statistical Association, 51 (1956), pp. 429–439.

[11] A.-L. Barabási, *Linked: How Everything is Connected to Everything Else and What it Means for Business, Science, and Everyday Life*, Plume, 2003.

[12] *Basketball-Reference.com.* http://www.basketball-reference.com/.

[13] R. M. Bell, Y. Koren, and C. Volinsky, *All Together Now: A Perspective on the Netflix Prize*, Chance, 23 (2010), pp. 24–29.

[14] E. R. Berlekamp, J. H. Conway, and R. K. Guy, *Winning Ways for your Mathematical Plays*, vol. 2, Academic Press, New York, 1982.

[15] D. P. Bertsekas and J. N. Tsitsiklis, *Introduction to Probability*, Athena Scientific, 2008.

[16] D. Bertsimas, M. V. Bjarnadóttir, M. A. Kane, J. C. Kryder, R. Pandey, S. Vempala, and G. Wang, *Algorithmic Prediction of Health-Care Costs*, Operations Research, 56 (2008), pp. 1382–1392.

[17] D. Bertsimas, F. Carr, and C. Noyes, *Analysis and Optimization of the Emergency Department at BIDMC via Simulation*, 2007. Working Paper, Operations Research Center, MIT.

[18] D. Bertsimas, D. Czerwinski, and M. Kane, *Measuring Quality in Diabetes Care: an Expert Based Statistical Approach*, SpringerPlus, 2 (2013). http://www.springerplus.com/content/2/1/226.

[19] D. Bertsimas, C. Darnell, and R. Soucy, *Portfolio Construction Through Mixed-Integer Programming at Grantham, Mayo, Van Otterloo and Company*, Interfaces, 29 (1999), pp. 49–66.

[20] D. Bertsimas, V. Farias, and N. Trichakis, *Flexibility, Fairness and Efficiency in Kidney Transplantation*, Operations Research, 61 (2013), pp. 73–87.

[21] D. Bertsimas, M. Frankovich, and A. O'Hair, *The Dynamic Crime Index*, tech. rep., Operations Research Center, MIT, 2011.

[22] D. Bertsimas and R. M. Freund, *Data, Models, and Decisions: The Fundamentals of Management Science*, Dynamic Ideas, 2004.

[23] D. Bertsimas, L. Kogan, and A. W. Lo, *Hedging Derivative Securities and Incomplete Markets: An ϵ-Arbitrage Approach*, Operations Research, 49 (2001), pp. 372–397.

[24] D. Bertsimas, N. Markuzon, and K. Shenk, *Patterns of Heart Attacks.* Working Paper, Operations Research Center, MIT, 2015.

[25] D. Bertsimas and J. N. Tsitsiklis, *Introduction to Linear Optimization*, Dynamic Ideas and Athena Scientific, 1997.

[26] *Beth Israel Deaconess Medical Center - Emergency Medicine.* http://www.bidmc.org/CentersandDepartments/Departments/EmergencyMedicine.aspx.

[27] F. BLACK, *How we came up with the Option Formula*, The Journal of Portfolio Management, 15 (1989), pp. 4–8.

[28] F. BLACK AND M. SCHOLES, *The Pricing of Options and Corporate Liabilities*, The Journal of Political Economy, 81 (1973), pp. 637–654.

[29] M. BLOUNT, M. R. EBLING, J. M. EKLUND, A. G. JAMES, C. MCGREGOR, N. PERCIVAL, K. P. SMITH, AND D. SOW, *Real-Time Analysis for Intensive Care: Development and Deployment of the Artemis Analytic System*, IEEE Engineering in Medicine and Biology Magazine, 29 (2010), pp. 110–118.

[30] A. BRAGA, D. HUREAU, AND A. PAPACHRISTOS, *Deterring Gang-Involved Gun Violence: Measuring the Impact of Boston's Operation Ceasefire on Street Gang Behavior*, Journal of Quantitative Criminology, (2013), pp. 1–27.

[31] S. BRUMELLE AND J. MCGILL, *Airline Seat Allocation with Multiple Nested Fare Classes*, Operations Research, 41 (1993), pp. 127–137.

[32] M. CAMPBELL, *Knowledge Discovery in Deep Blue*, Communications of the ACM, 42 (1999), pp. 65–67.

[33] M. CAMPBELL, J. A. HOANE, JR, AND F.-H. HSU, *Deep Blue*, Artificial Intelligence, 134 (2002), pp. 57–83.

[34] C. CATLEY, K. SMITH, C. MCGREGOR, A. JAMES, AND J. M. EKLUND, *A Framework to Model and Translate Clinical Rules to Support Complex Real-Time Analysis of Physiological and Clinical Data*, in Proceedings of the 1st ACM International Health Informatics Symposium, IHI '10, New York, NY, USA, 2010, ACM, pp. 307–315.

[35] CHESSBASE, *FIDE Ratings: Garry Kasparov Retires at 2812.* http://en.chessbase.com/post/fide-ratings-garry-kasparov-retires-at-2812, 2005.

[36] *Climatic Research Unit.* University of East Anglia.

[37] L. G. CONNELLY AND A. E. BAIR, *Discrete Event Simulation of Emergency Department Activity: A Platform for System-level Operations Research*, Academic Emergency Medicine, 11 (2004), pp. 1177–1185.

[38] J. C. COX, S. A. ROSS, AND M. RUBINSTEIN, *Option Pricing: A Simplified Approach*, Journal of Financial Economics, 7 (1979), pp. 229–263.

[39] D. Czerwinski, *Quality of Care and Drug Surveillance: A Data-Driven Perspective*, PhD thesis, Massachusetts Institute of Technology, Operations Research, 2008.

[40] *Daily Kos.* Kos Media, LLC.

[41] T. R. Dawber, F. E. Moore, and G. V. Mann, *Coronary Heart Disease in the Framingham Study*, American Journal of Public Health and the Nation's Health, 47 (1957), pp. 4–24.

[42] DHHS, *Organ Procurement and Transplantation Network Final Rule*, 2000. Electronic Code of Federal Regulations, Title 42–Public Health, Chapter I–Public Health Service, Department of Health and Human Services, Subchapter K–Health Resources Development, Part 121.

[43] D. Easley and J. Kleinberg, *Networks, Crowds, and Markets: Reasoning about a Highly Connected World*, Cambridge University Press, 2010.

[44] ——, *Networks, Crowds, and Markets: Reasoning about a Highly Connected World.* https://www.cs.cornell.edu/home/kleinber/networks-book/networks-book.pdf, 2010.

[45] B. Edelman, M. Ostrovsky, and M. Schwarz, *Internet Advertising and the Generalized Second Price Auction: Selling Billions of Dollars Worth of Keywords*, American Economic Review, 97 (2007), pp. 242–259.

[46] *Earth System Research Laboratory (ESRL).* U.S. Department of Commerce.

[47] J. Feldman, S. Muthukrishnan, M. Pál, and C. Stein, *Budget Optimization in Search-Based Advertising Auctions*, ACM conference on Electronic Commerce, (2006), pp. 40–49.

[48] D. A. Ferrucci, E. W. Brown, J. Chu-Carroll, J. Fan, D. Gondek, A. Kalyanpur, A. Lally, J. W. Murdock, E. Nyberg, J. M. Prager, N. Schlaefer, and C. A. Welty, *Building Watson: An Overview of the DeepQA Project*, AI Magazine, 31 (2010), pp. 59–79.

[49] B. Gannon, C. Loureiro, P. Luff, T. Nyakurimwa, and I. Pirvu, *Beth Israel Deaconess Medical Center Emergency Department Patient Care Process*, 2006.

[50] D. F. Gleich, *PageRank Beyond the Web*, CoRR: Computing Research Repository, abs/1407.5107 (2014).

[51] F. Glover, R. Glover, J. Lorenzo, and C. McMillan, *The Passenger-Mix Problem in the Scheduled Airlines*, Interfaces, 12 (1982), pp. 73–80.

[52] *Godard Institute for Space Studies.* National Aeronautics and Space Administration (NASA).

[53] C. Goffman, *And What Is Your Erdos Number?*, American Mathematical Monthly, 76 (1969), p. 791.

[54] E. Goode, *Sending the Police Before There's a Crime*, August 15, 2011. The New York Times.

[55] *Google AdWords.* https://www.google.com/adwords/.

[56] *Google Investor Relations.* Google, Inc. 2014. http://investor.google.com/.

[57] B. Graham, *The Intelligent Investor: A Book of Practical Counsel*, Harper & Row Publishers, 1986.

[58] B. Graham and D. Dodd, *Security Analysis*, McGraw-Hill, 2008.

[59] A. Hassan, *HPD's Real Time Crime Center Works Behind the Scene*, August 2012. Houston Chronicle.

[60] *History of Google.* Wikipedia, The Free Encyclopedia. Wikimedia Foundation, Inc. http://en.wikipedia.org/wiki/HistoryofGoogle.

[61] F.-h. Hsu, *Behind Deep Blue, Building the Computer that Defeated the World Chess Champion*, Princeton University Press, 2002.

[62] J. C. Hull, *Options, Futures, and Other Derivatives*, Prentice Hall, 2011.

[63] C. Humphries, *Dating Sites Try Adaptive Matchmaking*, December 27, 2010. Technology Review.

[64] *Kasparov vs. Deep Blue: The Rematch.* https://www.research.ibm.com/deepblue/, 1997.

[65] *First-of-a-Kind Technology to Help Doctors Care for Premature Babies*, July 23, 2008. IBM Press Release.

[66] IBM, *Memphis Police Department Reduces Crime Rates with IBM Predictive Analytics Software*, July 2010. IBM News Releases.

[67] *IBM Watson: Offerings.* http://www.ibm.com/smarterplanet/us/en/ibmwatson/offerings.html, 2015.

[68] *The DeepQA Research Team/Publications.* http://researcher.watson.ibm.com/researcher/view_group_pubs.php?grp=2099, 2015.

[69] *Frequently Asked Questions: Deep Blue.* https://www.research.ibm.com/deepblue/meet/html/d.3.3a.html, 1997.

[70] *Internet Movie Database.* http://www.imdb.com.

[71] G. James, D. Witten, T. Hastie, and R. Tibshirani, *An Introduction to Statistical Learning with Applications in R*, Springer Science+Business Media, 2013.

[72] N. Jegadeesh and S. Titman, *Returns to Buying Winners and Selling Losers: Implications for Stock Market Efficiency*, The Journal of Finance, 48 (1993), pp. 65–91.

[73] ——, *Profitability of Momentum Strategies: An Evaluation of Alternative Explanations*, The Journal of Finance, 56 (2001), pp. 699–720.

[74] W. B. Kannel, T. R. Dawber, A. Kagan, N. Revotskie, and J. Stokes, III, *Factors of Risk in the Development of Coronary Heart Disease – Six-Year Follow-up Experience: The Framingham Study*, Annals of Internal Medicine, 55 (1961), pp. 33–50.

[75] D. Kempe, J. Kleinberg, and E. Tardos, *Maximizing the Spread of Influence through a Social Network*, in Proceedings of the ninth ACM SIGKDD International Conference on Knowledge Discovery and Data Mining, New York, NY, USA, 2003, ACM, pp. 137–146.

[76] S. E. Kimes and J. A. Fitzsimmons, *Selecting Profitable Hotel Sites at La Quinta Motor Inns*, Interfaces, 20 (1990), pp. 12–20.

[77] B. Krauss, J. Lee, and D. Newman, *Optimizing the Assignment of Students to Classes in an Elementary School*, INFORMS Transactions on Education, 14 (2013), pp. 39–44.

[78] A. N. Langville and C. D. Meyer, *Google's PageRank and Beyond: The Science of Search Engine Rankings*, Princeton University Press, 2006.

[79] V. Lazova and L. Basnarkov, *PageRank Approach to Ranking National Football Teams*, CoRR: Computing Research Repository, abs/1503.01331 (2015).

[80] C. J. Levy and M. Luo, *New York Medicaid Fraud May Reach Into Billions*, July 2005. New York Times.

[81] D. Levy and S. Brink, *A Change of Heart: Unraveling the Mysteries of Cardiovascular Disease*, Vintage Books, a division of Random House, Inc., 2005.

[82] M. Lewis, *Moneyball: The Art of Winning an Unfair Game*, W. W. Norton & Company, Inc., New York, 2003.

[83] J. Li, K.-Y. Huang, J. Jin, and J. Shi, *A Survey on Statistical Methods for Health Care Fraud Detection*, Health Care Management Science, (2008), pp. 275–287.

[84] M. Lichman, *UCI Machine Learning Repository*, 2013.

[85] G. Linden, B. Smith, and J. York, *Amazon.com Recommendations: Item-to-Item Collaborative Filtering*, Internet Computing, IEEE, 7 (2003), pp. 76–80.

[86] J. Ma, *The House Advantage: Playing the Odds to Win Big in Business*, Palgrave Macmillian, 2010.

[87] B. Macdonald, *Greater Than Plus Minus*. http://www.greaterthanplusminus.com/p/realignment.html, 2013.

[88] B. Macdonald and W. Pulleyblank, *Realignment in the NHL, MLB, NFL, and NBA*, Journal of Quantitative Analysis in Sports, 10 (2014), pp. 225–240.

[89] J.-F. Marcotorchino and P. Michaud, *Optimisation en Analyse Ordinale des Données, Chap.X.*, Masson, Paris, 1979.

[90] H. Markowitz, *Portfolio Selection*, The Journal of Finance, 7 (1952), pp. 77–91.

[91] A. McAfee and E. Brynjolfsson, *Big Data: The Management Revolution*, Harvard Business Review, (2012).

[92] I. McCulloh, H. Armstrong, and A. Johnson, *Social Network Analysis with Applications*, John Wiley and Sons Inc., 2013.

[93] R. C. Merton, *Theory of Rational Option Pricing*, The Bell Journal of Economics and Management Science, 4 (1973), pp. 141–183.

[94] R. Metters, C. Queenan, M. Ferguson, L. Harrison, J. Higbie, S. Ward, B. Barfield, T. Farley, H. A. Kuyumcu, and A. Duggasani, *The "Killer Application" of Revenue Management: Harrah's Cherokee Casino & Hotel*, Interfaces, 38 (2008), pp. 161–175.

[95] B. Mezrich, *Bringing Down the House: The Inside Story of Six MIT Students who Took Vegas for Millions*, Free Press: A Division of Simon and Schuster, Inc., 2002.

[96] ——, *Busting Vegas: The MIT Whiz Kid Who Brought the Casinos to Their Knees*, HarperCollins Publishers, 2005.

[97] J. E. Mitchell, *Realignment in the National Football League: Did They do it Right?*, Naval Research Logistics, 50 (2003).

[98] G. O. Mohler, M. B. Short, P. J. Brantingham, F. P. Schoenberg, and G. E. Tita, *Self-Exciting Point Process Modeling of Crime*, Journal of the American Statistical Association, 106 (2011), pp. 100–108.

[99] *National Corrections Reporting Program.* United States Department of Justice.

[100] *Netflix Investor Relations.* http://ir.netflix.com/.

[101] *Netflix Media Center.* http://pr.netflix.com.

[102] M. Newborn, *Kasparov versus Deep Blue: Computer Chess Comes of Age*, Springer-Verlag, New York, 1997.

[103] ——, *Deep Blue, An Artificial Intelligence Milestone*, Springer-Verlag, New York, 2003.

[104] M. Newman, *Networks: An Introduction*, Oxford University Press, 2010.

[105] S. Norman, *Update on the Development of a New Kidney Transplant Allocation System*, Nephrology Dialysis Transplantation, 38 (2009), pp. 400–406.

[106] ODADK, *Organ Distribution: Allocation of Deceased Kidneys*, 3 (2010), pp. 1–13. United Network for Organ Sharing Policies.

[107] A. Ojo, F. Port, R. Wolfe, E. Mauger, L. Williams, and D. Berling, *Comparative Mortality Risks of Chronic Dialysis and Cadaveric Transplantation in Black End-Stage Renal Disease Patients*, American Journal of Kidney Diseases, 24 (1994), pp. 59–64.

[108] OPTNKTC, *Report of the OPTN/UNOS Kidney Transplantation Committee to the Board of Directors*, 2007. September 17-18, Los Angeles, California.

[109] ——, *Report of the OPTN/UNOS Kidney Transplantation Committee to the Board of Directors*, 2008. February 20-21, Orlando, Florida.

[110] B. Orr, *LAPD Computer Program Prevents Crime by Predicting It*, April 11, 2012. CBS News.

[111] L. Page, S. Brin, R. Motwani, and T. Winograd, *The PageRank Citation Ranking: Bringing Order to the Web*, (1999).

[112] P. Pardalos, F. Rendl, and H. Wolkowicz, *The Quadratic Assignment Problem: A Survey of Recent Developments*, In P. Pardalos and H. Wolkowicz, editors, Quadratic Assignment and Related Problems, DIMACS Series in Discrete Mathematics and Theoretical Computer Science, 16 (1994), pp. 1–42.

[113] P. Passell, *Wine Equation Puts Some Noses Out of Joint*, March 4, 1990. New York Times.

[114] F. Port, R. Wolfe, E. Mauger, D. Berling, and K. Jiang, *Comparison of Survival Probabilities for Dialysis Patients versus Cadaveric Renal Transplant Recipients*, JAMA, 270 (1993), pp. 1339–1343.

[115] RFI, *Kidney Allocation Concepts: Request for Information*, (2008). OPTN/UNOS Kidney Transplantation Committee.

[116] J. Rubin, *Stopping Crime Before it Starts*, August 21, 2010. Los Angeles Times.

[117] T. W. Ruger, P. T. Kim, A. D. Martin, and K. M. Quinn, *Competing Approaches to Predicting Supreme Court Decision Making*, Perspectives on Politics Symposium, 2 (2004), pp. 761–767.

[118] ——, *The Supreme Court Forecasting Project: Legal and Political Science Approaches to Predicting Supreme Court Decisionmaking*, The Columbia Law Review, 104 (2004), pp. 1150–1210.

[119] R. G. Santalla, *On the Digital Front Line of Policing*, September 2009. BBC News.

[120] C. E. Saunders, P. K. Makens, and L. J. Leblanc, *Modeling Emergency Department Operations Using Advanced Computer Simulation Systems*, Annals of Emergency Medicine, 18 (1989), pp. 134–140.

[121] J. Scarne, *Scarne's New Complete Guide to Gambling*, Fireside, 1986.

[122] B. M. Schmidt and M. M. Chingos, *Ranking Doctoral Programs by Placement: A New Method*, PS: Political Science and Politics, 40 (2007), pp. 523–529.

[123] M. S. Schmidt, *Have a Tattoo or Walk With a Limp? The Police May Know*, February 2010. New York Times.

[124] P. Schnuelle, D. Lorenz, M. Trede, and F. V. D. Woude, *Impact of Renal Cadaveric Transplantation on Survival in End-Stage Renal Failure: Evidence for Reduced Mortality Risk Compared with Hemodialysis During Long-Term Follow-up*, Journal of the American Society of Nephrology, 9 (1998), pp. 2135–2141.

[125] M. A. Schuster, E. A. McGlynn, and B. H. Brook, *How Good is the Quality of Health Care in the United States?*, The Milbank Quarterly, 76 (1998), pp. 517–563.

[126] P. Shakarian, J. Salmento, W. Pulleyblank, and J. Bertetto, *Reducing Gang Violence Through Network Influence Based Targeting of Social Programs*, in Proceedings of the 20th ACM SIGKDD International Conference on Knowledge Discovery and Data Mining, New York, NY, USA, 2014, ACM, pp. 1829–1836.

[127] J. Shambora, *eHarmony's Algorithm of Love*, September 23, 2010. Fortune Magazine.

[128] C. Shannon, *Programming a Computer for Playing Chess*, Philosophical Magazine, 41 (1950), p. 314.

[129] G. Shmueli, N. R. Patel, and P. C. Bruce, *Data Mining for Business Intelligence: Concepts, Techniques, and Applications in Microsoft Office Excel with XLMiner*, John Wiley & Sons, Inc., 2010.

[130] T. Simonite, *Watson Goes to Work in the Hospital*, April 13, 2011. Technology Review.

[131] B. C. Smith, J. F. Leimkuhler, and R. M. Darrow, *Yield Management at American Airlines*, Interfaces, 22 (1992), pp. 8–31.

[132] *SOLARIS-HEPPA Project.*

[133] A. L. Sorrel, *Woman's Death in Hospital Emergency Department Ruled a Homicide*, October 16, 2006. American Medical News.

[134] STATETECH Magazine, *Albuquerque Police Department Bridges the Data Gap*, 2014. STATETECH: Technology Insights for Leaders in State and Local Government.

[135] L. M. Sullivan, J. M. Massaro, and R. B. D'Agostino, Sr, *Presentation of Multivariate Data for Clinical Use: The Framingham Study Risk Score Functions*, Statistics in Medicine, 23 (2004), pp. 1631–1660.

[136] M. Suthanthiran and T. Strom, *Renal transplantation*, New England Journal of Medicine, (1994), pp. 331–365.

[137] K. T. Talluri and G. J. van Ryzin, *The Theory and Practice of Revenue Management*, Springer, 2005.

[138] L. Telegraph, *Barack Obama Visits Real Time Crime Center*, May 2010. The Telegraph.

[139] E. O. Thorp, *Beat the Dealer: A Winning Strategy for the Game of Twenty One*, Vintage Books, 1966.

[140] ——, *Beat the Market: A Scientific Stock Market System*, Random House, 1967.

[141] B. Tjaden and P. Reynolds, *Oracle of Bacon*. http://oracleofbacon.org.

[142] S. Tufféry, *Data Mining and Statistics for Decision Making*, John Wiley & Sons, Inc., 2011.

[143] A. Turing, *Computing Machinery and Intelligence*, Mind, 59 (236): 43360., 59 (1950), pp. 433–60.

[144] C. D. Uchida, *A National Discussion on Predictive Policing: Defining Our Terms and Mapping Successful Implementation Strategies*, May 2010. U.S. Department of Justice.

[145] UNOS, *United Network for Organ Sharing*, (2010). http://www.unos.org/.

[146] USRDS, *U.S. Renal Data System, Annual Data Report: Atlas of Chronic Kidney Disease and End-Stage Renal Disease in the United States*, (2009). National Institutes of Health, National Institute of Diabetes and Digestive and Kidney Diseases, Bethesda, MD.

[147] K. Uston and R. Rapoport, *The Big Player: How a Team of Blackjack Players Made a Million Dollars*, Holt, Rinehart and Winston, 1977.

[148] U. von Luxburg, *A Tutorial on Spectral Clustering*, Statistics and Computing, 17 (2007), pp. 395–416.

[149] *Deep Blue (chess computer)*. https://en.wikipedia.org/wiki/Deep_Blue_%28chess_computer%29.

[150] *Deep Blue versus Garry Kasparov*. https://en.wikipedia.org/wiki/Deep_Blue_versus_Garry_Kasparov.

[151] *Wikinvest*. http://www.wikinvest.com/.

[152] P. W. F. Wilson, R. B. D'Agostino, D. Levy, A. M. Belanger, H. Silbershatz, and W. B. Kannel, *Prediction of Coronary Heart Disease Using Risk Factor Categories*, Circulation, 97 (1998), pp. 1837–1847.

[153] R. Wolfe, K. McCullough, D. Schaubel, J. Kalbfleisch, S. Murray, M. Stegall, and A. Leichtman, *2007 SRTR Report on the State of Transplantation: Calculating Life Years From Transplant (LYFT): Methods for Kidney and Kidney-Pancreas Candidates*, American Journal of Transplantation, 8 (2008), pp. 997–1011.

[154] R. Xiao, *Tic-tac-toe*. https://en.wikipedia.org/wiki/Tic-tac-toe#/media/File:Tictactoe-X.svg, 2010. Licensed under the Creative Commons, CC BY-SA 3.0, based on the xkcd comic http://xkcd.com/832/.

[155] *YCharts*. http://ycharts.com/companies/.

Index